THE MANYŌSHŪ

REISSUED FOR THE
COLUMBIA COLLEGE PROGRAM
OF TRANSLATIONS FROM
THE ORIENTAL CLASSICS
WM. THEODORE DE BARY, EDITOR

NUMBER LXX OF THE
RECORDS OF CIVILIZATION: SOURCES & STUDIES
EDITED UNDER THE AUSPICES OF THE
DEPARTMENT OF HISTORY, COLUMBIA UNIVERSITY

安貴王歌一首 并短歌

遠嬬此間不在者玉桙之道乎多遠見思
空蠢真國豊不安物手水空徃雲尒毛
欲成高飛鳥尒毛欲成明日去而於妹
言問為吾妹毛不去為妹無毛其毛
久今花見如刻而毛欲得

反歌
敷細乃手枕不纒間置而年曽経来不
相念者

しきたへのたまくらまかすあひたおきてとしそへにける
あひおもはなくに

'KATSURA MS.' (11th century)

The 'Katsura MS.' is the oldest extant copy of the *Manyōshū*, and is so called because it was formerly in the possession of the House of Prince Katsura. It now belongs to the Imperial Household. It is in a form of a scroll, which, being made of sheets of paper of varied hues and decorated with figures of birds and flowers in gold and silver, is in itself a fine work of art. The illustration shows the part containing Poems Nos. 255–6.

THE MANYŌSHŪ

The Nippon Gakujutsu Shinkōkai Translation of

ONE THOUSAND POEMS

with the Texts in Romaji

With a New Foreword by Donald Keene

Columbia University Press   New York and London   1965

NIPPON GAKUJUTSU SHINKŌKAI

Japanese Classics Translation Committee

Seiichi Taki (Chairman), Imperial Academy
Masaharu Anesaki, Imperial Academy
Nobutsuna Sasaki, Imperial Academy
Izuru Shimmura, Imperial Academy
Torao Suzuki, Imperial Academy
Zennosuke Tsuji, Imperial Academy
Jirō Abe, Tōhoku Imperial University
Sanki Ichikawa, Tokyo Imperial University

Special Manyōshū Committee

Nobutsuna Sasaki, Imperial Academy
Yoshinori Yoshizawa, Kyoto Imperial University (emeritus)
Yoshio Yamada, sometime of Tōhoku Imperial University
Shinkichi Hashimoto, Tokyo Imperial University
Shigeyoshi Saitō, Imperial Academy of Arts and Letters
Yūkichi Takeda, Kokugakuin University

UNESCO COLLECTION OF REPRESENTATIVE WORKS—
JAPANESE SERIES

This work has been accepted in the Japanese Translation Series of the United Nations Educational,
Scientific, and Cultural Organization (UNESCO).

FOREWORD

The first translations from the *Manyōshū* into a European language date back more than a century, well before Japan was opened to the West. One "envoy" (*hanka*) to a long poem was translated as early as 1834 by the celebrated German orientalist Heinrich Julius Klaproth (1783–1835). Klaproth, having journeyed to Siberia in pursuit of strange languages, encountered some illiterate Japanese castaways, fishermen, hardly ideal mentors for the study of eighth-century poetry. Not surprisingly, his translation was anything but accurate. Other translations appeared from time to time, particularly after the Meiji Restoration of 1868, and in 1872 a fair-sized selection of *Manyōshū* poetry, some 200 poems in all, was published by the Austrian scholar August Pfizmaier (1808–87). Pfizmaier's absorption with *Manyōshū* studies may account for his reputation as a more than usually absent-minded professor: it is reported that he learned of the outbreak of the Franco-Prussian War by reading of the event, one year after it occurred, in a Japanese newspaper which had been slow in reaching Vienna. His versions, for all the singular devotion to scholarship they demonstrated, unfortunately were soon superseded by the work of the great generation of English Japanologists, notably that of Basil Hall Chamberlain (1850–1935). From the late nineteenth century onwards translations into English, German, French, or Italian frequently appeared, sometimes the work of a European scholar, sometimes that of a Japanese translating his country's literature into a foreign tongue.

The most satisfactory *Manyōshū* translations are those of the present volume. Originally prepared by a committee of Japanese, scholars of both English and Japanese

iii

literatures, they were subsequently revised by the English poet Ralph Hodgson, a resident of Japan at the time. Collaboration between Japanese and Western scholars has often been urged as the best solution to the eternal problem of how to produce translations of difficult works which are at once accurate and of literary distinction but, as far as I know, *The Manyōshū* is the only successful example of such collaboration. Generally, the Western member of the team unconsciously seeks to recast the literal translations from the Japanese prepared by his colleagues into an idiom which he himself favors, though it may be inappropriate, or else he intrudes foreign imagery and thoughts in an attempt to make the poetry more appealing to a Western audience. His Japanese collaborators in such cases tend to refrain politely from expressing any objections. Here, however, the combination worked exceptionally well, a tribute equally to the Englishman and the Japanese.

The original edition of this translation was published in 1940. Since then *Manyōshū* studies have been extremely active in Japan, and new discoveries have repeatedly affected our understanding of different poems. To cite a very simple example: the poem by the Emperor Tenji on the three hills Kagu, Miminashi, and Unebi (p. 5) was long considered to refer to two male hills (Kagu and Miminashi) quarreling over a female hill (Unebi), but scholars have recently suggested that Kagu and Miminashi were two female hills in love with the same male hill, Unebi. Other discoveries have a broader application; the most important, probably, being that the Japanese language in the *Manyōshū* period had eight vowels instead of the present five, a fact of enormous linguistic significance though it does not affect the translations of the poems.

Not only has Japanese scholarship continued to advance and refine previous knowledge of the *Manyōshū*, but Western scholarship, inspired in large part by Japanese achievements, has developed apace. The most impressive critical study to appear in a Western language to date, *Japanese Court Poetry* by Robert Brower and Earl Miner (Stanford University Press, 1961), treats the *Manyōshū* in considerable detail and also gives a general background to the themes and methods of Japanese poetry. Translations continue to appear, some profiting by the new interpretations of the texts, others representing little more than reworkings in somewhat more poetic language of existing versions.

Interpretations of the *Manyōshū* have inevitably reflected the outlook of the modern critic almost as much as they conveyed the intent of the original poets. Reading the Introduction to this edition of the *Manyōshū*, we cannot help but be struck by the repeated allusions to a philosophy of the Japanese state which, though normal in 1940, has largely been discredited since. Not only is the imperial authorship of many poems stressed (though more recent scholars cast doubt on these attributions, aware that anonymous poems were often dignified by associations—however unlikely—with rulers of the distant past), but the glory of the Imperial House itself is proclaimed in a manner as foreign to the Japanese of today as to ourselves: "Turning to human relations, Japanese clan morality in its purified form—namely, that which is based upon the consciousness of the Imperial House as the supreme head of all clans—manifests itself in the *Manyōshū* in spontaneous sentiments of the loveliest kind, giving the Anthology its chief distinction." During the war years of 1941–45, the "spirit of the *Manyōshū*" was constantly invoked by literary men. They meant by the phrase worship of the Emperor and an insistence on "pure Japanese" virtues untainted by foreign influence or by the over-refined, effeminate sentiments displayed in later poetry. As a result of the defeat of Japan in 1945, the *Manyōshū* acquired still another meaning: this time it was acclaimed as a "democratic" anthology that was given its chief distinction by the poetry of the common people (or of the humbler ranks of the nobility), unlike subsequent anthologies filled with jejune compositions by the decadent courtiers.

The poetry of the *Manyōshū* is sufficiently varied and abundant to afford corroborative evidence for all these theses, but though each is tenable as an interpretation of *part* of the work, it cannot be accepted as a judgment of the whole. The compilers of this edition, emphasizing the "cheerfulness" of an age when the Imperial family ruled without interference, declared that "the prevailing atmosphere is happy, bright and peaceful." Yet surely the "Dialogue on Poverty" by Yamanoe Okura (p. 205) offers unmistakable evidence that, whatever conditions may have prevailed at the court, all was not joy and light in the villages. The Introduction does not dwell on the darker aspect of the *Manyōshū* any more than postwar interpreters of its "democratic" character choose to examine, say, Hitomaro's profound devotion to the Imperial House. Again, such an assertion as "But filial piety, so sincere, intense and instinctive as shown in the Manyo poems is not likely to be duplicated by any other people and under any other social order" is certainly open to challenge, if not to being dismissed outright as absurd. But this nostalgic view of a distant golden age deserves our attention still, if only as a traditional, persistent Japanese interpretation of the ultimate meaning of the *Manyōshū*. Even with respect to poetics a preconception that the *Manyōshū*, in contrast to the artificial elegance of later Japanese poetry, is marked by a "genuineness of thought" unmarred by vanity or frivolity led the authors of the Introduction to discount technique as a major criterion of poetic excellence, and to dismiss as "a simple form of word-play" the highly complicated *kakekotoba* (pivot-words), which resemble less an ordinary pun than the portmanteau language of *Finnegan's Wake*.[1]

It might seem, in the light of the shortcomings of this Introduction, at least from a contemporary point of

[1] For a discussion of *kakekotoba*, see Keene, *Japanese Literature* (New York, Grove Press, 1935), pp. 4-5.

view, that an entirely new one is desirable. Certainly recent theories which trace the origin of the *choka* (long poem) to religious observances that were intended to quiet the souls of the dead by reciting their deeds on earth, or which suggest what the original functions of the "envoy" may have been, deserve attention. But although it is of urgent importance that the fruits of modern Japanese scholarship be introduced to Western readers, it clearly would be unfair to the translators of this edition to change arbitrarily the introduction which they deemed appropriate to their splendid translations. It has seemed preferable, both out of respect for the book as originally conceived, and for the sake of the valuable information presented, to reproduce the Introduction unaltered.

The great merit of *The Manyōshū*, it goes without saying, is the excellence of the translations. Surely no one could read these versions of the great *choka* by Hitomaro or Okura and remain unmoved. They make superb poems in English, and are worthy of the originals. Even some of the lesser works are so beautifully rendered as to acquire an importance in translation not often accorded them in Japan—for example, the poem from the "Tanabe Sakimaro Collection" (pp. 233–34). The selection too is exceptionally intelligent, offering not only such poems of an immediate emotional or aesthetic appeal as we might expect in a volume intended for Western readers, but others which, viewed against the subsequent course of Japanese poetry, seem atypical, and even un-Japanese. These include narratives (e.g., pp. 190, 216, 224), "beggar songs" (p. 275), admonitory poems (pp. 154, 178), commemorative odes (pp. 83, 150, 220), and poems prefaced by extended prose explanations (pp. 74, 272). These poems suggest possibilities of poetic development which either never materialized at all in Japan, or else were directed (as in the case of the poems with prose prefaces) into the domain of prose rather than poetry. Another feature of the selection is the inclusion of various poems

vii

on the same themes by men of different times; those which echo the themes and language of Hitomaro (e.g., pp. 42, 125, 313; 46, 227, 333) bear witness not only to his enormous influence on later poets but to the inimitable nature of his manner, no matter how slavishly the externals were followed.

The original texts were recorded in a script which used Chinese characters in an almost perversely difficult manner: sometimes for meaning, sometimes for sound when read as Chinese, sometimes for sound when read as Japanese. Many problems of decipherment remain to be solved, but for the general reader the pronunciations favored by Japanese philologists when *The Manyōshū* first appeared in 1940 are still acceptable, though it should be borne in mind that some vowel sounds had unfamiliar pronunciations in the eighth century, and many reconstructions are still tentative. The reader who wishes to follow the Japanese texts will not be far wrong if he consults the Romaji versions in the back of this volume.

For years *The Manyōshū* was out of print and virtually unobtainable. Its importance and excellence were widely recognized, but the difficulties of making arrangements with the various parties involved in the publication made it seem dubious that a reprinting would ever appear. Mr. Kensuke Tamai of the Iwanami Publishing Company proved especially helpful during the long negotiations; indeed, without his efforts the present edition might have had to wait for another five years or more of tedious correspondence. UNESCO sponsorship of the new edition also encouraged us to persevere despite repeated frustrations. Now that at last this fine translation of the greatest of Japanese anthologies has been included in the Records of Civilization series, it is hoped that *The Manyōshū* will be accorded by the reading public its rightful place of distinction among the poetic masterpieces of the world.

November 9, 1964   Donald Keene

PREFACE

The importance of rendering Japanese classics into foreign languages as a means of acquainting the world with the cultural and spiritual background of Japan cannot be over-emphasized. Few Japanese, however, have ventured into this field, the work so far having been largely undertaken by foreigners. It is in view of this regrettable fact that the Japanese Classics Translation Committee was appointed in 1934 by the Nippon Gakujutsu Shinkōkai, and the present English version of Manyō poems represents the first enterprise of the Committee.

The *Manyōshū* has long attracted the attention of foreign translators, and there exist several versions of its poems in English, French and German, which deserve high commendation. But the work is unwieldy material to deal with, abounding as it does in obscure and difficult passages, and the collaboration of a number of scholars and specialists is required in order to produce an adequate and authoritative translation. For this reason a Special Committee, consisting of eminent authorities on the subject, was formed.

The selection of the poems for translation was based upon : 1) their poetic excellence, 2) their rôle in revealing the Japanese national spirit and character, and 3) their cultural and historical significance. The selected poems were first paraphrased by the Special Committee into plain Japanese, and the paraphrases drafted by each member were submitted to joint sessions of the two Committees for criticism and correction. It was with the help of these paraphrases that tentative translations were made. These were then revised by an eminent English poet, and submitted to the Committees in full session for examination and final revision. Altogether it has taken four years since the work of paraphrasing was begun until the English version of the last poem was approved. It may be added that the preparation of the Romaji text entailed no small labour on the part of the Committees when investigating and deciding upon the various disputed readings.

The Committee desire to acknowledge the important contributions of Messrs. Haxon Ishii and Shigeyoshi Obata, who made the tentative translations, Mr. Ralph Hodgson who revised them, and Dr. Sanki Ichikawa who supervised all matters relating to the English. Their thanks are due also to Assistant Professor Yoshimoto Endō, of the Kyoto Imperial University, and Assistant Professor Fumio Tada of the Tokyo Imperial University, the former in connection with the preparation of the Romaji text and the latter with the making of the maps.

SEIICHI TAKI

Chairman of the Japanese Classics Translation Committee, The
Nippon Gakujutsu Shinkōkai*

Tokyo
December, 1939

*The Japan Society for the Promotion of Scientific Research.

CONTENTS

FOREWORD, *by Donald Keene*   iii

PREFACE   ix

INTRODUCTION   xiii

NOTES   lxxxi

PRE-ŌMI AND ŌMI PERIODS   1

ASUKA AND FUJIWARA PERIODS   15

NARA PERIOD   79

PERIOD UNKNOWN   269

TEXT IN ROMAJI   315

APPENDICES   455

    I.   BIOGRAPHICAL NOTES   457

    II. CHRONOLOGICAL TABLE   473

    III. FINDING LIST   479

INDEX   489

MAPS

I.   EASTERN ASIA   faces xxx

II. OLD JAPAN—JAPAN IN PROVINCES   xxxi

III. HOME PROVINCES   lii

IV. NORTHERN KYŪSHŪ   lxii

V. NOTO AND ETCHŪ   lxiii

INTRODUCTION

PART I

GENERAL REMARKS

The *Manyōshū* is the oldest of the early Japanese anthologies, and by far the greatest both in quantity and quality. It consists of 20 books and contains more than 4,000 poems, written for the most part by the poets who flourished in the Fujiwara and Nara Periods, which coincide with the Golden Age of Chinese poetry—the eras of Kaiyuan and Tienpao under the T'ang dynasty, when Li Po and Tu Fu lived and sang. In England it was the Anglo-Saxon period of Beowulf, Cædmon and Cynewulf. The Anthology reflects Japanese life and civilization of the 7th and 8th centuries, and not only does it record the indigenous thoughts and beliefs, but also touches, even if only casually, upon Buddhism, Confucianism and Taoism imported from the continent.

The *Manyōshū*, unlike the *Kokin Wakashū* (generally known as *Kokinshū*), and other 'imperial' anthologies later compiled by the sovereign's command, is rich in the poems of the people as well as in those of the court. It embraces and harmonizes both patrician and plebeian elements, and reveals the brilliance of city life side by side with the charm of the country-side. It forms a happy contrast that many sovereigns and members of the imperial family are represented in the Anthology, together with a great number of excellent works by humble and nameless poets. That no less than 300 poems in the rude dialect of eastern Japan should be grouped together at two different places, is an unparalleled phenomenon in the ancient anthologies of the Orient. These provincial poems consist not only of occasional and extempore pieces, but of what appear to be the then current folk-songs, altered or recast in the course of transmission from place to place; and there may also well be a few by city poets who composed them in imitation of the rustic style. It is to be noted that the strain of folk-song is also frequently encountered in the works, especially in the amatory verse, of some urban singers. In addition there are some ballad-like poems dealing with legendary stories, and a small number of humorous pieces, which will not escape the reader's notice. It should be added that the *Manyōshū* boasts a number of women poets representing various strata of society from the highest to the humblest.

Genuineness of thought and feeling pervades all the Manyō poems, with scarcely any trace of vanity or frivolity. The prevailing atmosphere is happy, bright and peaceful. Frontier-guards departing for distant shores pledge their loyalty to the Throne and frankly record their personal loves and the sorrows of separation, but never a murmur of grudge or resentment. A sanguinary and martial spirit is conspicuous by its absence : not a single war-song is to be found in the whole collection, there being only one poem which contains a passage describing a battle. Those who compare the *Manyōshū* with the *Shi King* ('Book of Songs'), supposed to have been compiled by Confucius, generally begin with the first poems of the respective anthologies—the one by the Emperor Yūryaku and the other regarding the consort of a Chinese king of the Chou dynasty. No matter what may be the alleged allegorical virtue of the Chinese poem, no one will fail to discover in the Japanese piece an artistic masterpiece, combining sincerity with dignity, and elegance with pastoral simplicity—a charming revelation of the close intimacy and friendliness that characterized the relationship between sovereign and subject in ancient Japan. It is scarcely necessary to say that the pervading spirit of the *Manyōshū* is the Japanese spirit of genuine simplicity and sincerity.

The *Manyōshū* with its infinite variety and the intrinsic

value of its superb poetry occupies a foremost place in the history of Oriental literature. In quality it stands inferior to none of the numerous Chinese collections of verse. In quantity it can compare with the *Greek Anthology*, surpassing the latter in pure lyricism, and in its ardour and vigour of spirit, probably due to the fact that the Greek epigrams are the products of a decadent civilization, while the Manyō poems are the flower of a culture at its zenith. Thus the importance of the *Manyōshū* in world literature cannot be gainsaid.

The name '*Man-yō-shū*,' though often translated as 'Collection of a Myriad Leaves,' is authoritatively interpreted to mean 'Collection for a Myriad Ages.' No name more fitting could have been chosen to indicate the faith and the blessing with which the Anthology was bequeathed to posterity and to the world.

The fact that the *Manyōshū* consists of 20 books has set a precedent for the majority of later imperial anthologies. In its manner of classification and arrangement also it has provided, to a certain extent, a model for later collections which followed the method used in some books of the *Manyōshū*. In the number of its poems, however, the *Manyōshū* exceeds all the imperial anthologies of later periods. According to the *Kokka Taikan* (1st edition, 1901–2), the popular reprint of all the old anthologies, in which the poems are numbered in the order they appear in each original collection, the *Manyōshū* contains 4,516 poems. This figure can be reduced slightly if the duplications and variants are subtracted, so that 4,500 is commonly given as the actual number of the poems in the *Manyōshū*, while the poets whose names are either mentioned or ascertainable, are about 450 in all.

COMPILATION

It is impossible to ascertain how and when the compilation of the *Manyōshū* was completed in the form in which it has been handed down to this day. It may, however, be safely said that the collection came into being some time during the late Nara Period—the latter half of the 8th century. Of course the entire 20 books were not compiled systematically, nor at the same time. Most likely a few of them were compiled early in the century, which served as a nucleus to which were added later—at least on two different occasions—the remaining books, while the entire collection was subjected to revision at frequent intervals before the Anthology assumed its present form. That is to say, it required a rather complicated process extending over half a century to compile the *Manyōshū* in 20 books as we now have it.

There existed no definite principle of compilation. The standard of selection varied according to individual compilers; nor was the manner of classification and arrangement uniform. The great poet Yakamochi, of the illustrious clan of Ōtomo, is generally regarded as the last man who had a hand in the compilation of the entire collection. Yakamochi, who was involved in various political incidents after reaching middle age, died in 785 in adverse circumstances, and his clan itself declined steadily down to the end of the 9th century. In the meantime, the vogue for Chinese prose and poetry took possession of court circles for over 100 years from the late Nara Period to the early Heian Period, during which Japanese poetry was more or less neglected. It is probably owing to these circumstances that the *Manyōshū*, still lacking the intended final touch, was handed down in an unfinished form.

Of the sources of the *Manyōshū*, historical works such as the *Kojiki* and the *Nihonshoki* are mentioned in the book itself. In addition, collections of the works of individual poets, miscellaneous papers, memoirs and diaries were drawn upon, as well as poems preserved only through oral transmission. Evidence is scattered throughout the Anthology of the efforts of the compilers to gather material from books and fragmentary documents, and other available sources, both public and private, old and new. In some cases the compiler gives, together with a poem, its original source, reference matter, or even his personal opinion of the poem itself. Because the task of compilation was not completed, the Anthology contains here and there indications of the process of selection and the traces of the conscientious labours of the compilers, which constitute a unique and interesting feature not found in the later anthologies. Repetition of the same poems and inclusion of slightly varied versions in different parts of the book are also another characteristic quality of the *Manyōshū*.

One of the most important source books is the *Ruiju-Karin* (Forest of Classified Verses), mentioned elsewhere, which was compiled by Yamanoé Okura—a pioneer of Manyō poetry as well as a profound student of Chinese literature. This book having long since been lost, nothing is known as to its form or the number of books into which it was divided, but from its title we may suppose the poems to have had some sort of classification. There are reasons to conjecture that this anthology may have served as a model for at least the first two books of the *Manyōshū*. The name ' Karin ' (Forest of Verses) appears in an Imperial Household document dated 751, a quarter of a century after the death of Okura, though it remains a question whether or not the book is to be identified with the *Ruiju-Karin*. Another anthology on which the *Manyōshū* draws heavily is *Kokashū* (Collection of Ancient Poems), which was in all likelihood an anthology of a general character. Besides these, the *Manyōshū* mentions four individual anthologies, known respectively as the Hitomaro, Kanamura, Mushimaro and Sakimaro Collection, but it is impossible to ascertain whether each was the collected work of the poet whose name it bears, or included poems by others ; or whether it was simply a collection of poems compiled by the poet.

As a general rule, an individual poem or a group of poems in the *Manyōshū* is preceded by the name of the author and a preface, and is frequently followed by a note. In these prefaces and notes are given the occasion, the date and place of composition, the source book or the manner of transmission, or anecdotes or legends concerning the authors or the poems. Occasionally in the notes the compilers' comments and criticisms are given. All the prefaces and notes and dates are written in Chinese. In some of the books the letters and introductions in Chinese prose, sometimes quite lengthy, which were sent together with the poems, are included. Even Chinese poems, though this is rare, find their way into these pages.

The texts of the poems are transcribed in Chinese characters. The syllabaries called *kana* which came into being a century or so later, were still at an incipient stage in their development. Accordingly, in writing Japanese poems, Chinese characters were borrowed for their phonetic values, or they were used ideographically in their original sense. Sometimes the first method was employed exclusively in copying a poem, but more often the two methods were used simultaneously. The so-called ' *Manyō-gana* ' are the Chinese characters which were commonly used as phonograms in the *Manyōshū*, from which the present system of *kana* was evolved. Besides the above two methods, Chinese characters were frequently used in playful and fantastic combinations like puzzles, to denote syllables or words. The problems arising from the difficulty of deciphering them in the last-mentioned instances, and more often from uncertainty as to the exact reading of the characters used ideographically, have been gradually solved in subsequent ages, but there remain certain words and passages of which the reading is still disputed among specialists.

In this connection it may be pointed out that while the *Manyōshū* had necessarily to be clothed in a Chinese garb, so to speak, in the absence of any other system of writing, the very idea of making such a collection of poems was in all probability inspired by the examples imported from China, where the work of compiling anthologies had early developed, and where in later ages it grew to be almost a national industry of unparalleled magnitude. The *Shi King* of Confucian canon, already mentioned, and the famous *Chu Tsu*, a collection of metrical compositions, compiled toward the end of the first century B. C., had long been known in Japan by the time the first two books of the *Manyōshū* are conjectured to have been completed. Later works, especially anthologies made in the 6th century, were widely read by Japanese. Of these the most important was the *Wên Hsuan* in 30 books, containing both prose and poetry, which was popular in and around the court of Nara, and which came to be the standard text-book of Chinese literature in Japan after the 8th century. The *Yütai Sinyung*, another collection of elegant and somewhat voluptuous lyrics, which appears to have been privately cherished, may also be mentioned. It is significant that of the Manyō poets, more than twenty are known as accomplished versifiers in Chinese, and that a small collection of Chinese poems composed by Japanese was published in 751 under the title of *Kaifūsō*, preceding by several years the supposed date of the completion of the *Manyōshū*. The wonder is that at a time when Japan had yet to possess a writing system of her own, and when the literature of the continent, as well as its arts and crafts, were being bodily transplanted and assiduously cultivated, there should have emerged the *Manyōshū*—a monumental collection of native verse in the purest Yamato speech. For an explanation of this point, the reader is referred to Part II, in which the political and social background of the Manyō age and the life and the spirit of the nation are dealt with at length.

VERSIFICATION AND RHETORICAL DEVICES

Manyō versification consists in combining in varied ways several or more lines, which as a rule are made up of five or seven syllables. The most prevalent form in the *Manyōshū*, which accounts for more than ninety per cent of the total number of its poems and which still flourishes to-day as the form *par excellence* of the national poetry of Japan, is the *tanka*—a verse of five lines of 5–7–5–7–7 syllables. On the other hand, the so-called 'long poem' or *chōka* consists of alternate lines of 5 and 7 syllables, finishing with an extra 7-syllable line. Though called 'long,' the longest *chōka* in the *Manyōshū* does not exceed 150 lines. The Anthology contains some 260 *chōka*, including many masterpieces by Kakinomoto Hitomaro, the 'Saint of Poetry.' The presence of these poems, unsurpassed in number as well as in quality by later anthologies, constitutes an outstanding feature of the *Manyōshū*. Generally speaking, the *chōka* is accompanied by one or two, or even several, short poems called *hanka*, somewhat in the manner of an 'envoy,' summarizing, or supplementing, or elaborating on, the contents of the main poem. The word *hanka* meaning 'verse that repeats,' was derived from Chinese classical poetry, in which the term is applied to a similar auxiliary verse. Though such repetition was not unknown in ancient Japanese poetry, its development and standardization in the Manyō age may have been due to Chinese influence. A third verse-form is called *sedōka*—a name presumably of Japanese invention—which repeats twice a tercet of 5–7–7. This form fell into desuetude in later ages, the *Manyōshū* itself containing only about 60 examples. There is yet another curious form called ' Buddha's Foot Stone Poem' by virtue of the fact that there are extant 21 poems of this type commemorating a stone monument bearing Buddha's foot-mark, which was erected in 752 in the precincts of the Yakushi-ji temple near Nara. The poem consists of 6 lines of 5–7–5–7–7–7 syllables, and only a few specimens are found in the *Manyōshū*. Finally it may be mentioned that there is in Book VIII (Orig. No. 1635) a brief form of *renga* (' poems-in-series ') which became extremely popular in the 14th century and after, and in the composition of which a number of persons participated.

Japanese verse is generally based on the combination of

syllables in fives and sevens. It takes no account of the question of stress, pitch, or length of syllable ; nor is rhyme employed for poetic effect. This is an inevitable consequence of the phonetic system of the Japanese language, in which, as far as concerns its standard form, known since the beginning of history as the Yamato language, all syllables end in vowels, and there is no clear distinction between accented and unaccented, or long and short syllables, thus rendering impossible a metrical system based upon rhyme or accent. Thus, the number of syllables, which serves usually as only one of the bases of metrical structure in other languages, has become the sole principle of Japanese prosody.

Of the different rhetorical devices, alliteration, which is so conspicuous in old Germanic poetry, is employed consciously or unconsciously, and frequently with considerable effect in the *Manyōshū*, as it is also in all forms of Japanese poetry, both ancient and modern. On the other hand, parallelism, as it is found in Shinto litanies and more commonly in Chinese verse, is used invariably in *chōka*, often with consummate skill.

Among the other devices in Japanese poetry, what are known as *kake kotoba* (pivot-words), *makura kotoba* (pillow-words) and *joshi* (introductory verses) are the most peculiar, the effect of which depends upon a subtle association produced by similarity or identity of words in sound or sense. Of the three, the *kake kotoba* is the simplest, being a form of word-play which, however, occupies in Japanese poetry a legitimate and important place.

The ' pillow-word ' modifies the word that follows it in various ways, either through sound or sense association. As a poetic technique the use of pillow-words had been practised from the earliest times so that by the Manyō age many of them had become conventionalized, while others were obscure and unintelligible. There are pillow-words which may be construed in more than one way, and there are some which invoke images extraneous and incongruous, confusing to the uninitiated reader. But where they are used properly, and in a proper place, the effect is extremely felicitous. The nearest counterpart in Occidental poetry is the 'permanent epithet' in Homer. But the pillow-word is far more free, daring and imaginative. It is not necessarily an adjective, but may be an attributive form of a verb, a noun in the possessive or objective case, and so on, and considerable freedom and ingenuity is shown in its application. Thus, 'grass for pillow' is natural and appropriate as a pillow-word for 'journey,' reminding one of the hardships of a traveller in primitive ages, but where the word *azusa yumi* (birchwood bow) is applied to the noun *haru* (spring time), the connection cannot be established except through another word *haru*, a verb meaning 'to string.' The phrase *akane sasu* (madder-root coloured) for the 'morning sun' may be applied by gradual transference of association to 'sunlight,' 'day,' 'purple' and finally even to 'rosy-cheeked youth.' *Taku tsunu* (fibre rope) is made to serve as a pillow-word for *Shiragi*, because the *taku* fibre is white, and the Japanese word 'white,' *shiro* or *shira*, is partly homophonous with the name of the Korean state. These are just a few examples. While many of these pillow-words had been, as has already been stated, partly conventionalized by the 8th century and handed down to poets as stock phrases, their vitality had by no means been exhausted. In fact, it appears that there was still room for the invention of new pillow-words, for the *Manyōshū* contains a number of epithets not found in poems of earlier date.

The *joshi* or 'introductory verse' is based on somewhat similar principles, but it is longer and admits of greater freedom in application than the pillow-word. More than 5 syllables in length, the introductory verse modifies the contents of the succeeding verse, usually by way of metaphor. For instance, in Poem No. 205, the lines describing a warrior standing with his bow, etc., constitute an introductory verse to the Bay of Matokata, the target (*mato*) he is aiming at being partly homophonous with the name of the bay. Here between the introductory verse and the main part of the poem there is no connection whatever, either actual or logical, and their juxtaposition may appear unnatural and perplexing ; but such abrupt transition from one image to another, without destroying the latent association, is one of the characteristics of Japanese poetry, in which lies also the secret of the technique of modern *haiku*. Without investigation of such points it is perhaps not possible to elucidate the psychological foundation and historical development of Japanese poetry.

The characteristic rôle of the introductory verse is to invoke images lying outside the mental vista of the reader. After having carried him aloft into an unsuspected realm, it suddenly but gently sets him down in another world (Nos. 205, 316, etc.). The very absence of actual connection or co-relation between the modifier and the word modified is what makes this form of oblique comparison so effective. Since it is the way of the Japanese language to introduce a comparison with no connective term corresponding to ' as ' or ' like,' the blending of different ideas and images is achieved in a most direct manner and examples of the felicitous employment of the introductory verse abound throughout the *Manyōshū*.

Individual Books

In order to indicate the general appearance and composition of the *Manyōshū* as a whole, it may be useful to give here a brief account of the individual books, their characteristics, and the periods with which they are concerned.

The first two books are sometimes regarded as collections compiled by imperial order, so carefully are they edited as to matter and form. Book I contains poems written between the reign of the Emperor Yūryaku (456–79) and the early Nara Period (*circa* 712), whereas Book II covers a more extended period, with poems believed to have been written in the reign of the Emperor Nintoku (313–99) and those dated as late as 715. 16 *chōka* are found in the former and 19 in the latter. In both books the poems generally are arranged in chronological order, and Hitomaro is the poet most copiously represented, while imperial progresses constitute the favourite theme of Book I. Though small in size as compared with others, these two books are of great importance for their poetry of the so-called 'Early Palace Style.' Book III covers the long interval between the reign of the Empress Suiko (592–628) and the 16th year of Tempyō (744), including the brilliant periods of Fujiwara and Nara. In contrast to its predecessors, which contain large numbers of poems by sovereigns, princes and princesses of the blood, this book includes more works by courtiers. Here we encounter for the first time the poems of Akahito. Tabito and Yakamochi and the illustrious company of poets centreing about the Ōtomo clan also make their appearance. Book IV, with the exception of a few earlier works, consists largely of poems of the Nara Period, especially those of Tabito and his group and those exchanged between young Yakamochi and his lady-loves ; while Book V consists of poems exchanged between Tabito and his friends, to which are added the works of Okura, covering the years between 728 and 733, and containing a number of important *chōka*, besides verse and prose in Chinese. Book VI, covering the years between 723 and 744, is more or less identical with Books IV and VIII as regards period and poets. It contains as many as 27 *chōka*, and is distinguished by the inclusion of a large number of poems of travel, of imperial progresses and poems composed on the occasion of banquets. Book VII, like Books X, XI and XII, contains anonymous poems which may be ascribed roughly to a period extending from the reign of the Empress Jitō (686–96) to that of the Empress Gemmyō (715–23). Many poems from the 'Hitomaro Collection' are included, while the inclusion of 26 *sedōka* forms a notable feature of this book. Book VIII, as stated above, resembles Book IV, the earliest

poem in the collection being a *tanka* by the Emperor Jomei
(629–41), while the latest are dated 743–45. The poems are
divided into 'miscellaneous poems' and 'epistolary poems'
(largely amatory), and each kind is subdivided under the
heads of the four seasons—a form of classification which
served as a model for later imperial anthologies. Book IX,
except for a single *tanka* by the Emperor Yūryaku, contains
poems written between the reign of the Emperor Jomei and
744, which are drawn largely from the Hitomaro and Mushimaro Collections; it also includes 22 *chōka* and many on
legendary subjects. Book X, while consisting of anonymous poems, as does Book VII, appears to include more of
later work—many pieces being delicately and beautifully
finished. Its nature poems reveal a new tendency, as in the
case of those dealing with gardens. Poems in Books XI
and XII, which are also anonymous, may be ascribed to the
Fujiwara and the early Nara Periods, and many of them are
in the style of folk-songs. Book XIII is a unique reposi-
tory of 67 *chōka* of unknown authorship. Although many
of these may be traced to the transitional period between
the age of the *Kojiki* and the *Nihonshoki* and the Manyō age,
there are included poems of unmistakably later origin, so
that it is difficult to ascribe the book as a whole to any
definite period.

Book XIV is a collection of the so-called 'Eastland
poems,' of which neither the authors nor the date of compilation can be ascertained, but which stand apart as provincial
poetry, unique in language and style. Book XV contains
among others a group of sea poems written by the members
of the embassy despatched to Korea in 736 and a series of
63 impassioned love poems exchanged about the year 740
between the courtier Nakatomi Yakamori and his sweetheart Sanu Chigami. Book XVI is distinguished by its
inclusion of legendary poems and humorous verse, covering a period from the reign of the Emperor Mommu (697–
706) to the Tempyō era. It is generally conjectured that
these first 16 books were put more or less into their present

shape by Yakamochi. Some scholars believe that certain books, especially Book XIV, were completed some time after the year 771. Though no final conclusion has yet been reached in this matter, it is evident that there is a gap between the first 16 books and the 4 following.

Books XVII–XX appear to be personal compilations made by Yakamochi of his own poems and those of others about him. All the poems are of the Tempyō era—the glorious years of the Nara Period: Book XVII covers the years from 730 to 748 ; Book XVIII, from 748 to the early part of 750 ; and Book XIX, thence to the beginning of 753. These 3 books contain altogether 47 *chōka*, some of which are of great literary and historical value. It should be noted that the works of Yakamochi constitute the principal contents of these books—especially Book XIX, of which fully two-thirds of the poems are his ; and while there are numerous exchange and banquet poems in the conventional vein, there are also found many born of pure creative impulse. It is this book which contains the majority of Yakamochi's masterpieces, and provides the richest source for the study of his poetic genius. Book XX covers the years from 753 to 759, and contains many banquet poems. There are also poems composed by the frontier-guards—brave Eastlanders who went to defend the coast of Kyūshū—and their parents and wives, expressing their patriotism and genuine personal emotions. The name, native province and district, status and rank of each soldier are carefully set down, together with his verse. In conjunction with the other group of Eastland poems by anonymous singers in Book XIV, these poems are of exceptional interest to the reader. The year 759 is the latest date mentioned in the *Manyōshū*, and is attached to the last poem in Book XX, written by Yakamochi, at that time Governor of Inaba Province. It is a date that provides a clue to fixing the time when the whole *Manyōshū* was finally completed.

PART II

POLITICAL AND SOCIAL BACKGROUND

Behind the *Manyōshū* there looms the epochal Reform of Taika (646), which brought in its train, in rapid succession, a series of political and social changes, progressive and reactionary. Some acquaintance, therefore, with the significance and far-reaching influence of that reform is indispensable to a proper appreciation of the Manyō poetry.

From the beginning of history Japanese society was built upon a patriarchal foundation. The unit in the system was the *uji*, or clan, consisting of a group of families headed by the main house and bound into a compact and well-ordered community by the ties of common ancestry. Each clan was under the control and leadership of a chief called *uji-no-kami*, and the members of the clan were known as *uji-bito* or clansfolk. Generally a clan embraced within its system alien people working for it as serfs and enjoying its protection. These were called *kakibé*. As is usual in an agricultural society, the clans possessed lands of their own, which they exploited with the help of the man-power at their disposal, so that even economically each formed a sort of commonwealth independent of the others. When thus stated, it would appear that the social order of old Japan was nothing but a primitive and decentralized one that had grown up naturally on the soil. But such was not the case. Though there were numerous clans, with their three ' divisions ' according to ancestry—(1) scions of the Imperial House, (2) descendants of the imperial followers or of the aboriginal tribal chiefs who had submitted to the imperial rule, and (3) descendants of alien settlers,—they were officially recognized only by virtue of their respective services to the Throne ; and, theoretically as well as actually, they formed a vast and unified society with the Imperial House as its centre.

The reality of the imperial prestige and power lay in the very principle of this clan system. The emperor was the supreme head of all clans. Every man born in Japan owed allegiance to him, served and obeyed him as he would serve and obey the chief of his own clan, and looked up to the Imperial House as the head of his own family. With a sovereign of unbroken lineage reigning above, Japan's clan system formed a great family state, transcending the rivalry and strife of individual clans. Under this system the chiefs of various clans were subjects of the Imperial House for which they performed their respective hereditary functions, some as priests or ministers of state, others as soldiers or artisans.

It should be noted, however, that the system permitted the authority of an individual clan chief to intervene between the people and the Imperial House, for the latter ruled directly only over state lands and the people living thereon, while the rest of the country and its population were subject to the Throne through the clan chiefs. And wherever the chief of a clan controlled a wide domain and large numbers of clans-folk and *kakibé*, there was likely to emerge an independent local régime which cut off the people from the Imperial House. Moreover, greed for power and wealth on the one hand, and the growth of population and land development enterprises on the other, led to a struggle between clans for territory and serfs and to the evil practice of annexation, which destroyed the peace and stability of the country. In fact, from the 6th to the middle of the 7th century, this tendency became more and more pronounced. The lands of the weaker clans were annexed or absorbed by the more influential families. There were quarrels among powerful houses over spoils, especially in connection with the newly conquered territories in Korea. The period was marked by deep social unrest and frequent political upheavals, culminating in the rise of the Sogas, father and son, who conspired to augment their own power at the expense of the Imperial House. It was this situation that called for the Reform of Taika.

What had to be done at that time was clear. It was necessary in the first place to check the domination of the mighty families at court and in the country, and to eliminate the excesses of intermediate powers so as to enable the people at large to enjoy the direct rule of the Imperial House; and in the second place, to suppress the practice of annexation, to strengthen the national finance and to promote the welfare of the people. The need of these remedial steps was well realized without any prompting from abroad. At the same time, as regards the actual procedure, Japan could, and did, learn much from China.

Some historians call this period the ' age of imitation of China under the Sui and the T'ang dynasties,' and in a sense they are justified. The significance of the Reform of Taika could never be grasped without taking into account its continental elements. It should, nevertheless, be remembered that those elements were adopted only in so far as they suited the conditions in Japan, and moreover that it was not a case of blind imitation, for the reforms were carried on with an ardour and ambition which not only equalled but surpassed the examples set by the continent.

Japan's political and cultural contact with the Asiatic continent was first established through Korea. The Japanese-Korean intercourse, which may probably be traced back to remotest times, becomes a matter of recorded history with the expedition of the Empress Jingu to the peninsula in the year 200 (according to the *Nihonshoki*). For several centuries subsequently Korea proved politically a source of perpetual trouble for Japan, but from the cultural standpoint that country rendered a signal service by acting as an intermediary for the introduction of Confucianism along with Chinese arts and letters, and also by sending her own scholars and craftsmen, and large numbers of immigrants. In the middle of the 6th century the King of Kudara, a state in the south-western part of Korea, presented to the Japanese court an image of Buddha together

xxix

with some Buddhist scriptures and ritual furnishings. This was an event that marked a decisive stage in the history of Japanese cultural contact with the continent.

With the advent of Buddhism there developed a new situation that had two important aspects. One was that this sudden confrontation of the native cult of Shinto, the backbone of Japanese life, by a strange faith from abroad, had considerable repercussions. So violent was the shock that it caused an open breach between the new and the old schools of thought and even produced a movement among the conservatives against the importation of foreign culture in general. The other was that the continental culture now entering Japan had assumed a cosmopolitan character, considerably widening the field of Japanese vision. Concerning the former of these two aspects more will be said later. Here a few words will be added regarding the latter.

In the year 589 China was unified under the Sui dynasty —China that had been torn for many centuries, during which the so-called ' Three Kingdoms ' and the ' Six Dynasties ' rose and fell. It is recorded that during these periods of internecine strife, bands of war-stricken Chinese sought refuge in Japan, but it appears improbable that any attempt was made on the part of Japan to establish friendly intercourse with any of the Chinese states for the sake of cultural benefits. There was, of course, prior to those periods, the mighty empire of the Hans ; but of its civilization, only a meagre stream, trickling through Korea, had entered Japan. But when under the Sui a new China emerged, reunited and re-vitalized, and a swelling tide of Asiatic culture began to sweep the continent, Japan, with new vistas opened up to her by Buddhism, was in a ferment, eagerly seeking to import the continental civilization. The movement was headed by the great and progressive national leader—Prince Shōtoku (d. 622). In 607 Ono Imoko was despatched as ambassador to the court of the Sui emperor. Friendly intercourse with China being

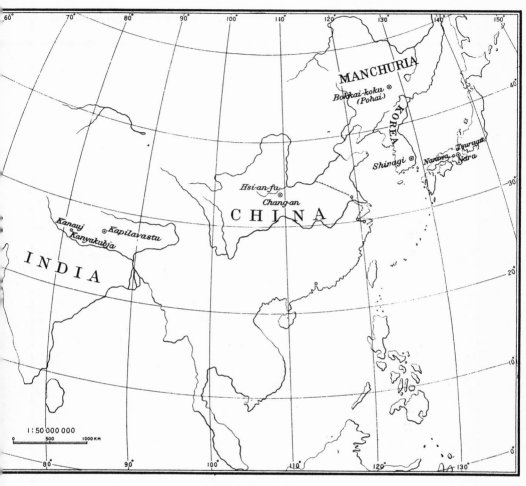

EASTERN ASIA

JAPAN in PROVINCES

thus formally inaugurated, Japan herself joined in the broad current of Asiatic civilization.

The civilization of the Sui dynasty and its successor, the T'ang, was characterized by its cosmopolitanism. Militarily and politically the Han empire, whose armies marched far into foreign lands and whose government effectively held the conquered territories, was also cosmopolitan. But the Han culture possessed few international elements. It is this essentially Chinese civilization of the Han race that was preserved and even enhanced by the Three Kingdoms and the Six Dynasties, notably by the state of Wei in the north, and by the states of Tsi and Liang in the south, and that had found its way to Korea, and thence to Japan. The Sui and T'ang, showing a far more liberal and tolerant attitude towards alien races and alien cultures, proceeded to create a new cosmopolitan fusion of all cultural elements.

Military campaigns opened new routes of travel and commerce. Products of Persia and India and their arts and religions were brought into China through Central Asia. Even traces of Graeco-Roman civilization from farther west were discernible. Above all, Buddhism played an important part in stimulating the creation of a new culture as it brought not only its tenets and creeds but also the music, arts and learning of the countries which were situated along its long road to China. Thus, contact with the Sui and T'ang meant that Japan was able to be in touch with the rest of the world as far as was possible at that time.

The Sui dynasty, which fell in less than 30 years, was followed by the T'ang dynasty, under which the new civilization continued to make swift strides toward its consummation and usher in the golden age of China. Such a brilliant cultural progress could not have been achieved without political and economic stability. Naturally, attention was first focussed upon the centralization of power with a view to reuniting the country that had suffered so long from being a house divided. In order to execute this policy, men of talent were required to serve in various Government posts. Accordingly, an elaborate system of civil service examinations was inaugurated. Something like a socialization of land was also adopted, to ensure revenue from taxation and to put national finance upon a solid basis. The so-called 'Land-allotment Law' which was promulgated in this connection was designed to render plastic the private title to immovable property and to effect wider and more equitable distribution by prohibiting perpetual ownership and forestalling unrestricted expansion of large estates. It was these and other laws and institutions of the early T'ang that supplied Japan with valuable models and examples.

Centralization of power was also one of the crying needs of Japan for which the country with its patriarchal system headed by the Imperial House had long been prepared. The principle of government by a central authority was already there, deep-rooted like a religious faith in the minds of the people. What was necessary was to remove the noxious incrustations of later centuries that had obstructed its operation. Consequently, in Japan the desired reform was accomplished far more smoothly and thoroughly than in China. The first task of the reformers was the elimination of the extraordinary political powers and economic privileges enjoyed by the great clans which had grown semi-independent of the Imperial House, and of which the Soga family was the most powerful, arrogant and unscrupulous. In the 4th year of the Empress Kōgyoku's reign (645) the Soga usurpers were put to death, Emishi, the father, at his home and Iruka, the son, in the Council Hall of the Palace. The heroes of this historic drama which paved the way for the Taika Reform, were the Prince Naka-no-ōé (later, the Emperor Tenji) and Kamako (later, Fujiwara Kamatari) of the priestly clan of Nakatomi. In the same year the system of eras was established, to the first of which the name Taika was given. Hence the name of the series of reforms which were begun with that year.

Thus the first obstacle to the proposed reform was removed, but the real work still lay ahead. After having disposed of the obnoxious clan system, what new order was to be set up in its place? What steps were to be taken to facilitate the transition from the old order to the new? These were large and difficult problems. However, judging from the manner in which the Prince embarked upon a series of innovations immediately after destroying the Soga family, it may be that his programme had been carefully formulated in advance in consultation with Kamatari and other advisers. Be that as it may, the principal features of the reform were as follows. All free citizens, instead of being left under the control of their clan chief, were made subject to, and protected by, the Central Government. All lands were turned over to the Government and re-distributed among individuals according to their family standing, their services to the state, and their needs of a livelihood. The country was newly divided into provinces, provinces into districts, and local administration was put in the hands of officials appointed by the Central Government. Hereditary office-holding was considerably curbed to make room for the appointment of the most talented to government posts. Such drastic innovations were bound to be attended by profound and alarming social changes. Practical statesmanship was obliged to face the question of how to adjust to the new age the old forces that still remained unextinguished. The Government instituted a new system of court ranks and grades and conferred various caps and titles upon persons of distinguished lineage, or appointed sons of great families to offices and provided them with emoluments from the national treasury, in an attempt to compensate the clans for the loss of their former powers and prosperity. Although such measures tended necessarily to obscure the principle underlying the socialization of land or the mobilization of the country's best talents, the prevailing spirit of progress was not so weak as to be checked by mere compromises of this kind. Those nobles without ability, although some out of sheer discontent offered a feeble resistance, had no alternative but to follow the road of steady decline, while new forces with a new spirit gained ascendancy and proceeded to build up a new Japan. All such innovations, of course, are bound to be attended with excesses. As time passed the new order disclosed its maladjustment with reality at various points : the Reform of Taika had to be modified and revised in many ways according to the actual conditions of the country. The earlier part of the Manyō age, i. e. the three decades from 673, when the Emperor Temmu moved the court to Asuka, to 710 when the capital was established at Nara by the Empress Gemmyō, was a period of political experiment and innovation. It was in the next 50 years, the later Manyō age, that the Reform of Taika was brought to a stage of completion, and this period coincides with the reign of the T'ang emperor Hsuantsung under whom China reached the zenith of her civilization.

As for the new Japan born of the Taika Reform, its most conspicuous aspect was a deep and pervading devotion to the Throne and the thorough consolidation of its authority. In a way, of course, this was nothing new either in fact or in idea, since the Imperial House as political centre was a thing as old as Japan itself. What was new was the free and untrammelled operation of the old principle now that it had been embodied in a proper political frame-work. The common people throughout the land, delivered from the control of intermediate powers, rejoiced in the direct rule of the Imperial House. The newly-awakened sense of loyalty in all its freshness and fullness may be perceived on almost every page of the *Manyōshū*. It was a joyful devotion arising from the close relationship between sovereign as parent and subjects as children—a relationship based upon the idea of a great family-state, which was then so forcibly projected upon the national consciousness. The clan system was not destroyed, but refined and elevated. Each clan, rising above its selfish interests, re-discovered its *raison-d'être* in the light of its obligations to the Imperial House. The clansman realized his responsibility to uphold the reputation of his ancestors and strove to live and act accordingly, as may be readily seen from the works of the poets of the Ōtomo clan. This moral awakening was not confined to great families alone : that even the humblest people in the provinces were animated by a noble spirit of loyalty is amply demonstrated by the poems of the frontier-guards.

Centralization of power required the maintenance of close contact between the capital and the provinces. For purposes of efficient local administration it was necessary to construct new roads and to develop a courier service, posts, ports and other facilities for travel and communication. The growing intercourse with the capital meant for the provinces a gradual elevation of their culture and living standards. Moreover, with the firm establishment of internal order and security, and the enhancement of the Government's power and prestige, the borders of the empire were extended into remoter regions occupied by untamed tribes such as the *Yezo* in northern provinces or the *Hayato* in south-eastern Kyūshū. Thus, the Manyō age was one of unprecedented cultural progress and political expansion. Viewed from the present day, what was then actually accomplished appears quite small in scale, but its significance is to be discovered in the temper of the Manyō man in the course of this expansion and growth. An exuberant enthusiasm, a buoyant spirit and a highly imaginative and susceptible mind gave to his emotional life a refreshing and colourful glow, as of the dawning sky, and produced this rich crop of poetry. That there are so many fine poems of travel is but an indication of the pioneering nature of the age.

Places which had an important bearing on the Manyō poems are, with the exception of the metropolitan area surrounding the capital, more or less outlying provinces, such as Izumo, Iwami, Koshi, Hitachi, of which the last three are associated respectively with Hitomaro, Yakamochi, and Mushimaro. The island of Tsukushi, which recalls the names of Tabito and Okura, has a wider significance; it invites our attention to Japan's foreign relations at that time and their influence upon the life of the nation.

The Asiatic continent was not only the motherland of a new culture, with which Japan had to keep on good terms, but also a conceivable enemy against which she had to make military preparations to defend herself. Thus, the Government General of the Dazaifu in northern Kyūshū, which was charged with foreign affairs and the local administration of the island, was also a military centre directing the frontier-guards garrisoned along the coast. Numerous officials plied back and forth along the way between the capital and the Dazaifu. The soldiers were obliged to spend long years at forlorn outposts on islands or capes far from their homes in Eastland: embassies despatched to Shiragi (a Korean state in the south-east of the peninsula) or to China sometimes passed through the Dazaifu before they set out on their perilous journeys across the ocean. The envoys to Po-hai (in Manchuria), it should also be mentioned, departed from the port of Tsuruga on the Japan Sea.

The sea journey was fraught with dangers, and all the more poignant was the sorrow of leave-takings and the longing for home. It was due to these circumstances that the Manyō age produced hosts of sea poets, such as are encountered nowhere else in Japanese literature; and the poems by members of the Embassy to Shiragi found in Book XV (Nos. 738–763) afford a most conspicuous instance of this. On the other hand, there were in the Nara Period not a few foreigners who came to Japan on their own account, like the ' Brahmin Prelate,' who came from India, with an Annamese priest Buttetsu, or Abbot Ganjin of China who arrived as a blind man after a series of trying hardships at sea, or the nun Rigan (Nos. 388–9) who immigrated from Shiragi and spent the rest of her life in modest seclusion as a guest of the Ōtomo family.

The fruits of this intercourse were many and varied, rich and dazzling. Not only religion and learning were imported, but also Buddhist sculpture and architecture, together with their auxiliary arts and crafts. These gave Japan temples and palaces of unheard-of splendour and grandeur. Musical instruments, like flutes, drums, gongs and cymbals brought from India, Central Asia, China and Korea sounded, as it were, the sweet music of the Land of Bliss. There arrived cargoes of rare treasures and articles of exquisite beauty and workmanship, such as may be seen to-day in the Shōsō-in (Nara), where have been preserved under imperial seal the personal belongings of the Emperor Shōmu. No wonder then that on this new rich soil poetry blossomed like flowers in spring. It is rather surprising that the *Manyōshū* contains comparatively few allusions to these articles of alien cultures and civilizations, but we should not overlook the rôle they had played in creating the necessary atmosphere for an efflorescence of poetry. It is not difficult to imagine, for instance, with what wonderment, with what ebullition of enthusiasm and joy the Manyō men hailed the dedication of the Great Buddha of the Tōdai-ji temple, in 752, which was performed with great pomp and magnificence.

The Manyō age naturally fostered the growth of cities. The immemorial custom of removing the court at each change of reign was broken, and Nara remained the capital for seven successive reigns. There may have been many reasons for this, but the growth of the city's population, the permanence of its various establishments, the importance of its trade and industry, were no doubt some of the most important considerations against the transference of the court. At that time Nara was a great metropolis, four miles long and more than three miles wide, with its imperial palaces and official mansions, its beautiful temples and towers, and its broad avenues planted with willows and orange-trees. The city had two markets—one on the east side, the other on the west. Money economy was beginning to prevail, and trade was steadily expanding. Poems with reference to commerce (e. g. No. 885) which are occasionally found in our Anthology are the reflections of yet another aspect of this new age.

THOUGHTS AND BELIEFS

The Manyō man lived in a world peopled by multitudes of gods and spirits, genii and fairies. And it is noteworthy that despite the wide acceptance of Confucianism and Buddhism, almost all the gods whom he sang, or who fed the well-spring of his lyric inspiration, were purely Japanese. They were gods of the indigenous cult which was named Shintō, or the Way of the Gods, in contradistinction to Buddhism.

There is here no need of attempting to explore the whole field of Shintō mythology. So far as the *Manyōshū* is concerned, it suffices that on the one hand there were the spirits, which had survived from the remote past in folklore, and which still affected daily life ; and on the other, those whose influence was steadily rising as gods of the clan or nation. When analyzed historically, it will be seen that the Manyō idea in this connection was really an admixture and fusion of concepts which had different origins and which were in various stages of development. There were mysterious powers which moved and had their being in nature but which were too vaguely felt to be personified : lands and provinces, mountains and rivers, trees and herbs, and even human acts such as speech, were believed to be endowed with spirits, and as such were made objects of reverence or fear. There were gods possessing full personalities, namely the ancestors of the Imperial House and of various clans, the patrons of arts and industries, the tutelary deities of communities and the spirits of nature. Thus, individual objects of nature in their various capacities, sometimes as mediums through which gods manifested themselves to man, sometimes as gods in themselves, and sometimes as divine property or demesne, occupied their respective places in the religious life of the nation. The practice of taboo, charm and divination, so frequently alluded to in the *Manyōshū*, points unmistakably to a belief in the mysterious powers of the first category. Belief in gods of the second category in all its simplicity and naivety is illustrated in the poems of the ' Three Hills ' (Nos. 9–10), although similar cases of the deification of mountains or districts are to be met with frequently throughout the Anthology. The spirits of nature, such as storm and thunder, fire and water, seem to occupy an intermediate place between the first and second categories. The transition from the second to the third is exemplified in Tatsuta-hiko—the deity who ruled the wind. Finally there were gods conceived as personalities. This concept, which has all the other feelings for the supernatural as its background and as its intrinsic element, is best embodied in the ancestral gods. It is this concept which developed as the central idea, purifying, assimilating and unifying all other beliefs, and whose growth was parallel with the progress of the political unification of the country. The Goddess Ama-terasu—the ancestral deity of the Imperial House—was the chief guardian of agriculture, as well as the supreme god of heaven and earth. Consequently all the gods of heaven and earth and all the ancestral gods of clans were gradually systematized into a cult on the basis of communal and national life. It is, therefore, most natural that the ' eight hundred myriad gods ' came to form a pantheon with the Goddess Amaterasu as its central figure.

Now how did the Manyō man seek to communicate with his deities ? Generally in worshipping his god, he set in the earth before the altar a sacred wine-jar filled with saké brewed with special rites of purification ; hung up mirrors and beads on the sacred posts ; tied his shoulders with a cord of *yū*-fibre, presented the sacred *nusa*, 'with the *sakaki* branch fresh from the inmost hill ' (No. 386), and bending on his knees, recited his litany (*norito*). The greatest impediment to his prayer reaching the god was 'uncleanliness' of body and mind. He did not therefore neglect to redeem himself in the eyes of his deity by performing the rites of ablution (*misogi*) and purification (*harai*) (No. 803). It was his ideal of life that he should keep himself clean in body and soul, and in constant communion with his gods, to obtain their protection and thereby live and work in a happy world.

Gods were worshipped either in supplication or in thanksgiving. There were national feasts and communal feasts and those observed by individual households. Of the national feasts the most important were those held to pray for good crops and to give thanks for harvest, as was quite natural with an agricultural country like Japan. The first took place in spring, in the second month of the year, and the latter in autumn after the harvest. On the latter occasion the emperor himself offered new rice to the gods, after which he himself partook of it. Hence the feast was called *niinamé* or 'new-tasting.' On the following day, at the palace, the court nobles and officials were invited to a grand banquet of *Toyo-no-akari* (Nos. 730–1, etc.). The observance of the 'Feast of New-tasting' was not confined to the court but was celebrated throughout the country by each community and family.

Life had many trials and tribulations in the Manyō, as in any other, age. There were, for instance, the universal pitfalls of love. Equally unforeseen and vexing were the dangers of travel and military campaigns. The Manyō man before starting on a voyage would pray to the Gods of Suminoé for safety, or he would worship at the Shrine of Ḳashima, if he were setting out as a soldier. Even in crossing a steep mountain he would make offerings to the god of the 'awesome' pass (Nos. 882, 812, 237, 781, 782, 533, etc.). Prayer was also the usual recourse for the love-lorn (Nos. 161, 165). But when hope was fast waning and his fate seemed uncertain, the Manyō man resorted, now to charms to exorcize evil spirits, now to magical spells for the fulfilment of his desires ; and for telling his fortune he relied on omens and divinations. The use of the *shimé* (sacred rope) to mark off a place, or an object, was the principal method for making taboo (No. 35), while the binding of a stalk or spray of a plant for happiness and long life (No. 21, etc.) and sleeping with one's sleeves turned back to anticipate a visit from a lover or friend, were some of the commonest forms of sympathetic magic (No. 442). Among the omens, which were believed to be auguries of the coming of one's lover, an itch in the eye-brow, a sneeze, or unfastening of the girdle, may be cited as examples. It was believed that desired information was transmitted to a person in mysterious ways through certain mediums. Dreams served as this medium while one was asleep (Nos. 865–6) ; while in waking hours it consisted of such physical phenomena as mentioned above, to which may be added the stumbling of a horse a man was riding, which was regarded as a sign of the anxiety and longing of his people at home (No. 284). Apart from these natural and unsolicited signs there was another means by which the divine will was sought and man's fortunes told. This was divination, which was widely practised and for which there was even an hereditary office called *urabé*. Many were the forms of divination. There was one of native origin called 'deer oracle,' of which the exact character is not known. There was another introduced from China, according to which a forecast was made by the cracks appearing in a tortoise-shell roasted over the fire (No. 330). But among simpler and more popular forms were the 'evening oracle' and 'foot divination,' of which the first was supposedly performed by standing at a cross-roads in the evening and listening to the words spoken by those passing, and the second by counting the number of steps from one place to another, or by noting which foot, the right or the left, was required for the last step in covering a given distance. There was divination by dreams, and also divination by stone, based on a superstition that a stone varied in weight according to whether the occasion was evil or auspicious. The Manyō man's world was pervaded by mysterious powers, even to its minutest detail. These beliefs, generally held by the Manyō man, which appeared to comprise all the religious notions of his ancestors from primordial times, were undergoing changes with the progress of the age and through contact with alien influences. There were indications that some had already lost their positive ' awesomeness ' and were being treated with levity and freedom, while others were being elevated to a predominant place in the religious life of the people. Among decaying beliefs, we may cite, for instance, a poem (No. 837) in which a readiness is expressed to commit sacrilege for the sake of love. This is a romanticism exalting passion at the expense of the gods, and it is significant that such a sentiment is discovered in the works of apparently common people. In another poem (No. 833) its author, in his grief and despair, having lost his beloved wife, doubts the existence of any gods. Still another poem (No. 249) falls into sheer fantasy, as it speaks of persuading the moon-god to prolong a beautiful moonlight night! There occurs even a cynical poem by a disillusioned poet who demands the return of the offerings made to a god because his prayers for a tryst with his maid had failed. Obviously in many cases magic, taboo, and divination were practised not through a complete reliance upon their efficacy, but more or less as sentimental exercises. They were even sometimes treated in a whimsical spirit and their failure was of little concern. While the folklore beliefs, retained in the twilight of sentimental attachment, were being transferred into the province of poetic symbolism, the belief in ancestral gods, gaining more and more in its solemn and spiritual qualities, came to be clothed with high authority. This development went, as we have seen, hand in hand with the process of centralizing the political power. The ancestral gods of clans being placed in subordinate positions under the ancestral gods of the Imperial House, the emperor, as 'succeeding to the Celestial Throne,' was to wield its divine authority over the land. He was called Akitsu-kami (Manifest God) who stood above and over all other deities of heaven and earth, commanding their devotion and services. (Nos. 79–80, etc.)

> Lo, our great Sovereign, a goddess,
> Tarries on the Thunder
> In the clouds of heaven. (No. 118)

So sang a poet, with genuine conviction in the divinity of the sovereign, which was one of the basic concepts underlying the Shintō faith. Since the authority of the emperor was derived from the virtues and powers of his imperial ancestors which he had inherited, the poems magnifying a sovereign usually begin with a solemn description of the tradition concerning the Celestial Throne, and sometimes imperial princes are spoken of, by anticipation, as possessing the prerogatives of the sovereign. (Nos. 94, 103, etc.)

The emperor clearly occupied a place in which, not only as political but also as religious head of the country, he was to rule over the state with divine authority. As a matter of fact all the efforts of the reformers were concentrated upon moulding Japan into a great state with the emperor as its central figure; and it was with this high purpose that foreign cultures and civilizations were transplanted, adopted and assimilated. The ultimate aim was to bring into being a new Japan that should rival and surpass China or India in splendour. The fact that continental institutions and systems of government were imported in accordance with this policy is plainly seen by comparing the laws and statutes of the T'ang empire with those which were promulgated in Japan subsequent to the Reform of Taika. The acceptance of Buddhism was also part of the same programme. In other words, the new faith was embraced with the avowed purpose of making it serve as a mighty spiritual power to guard the state, and to provide the nation with new and high ideals in the field of culture.

When Buddhism was officially imported, it produced repercussions far more profound than those caused earlier by the introduction of Confucianism, for Buddhism came as a distinctly new religion to confront the native cult of Shintō, whereas Confucianism was largely a system of moral teachings. Buddha was, it was contended, a strange god from a strange land, who would compete with the deities of the nation. Acceptance of Buddhism would incur the displeasure of those gods of old and invite calamities to fall upon the country. In the face of bitter opposition and dire warnings Prince Shōtoku displayed both wisdom and statesmanship by accepting Buddhism, as he had accepted Confucianism before, when he installed the alien god in the pantheon of native deities. The prince himself welcomed and fervently embraced the new faith in order that it might be made, together with the continental culture behind it, an important factor of national progress and enlightenment. It is this progressive policy of tolerance that won over, as it did repeatedly thereafter, the temporary opposition from conservative and reactionary forces, and laid the foundation of the Japan that was to be.

From the Taika era to the Tempyō the above policy of Prince Shōtoku was followed. What was expected, then, of Buddhism was that it should provide the country with guardian deities and patrons of national well-being and progress. In this spirit 'provincial temples' and also the Great Buddha at Nara, which constitute the most conspicuous monuments of those times, were constructed. Similarly, the Sutras of the Golden Light (*Konkōmyō-gyō*) and of the Benign King (*Ninnō-gyō*) were, in all probability, taught, read, and copied more widely than any other of the numerous Buddhist books. After all, these were more or less cultural enterprises differing little from the compilation of books and the decoration of the capital for the basic purpose of rendering Japan a happier land to live in.

The external manifestations and proselytizing methods thus preceded the spiritual penetration of Buddhism. The view of the earthly existence as one of sorrow and pain, the ardent desire inspired thereby for deliverance, the idea of *karma*, and the practice arising therefrom of pious dedication —to these phases of the new religion, the *Manyōshū* contains few direct references, although Buddhistic thoughts and allusions are scattered here and there. The fact that sentiments concerning life's vanity and evanescence, such as ‘life frail as foam’ (Nos. 141, 543), ‘all is vain’ (Nos. 716, 69, 809, 276, 443), ‘nothing endures’ (Nos. 368, 388, 809, 499, 500, 513), are frequently encountered, indicates that it is at this point that Buddhism first entered the province of Japanese poetry. Nevertheless, it should be recalled that to the Manyō man who had accumulated rich personal experiences, having witnessed stupendous political upheavals and social changes and standing at a concourse of sundry cultural streams, this sort of idea made a great appeal. It should, however, be remembered that it gave rise to no intense religious aspirations ; nothing more than what appear to be rather lukewarm and conventional sentiments (Nos. 828, 541–2). More genuine, perhaps, is the calm contemplative attitude which was induced by the same view (Nos. 501, 515). In the poems of the later Nara Period, there is to be found a pensive mood, ready to respond to the slightest quivering of nature, presaging the approach of a new age of lyricism. (Nos. 521–2, 523)

As regards what is to come after death, generally speaking, the traditional notions prevailed. The dead are either to rise to heaven (No. 94), or to descend to the netherworld (No. 639), or wander in the vague space between (No. 640). The Buddhistic belief in a life to come crops up as a solace in a hopeless case of love (No. 267), but the Manyō man was not seriously concerned over the vexed problem of metempsychosis. The idea of the possibility of a man's being born an insect or a bird in his next life is introduced in one of a series of Anacreontic verses of Taoistic inspiration (No. 369) for no other purpose than to emphasize the importance of the pleasures that the

xlv

present life holds in store.

Chinese learning was introduced into Japan much earlier than Buddhism. In the days when embassies were despatched to China, each ship bearing an ambassadorial suite, accompanied by students and monks, returned with a cargo of books on laws and institutions, astronomy and mathematics, arts and crafts, and various other subjects. Confucianism was a new lore imported thus from China and was readily accepted in Japan as a practical system of social morality and statecraft. To say this is not to deny the essential difference in character between the Japanese ' way of living' of those days and the Confucian attitude of mind. In the moral sphere the Japanese valued honesty and sincerity, and regarded uncleanliness in any form as a vice. As for individual conduct, importance was attached to candour and spontaneity. Difference there was indeed between the Japanese way of living and the Confucian attitude, which was didactic and disciplinary, and which strove in the main to regulate life socially and institutionally by the application of external laws and standards. But the realization of this basic incompatibility was to come later. Japan in the Manyō age, in the midst of rapid social changes, needed order and discipline. Confucianism must have been gratefully accepted since it ministered to this need and supplied something like a canonical basis for those social values that had already prevailed. Loyalty, filial piety, brotherly affection, conjugal devotion, faithfulness, etc. taught by Confucianism, were virtues that had naturally grown within, and been fostered by, the clan system of Japan. Then why is it that Confucianism has left so few traces of its influence in the *Manyōshū* ? The first and simple reason is that few Japanese at that time had any proper training for reading Chinese classics and assimilating the mental attitude of Confucianism. The second reason is that Confucianism by its own nature as a teaching of social adjustment through ' etiquette and music ' has little to do with pure lyricism ; only in the realm of didactic poetry may it become a source of inspiration. In these circumstances Confucianism possesses among the many Manyō poets only a single representative in the person of Yamanoé Okura. A scholar sufficiently distinguished to be chosen and sent to China, and a man of the utmost honesty with a keen concern in social welfare, Okura was naturally inclined to didacticism. Although he has but few followers among the lyric poets of later ages, he occupies an important place in the history of Japanese thought, as the one poet in the *Manyōshū* reflecting the doctrine of Confucianism which, starting from its encouragement by Prince Shōtoku, was to spread over the entire country.

Taoism is another cult that was imported from China. Largely derived from the transcendental teachings of Laotsu and Chuangtsu, but compounded with all manner of folklore and superstition, it had fostered on the continent a belief in fairies and genii, and gave rise in certain circles to the vogue of the so-called 'serene conversations' and voluntary retirement from the world; and through its varied and startling manifestations it had left indelible marks on Chinese thought. It was received, however, in Japan with divided interest, in some quarters with an apparently evasive, even hostile attitude. Its spiritual influence on the *Manyōshū* is even less, as compared with that of Buddhism. In the Anthology we find sometimes meditative tendencies and Arcadian longings, Taoism serving as an adjunct to Buddhistic thought and providing a certain vocabulary, or sometimes supporting an Epicurean philosophy of life, as in the case of the series of verses composed by Tabito in praise of saké. Of course it should not be forgotten that, as regards subject matter for poetry, Taoism contributed, as is noted elsewhere, a rich store of parables and fables of a highly imaginative character.

LIFE, MANNERS AND CUSTOMS

How did the Japanese live in the Manyō age ? What

did they wear? What did they eat? And how were they housed?

Let us turn first to the clothing. The common materials in use were fabrics of *taku* (paper-mulberry fibre) and hemp. In the finer class stood silk, while the coarsest material was cloth woven of the *kuzu*-vine fibre (*Pueraria Thunbergiana*). Rarely were furs worn. All fabrics were ordinarily plain; but there existed, besides the much-prized native weave of striped patterns called *shizu*, various richly-figured silks obtained by the weaving methods imported previously from Korea and China, such as *aya* (twill) or *nishiki* (brocade) or even a gauze 'shining like the wings of a dragon-fly.' A primitive mode of dyeing was retained in the *suriginu* or ' rubbed cloths '—so called because they were obtained by rubbing with the flowers or leaves of the season such as bush-clover (*Lespedeza bicolor*), iris and ' mountain-indigo ' (*Mercurialis leiocarpa*). At the same time there were dyes for red, purple, green, blue, black, etc. and numerous half-tones compounded thereof, so that it was possible to produce fabrics of many colours and shades. Although the common people were usually clad in plain white, the wearing of coloured dresses was by no means rare. The court prescribed different hues and shades for officials and nobles according to their ranks and grades; one can, therefore, imagine what processions of gorgeous colours must have moved up and down the broad avenues of the capital city!

The style of dress differed between the periods before and after the introduction of the T'ang customs. But most commonly a tight-sleeved coat of a comparatively short length was worn by both men and women. This coat was either unlined, lined, or wadded, according to season. Over the coat, a sort of loose trousers, called *hakama*, was worn by both sexes, while women put on, in addition, a long skirt (*mo*), or let the girdle-ends hang down. Among special accessories, the *osuhi*—probably a cape or shawl of a sort—was worn by men as well as women, while on a journey or in worshipping the gods, the *ayui* (leg-ties) were used by soldiers, travellers and workmen to bind their *hakama* at the knees, and women wore *hiré* (scarfs) about their shoulders.

As for personal adornments, there were gems or beads of various shapes and colours, which had been extensively used from the earliest times. Strings of these worn round the neck, on arms and ankles, were prized, especially as female ornaments. Young girls clinking their bracelet gems as they danced (No. 152), or the 'Weaver Maid' at work with all the jewelled bangles on her wrists and ankles swinging (No. 921), were visions invoked by the poets and sung with a genuine warmth of feeling. *Kushiro*, or rings of metal or stone worn on the arm, were also favourite ornaments for men as well as women. The coiffure changed from time to time. The typical mode for men was to bind the hair into two knots on either side of the head, or in a single large knot on the top. The style for women varied according to age. A child had the hair bobbed short, while a young girl wore it long, sometimes parted and hanging down to the shoulders ; but as soon as she reached marriageable age it was either done up, or left to hang down still longer. Both sexes wore combs in the hair, a boxwood comb being considered a precious addition to female charm. Thus, the comb-case, together with mirror, made an indispensable and most intimate item of a lady's personal effects. In their full attire, gentlemen of rank wore the prescribed caps, which sometimes were decked with garlands, either artificial or of fresh flowers and leaves. A pretty custom of breaking off sprays of flowers or autumn leaves and wearing them on the head as ornaments prevailed with both sexes. For foot-wear, shoes of leather or cloth were worn by the upper classes. However, since even the beautiful maid of Mama, famous in story, is going barefoot (No. 672), the use of shoes appears to have been rare in rural communities. A simpler wear for the commoners was sandals made of rice-straw.

Turning to food, the main article of diet was, of course, rice—a staple which was destined to shape Japan's industrial structure for all the succeeding ages, and even to colour the religious life of the nation. Millet, *kibi* (*Panicum milia-ceum*), barley and *hié* (*Panicum frumentaceum*) served as supplements to, or substitutes for, rice. The subsidiary dishes included vegetables, both cultivated and wild, such as wild celery, bracken shoots, yam, lettuce and other greens, onion and garlic, and sea-weeds of various kinds ; such fish foods as bream, bonito, bass, carp, trout, eel, abalone, crab, mussel, etc. ; birds like the wild goose, duck, pheasant, quail, snipe, and so on. It is interesting to note that no beef or horse-flesh was used, but whale-meat was undoubtedly eaten. The chief game animals were deer, boar and rabbit. All these things were served raw, boiled, broiled, or pickled. As may be gathered from the above list, fishing was a flourishing industry all along the sea-coasts. Hunting was also an occupation, but it was quite frequently done by the aristocracy as a knightly exercise or merely for sport. The *Manyōshū* mentions specifically hawking and the ' medicine hunt,' the latter being undertaken to obtain the horns of young deer for medicinal use. As for fruits, there were melons, chestnuts, oranges, peaches and many others. The principal beverage of the time was saké brewed from rice, which was universally drunk and used also as a sacred offering to the gods.

Thirdly, housing. Buildings varied widely in size and appearance and in their manner of construction, ranging from a hut in the primitive style to the palaces and temples constructed according to architectural plans and methods introduced from the continent. A rural dwelling had logs for posts, grass or board for roofing, and its earthen floor was covered with rushes or rice-straw. Wealthier families lived in larger, sometimes two-storied, houses, which had wooden floors, and also barns and stables. The fences were sometimes of living bushes, and sometimes of dead brushwood, reed or bamboo. Alongside such humble quarters, there rose palaces and temples in the new style. The building material for these edifices was still mainly timber, but construction was on a grand scale with vermillion-tinted pillars and beams and tiled roofs. The mansions of the nobles and the rich followed suit. And in consonance with this architectural magnificence, many a great garden was laid out with its rocks, artificial lakes and islets, its pines, willows and plum-trees and clumps of staggerbush and azalea and flowers of the four seasons, and even with mandarin-ducks in the lakes. With the increasing luxury in house and garden, the old ritual feasts always held in connection with the construction of a new dwelling (No. 152, etc.) were celebrated all the more heartily.

The mode of life differed radically between town and country. The contrast was not perhaps so marked in the early part of the Manyō age—namely, the Ōmi Period and the Asuka and Fujiwara Periods—when the court was being removed from place to place and the influence of the capital remained comparatively insignificant despite the steady enhancement of the metropolitan greatness through the importation of T'ang culture and civilization. That the prosperity of a capital in those periods was altogether transitory may be seen from the fact that as soon as it was evacuated by the court, it fell rapidly into ruin, so that the decay of an ' old Imperial City ' came to be one of the stock themes for poets. But with the Nara Period, the capital was really the glorious centre of national life. The Emperor Shōmu transferred the court once to Kuni, and then to Naniwa, but each time he was drawn back irresistibly to Nara, so powerful had that city grown.

> The Imperial City of fairest Nara
> Glows now at the height of beauty,
> Like brilliant flowers in bloom. (No. 282)

Young gallants wearing silver-wrought swords paraded the wide boulevards while ladies of the court walked along the tree-shaded avenues trailing their crimson skirts. It was such a picture of the gay metropolis which the officials stationed at the Empire's outposts, ' the far courts of the Sovereign ', could never forget and which caused them the most unbearable pangs of nostalgia (Nos. 558–9). Various functions, temple services, holiday outings, banquets and entertainments, occurring from day to day, made life in Nara a delightful thing not only to those ' lords and ladies of the Great Palace ' (No. 912), but to the common run of its citizens. Of course there were the poor who grieved of having ' no sackcloth for my children to wear ' and envied ' those silks and quilted clothes ' thrown away by the rich (Nos. 634–5). But that, in the face of the general temper and actual prosperity of the metropolis, was allowed to cast no shadow to mar its brilliance and gaiety.

On the other hand, life in the country, keeping the tenor of the ancient days, went on with charming simplicity. In the *Manyōshū* we find a village maid who, at a river-side overgrown with green willows, draws no water from the stream but waits for her lover, ' ever stamping the ground ' (No. 856), or a working girl worrying how her hands, chapped from rice-pounding, might distress ' my young lord of the mansion ' (No. 850), and again a lad asking his lass to give him water out of the well-pool for the post-horses : ' Mind you, straight from your own sweet hand ! ' (No. 847). This last instance recalls the system of high-ways and posts, which in those days carried the exhilarating air of the country into the town and at the same time preserved rural communities from falling into stagnation and decay.

Mention has been made of embassies to the continent, of frontier-guards, and of province officials. It was their comings and goings that enlivened and invigorated the entire nation. Besides, a direct link between the court and the country was found in the occasional or periodical progresses of the sovereign to various hot spring resorts (Arima Hot Springs in Settsu Province and the spas of Iyo and Kii) or to the imperial villas at Yoshino and elsewhere.

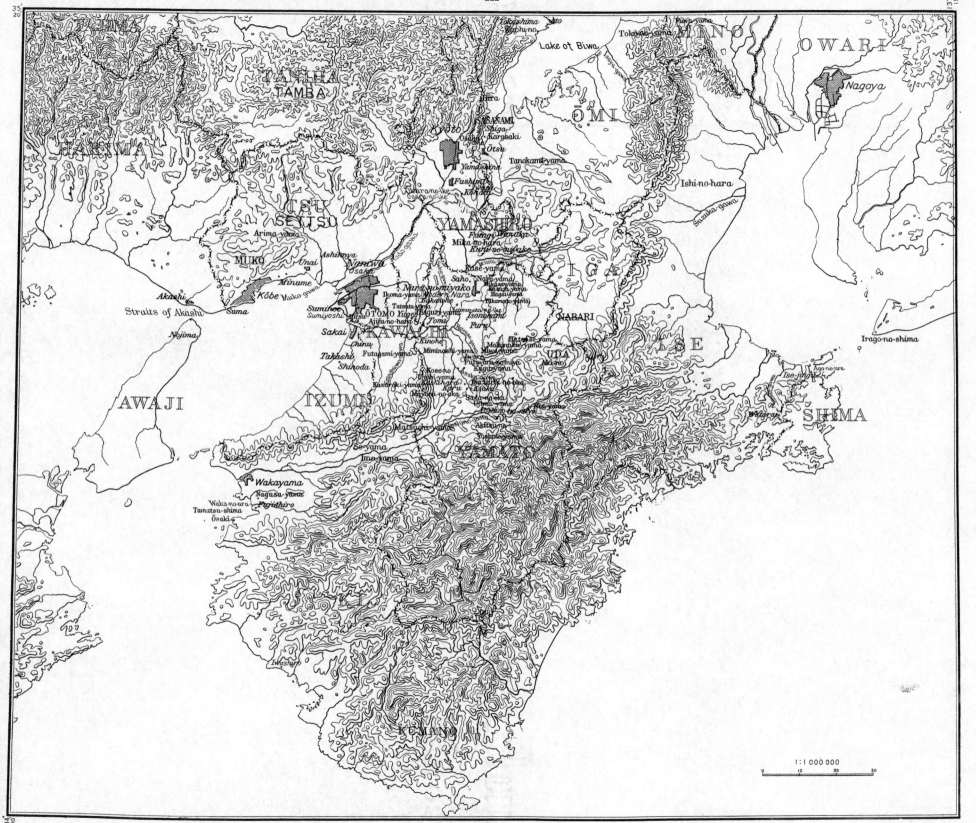

HOME PROVINCES

The journeys of palace-guards between the capital and their homes in the provinces, and the imperial excursions and hunting-trips may also be mentioned in this connection. All these things not only enlivened the country-side and served as a tonic for the city-dwellers, but provided the Manyō poets with an inexhaustible source of inspiration.

Distant journeys on land and sea were attended with dangers and difficulties. Although there were already in existence large vessels that could carry hundreds of passengers and a considerable quantity of goods, in most cases the ships were small and frail. The seafarer had to wait for favourable winds before he could hoist sail ; and relying upon good weather, he steered his uncertain course along rugged coasts and from island to island. Neither was the lot of the land traveller to be envied, for he had to make his way over steep hills or by a ' new-cut ' road bristling with tree-stumps. Hostels were few and far apart, so that even a prince of the blood was sometimes obliged to spend the night in a hurriedly improvised hut, to say nothing of the common wayfarer who frequently had to sleep literally ' with grass for pillow.' The *Manyōshū* contains a number of poems on the drowned or starved found on the roadside, giving a vivid proof of the extreme hazards of travel in those days. These hardships and privations, however, only served to reveal the depths of human existence, as contrasted with the amenities afforded by imperial progresses and hunting excursions, of a few days' duration and not even very far away from the capital. It was indeed a delightful privilege for courtiers to accompany their sovereign on these occasions and to wade through the dewy grass, starting the birds to flight, or to stain their clothes with the bloom of lespedeza in the autumn fields, or to stroll along the seashore and gather shells for their wives at home ; and in this way to disport themselves in the very bosom of nature.

Now let us follow from season to season the principal festivals in the calendar of the Manyō age. New Year's

Day is celebrated with a state banquet at court, and with the feastings of relatives and friends in private homes. On the first Day of the Rat, in January, another banquet is held in the palace and 'jewelled brooms' are distributed— a symbolic act for the encouragement of sericulture, a broom being used to collect young silk-worms. On the same day, people went out into the country, and gathered the young spring herbs, which were boiled and eaten. On the 7th of January the Feast of the Blue Horse is celebrated at the court. Blue being the colour of spring, according to Chinese tradition, ' blue ' (black) horses were led before the Throne and prayers were offered for a prosperous year. The 15th and 16th days were reserved for a song-feast, also of Chinese origin, at which the participants sang, keeping time by stamping on the ground. Early in February the important rites of praying for a good crop were performed. Also during this month some clans held the festivals of their respective tutelary gods. These clan festivals took place twice annually, in spring (either in February or in April) and in winter (November). Now, as the balmy spring invites country-folk as well as townsmen out-of-doors, the roads and the fields are crowded with holiday-makers. On March 3, the court holds in some years a poetry festival in the Chinese style, in which the courtiers sit here and there alongside running water and compose Chinese poems, while cups of saké float down the stream towards them. Between April and May the ' medicine hunt ' takes place, the young nobles on horseback presenting a beautiful and thrilling spectacle. May 5 is the Feast of *Tango*—now popularly known as the Boys' Festival—on which day anciently bags filled with spices were hung on the door-posts together with sweet-flag leaves or orange-flowers as a means of warding off uncleanliness and evil spirits. This is about the time when the cuckoo begins to sing. In fact, all the birds and flowers of the season seem to join in the festival. On the last day of June the rites of *Ōbarai* (Great Purification) are observed. Great importance was attached alike by court and people to the sacred rite of *misogi* by which mortals were to be cleansed of their sins and stains. With the autumn comes the Feast of *Tanabata*—on the Seventh Night of the Seventh Month. The feasts of *Tango* and *Tanabata* are both Chinese in origin, but they were assimilated and absorbed into Japanese folklore just about this time, and have since been preserved even to this day. The number of 'Seventh Night' poems in the *Manyōshū* exceeds 120 ; which helps us to judge how deeply the 'Romance of the Milky Way' thrilled the hearts of the Manyō man and kindled his imagination. The story is about the love of two stars—the Oxherd and the Weaver Maid who, having incurred the displeasure of the Ruler of Heaven, were doomed to live on the opposite shores of the Heavenly River, and were allowed to meet only once in the year—namely on the Seventh Night of the Seventh Month, which as such is celebrated by mortals to share in the joy of the celestial lovers. It is to be noted that in the Manyō poems, man goes to maid instead of maid going to man as the original Chinese version has it, and the boat used by the Oxherd for crossing the Heavenly River and the costumes and the loom of the Weaver Maid are all quite naturally in the Japanese style of that time. As the season advances, autumn flowers and foliage, with an appeal no less tender and irresistible than spring flowers, call out the people once more to hill and field. Towards the end of November, Thanksgiving, the 'Feast of New-tasting,' is solemnly observed at court and throughout the land. This is the last and most important of the series of agricultural feasts and festivals of Japan held in the year, beginning with the prayer for a good harvest early in February. Finally, another 'Great Purification' takes place in December. Having been purified thereby, body and soul, the nation is now ready to welcome the New Year.

Turning to human relations, Japanese clan morality in its purified form—namely, that which is based upon the consciousness of the Imperial House as the supreme head of all clans—manifests itself in the *Manyōshū* in spontaneous sentiments of the loveliest kind, giving the Anthology its chief distinction. Parental love, such as pervades the poems of Okura, may be regarded as a natural human feeling, common to all races and to all ages. But filial piety, so sincere, intense and instinctive as shown in the Manyō poems is not likely to be duplicated by any other people and under any other social order. Among the upper classes this virtue was so extended from parents to forefathers as to include an obligation to keep one's ancestral name unspotted and to enhance the prestige of one's family; and in that sense it was necessary to guard jealously one's integrity and honour (Nos. 470, 538–40, etc.). How warm and genuine filial devotion was also in the lower strata of society may be seen in the poems of the frontier-guards, who, on taking leave of their families, exhibit as much, if not more, tenderness and solicitude toward their parents as toward their wives and children (Nos. 766, 767, 772, 774, 775, 789, etc.). From this love between parents and children is derived the love between brothers and sisters, such as is revealed in the *tanka* of Princess Ōku on her ill-fated brother Prince Ōtsu (Nos. 54–5, 56–7), or in the *chōka* composed by Yakamochi on the death of his younger brother (Nos. 496–8). Because of the custom of that time, the sense of consanguinity tended to be restricted to the children born of the same mother and brought up under one roof. As a notable case we may mention that of Lady Ōtomo of Tamura who displayed intense love for a half-sister, Lady Ōtomo of Sakanoé's Elder Daughter (No. 408, etc.).

Then there was the love between man and woman—the most personal of all attachments. What attitude did Japanese society assume towards it under a clan system? Here will be discovered conflicting circumstances. The individual man or woman seeks to unite with his or her partner in love according to a natural and spontaneous inclination. But the 'family' which was always growing in complexity and more rigid in its demands on all its members to conform to its needs, does not always give countenance to such a union. Already in the Manyō age there was a law requiring the consent of parents and the formal recognition by society as a *sine qua non* of marriage. Hence passionate love had often to chafe at insuperable obstacles. A girl must keep her lover's name secret at the risk of her life. It became a desperate task to guard against the prying eyes and the busy mouths of the world. But tameless, bold, and unconquerable is the Manyō lover ; intense passion pursues its course like a mountain torrent that sweeps on—swirling, splashing and crashing against the rocks. Herein lies the glory of the Manyō love-poems. The piteous tale of the forbidden love between the courtier Nakatomi Yakamori and Sanu Chigami is a good example (Nos. 339-48).

But unless love is forced to flounder tragically, as in the above example, it will eventually arrive at its goal, which is marriage. And as far as we may judge from the poems, conjugal love, reflecting and retaining the ardour of court-ship days, is fraught with genuine warmth and tenderness. The wife cherished the husband with a single-hearted devotion, which was reciprocated by him with loving care and attention, though this, under the existing social system, may not have been altogether undivided. At any rate, our Anthology contains a poem in dialogue—a *chōka* by a wife and a *tanka* (given as its envoy) by her husband—which tells of a conjugal love as unassuming as it is tender. The story is worth recounting. The husband is evidently one of those men whose business takes him regularly to the Province of Yamashiro over a mountain road. The wife cannot bear to see him go on foot while others travel on horseback. She takes out a mirror and a scarf which she has treasured as a keepsake of her mother, and offering them to her husband, she asks him to exchange them for a horse. The husband declines the present, since his wife must walk even if he gets a horse. ' Though we tread the rocks,' says he, ' let's walk, the two of us, together ! ' (Nos. 871–4).

There was one sentiment which demanded, when the occasion arrived, a willing sacrifice of all these personal affections, no matter how dear, and of which the nobles and peasants were always deeply aware. This supreme devotion was due to the sovereign, under whose rule Tabito at the Dazaifu was content to say : ' In Yamato or here in this far province, I feel ever the same ' (No. 381). ' At the dread Sovereign's word,' the embassies to China defied storms and went ' whither his royal ships took them ' (No. 753). Courage and military prowess were prized by the warriors as necessary qualities in their service to the Throne. Carrying sword, spear, or shield, or shouldering a quiver and grasping a birchwood bow, they went to meet their foe in the field. All was for their lord and sovereign. It was not only among the educated or the higher classes that this sentiment of loyalty to the Throne prevailed.

Let us once more turn to the poems of frontier-guards (Nos. 769, 783, etc.). These young men, taken out of their lowly cottages in Eastland, bravely set forth for the far island of Kyūshū, leaving behind them their beloved parents, their wives and their sweethearts—who clung to them, ' even as the creeping bean-vine clings to the wild rose-bush by the wayside ' (No. 777), or who ' wept, standing in the reed-fence corner ' (No. 778). Their patriotic zeal is well illustrated by the following poem :

> I will not from to-day
> Turn back toward home—
> I who have set forth
> As Her Majesty's humble shield. (No. 783)

Thus, all the threads of human relations are drawn to a single point—the Throne, Japanese morality ending where it ought to end.

The Manyō poems display an outlook on nature, which excels the later anthologies of Japan in scope and in depth of sympathy ; it would perhaps be difficult to find a like intimacy with nature in the contemporary lyric poetry of any other country in the world.

Japanese appreciation of nature, deep-rooted in religious sentiment, had long been cultivated through an intimate contact between nature and man. In the Manyō age nature was animated directly by such of its phenomena as were still looked upon with religious deference and were identified with personal emotions. There were, of course, things in nature which had become objects of affection and admiration by virtue of their beauty or loveliness. There were things which were regarded as resounding with human emotions in that they reflected the joys and sorrows of man. Even in such cases, where natural objects are dealt with purely as poetical material, they seem to retain each their individuality and life—a spiritual entity permeated by a mysterious atmosphere. Never are they allowed to lapse into cold lifeless rhetorical ornament, or metaphor without some fringe of emotion. In the great majority of cases natural phenomena are still divine manifestations, or guardians of life in one way or another to whom man's gratitude is due, or else powers of destruction to be feared and dreaded. When their spiritual import or acute bearing on life are forgotten—as, for instance, when a man goes out gathering violets, and spends the night in the field (No. 599), or when young girls are boiling starworts on Kasuga Plain (No. 819), or when a poet, mourning his wife, ascribes the fog rising on the hill to his sighing breath (No. 610),—even then nature is man's friend and companion and there still exists a sense of mutual sympathy. It is this profound feeling of mutual sympathy that made the Manyō man look far and wide and search deeply with lively emotions into all aspects of nature and grasp them with such eminent success. Probably every phase of nature that had anything to do with the life of those days appears in the *Manyōshū* in one form or another.

Mountains were considered the most divine of all natural phenomena. It is scarcely necessary to recall that Mount Fuji, then an active volcano, was worshipped as the tutelary god of Japan. The peak is immortalized also by Yamabé Akahito (Nos. 567-8), and by another, unknown, poet (Nos. 651-3). As these poets sing of Fuji the majestic and beautiful, or of Fuji the sublime and mysterious, Japanese poetry itself seems to soar to a rapturous height nowhere else surpassed. Among other mountains that were revered as deities, there is Tateyama, sung by Ōtomo Yakamochi (Nos. 550-2, 553-5); also the Tsukuba Mountain, famous for its festival of *Kagai* which was held in spring and autumn, and in which men and women gathered to pass the night dancing and singing (Nos. 668-9). All these mountains, which were greatly revered, are located far from the capital; but there are a number of mountains and hills nearer the capital, especially in the province of Yamato, which, either by their divinity or by virtue of their graceful features, were famous in song and story. In the south of Yamato Plain there is Unebi, a female mountain, with the two male mountains of Kagu and Miminashi standing near by. An old legend of the quarrels of the latter for the love of the former forms the subject of Poems Nos. 9-11. Further southwards, there is Mount Kamunabi of Asuka, overlooking the site of the former capital (Nos. 571-2). Beyond, rise the Yoshino Mountains which, with an imperial villa, their scenic beauties of green slopes and tumbling waters, spring flowers and autumn leaves, invoked an endless chorus of pious admiration and praise (Nos. 77-8, 79-80). Midway between Asuka and Nara and in a slightly easterly direction there stands the sacred hill of Miwa, and to its north a higher hill, Makimuku. The hill of Tatsuta, situated on the way from Nara to Naniwa and celebrated in those days for its cherry-flowers, was held in fee by Tatsutahiko, the god of wind. Ikoma is a large mountain that dominates not only Yamato Plain, but also the province of Settsu and the bay of Ōsaka on the opposite side. It was to its blue peak that the men of Nara, sailing out from the port of Naniwa, turned with wistful eyes to bid a last farewell to their beloved land of Yamato. In the immediate neighbourhood of the capital the hills of Kasuga, Mikasa and Takamado provided the urban population with convenient and beautiful grounds for outings and excursions.

The river most praised in the *Manyōshū* is the Yoshino, which rises in the mountains of Yoshino already mentioned, and the scenic beauty of its rock-strewn rapids delighted visitors from the capital. The Saho, the Hatsusé, and the Asuka, sometimes known as the Kamunabi, all flowing through Yamato Plain, were also favourite streams of the Manyō poets, who sang of their plovers and singing-frogs, or the yellow-roses on their banks. The Izumi River and the Uji River of Yamashiro were used for the transportation of timber required in the construction of a new capital. Yet another important waterway was the Horié Canal in Naniwa, which was crowded with ships from far provinces. Other rivers mentioned in the *Manyōshū* include the Tama and the Toné in eastern Japan, the Chikuma of Shinano Province, the Ogami, the Imizu, and the Haétsuki in northern Japan, and the Matsura in the island of Kyūshū. The lake that almost monopolized the attention of the Manyō poet is the Biwa in Ōmi, the largest lake in Japan, on whose shore stood at one time Shiga—the seat of the Emperor Tenji's court. Even in the Nara Period only ruinous traces of his palace and city remained for the melancholy contemplation of poets. The lake offered a convenient passage to the northern provinces of Japan, but a traveller crossing it in the frail boat of those days must have been seized by a sense of helplessness, as upon the open sea. Of the Fusé Lake, made famous by Yakamochi's poem, the name alone survives to-day, most of it having since been converted into cultivated fields.

The ocean represented, quite as forcefully as did mountains, the mighty powers of nature to the Manyō man, who travelled so much by sea and was personally and intimately acquainted with its manifold aspects, fair and genial, awesome and terrible. Of the many beautiful bays of Japan, the most famous, lying on the route from Yamato to the eastern provinces, was Miho Bay with its beach of white sand and green pine-trees and with its magnificent view of the sacred peak of Fuji in the distance. Between the bay of Naniwa and the Straits of Akashi in the west, or along Waka Beach in the south, the sea-coast unfolded a panorama of beautiful scenes that charmed excursionists from the capital. But the courtier on a journey to the south of Kii Province, even as a member of the imperial suite accompanying the sovereign on his visit to the spa of Muro, begins to yearn for home, wearied and awe-stricken by the waves of the vast Pacific beating upon the shore. As for the official journey to his post in Tsukushi, he has to sail the whole length of the Inland Sea, trusting his fate to a small ship. He crosses the thundering whirlpool of Ōshima and sails on westwards—sometimes stopping storm-bound in an island lee, sometimes steering ahead in the darkness of night. The insufferable anxieties and uncertainties of such a voyage are graphically told in many a Manyō poem. But above all, the most solemn and indelible impressions of the sea's 'awefulness' were engraved in the minds of those envoys to China or Korea who, leaving the shores of Kyūshū behind them, sailed over the rolling billows of the boundless ocean. The difficulties of the voyages seem to have added to the enthusiasm with which the Manyō poets sang of ports and harbours. From the travel poems by those who went to Tsukushi or abroad, it is possible to conjecture regarding the ports of call on their route through the Inland Sea. Mitsu of Naniwa, as the principal port of embarkation and debarkation, is mentioned most frequently in the Anthology. Next comes the port of Tomo in Bingo Province. Both

NORTHERN KYŪSHŪ

1 : 500 000

Genkai-nada

MUNAKATA-NO-KŌRI

KASUYA-NO-KŌRI

Kashii

Fukuoka

Noko-no-shima

Fukuoka-wan

Karadomari

Shika-no-shima

Shio

ŌnoyAma

Mizuki

Dazaifu

Ashiki-no-uhaya

TSUKUSHI

CHIKUZEN

NAKA-NO-KŌRI

SHIMA-NO-KŌRI

ITO-NO-KŌRI

Fukae-mura

Kofu-no-hara

HI

HIZEN

Tama-shima

Hirefuri-no-ne

MATSURA

Karatsu

Matsura-gawa

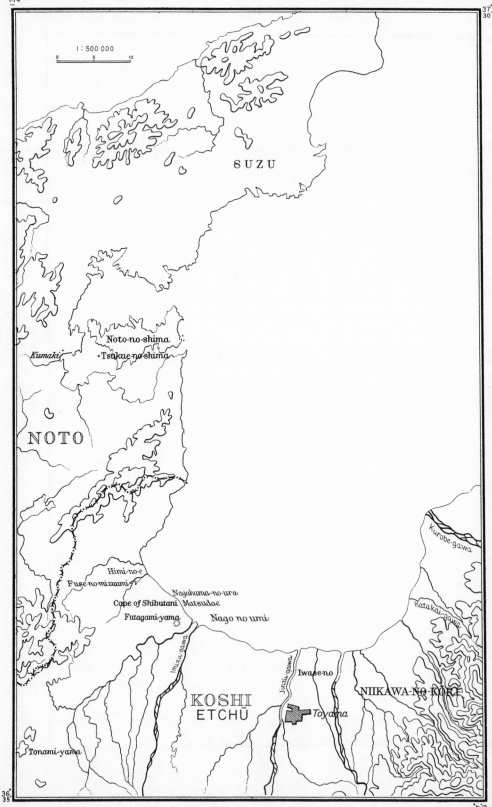

1 : 500 000

SUZU

Noto-no-shima
Tsukue-no-shima

Kumaki

NOTO

Himi-no-e
Fuse-no-mizuumi
Nagahama-no-ura
Cape of Shibutani Matsudae
Futagami-yama
Nago no umi

Kurobe-gawa

Katakai-gawa

Imizu-gawa
Jinzū-gawa
Iwase-no
NIIKAWA-NO-KŌRI

KOSHI
ETCHŪ
Toyama

Tonami-yama

NOTO AND ETCHŪ

of these served also as ports of landing for foreign embassies to the court of Nara. The latter, owing to its beautiful scenery, was a harbour specially dear to the hearts of all travellers in the Inland Sea.

As for the names of animals and other creatures appearing in the *Manyōshū*, the *Kogi* lists 37 kinds of birds, 13 of insects, etc., 11 of beasts, 9 of fishes, 6 of shells, or 76 kinds in all. With the rare exception of a foreign animal, the tiger, and a fabulous creature, the dragon, they were all familiar in various ways, so that they are treated with intimate knowledge and understanding in the poems. Fish and shell-fish; domestic animals like oxen and horses; domesticated birds such as fowls and hawks; silkworms; all these were of great importance for their practical uses, but they also occupied their respective places in the realm of poetry as familiar objects of nature, quite irrespective of practical consideration. For instance, the univalvular appearance of the abalone shell suggested unrequited love, while the silkworm cocoon recalled a lady secluded in her bower (No. 168). But it is not merely utilitarian purpose that binds the animal world to human society. The birds and beasts that come and go with the seasons and visit hill or field, or waterside, never fail to stir the Manyō man's emotions. What is noteworthy is that the poetic appeal of these animals lay apparently not so much in their colours or shapes as in their cries and sounds. The *uguisu* is the harbinger of spring. Though the picture of this dainty warbler flitting among the branches of bamboo or plum-trees does certainly attract the attention of the Manyō poet, his heart is more thrilled by its sweet hymn of joy. In contrast to the *uguisu*, the 'night-thrush' (*nue*) is mentioned for its plaintive note. When the sound of the singing-frogs is heard from clear streams, the spring is almost over. Summer brings the cuckoo. This bird, with its rich legendary and other associations, is apt to move the heart of a poet brooding over long-past ages. Summer dies amid the mournful shrillings of cicadas. Now the wild geese come crying, riding the autumn wind. As the dews thicken on the bush-clovers (*hagi*), the stag calls for his mate in the wakeful night-hours of a lonely lover. The cricket's chirping in the garden only deepens the melancholy. Winter draws near. The sanderlings call on the river-beaches, and the wild duck among the reeds. Numerous references to the voice of the cranes indicate that they were not then rare in central Japan. It is these birds, beasts, and insects, with their widely varied notes, that played the accompaniment to man's emotional life through all the seasons of the year.

As for the plants, the *Kogi* is again our authority for stating that there are 157 in number, consisting of 86 herbs and grasses, 67 trees and 4 kinds of bamboo. The familiar plants used for food have already been mentioned. These and many other useful plants, including the mulberry which supplied fibre for cloths, birch and spindle-tree for bows, bamboos for baskets, arrows and other articles, boxwood for combs, the gromwell, madder and other herbs for dyes—all served as poetic material exactly in the same manner as the useful animals. And it goes without saying that the number was especially large of those plants, cultivated or wild, which were regarded purely as objects of admiration because of their beauty and loveliness.

The earliest of all flowers was the plum-blossom which is described fancifully as offering a hospitable shelter to the *uguisu*, or realistically in a delectable word-picture of its white petals fluttering and falling together with the snow-flakes. Being a comparatively late importation from the continent, the plum-tree must have had a specially fresh appeal and charm. Then followed the peach-blossom, somewhat neglected by poets who were eager to welcome the cherry-flowers, which soon burst forth in all their glorious profusion. Here we must not forget to mention the fragrant little violets which were sure to attract the poet's eye and capture his heart. The long-blooming camellia, symbolic of the lengthening spring day, the staggerbush, still abundant in Kasuga Plain, the wild azalea—so passed by the gay procession of vernal flowers with wistaria and yellow-roses bringing up the rear.

In summer bloomed the *kakitsubata*, a species of iris, which is often cited in love poems, owing probably to its colour and form, in which there is something that suggests feminine beauty. The fragrant sweet-flag, as a plant capable of warding off evil spirits, was used together with the mugwort to decorate the 'medicine bags' that were hung up for the Feast of *Tango* on May 5th. The sweet-flag is also mentioned frequently in Manyō poems with the cuckoo, the favourite summer bird, as are also the *unohana* (*Deutzia crenata*) and the orange-flower. The orange-tree, brought over with great difficulty from the continent early in the history of Japan, was highly valued both for its flowers and fruit. Of other flowers of this season two more are worthy of mention, the *auchi* (bead-tree) and the lily—' the deep-grass lily on the wayside.'

' The seven flowers that blow in the autumn fields ' are attractively catalogued by Okura (Nos. 645–6). Of these, the more particularly liked were the bush-clovers that grow in thick clumps, profusely covered with purplish flowers, the 'tail flower' (*Miscanthus sinensis*) with its glossy ears of dark red, waving as if beckoning a friend to its side, and the patrinia, with its clusters of little yellow flowers twinkling like golden grains.

The green willows of spring and the yellow and crimson foliage of autumn were also universally admired, perhaps in the same sense as flowers were, for the richness and brilliance of their colours. But there was another side to the Manyō taste for plants. Non-flowering and unostentatious plants like bamboo, reeds, and rushes also attracted the poet. The pine-tree held a place of honour because of the noble and masculine character of its sturdy limbs, or because of the clear tone of the wind soughing through its branches. There still survived the primitive tendency to worship a large elm, or cryptomeria of great age, as a sacred object, demonstrating the presence of religious elements in the Manyō man's love of plants. The epithet *maki tatsu* (true-wood standing) was a favourite pillow-word for *yama* (mountain). It is quite likely that the sanctity of a mountain was believed to be enhanced by the luxuriance of its vegetation.

Finally, what was the attitude of the Manyō man towards the celestial and atmospheric phenomena which hung over, surrounded, and enfolded all these terrestrial things? Poetically and symbolically, and no doubt animistically also, homage was paid to the sun as the source of light and life. The moon was looked upon as a mirror to reflect the face of one's beloved far away. The star Vega shining high in the autumn sky was the 'Weaver Maid' in a romantic legend of the heavens. A floating cloud was spoken of as a messenger making for one's distant home, and the fog as rising up with the sigh of one in grief. While it is true that these phenomena were regarded with reverence or affection as living things possessing intimate ties with man, we should also remember that the Manyō man was a keen observer of all their multiple aspects. It is to his objectivity, combined with his sensitiveness, that we owe the rich variety of description that we find in the Manyō poems. Take the moon, for instance. We read of a young moon as being reminiscent of 'the eyebrow of you whom I have seen but once'; the evening moon that rises before the day is over; the full moon bright and clear; the moon past its full for which one must sit up and wait; the moon that remains in the dawning sky; again, of the hour when the sky glows before moon-rise; when the moon traverses the sky at night or when it hangs low; or the dusk of dawn produced by the sinking of the moon: in fact every phase of the moon as it waxes and wanes in the course of a month and all the hours as they are affected by it are touched upon. The beauty as well as the movements of the *yūzutsu* (Venus), which both as evening- and morning-star 'wanders hither and thither,' had been noted so early that in the Manyō time 'the star of eve' is used as a pillow-word for 'wavering of the mind.'

Since Japan's range of temperature is rather extreme for the temperate zone, and the atmospheric changes are varied and startling, the rainbow, hail and thunder, to say nothing of the spring haze, the autumn mist, the dew-drop or ' the frost that falls at night' are all used as poetic material. As for the clouds, they are mentioned in infinite variety, including ' banner clouds,' ' heaven-flying clouds,' ' swinging clouds,' ' fading clouds,' and ' horizontal clouds '; while rain is differentiated according to certain poetic characteristics into *harusamé* (spring rain), *yūdachi* (sudden shower), *shiguré* (passing shower), and so forth. In Japan, the four seasons, though not abrupt in transition, are clearly marked off from one another, so that from early times each season was associated with a distinct set of poetic sentiments, and began to possess a poetry of its own, springing from a separate source of inspiration. The sense of the seasons and a delicate susceptibility to the peculiar aspects of each, which were cultivated more and more, came to constitute one of the more important characteristics of Japanese literature in all the succeeding centuries. But this literary tradition was well established in the Manyō age, whose poets showed a very great and lively concern for all the seasonal changes.

POETRY AND POETS

Manyō poems are characterized by directness and frankness in their expression of life's joy, love, grief and indignation. No poetry of later ages can attain to the level of beauty of these poems, alive as they are with sentiments that are instinctive, robust and undisguised. This does not mean, however, that the *Manyōshū* forms the primeval poetry of the Japanese race, for, as a matter of fact, the Anthology represents a literature which presupposes the development and cultivation of a language extending over centuries. The Manyō man himself was aware of this historical background. His emotional reactions to the events in his daily life or in his natural environment were directly or indirectly linked to the 'times of old.' The *Manyōshū* is by no means primitive. Its artistic value and significance are to be found in the fact that it reflects a culture that retained its primitive freshness and vigour. A conscious effort is visible throughout the book to discover in mythology a basis for the present life. A longing for the past, and regret for its disappearance are conspicuous everywhere, especially in the poems lamenting the decay of former capitals. Such tendencies served to introduce, in addition to the realms of life and nature, a third class of subject-matter for poetry—namely the realm of tradition and legend.

Rivalry in winning a wife is the theme of many legends. In the 'Age of the Gods' even mountains, as already noted, quarrelled over a prospective spouse (Nos. 9–11). The well-known tales of the Maiden Unai (Nos. 674–6) and Tekona of Mama (Nos. 575–7, 672–3), or of the Cherry-Flower Maid (Nos. 823–4) and Kazurako, all tell of fierce contentions between lovers. In every case, it is to be noted, the story ends with the self-destruction of the poor helpless girl. Among the legends concerning the origin of place-names, those of the 'Scarf-Waving Hill' (No. 802) and the 'Yōrō Waterfall' (No. 556) are best known. The latter story, having to do with the 'elixir of youth,' directs our attention to the Taoistic elements in the *Manyōshū*. All the poems dealing with the supernatural, the life of perpetual youth and happiness, or the marriage between a mortal and a fairy maid, and others on like subjects, are to be considered as more or less connected with Taoistic superstitions. As for the famous legend of Urashima (Nos. 656–7), while no hasty conclusion is permissible regarding its origin and evolution, it is not difficult to detect the Taoistic influence in its description of the 'Everlasting Land' without age and without death. Of a similar and even deeper significance are the stories of 'Yamabito Tsuminoé' (No. 712) and the Maidens of Matsura (Nos. 793–6). Thus those

Taoistic ideas, which extend the concept of life beyond the bounds of earth, served to enrich considerably the Manyō world of poetry. Here one finds an instance of the influence of Chinese literature on our Anthology.

Now, having before him this world of rich poetic material, embracing life, nature and history, together with mythology and legend, how did the Manyō poet grasp it ? How did he portray it ? These questions bear upon another historical aspect of the Anthology. In the Manyō age, though it possessed an artistically finished language and a certain tradition in world outlook, Japanese poetry still retained its primitive vitality, and was in the process of a steady and wholesome development. Hence, the Manyō poems are impregnated with the health and virility of youth—a fact which has made the Anthology an inexhaustible reservoir of strength for Japanese literature of all subsequent ages.

The language of the *Manyōshū* is highly sensuous ; that is to say, a psychological reaction, instead of being described in an abstract and general way, is expressed in terms of the physical senses, visual or auditory, gustatory or tactual. When a man is in love with a maid, it is said that ' she rides on my heart,' even as the wave rolls and spreads over the beach. The intensification of passion is represented in terms of respiration, such as ' breath-choking.' Of course, such phrases were not inventions by individual poets ; they constituted a literary heritage of the race which was held in common by all the people, high and low, in town and country. The prevalent use of pillow-words is a good illustration of this point.

We have already spoken of the danger of pillow-words becoming meaningless appendages or repetitions. In the case of the *Manyōshū*, however, a pillow-word usually serves as an overtone to magnify the amplitude of the tone of the head-word, leading us to the contemplation of a wider vista. Such juxtaposition of two different ideas does not merely affect the question of the structure or rhetoric of a language ; it involves the question of how the Manyō man grasped his world. When a poet is inspired to put into verse a certain emotion that burns within him, he seldom stops at giving the mere description of the internal state of his mind but, by association, he introduces into the realm of his feeling the things about him—especially the objects and phenomena of nature—which he has seen or felt or which are claiming his attention at that very moment. It is by the employment of these things as 'sympathetic chords,' so to speak, that he proceeds to play the main string of his feeling. Herein lies the function of another rhetorical device, the 'introductory verse.' There are, consequently, a great many lyrics in the *Manyōshū*, which have what might perhaps be called harmonic construction.

To summarize the foregoing, the characteristics of the Manyō poetry consist in its freshness of language, its harmonic construction and its firm grasp of life and nature, and these may be regarded as a continuation and development of the old traditions of indigenous Japanese culture. In this respect the Manyō lyrics stand in marked contrast to the plastic arts which flourished in the same period, but which were largely continental in style and technique. Plastic art, by its very nature, is capable of being transplanted from one country to another and of thriving on the new soil practically in its original form—especially when it meets with no competition from a native source, as was the case in Japan of the 8th century, which could boast no greater tradition in this line than what was represented by the crude and primitive clay figures known as *haniwa*. Even among the sculptural masterpieces of the Asuka and Nara Periods, which mark one of the highest points in the history of Japanese art, it is usually difficult to distinguish which are the most typically Japanese specimens and which the general Asiatic type. The Manyō poetry, on the contrary, was eminently successful in preserving and developing characteristically Japanese elements. This is no doubt due to the fact that poetry is a word-art forming part and parcel of the very life of a race. At the same time, it indicates how strong and deep-rooted were the literary traditions that the Manyō age inherited from the ages past.

While the *Manyōshū* possesses as a whole a unique distinctive quality of its own, its poems naturally change in style with the changing times. Apart from those few works that belong to earlier periods antedating the reign of the Emperor Tenji, the bulk of the poems may be roughly divided into two groups—one belonging to the Asuka and Fujiwara Periods (673–710) and the other to the Nara Period (710–84). The poems of the former group are imbued with the freshness of elemental emotions and animated with a sturdy pioneering spirit. They possess an archaic solemnity, as well as masculine and vigorous qualities of tone, although marred at times by a crudeness or extravagance of expression. The latter group shows a marked gain in smoothness and lucidity of style; sometimes breathing a note of melancholy, and sometimes striving for rhetorical elegance with a tendency to substitute a refinement of sensibility for fervour of sentiment. This meant, of course, only an internal change within the healthy, honest and unsophisticated Manyō mind, and the process was influenced and complicated by the genius of individual poets. Nevertheless, it may be broadly stated that such is the general direction that Manyō poetry followed in the course of its development.

Among the poets prominent in the *Manyōshū* there are, as stated before, many members of the imperial family, beginning with the Emperor Yūryaku and the Empress Yamato-himé of the more remote periods. The most representative poet, however, of the early Manyō age, both in style and ability, is Kakinomoto Hitomaro, who excelled both in *chōka* and *tanka*, and whose works include elegies and hymns of praise, as well as poems of love and travel. In his poems every scene glows with the fire of his feelings, and he often uses sonorous cadences such as recall the sound of the sea. In travel poems Takechi Kurohito is con-

sidered Hitomaro's equal, but the poet, who has always
been accorded the place of honour with Hitomaro as one
of the two ' Saints of Poetry,' is Yamabé Akahito who
flourished in the early Nara Period.   In contrast to the
former's impassioned attitude towards life, the latter, contemplating the world before him calmly and with unclouded
eyes, wrote poems in a pure and limpid style.   Takahashi
Mushimaro, of whom a number of ballad-like poems
treating of legendary subjects are preserved, is another
important representative of this period.

The later Manyō age, i. e. the Nara Period, is best represented by a galaxy of poets centreing round the Ōtomo
clan, of whom Tabito, his son Yakamochi, and his one-
time subordinate, Yamanoé Okura, are the best known.
They were all civilized men of the age, steeped in continental culture and well acquainted with the teachings of
Confucius and Buddhism, by which they were consequently
influenced to a considerable degree.   Okura, a Confucian
scholar, was seriously interested in human relations and
social questions.   On the other hand, it is worthy of note
that Tabito, while showing in the prefaces to his poems
a profound knowledge of Chinese literature, remained
throughout his life a passionate and truly Japanese poet.
But in his son, Yakamochi, we have the pre-eminent figure
of this period.   From the many, and occasionally frivolous,
love poems which he wrote as a young court noble surrounded by a bevy of beautiful women, to those in which
he gravely exhorts his clansmen to tread the path of recti-
tude and honour, his work ranges widely in content and
tenor.   Specially notable is that group of *tanka* (Nos. 521–2,
523) which shows the poet's soul, pensive and subdued,
free from all violent emotions, and responding to every
casual phenomenon of nature.   They constitute in fact a
new brand of poetry created in the closing years of the Manyō age.

Lady Ōtomo of Sakanoé—a sister of Tabito and a member of the above-mentioned group—is only one of the many

distinguished women poets of the *Manyōshū*. There are also Princess Nukada who flourished in the reign of the Emperor Tenji, and Princess Ōku (elder sister of Prince Ōtsu) whose genius was prompted to blossom forth under the star of an evil fortune. Then there is the Maiden Sanu Chigami, author of a series of impassioned poems inspired by her tragic love. Further, there are those ladies who exchanged verses with Yakamochi, and many others, known or unknown by name, whose works deserve to rank among the best by virtue of the delicacy or tenderness or intensity of their feeling.

Finally, it should be noted that the *Manyōshū* contains a great number of excellent poems by anonymous authors and common folk, as may be readily seen in the Eastland poems, or those by frontier-guards, and some others which are scattered in Books XI, XII and XIII. In point of style, idea and simile, they are simpler and plainer, as compared with the works of court poets ; but their rusticity has a rich charm of its own, and they are moreover no whit inferior in the genuineness of sentiment and in their observation and treatment of nature. Many of these poems have the qualities of folk-song, which makes the *Manyōshū* truly a ' people's anthology.' Those humble poets who sang, borrowing old familiar ditties of the country-side and weaving their own feelings into them, inject a refreshing and vital element into the Anthology, and throw interesting sidelights on the thoughts and beliefs of the age and the sentiments and modes of life in the provinces.

PART III

THE *MANYŌSHŪ* IN LATER AGES

The *Manyōshū* seems to have been almost totally neglected for some time after its compilation. The first evidence we have of its having attracted any attention is a poem which was composed in the latter half of the 9th century in reply to a question of the emperor regarding the Anthology, and which is included in the *Kokinshū*, the first of the anthologies compiled at imperial command, which appeared in 905, and which was itself claimed to be a continuation of the *Manyōshū*. A small collection of *tanka*, called *Shinsen* (newly compiled) *Manyōshū*, dated 893, is also extant.

The *Kokinshū* and the subsequent 'imperial anthologies' continued to include some Manyō poems, though not without errors and misquotations. Of the Manyō poets, Hitomaro, Akahito and Yakamochi were honoured each by a book of random collections of their works. Especially Hitomaro and Akahito, as 'Saints of Poetry' among the 'Thirty-six Master-Poets,' came to receive universal veneration from this time onward. But little appreciation was shown of the true value and spirit of Manyō poetry.

It was some 200 years after the supposed date of its completion, that the first attempt was made at a textual study of the Manyō poems. By order of the emperor, Minamoto Shitagō (911–83), the leading poet and scholar of that time, who was also a lexicographer, produced a Manyō text to render its reading easier. For this work he has been accorded the first place in the long list of Manyō scholars. Subsequently for three or four centuries, gleanings, selections and classified collections of Manyō poems continued to be made, as well as a certain amount of textual emendation, and even investigation into the date and circumstances of the compilation. There is no doubt that the Anthology was cherished by court circles and the Shoguns; and the copying of it was a pious exercise, to which fact we owe the scattered volumes and stray leaves of manuscript copies of the *Manyōshū* done by master calligraphers. Of these the most famous are a fragment of the 'Katsura MS.'—apparently a copy of selected poems made in the middle of the 11th century—now one of the 'imperial treasures'; the 'Genryaku Comparative Texts' consisting of parts of a manuscript copy dated 1184, and the 'West Hongan-ji Temple Book'—a complete copy of the 13th century.

A priest named Sengaku (1203–? 73), at Kamakura, by order of the Shogun Fujiwara Yoritsuné, carried on a thorough revision of the Manyō texts. His commentary in 10 volumes, completed in the middle of the 13th century, marks the beginning of really scholarly labour in this field. During the 15th and 16th centuries the *Manyōshū* gained in prestige and popularity, but no advance was made in the field of critical studies. It may be noted in passing that to the new school of *renga* poets the *Manyōshū* became an object of special esteem, and its great leader Sōgi (d. 1502) tried his hand at commenting on the Anthology. With the 17th century a new age of revival of classical learning dawned upon Japan. The first printed edition of the *Manyōshū* was made possible by the use of movable wooden types. The third edition, revised and corrected and superseding the previous editions, was published in 1643, and this is an epoch-making edition that has remained to this day as an authority for general consultation concerning the Manyō text.

Studies and researches, based strictly on bibliographical sources, were inaugurated by Keichū (1640–1701), a learned monk of Ōsaka. Tokugawa Mitsukuni (d. 1700), head of the Mito branch of the Shogunate family, who was one of the greatest patrons of learning in modern Japan, sponsored the labours of Keichū, which bore fruit in the *Manyō Daishōki*—a voluminous commentary in 20 books. For two centuries this book circulated, in the form of manuscript copies, as a valuable store of information. Keichū, a profound Buddhist scholar, was not only acquainted with Sanskrit, but was also versed in Chinese literature. He was thus well-equipped for his researches into ancient classics, and became the pioneer of Japanese philology as well as the founder of Manyō learning.

Sixty years after Keichū's death, Kamo Mabuchi (1697–1769), a great scholar of Japanese classics, carried on further studies in the *Manyōshū*. Without confining himself to exegetical work, he investigated the dates of compilation of all the books of the *Manyōshū* and formulated theories regarding their original order, the results of which are embodied in the book entitled the *Manyōkō*. Moreover, endowed with an extraordinary capacity for understanding and appreciation, he extolled the true spirit of the Manyō and demonstrated his devotion by writing poems in the Manyō style, so that many eminent scholars and poets, some of whom are mentioned below, appeared from among his pupils. Considerable as was his academic contribution, his influence upon the generation of Manyō scholars who followed him was no less.

Tachibana Chikagé (1734-1808) of Yedo, a disciple of Mabuchi, brought out the *Manyōshū Ryakugé*, a concise and convenient commentary, in 1812, which proved most successful in spreading Manyō knowledge. In contrast to this popular book, a monumental work in 141 volumes, embodying most elaborate commentaries and studies, known as the *Manyōshū Kogi*, was compiled by a scholar in the remote province of Tosa in southern Japan, Kamochi Masazumi (1791–1858), and it is still valued as an authoritative work of reference. A fine edition of the book was published under imperial patronage in the year 1891, which has since been followed by smaller editions. It was while the work on the *Kogi* was in progress, that Kimura Masakoto (1827–1913), who became a great Manyō bibliographer, and an indefatigable collector and commentator of various texts, was born in eastern Japan. He conducted special researches in the field of Manyō script and phonology, and has left a critical commentary, which, though not complete, was the most exhaustive in existence at the time. Of this book the parts dealing with bibliography and methodology are still valuable, while many of the author's views regarding textual interpretation compel attention and respect, representing as they do profound and conscientious scholarship.

The ground-work for Manyō textual criticism was

completed by Dr. Nobutsuna Sasaki and his collaborators after many years' labour. The *Kōhon Manyōshū*, a variorum edition in 24 volumes (10 vols. in 2nd edition), published in 1924, is based on the standard edition of 1643 mentioned above, and takes note of all the variant readings found in 20 different sources, including such rare manuscripts as the 'Katsura MS.' and others already described. It also contains facsimile reproductions from old manuscripts and editions. Though it may yet have to be enlarged or revised in future, this book is final for the present, and anticipates the compilation of a definitive edition of the *Manyōshū*.

During the four decades from the beginning of the 20th century, when the first volume of Kimura's commentary was issued, more manuscripts have been discovered, and those already known have been reproduced. Old commentaries have been reprinted and new ones, large and small, have been written. Biographies, geographies and natural history books concerning the *Manyōshū*, indexes and concordances of various kinds, monographs and dissertations, giving original theories or the results of independent studies, books and essays, some critical, some popular, some cultural-historical,—thousands of publications have come from the press. Details of these are to be found in the *Manyōshū Kenkyū Nempō* (Year's Work in Manyō Studies) which has been issued regularly since 1930. It only remains to add that important contributions have been made in recent years by several members of our Committee to this Manyō renaissance.

The *Manyōshū*, which has given later scholars a store-house of historical materials regarding Japanese poetry and culture, has in more recent times served for poets as an undefiled well of thought and language. It is true that superficial followers of the Manyō style began to appear early in the mediaeval age, and they grew more numerous in the 12th century, but they were mere imitators, and their number continued to multiply throughout the subsequent ages. The name of Minamoto Sanetomo (d. 1219), however, deserves mention, since this ill-starred Shōgun at Kamakura was a poet, young and sensitive, who in some of his poems showed a fine grasp of the Manyō spirit and style. In the modern age, despite the active interest aroused in Manyō studies, scholars did not necessarily write their poems in the Manyō style. We have already discovered in Kamo Mabuchi an early propounder of Manyōism in the 18th century. His pupils, Tokugawa Munetaké (d. 1771) of Yedo and Katori Nahiko (d. 1782), were both excellent neo-Manyō poets. More poets of the same school appeared in the 19th century in northern and western Japan, of whom Ryōkan the monk (d. 1831), Hiraga Motoyoshi (d. 1865) and Tachibana Akemi (d. 1868) may be mentioned. As for those of the Meiji era and after, there were—to confine ourselves to those poets who are dead—first of all Shiki Masaoka (d. 1902), who is remembered for his brilliant achievements as a reformer of *tanka* and *haiku*; Sachio Itō (d. 1913), Shiki's pupil, and Akahiko Shimaki (d. 1926), Sachio's pupil, who are also famous for their poems in the Manyō style. This trio of master-and-disciples wrote not only excellent poems but also useful books for popularizing the appreciation and the spread of the Manyō style; and future historians of Japanese poetry are not likely to overlook the contributions they made, in concert with other master-singers of their time, to the unprecedented vogue of *tanka* in Japan to-day.

TRANSLATIONS

European acquaintance with the *Manyōshū* began with the 19th century. It was in 1834 that Klaproth, a noted Orientalist, translated into French one of the envoys to Yakamochi's *chōka* (No. 471) concerning the discovery of a gold mine in 749. In the middle of the 19th century a specimen of some printed edition found its way into Holland, for the *Manyōshū* is listed in Siebold's catalogue of books imported from Japan. Translations, though of but a few poems in each case, began to appear from 1870 onward, after intercourse was firmly established between Japan and Europe.

The first of these was attempted by a French scholar, Léon de Rosny (1837–1914), who published his *Anthologie Japonaise* in 1871, which contained 9 Manyō poems. In the following year, 1872, an Austrian Orientalist, August Pfizmaier (1808–87) published in the Proceedings of the Imperial Academy of Vienna translations of more than 200 poems—a half of Book III and a great part of Book IV. But all these early translations are, as would be expected, extremely inaccurate. The first adequate work in this field appeared in 1880 in *The Classical Poetry of the Japanese* which was written by Basil Hall Chamberlain (1850–1935), then Professor of the Tokyo Imperial University and a foremost authority on Japanese classics. The book contains a few score of the more important poems from the *Manyōshū*. Since then, with the growing appreciation of the Anthology, good translations have been published one after another. Karl Florenz (1865–1939), formerly Professor of the Hamburg University and also Professor of the Tokyo Imperial University for many years, included 30 poems from the *Manyōshū* in his *Dichtergrüsse aus dem fernen Osten*, published in 1894. He also wrote in 1904 a history of Japanese literature, giving therein a brief exposition of the *Manyōshū* together with a few sample translations, as G. Aston (1841–1911) had done previously in 1899 for the English reading public.

The *Primitive and Mediaeval Japanese Texts*, brought out in 1906 by F. V. Dickins (1838–1915), contains metrical translations of practically all the *chōka* and a scholarly and comprehensive introduction to the Manyō age and poetry. Michel Revon's *Anthologie de la Littérature Japonaise des Origines au 20ᵉ Siècle*, published in 1910, has also a good many pieces, including 5 *chōka*. The little book by Arthur Waley, *Japanese Poetry* (1919), gives literal translations of some 90 poems, mostly *tanka*, with a view ' to facilitate the study of the Japanese text.' The German translation of all Hitomaro's poems and a study of the poet made in 1927 by Alfred Lorenzen, one of the pupils of Professor Florenz, should be mentioned as a notable contribution, while the work of Dr. Georges Bonneau, who has been staying in Japan and devoting his time to the translation of the *Kokinshū* and Japanese folk-songs, and who in the meantime has published a few translations from the *Manyōshū*, deserves notice. Dr. Bonneau claims that French is *the* European tongue best suited for translating Japanese poetry into because of certain intrinsic similarities between the two languages. By far the most colossal enterprise ever attempted in this field is being undertaken by Dr. J. L. Pierson, Jr., a Dutch scholar well versed in the Japanese language, who has embarked upon a complete translation of the *Manyōshū* with copious annotations 'from the point of view of the linguist,' of which the fifth volume, covering Book V of the original, has recently been published.

As regards the labours of Japanese scholars in this field, it may be recalled that in 1897 Tōmitsu Okazaki submitted to the University of Leipzig a doctoral dissertation, which contained an exposition of the *Manyōshū* and translations of its poems. Okazaki also gives translations of some Manyō poems in his *Geschichte der japanischen Nationalliteratur*, which was published in the following year. Among the contemporary writers of English, Professors Tetsuzō Okada and Asatarō Miyamori may be mentioned, the former being the author of *Three Hundred Manyō Poems*, published in 1935, and the latter of *Masterpieces of Japanese Poetry Ancient and Modern* (1936) in two volumes, of which fully one-third of the first is devoted to the *Manyōshū*.

NOTES

The present translation is based largely upon the popular printed edition of the 20th year of Kan-ei (1643), while older editions and ancient manuscripts have also been consulted.

Of the total number of poems, 4,516 in all according to the *Kokka Taikan* (Conspectus of National Poetry), 1,000 have been selected. These have been re-arranged according to periods, and are further classified into those of individual poets, those forming special groups, and those whose authorship is unknown. Poets whose years extend over two periods are placed under one or other of the two for the sake of convenience.

The translated poems are numbered according to the order in which they are given, a *chōka* with its envoys or a special group of poems being marked with the numbers of the first and last poems, placed together at the beginning, as for instance, 4–5, or 12–5. The original numbering in the *Kokka Taikan* for each individual poem is given on the right side in square brackets, Roman numerals indicating the number of the book, Arabic the number of the poem.

Titles and Prefatory Notes have often been abbreviated; and Original Notes have been abridged or transferred to foot-notes, where also the more important alternative readings and interpretations are to be found.

Titles and Original Notes, etc., are omitted from the Romaji text, in which the original four lines are printed as one line in order to economize space.

The reading given in the Romaji text is mainly that of Modern Japanese, as it is impossible to ascertain exactly the pronunciation of the Manyō age, but in the case of obsolete or archaic words an attempt has been made at restoring an older pronunciation. Some inconsistency is unavoidable owing to the disagreement between the theoretical pronunciation suggested by scholars and the traditional manner of reading followed by poets.

In the Romaji transcription the Hepburn system has been followed, in which the consonants are pronounced as in English and the vowels as in Italian. The final *E* is always pronounced, two vowels coming together are pronounced separately, and *G* is always hard, even before *I* or *Y*. To guard against error and confusion in connection with the final *E* some Japanese names or words are marked with the acute accent (saké, Prince Yugé, etc.).

In writing personal names, the conjunctive particle, *no*, so frequently introduced in Japanese between the surname and the given name, is omitted; thus, *Kakinomoto Hitomaro* instead of *Kakinomoto no Hitomaro*. Place-names are occasionally translated, as, for instance, 'Mirror Mountain' for *Kagami Yama*.

In the case of animals, plants, clothes, etc., it is often difficult to find exact counterparts in English. Sometimes, the original Japanese names (*susuki*), or approximate translations ('elm-tree' for *tsuki*), are given; sometimes new names have been invented through literal translation ('morning face' for *asagao*), or by way of description ('night-thrush' for *nué*). The names of offices and ranks are usually given in terms of the corresponding offices and ranks of to-day (Prime Minister for *Naidaijin*); or translated ('Minister of the Left' for *Sadaijin*); or in the original (*Taishok-kan*). In all cases dates, unless otherwise mentioned, refer to the Christian era, but A. D. is omitted.

The names of months are sometimes translated. It should be borne in mind that as the lunar calendar was in use, 'the first month' or 'January' in the translation is about a month behind in season, corresponding more closely to February of the present calendar. 'Pillow-words' are translated or suggested as far as possible, but many have been omitted because of the uncertainty of their original meanings.

The Biographical Notes are given according to the order in which the poets are arranged in the translation. Only the more important offices which they held are mentioned, their court ranks being omitted.

PRE-ŌMI AND ŌMI PERIODS

Emperor Yūryaku

1   YOUR basket, with your pretty basket,   [1 : 1]
       Your trowel, with your little trowel,
Maiden, picking herbs on this hill-side,
I would ask you : Where is your home?
Will you not tell me your name?
Over the spacious Land of Yamato
It is I who reign so wide and far,
It is I who rule so wide and far.
I myself, as your lord, will tell you
Of my home, and my name.

Emperor Jomei

2   *Climbing Kagu-yama*[1] *and looking upon*   [1 : 2]
              the land.

COUNTLESS are the mountains in Yamato,
    But perfect is the heavenly hill of Kagu;
When I climb it and survey my realm,
Over the wide plain the smoke-wreaths rise and rise,
Over the wide lake[2] the gulls are on the wing;
A beautiful land it is, the Land of Yamato!

3   THE stag of the Ogura Mountain   [VIII : 1511]
       That cries when evening comes,
Cries not to-night—
Is it that he sleeps?

---

[1] The hill stands in Yamato Plain. According to legend, it descended from heaven.

[2] i. e. the lake of Haniyasu at the northern base of Kagu-yama. Though there remain only traces of it now, the lake was apparently very large.

3

Empress Kōgyoku

4–5　　　*Presented to the Emperor Jomei by a mes-*　　　[1 : 3–4]
　　　　　senger, Hashibito Oyu, on the occasion
　　　　　of his hunting on the plain of Uchi.[1]

I HEAR the twang of the mid-string[2]
　Of his royal birchwood[3] bow,
Which my Sovereign, ruling in peace,
Loves to handle at break of day,
And fondly leans against with dusk.
Now he must be out for his morning hunt,
Now he must be out for his evening chase;
I hear the twang of the mid-string
Of his loved birchwood bow!

Envoy

With horses drawn abreast
On the open waste of Uchi,
This morning he must be trampling
That grassy land!

6–84　　　FROM the age of the gods　　　[IV : 485–7]
　　　　　Men have been begotten and begetting;
They overflow this land of ours.
I see them go hither and thither
Like flights of teal—
But not you whom I love.
So I yearn each day till the day is over,
And each night till the dawn breaks;

---

[1] In Uchi District, Yamato Province.

[2] An alternative reading of the text is ' *nagahazu* ' (long notches).

[3] *Azusa*, a kind of birch, chiefly used for making bows in ancient times.

[4] Composed presumably during the absence of her husband, the Emperor Jomei. The author's name given in the text is *Okamoto-no-miya*, which may mean either the Emperor Jomei or the Empress Kōgyoku. However, judging from their character, the poems are generally regarded as being by the Empress.

Sleeplessly I pass this long, long night!

Envoys

Though men go in noisy multitudes
Like flights of teal over the mountain edge,[1]
To me—oh what loneliness,
Since you are absent whom I love.

By the Toko Mountain in Ōmi[2]
There flows the Isaya,[3] River of Doubt.
I doubt whether now-a-days
You, too, still think of me?

Emperor Tenji

9-11[4]   *The Three Hills.*[5]   [1 : 13-5]

Mount Kagu strove with Mount Miminashi
   For the love of Mount Unebi.
Such is love since the age of the gods;
As it was thus in the early days,
So people strive for spouses even now.

Envoys

When Mount Kagu and Mount Miminashi wrangled,
A god[6] came over and saw it

---

[1] The first two lines may be construed to read:
    'Though in noisy multitudes
    Flights of teal go over the mountain edge,'
[2] Now Shiga Prefecture, in which Lake Biwa is situated.
[3] The first part of the poem is a rhetorical introduction, the word Isaya being employed in a double sense, viz. as the name of a river and also as an exclamation of doubt. However, the use of this and other place-names points to the probability that the Emperor was then travelling in the province of Ōmi.
[4] Composed by the Emperor while he was still Crown Prince during the reign of the Empress Saimei.
[5] In Yamato Plain. The poem is based on an old legend.
[6] The God of Abo.

Here—on this plain of Inami![1]

On the rich banner-like clouds
That rim the waste of waters
The evening sun is glowing,
And promises to-night
The moon in beauty![2]

Empress Iwa-no-himé

12-5   *Longing for the Emperor Nintoku.*   [II : 85-8]

SINCE you, my Lord, were gone,
    Many long, long days have passed.
Should I now come to meet you
And seek you beyond the mountains,
Or still await you—await you ever?

Rather would I lay me down
On a steep hill's side,
And, with a rock for pillow, die,
Than live thus, my Lord,
With longing so deep for you.

Yes, I will live on
And wait for you,
Even till falls
On my long black waving hair
The hoar frost of age.

---

[1] In Inami District, Harima Province. Legend has it that at the quarrel of the Three Hills, the God of Abo, intending to compose the dispute, left Izumo Province and came as far as the plain, where he settled, on hearing of the end of the strife.
[2] This poem does not seem to be an envoy, but as it is so given in an older book it is retained here.—Original Note.

How shall my yearning ever cease—
Fade somewhere away,
As does the mist of morning
Shimmering across the autumn field
Over the ripening grain?

Empress Yamato-himé

16   *Presented to the Emperor Tenji on the*   [II : 147]
               occasion of His Majesty's illness.

I TURN and gaze far
  Towards the heavenly plains.
Lo, blest is my Sovereign Lord—
His long life overspans
The vast blue firmament.[1]

17   *[After the death of the Emperor.]*   [II : 148]

THOUGH my eyes could see your spirit soar[2]
  Above the hills of green-bannered Kohata,
No more may I meet you face to face.

18   OTHERS may cease to remember,   [II : 149]
    But I cannot forget you—
Your beauteous phantom shape
Ever haunts my sight!

---

[1] The poem recalls the ancient practice of seeking omens in the skies. The latter half of the original poem literally means : His life is long and fills full the sky (that is, is endless as is the sky).

[2] It was believed that the spirit of the dead would rise from the earth and fly to heaven. The Emperor's tomb was situated at Kohata (near Kyōto). The phrase *aohata no*, here rendered ' green-bannered,' is a pillow-word for Kohata. But it may be construed as an ordinary phrase referring to the green banners that were actually used on the occasion of a state funeral.

On the occasion of the temporary enshrine-   [II : 153]
            ment of the Emperor Tenji.

O<small>N</small> the vast lake[1] of Ōmi
      You boatmen that come rowing
From the far waters,
And you boatmen that come rowing
Close by the shore,
Ply not too hard your oars in the far waters,
Ply not too hard your oars by the shore,
Lest you should startle into flight
The birds beloved of my dear husband !

Prince Shōtoku

20   *On seeing a man dead on Mount Tatsuta*   [III : 415]
            during his trip to the Well of Takahara.

H<small>AD</small> he been at home, he would have slept
      Upon his wife's dear arm;
Here he lies dead, unhappy man,
On his journey, grass for pillow.[2]

Prince Arima

21–2[3]   *Lamenting his plight, and binding*   [II : 141–2]
                  pine branches.

A<small>T</small> Iwashiro[4] I bind[5]
      The branches of a shore pine.

---

[1] i. e. Lake Biwa.   [2] Pillow-word for ' journey.'

[3] Prince Arima was being taken to the hot springs of Muro in the province of Kii, where the court was temporarily in residence. The prince, who was to be punished for his rebellious conduct, was put to death during the journey before reaching his destination.

[4] Located near the sea on the route to the hot springs.

[5] Binding pine branches was practised as a sort of charm.

If fortune favours me,
I may come back
And see the knot again.

Now that I journey, grass for pillow,
They serve rice on the *shii*[1] leaves,
Rice they would put in a bowl,
Were I at home!

Prince Ikusa

23-4 *Seeing the mountains when the Emperor Jomei* [1 : 5-6]
sojourned in Aya District, Sanuki Province.[2]

Not knowing that the long spring day—
    The misty day—is spent,
Like the 'night-thrush'[3] I grieve within me,
As sorely my heart aches.
Then across the hills where our Sovereign sojourns,
Luckily the breezes blow
And turn back my sleeves[4] with morn and eve,
As I stay alone;
But, being on a journey, grass for pillow,
Brave man as I deem me,
I know not how to cast off
My heavy sorrows;
And like the salt-fires the fisher-girls
Burn on the shore of Ami,
I burn with the fire of longing

---

[1] i. e. *Castanopsis cuspidata*, an evergreen tree with thick oblong leaves.

[2] According to the Original Note, the Emperor visited Sanuki presumably on the occasion of his journey to the hot springs in Iyo in the 12th month of the 11th year of his reign (639).

[3] *Nué*, identified with *tora-tsugumi*, a kind of thrush which sings at night or in cloudy weather in a mournful tone. Its back is yellowish brown.

[4] 'Turn back one's sleeves' was an auspicious happening for a traveller, anticipating a safe journey home. (See Introduction p. xli.)

In my heart.

Envoy

Fitful gusts of wind are blowing
Across the mountain-range,
And night after night I lie alone,
Yearning for my love at home.

Princess Nukada

25   WHILE at Nigitazu we await the moon   [1 : 8]
        To put our ships to sea,
With the moon the tide has risen;
Now let us embark![1]

26   *When the Emperor Tenji commanded Fujiwara*   [1 : 16]
        Kamatari, Prime Minister, to judge between
        the luxuriance of the blossoms on the spring
        hills and the glory of the tinted leaves on
        the autumn hills, Princess Nukada
        decided the question with this poem.

WHEN, loosened from the winter's bonds,
    The spring appears,
The birds that were silent
Come out and sing,
The flowers that were prisoned
Come out and bloom;
But the hills are so rank with trees
We cannot seek the flowers,
And the flowers are so tangled with weeds

---

[1] This poem, according to the Original Note, is attributed to the Empress
Saimei, who composed the poem in Iyo, when her imperial ships set sail westward.

We cannot take them in our hands.

But when on the autumn hill-side
We see the foliage,
We prize the yellow leaves,
Taking them in our hands,
We sigh over the green ones,
Leaving them on the branches;
And that is my only regret—
For me, the autumn hills !

27–8   *On the occasion of her journey to Ōmi.*[1]   [I : 17–8]

O THAT sweet mountain of Miwa[2]—
     I would go lingering over its sight,
Many times looking back from far upon it
Till it is hidden beyond the hills[3] of Nara
And beyond many turnings of the road ;
Then should the clouds be heartless
And conceal the mountain from me ?

Envoy

Must they veil Mount Miwa so ?
Even clouds might have compassion ;
Should ye, O clouds, conceal it from me ?

29   *Yearning for the Emperor Tenji.*   [IV : 488]

WHILE, waiting for you,
     My heart is filled with longing,
The autumn wind blows—

---

[1] Composed on viewing Mount Miwa when the Emperor Tenji removed his
court to Ōmi, in spring, in the 3rd month of the 6th year of his reign (667).—From
the Original Note.
[2] A shapely hill in Shiki District, looking over Yamato Plain from the east.
[3] A low range of hills to the north of the city, through which runs the highway
to the province of Yamashiro.

As if it were you—
Swaying the bamboo blinds of my door.

30　　　*Departing from the imperial tomb at*　　[II : 155]
　　　　　Yamashina.[1]

TENDING the hallowed tomb
　Of His Majesty our Sovereign Lord,
No more can they remain
In the Mirror Mountain of Yamashina
To weep aloud night-long and the long day
　　through—
The lords and ladies of the Great Palace
Must now depart and scatter !

Princess Kagami

31　　EVEN a breeze may fail me　　　　[IV : 489]
　　　　When I desire it.
　　Little I should grieve,
　　If only, sure of its coming,
　　I could await even a breeze.[2]

[1] The district where the Mirror Mountain is situated, the site of the tomb of the Emperor Tenji.　It is now a part of Higashiyama Ward of Kyōto.
[2] The poem is evidently intended to match No 29.　The word *tomoshi* in the text, here rendered ' fail,' can be taken to mean ' envy,' in which case the first two lines may be translated :
　　' How I envy you
　　Who wait even for a breeze ! '

Fujiwara Kamatari

32   *On the occasion of his marriage to*   [II : 95]
      Yasumiko, a palace attendant.

OH, Yasumiko I have won!
    Mine is she whom all men,
They say, have sought in vain.
Yasumiko I have won!

*   *   *

33–4   *Poems composed on the occasion of the*   [IX : 1665–6]
        Sovereign's visit to Ki Province.

I GATHER shells and pebbles
    For my darling at home;
O bear me those jewels from the open sea,
Ye white surges on the distant foam.

In clothes wet as they are with morning fog,
Since none is by to dry them,
All alone over the mountain road
Will my husband press his way!

35–6   *Two poems[1] on the occasion of placing*   [II : 151–2]
        the remains of the Emperor in the
        Mortuary Palace.

HAD we foreknown
    That thus it would be,
We would have roped off the mooring-place
Where lay the great imperial barge.
                              —By Princess Nukada.

---

[1] These poems are based on the pleasant reminiscences of the imperial excursion on Lake Biwa shortly before the death of the Emperor.

PERHAPS, Cape Karasaki of Shiga
    Is waiting and longing
For the great imperial barge
Of our Sovereign Lord who ruled in peace.
                                    —*By Toneri Kiné.*

A Lady of the Court

37 *On the occasion of the death of the* [II : 150]
                    Emperor Tenji.

MORTAL creature as I am,
    Whom the gods suffer not on high,
Wide sundered,
Each morning I lament my Lord;
Far divided,
I long and languish after my Lord.
Oh, were he a jewel
That I might put about my arm and cherish!
Oh, were he a garment
That I might wear and not put off!
The Lord whom I love so,
I saw but last night—in dream.

ASUKA AND FUJIWARA PERIODS

Emperor Temmu

38　ON the peak of Mimiga of fair Yoshinu[1]　　[1 : 25]
　　　The snow is falling constantly,
　　The rain is falling ceaselessly;
　　Constantly as falls the snow,
　　Ceaselessly as beats the rain,
　　Ever thinking I have come,
　　Missing not one turning
　　Of that mountain-path !

Emperor Temmu and Lady Fujiwara

39　MAGNIFICENT snow　　　　　　　　[II : 103]
　　　Has fallen here at my place.
　　But at your tumble-down old village of Ōhara,
　　If ever, later it will fall.—*By the Emperor.*

40　IT was I who did command　　　　　[II : 104]
　　　The Dragon God of these hills
　　To send down the snow,
　　Whereof a few fragments, perchance,
　　Were sprinkled over your home.—*By the Lady.*

Empress Jitō

41　SPRING has passed away　　　　　　[1 : 28]
　　　And summer is come;

　　　¹ Yoshinu, i. e. Yoshino, is the mountainous district occupying the southern
half of Yamato Province.

17

Look where white clothes are spread in the sun
On the heavenly hill of Kagu !

42   *After the death of the Emperor Temmu.*   [II : 159]

OH, the autumn foliage
    Of the hill of Kamioka ![1]
My good Lord and Sovereign
Would see it in the evening
And ask of it in the morning.
On that very hill from afar
I gaze, wondering
If he sees it to-day,
Or asks of it to-morrow.
Sadness I feel at eve,
And heart-rending grief at morn—
The sleeves of my coarse-cloth robe
Are never for a moment dry.

43-4   *Two poems said to have been composed*   [II : 160–1]
            by the Empress after the death of
                the Emperor Temmu.

Even a flaming fire can be snatched,
    Wrapt and put in a bag—
Do they not say so ?
But they say not that they know
How I may meet my Lord again !

Above the north mountain-range
That rims the blue firmament
The stars pass on,
The moon passes on—

---

[1] i. e. the so-called Thunder Hill in the village of Asuka near Nara. See No. 118.

Empress Jitō and Old Lady Shihi

45   'No more,' I say to her,   [III : 236]
       Yet Shihi insists on telling me her tales;
   Lately I have not heard them,
   And I miss them now !—*By the Empress.*

46   'No more,' I say to you,   [III : 237]
       Yet you urge, ' Tell me, tell me.'
   So I continue ; then you say,
   ' It is Shihi who insists.'—*By Shihi.*

Prince Ōtsu

47   *Composed in tears when he died by im-*   [III : 416]
      perial order on the bank of Iwaré Pond.

   To-day, taking my last sight of the mallards
      Crying on the pond of Iwaré,
   Must I vanish into the clouds !

Prince Ōtsu and Lady Ishikawa

48   Waiting for you,   [II : 107]
       In the dripping dew of the hill
   I stood,—weary and wet
   With the dripping dew of the hill.—*By the Prince.*

49   Would I had been, beloved,   [II : 108]
       The dripping dew of the hill,
   That wetted you
   While for me you waited.—*By the Lady.*

Prince Yugé

50   *On the occasion of his visit to Yoshinu.*   [III : 242]

UNLIKE the cloud that dwells on Mount Mifuné[1]
    Far above the rapids,
I cannot hope to live
Unchanging for ever !

Prince Shiki

51   *Composed after the Empress Jitō had removed*   [I : 51]
      from the Palace of Asuka to that of Fujiwara.[2]

THE gentle winds at Asuka
    That fluttered the ladies' sleeves[3] —
Now that the court is far removed,
Those breezes blow in vain.

52   *Composed when the Emperor Mommu visited*   [I : 64]
      the Palace of Naniwa[4] in the third year of
      Keiun (706).

THIS evening so cold and chill
    That the mallards' wings are white with frost
As they skim the reedy shore,
How I think of Yamato ![5]

---

[1] Said to be the mountain to the south of Miyataki (Palace Rapids), a division of Nakajō Village on the River Yoshino.
[2] The removal of the court to Fujiwara took place in the 12th month of the 8th year of Shuchō (694).
[3] *Uneme*, young women serving at court, chiefly at the imperial table. They were selected from among the daughters of influential families or of higher officials in the provinces.
[4] The Palace of Naniwa was in what is now the city of Ōsaka.
[5] The province in which Nara, the capital, was situated.

Aᴮᴼᵛᴱ the cascade² tumbling down the rocks
  The bracken sprouts and burgeons on the hill—
Ah, the happy spring is come !

Princess Ōku

54-5   *Upon the departure of Prince Ōtsu for*   [II : 105-6]
        the capital after his secret visit to
                the Shrine of Isé.

Tᴼ speed my brother
  Parting for Yamato,
In the deep of night I stood
Till wet with the dew of dawn.

The lonely autumn mountains
Are hard to pass over
Even when two go together—
How does my brother cross them all alone !

56-7   *On her arrival at the capital after the*   [II : 163-4]
                death of Prince Ōtsu.

Wᴼᵁᴸᴰ that I had stayed
  In the land of Isé
Of the Divine Wind.
Why have I come
Now that he is dead !

Now that he is no more—

---

  ¹ It is said that the poem alludes to the personal fortune of the Prince. But it
may be regarded simply as an extempore composition on the occasion of an outing.
  ² Tarumi, translated as ' the cascade,' is believed by some scholars to be the name
of a place in the province of Harima.

My dear brother—
Whom I so longed to see,
Why have I come,
Despite the tired horses !

58-9   *Lamenting Prince Ōtsu on the occasion of*   [11 : 165–6]
        the removal of his remains to the tomb
        in the Futagami Mountain.

FROM to-morrow ever
   Shall I regard as brother
The twin-peaked mountain of Futagami—
I, daughter of man !

I would break off a branch
Of the flowering staggerbush[1]
Growing on the rocky shore;
But no one says he lives
To whom I would show it !

Princess Tajima

60   *Composed when Prince Hozumi was des-*   [11 : 115]
        patched by imperial command to a moun-
        tain temple of Shiga in Ōmi.

RATHER than stay behind to languish,
   I will come and overtake you—
Tie at each turn of your road
A guide-knot, my lord !

[1] *Ashibi* (*Pieris japonica*), an evergreen wild shrub, whose tiny nodding white flowers open in clusters in early spring.

Composed when her clandestine relations   [II : 116]
       with Prince Hozumi during her residence in
       the palace of Prince Takechi became known.

BECAUSE of the slanderous tongues,
    The busy mouths abroad,
Now I cross the morning river
I have never crossed in my life before.

Prince Omi and an Anonymous Person

62   *Composed in sympathy for Prince Omi when*   [I : 23]
       he was exiled to the isle of Irago¹ in the
       province of Isé.

Is the Prince of Omi a fisherman ?
    Alas ! he gathers the seaweed
At the isle of Irago.

63   *Reply by the Prince, grieving at his lot.*   [I : 24]

CLINGING to this transient life
    I live on the seaweed,
Which I, drenched with the waves,
Gather at the isle of Irago.

Prince Yamakuma

64–6   *An elegy on the death of Prince Iwata.*   [III : 423–5]

A LONG the path of Iwaré
    Each morning he would pass,

¹ In Mikawa Province. But it was often regarded as belonging to Isé because
of its proximity to that province.

Thinking how to make garlands
Of flags and orange[1] flowers
In the fifth month when the cuckoo calls,
Or how to deck the hair with yellow leaves
In the ninth month of autumn showers,
Well believing the love would last,
Long as a creeping vine,
Endless for a myriad ages.
Alas ! from to-morrow on
Must we regard that prince
As belonging to another world !

Envoys

The jewels she wore on her arms,
That maiden of secluded Hatsusé,
I fear they are unstrung
And in confusion lie !

In the coldness of the river-breeze,
Grieving he plodded through Hatsusé;[2]
O that we could meet
One like that prince !

Prince Niu

67-9   *An elegy on the death of Prince Iwata.*   [III : 420–2]

M[Y] prince, graceful as the pliant bamboo,
    My lord, with beauteous ruddy face,
Was enshrined as a god
In the hills of secluded Hatsusé :
So a messenger has told me.
Is this a rumour that I hear ?

---

[1] *Tachibana*, a kind of citrus bearing small fruit.
[2] The River Hatsusé runs through the village of that name.

Is it a mockery that I am told?
My greatest sorrow under heaven,
My wildest grief in this world,
Is that I failed to travel,
With my staff or without it,
Far as the clouds of heaven wander,
Far as the ends of heaven and earth,
To consult the evening oracle,[1]
To consult the oracle of stones;
Whereupon to build a shrine at my home,
With a wine-jar[2] at my pillow,
Stringing many a bamboo-ring,[2]
With bands of mulberry-cloth[3] hanging on my arms,
And in my hand a seven-jointed sedge
From the Sasara Field of Heaven,
To purify myself and pray
On the Heavenly River's shore.
Ah that I must leave him lying
Among the rocks of that lofty hill!

Envoys

It is nothing but a trick
And a mere mockery,
That he, my prince, is laid
Among the rocks of that lofty hill!

Unlike the growth of the *sugi*,[4] the 'pass'-trees,
On Furu's hill at Isonokami,[5]
He is no such prince
As will pass from my mind!

---

[1] A form of divination from words spoken by passers-by in the evening.
[2] The wine-jar and bamboo-rings were used at religious services.
[3] Woven of *yū*, the fibre of the paper mulberry.
[4] i. e. *Cryptomeria japonica*, an evergreen needle-leaf forest tree allied to the cypresses, native to Japan. Its name being homophonous with the verb *sugu*, which means 'to pass,' it is often used as an introductory word to the verb.
[5] In Yamato Province. In the town of Tambaichi there is the Isonokami Shrine.

Princess Tamochi

70–2   *At the burial of Prince Kauchi in the*   [III : 417–9]
                Mirror Mountain¹ in Toyo.

Was it pleasing to my prince's soul?
    This Mirror Mountain in Toyo
He chose for his eternal palace.

In the Mirror Mountain in Toyo,
With its rock-doors shut,
Has he hidden himself?
However long I wait, he never returns.

O for strength to break the rock doors!
Weak woman that I am,
I know not what to do!

Wife of Tagima Maro²

73   Where is my husband trudging on his   [I : 43]
          journey?
Will he to-day force his road
Over the mountains of Nabari³
Hidden like the deep-sea weed?

---

¹ Kagami-yama in Tagawa District in Buzen. Buzen, one half of the land of Toyo, now forms part of Fukuoka and Ōita Prefectures.
² Her husband was travelling in Isé Province.
³ The present town of Nabari and its neighbourhood in Mié Prefecture.

Kakinomoto Hitomaro

74-6   *On passing the ruined capital of Ōmi.*[1]   [1 : 29–31]

SINCE the era of that sage Sovereign[2]
   At the palace of Kashihara[3]
Under the hill of Unebi,
All the Sovereigns born to the Throne,
Reign after reign, ruled the under-heaven,
Remaining in Yamato;
Then the Emperor, a god,
Forsaking the ancient land,
Crossed the hills of Nara,
And, though I know not what he meant,
Held court at Ōtsu of Sasanami[4]
In the land of Ōmi,
Remote place as it was.

But now, though I am told his royal palace towered
   here,
And they say here rose its lofty halls,
Only the spring weeds grow luxuriantly
And the spring sun is dimmed with mists.
As I see these ruins of the mighty palace
My heart is heavy with sorrows !

Envoys

Although it lies unchanged,
The cape of Karasaki
Of Shiga in Sasanami,
It waits and waits in vain
For the courtiers' barges.

---

  [1] The Emperor Tenji removed his court to Ōtsu in Ōmi in 667. The city was laid waste by the War of Jinshin in 672. In the following year a new capital was established again in Yamato.
  [2] i. e. the Emperor Jimmu, the first Emperor.
  [3] At the south-eastern foot of Unebi.
  [4] A district comprising Shiga and Ōtsu.

Though the vast waters stand still
At Shiga in Sasanami,
Could they ever meet again
The people of the former days?

77-8   *On an imperial visit[1] to the pleasure-palace*   [1 : 36–7]
of Yoshinu.

THOUGH, in the Land where rules our Sovereign,
   The provinces are many,
She loves, in Yoshinu,[2] the field of Akitsu,
Encircled by clear streams and towering mountains,
Where cherry-flowers fall,
And there she has reared herself
A mighty-pillared palace.

Here the courtiers row their barges
Side by side across the morning waters,
And race upon the evening stream.

Endless as this river flows,
Lofty as these mountains,
Will it stand for aye,
And never tire my eyes,
This palace by the stream!

Envoy

Endless as the smooth rocks lie
In the rapids of Yoshinu,
That never tire my eyes,
Will I come and gaze upon the palace.

---

[1] The Original Note says that, according to the *Nihonshoki*, the Empress Jitō visited the Palace of Yoshinu several times during her reign. But it is not clear on which occasion these poems were composed.
[2] Yoshinu was at one time a province.

Our great Sovereign, a goddess,   [1:38-9]
    Of her sacred will
Has reared a towering palace
On Yoshinu's shore,
Encircled by its rapids;
And, climbing, she surveys the land.

The overlapping mountains,
Rising like green walls,
Offer the blossoms in spring,
And with autumn, show their tinted leaves,
As godly tributes to the Throne.
The god of the Yū River,[1] to provide the royal table,
Holds the cormorant-fishing
In its upper shallows,
And sinks the fishing-nets[2]
In the lower stream.

Thus the mountains and the river
Serve our Sovereign, one in will;
It is truly the reign of a divinity.

Envoy

The mountains and the waters
Serve our Sovereign, one in will;
And she, a goddess, is out on her pleasure-barge
Upon the foaming rapids.

---

[1] The name of part of the river Yoshino.
[2] Strictly speaking, fishing-nets in the form of a winnowing-fan. They were sunk in the water.

81-2 *Composed by Hitomaro, who remained in the*   [1 : 40, 42]
        capital¹ when the Empress Jitō visited the
        province of Isé,² in spring, in the third
        month of the sixth year of Shuchō (692).

THE court ladies may board a boat
   On the bay of Ago ;³
Will the tide swell up
To the hems of their elegant skirts ?⁴

In the boat that sails about the isle of Irago
When the tides clash and brawl,
Will the court ladies venture forth ?
Ah, those raging waters round the isle !

83-7 *On the occasion of the night-sojourn of Prince*   [1 : 45–9]
        Karus on the plain of Aki.⁶

OUR prince, offspring of the Bright One on high,
   Of his godlike will,
Leaves the Imperial City;
Then, along the wild path through the cypresses,
And brushing the thicket in the rocks,
Crosses the hills of secluded Hatsusé
With morning;
And, as evening comes,
He bends the waving *susuki*⁷ and bamboo
On the snow-falling plain of Aki,

---

¹ Then situated at Asuka in Yamato Province.
² From Isé the Empress went to visit Shima Province, according to the *Nihonshoki*.
³ In Shima.
⁴ i. e. *mo*, a part of the lady's full dress.   It hung from the waist and covered only the back part.   (See Introduction p. xlviii.)
⁵ Son of the Crown Prince Kusakabé who was a son of the Emperor Temmu.   He later ascended the throne as Emperor Mommu.
⁶ In Uda District in Yamato.
⁷ A perennial grass, the ears of which look like the tail of an animal ; hence, its other name *obana* (tail flower).   See No. 646.

And stays the night long,
With grass for his pillow,
Remembering the days gone by.

Envoys

The travellers taking shelter
On the plain of Aki,
Can they sleep at their ease,
Remembering the days gone by?

Though this is but a desolate plain
Where people mow the grass,
They journeyed all the way
To remember him, gone like the yellow leaf.

On the eastern plain
The purple dawn is glowing,
While looking back I see
The moon declining to the west.

That Prince of Hinamishi[1]
Held here his royal hunt,
With horses bridle to bridle;
Again that time has come.

88–90   *On leaving his wife as he set out*   [II : 131–3]
           from Iwami[2] for the capital.

ALONG the coast of Tsunu[3]
     On the sea of Iwami
One may find no sheltering bay,
One may find no sequestered lagoon.
O well if there be no bay!

---

[1] An honorific title of the Crown Prince Kusakabé. He died in the 4th month
of the 3rd year of the Empress Jitō's reign.
[2] A province in western Honshū, facing the Japan Sea.
[3] Tsunotsu of the present day.

O well if there be no lagoon!
Upon Watazu's[1] rocky strand,
Where I travel by the whale-haunted sea,
The wind blows in the morning,
And the waves wash at eve
The sleek sea-tangle and the ocean weed,
All limpid green.

Like the sea-tangle, swaying in the wave
Hither and thither, my wife would cling to me,
As she lay by my side.
Now I have left her, and journey on my way,
I look back a myriad times
At each turn of the road.
Farther and farther my home falls behind,
Steeper and steeper the mountains I have crossed.
My wife must be languishing
Like drooping summer grass.
I would see where she dwells—
Bend down, O mountains!

Envoys

From between the trees that grow
On Takatsunu's mountain-side
In the land of Iwami
I waved my sleeve to her—
Did she see me, my dear wife?

The leaves of bamboo grass
Fill all the hill-side
With loud rustling sounds;
But I think only of my love,
Having left her behind.

[1] Presumably the vicinity of the present-day Watatsu Village, Naka District.

IN the sea of Iwami,
   By the cape of Kara,[1]
There amid the stones under sea
Grows the deep-sea *miru*[2] weed;
There along the rocky strand
Grows the sleek sea-tangle.

Like the swaying sea-tangle,
Unresisting would she lie beside me—
My wife whom I love with a love
Deep as the *miru*-growing ocean.
But few are the nights
We two have lain together.

Away I have come, parting from her
Even as the creeping vines do part.
My heart aches within me;
I turn back to gaze—
But because of the yellow leaves
Of Watari Hill,
Flying and fluttering in the air,
I cannot see plainly
My wife waving her sleeve to me.
Now as the moon, sailing through the cloud rift
Above the mountain of Yakami,[3]
Disappears, leaving me full of regret,
So vanishes my love out of sight;
Now sinks at last the sun,
Coursing down the western sky.

I thought myself a strong man,
But the sleeves of my garment
Are wetted through with tears.

---

[1] A headland of Takuno, Nima District, jutting out towards an island called Karashima.
[2] A seaweed, edible when young.
[3] Unknown, though sometimes it is identified with Mount Takazen.

My black steed
Galloping fast,
Away have I come,
Leaving under distant skies
The dwelling-place of my love.

Oh, yellow leaves
Falling on the autumn hill,
Cease a while
To fly and flutter in the air
That I may see my love's dwelling-place!

94–6 *At the time of the temporary enshrinement* [11 : 167–9]
    of the Crown Prince Hinamishi.[1]

At the beginning of heaven and earth
    The eight hundred, the thousand myriads of
    gods,
Assembled in high council
On the shining beach of the Heavenly River,
Consigned the government of the Heavens
Unto the Goddess Hirumé, the Heaven-Illumining
    One,
And the government for all time,
As long as heaven and earth endured,
Of the Rice-abounding Land of Reed Plains[2]
Unto her divine offspring,
Who, parting the eightfold clouds of the sky,
Made his godly descent upon the earth.

Our noble Prince,[3] child of the Bright One above,

---

[1] See note to No. 87.
[2] An ancient name for Japan.
[3] Sometimes taken to mean the Emperor Temmu, in which case the ensuing lines have to be construed differently.

Regarding this—the land over which
The gracious Sovereign reigns as a god
From the Kiyomi Palace[1] of Asuka, stout-pillared,
Has ascended the Plain of Heaven,
Opening wide the gate of stone.

Alas, our mighty lord and prince,
On whom the folk everywhere in the land leaned,
Trustful as one riding a great ship,
And to whom they looked up as eagerly
As to heaven for rain, hoping
That if he came to rule the under-heaven
He would bring to his reign
A glory of the spring flowers
And such perfection as of the full moon!

Ah, how was he minded that he chose
To plant stout pillars
And build him a palace high
On Mayumi's[2] alien hill!
There we wait on him each morning,
But no word he speaks—
So have passed days on days,
Wherefore now the servitors of the Prince
Must go, but know not where.

Envoys

The stately palace of our Prince
To whom we looked up
As we look up to high heaven,
Alas, must fall into ruin!

Though the ruddy sun shines,
The fair moon, that sails

---

[1] Built by the Emperor Temmu as an imperial residence, and maintained as such till the 8th year of the Empress Jitō's reign.

[2] Located in Sakari Village, Takaichi District, Yamato Province. The tomb of the prince, built on the hill, is still extant.

The darkness of night,
Is hidden for ever—alas!

97 THE birds of the Island Palace,¹ [II : 170]
  Kept in the lake of Crescent Gem,²
Will not dive under water,
Craving the sight of men.³

98-9 *Presented⁴ to Princess Hatsusebé⁵* [II : 194-5]
   and Prince Osakabé.⁵

DAINTY water-weeds, growing up-stream
 In the river of the bird-flying⁶ Asuka,⁷
Drift down-stream, gracefully swaying.
Like the water-weeds the two would bend
Each toward the other, the princess and her consort.

But now no longer can she sleep,
With his⁸ fine smooth body clinging
Close to hers like a guardian sword.
Desolate must be her couch at night.
Unable to assuage her grief,
But in the hope of finding him by chance,
She journeys to the wide plain of Ochinu,
There, her skirt drenched with morning dew
And her coat soaked with the fog of evening,

---

 ¹ *Shima-no-miya*, so called, referring to the islet in the lake of the palace garden. Shimanoshō in Takaichi Village, Takaichi District, Yamato Province, is regarded as the site of the ancient palace.
 ² Probably so named because of its shape.
 ³ This poem is attributed to Hitomaro in a certain book.
 ⁴ These poems were presented, according to a certain book, to Princess Hatsusebé on the occasion of the burial of Prince Kawashima.—Original Note.
 ⁵ Both were children of the Emperor Temmu ; they had the same mother.
 ⁶ A pillow-word for Asuka.
 ⁷ Traversed the metropolitan area of those days, now Takaichi District.
 ⁸ Prince Kawashima, if it may be assumed that the Original Note is correct.

She passes the night—a wayfarer with grass for
  pillow—
Because of him whom she nevermore will meet!

Envoy

Her lord and husband with whom she had slept,
The sleeves of their robes overlapping,
Has passed away to the plain of Ochinu.
How can she ever meet him again!

100–2   *On the occasion of the temporary enshrine-*   [II : 196–8]
              ment of Princess Asuka.[1]

ACROSS the river of the bird-flying Asuka
    Stepping-stones are laid in the upper shallows,
And a plank bridge over the lower shallows.
The water-frond waving along the stones,
Though dead, will reappear.
The river-tresses swaying by the bridge
Wither, but they sprout again.

How is it, O Princess, that you have
Forgotten the morning bower
And forsaken the evening bower
Of him, your good lord and husband—
You who did stand handsome like a water-frond,
And who would lie with him,
Entwined like tender river-tresses?

No more can he greet you.
You make your eternal abode
At the Palace of Kinohé[2] whither oft in your life-
  time

---

[1] Daughter of the Emperor Tenji. Died in the 4th month of the 4th year of the
Emperor Mommu's reign.
[2] A place in Hirosé District, Yamato Province (now included in Kita-Kazuraki
District).

37

He and you made holiday together,
Bedecked with flowers in spring,
Or with golden leaves in autumn-tide,
Walking hand in hand, your eyes
Fondly fixed upon your lord as upon a mirror,
Admiring him ever like the glorious moon.

So it may well be that grieving beyond measure,
And moaning like a bird unmated,
He seeks your grave each morn.
I see him go, drooping like summer grass,
Wander here and there like the evening-star,
And waver as a ship wavers in the sea.

No heart have I to comfort him,
Nor know I what to do.
Only your name and your deathless fame,
Let me remember to the end of time;
Let the Asuka River, your namesake,
Bear your memory for ages,
O Princess adored!

Envoys

Even the flowing water
Of the Asuka River—
If a weir were built,
Would it not stand still?

O Asuka, River of To-morrow,
As if I thought that I should see
My Princess on the morrow,
Her name always lives in my mind.[1]

---

[1] The poem is intended to convey regret over the impossibility of preventing the passing of the Princess. There is a play on the word *asu* which forms part of the name of the River, and at the same time means 'to-morrow,' or 'on the morrow.'

Awesome beyond speech,
    O dread theme for my profane tongue!
That illustrious Sovereign, our mighty Lord,
Who reared his imperial palace
On the Makami plain[2] of Asuka,
Now keeps his divine state,
Sepulchred in stone.

He it was who descended to dwell
At the pavilion of Wazami Field[3]
In yonder province of the realm,
Across the pass of high-forested Fuwa,[4]
There to rule the under-heaven—
To wield the sceptre over his wide domain;
Who summoned his Eastland host;
And ordered our prince, Imperial son as he was,
To pacify the furious men
And subjugate all the unruly lands.

Forthwith our prince buckled on a sword,
And in his august hand
Grasped a bow to lead the army.
The drums marshalling men in battle array
Sounded like the rumbling thunder,
The war-horns blew, as tigers roar,
Confronting an enemy,

---

[1] Son of the Emperor Temmu.   He was appointed Commander-in-Chief of the Imperial Army in the famous War of Jinshin (672).   Under the Empress Jitō he was made Prime Minister and became the Crown Prince.   He died in 696.   Princess Asuka was also temporarily enshrined at Kinohé (cf. Nos. 100–2).   Of course, the sanctuary of the Prince was not built on the same spot.   His tomb still exists on a hill called Mitachi-oka.
[2] Part of Asuka, where the court of the Emperor Temmu is said to have been situated.
[3] Not definitely known, although it is sometimes identified with the Sekigahara of to-day.
[4] Fuwa Mountain is in Fuwa District, Mino Province.

Till all men were shaken with terror.
The banners, hoisted aloft, swayed
As sway in wind the flames[1] that burn
On every moorland far and near
When spring comes after winter's prisonment.
Frightful to hear was the bow-strings' clang,
Like a whirlwind sweeping
Through a winter forest of snow.
And like snow-flakes tempest-driven
The arrows fell thick and fast.
The foemen confronting our prince
Fought, prepared to a man to perish,
If perish they must, like dew or frost;
And vying with one another like birds upon the
    wing,
They flew to the front of battle—
When lo, from Watarai's holy shrine[2]
There rose the God's Wind confounding them,
By hiding the sun's eye with clouds
And shrouding the world in utter darkness.

Thus was turmoil quelled,
And peace established once again
In this Rice-abounding Land,
Our glorious prince then administered
The affairs of government under heaven.
And his rule, men hoped, would endure
For ten thousand ages and prosper
Like the fadeless *yu*[3]-flower.
Alas, our dear Prince Imperial!
His resplendent palace was transformed
Into a sanctuary for a god,
And his servitors clad in white hempen clothes

---

[1] The simile refers probably to the use of red banners.
[2] i. e. the Great Shrine of Isé, Watarai being the name of the place where the shrine stands.
[3] Fibre of the paper mulberry, used for making cloth.

Daily fell prostrate like boars
In the palace grounds of Haniyasu,[1]
And at sunset wandered, bending low
Like quails and gazing toward the palace.
They would serve their prince,
But serve him now they could no more;
Grieving they moaned like spring birds,
But before their sorrow ended
And their sighing ceased,
The prince was borne over the Kudara Plain[2]
For sacred burial in the tomb of Kinohé,
Where, a god enshrined high,
He makes his eternal abode.

Even so, there remains the palace of Kagu-yama,[3]
Built by our prince to stand for ages—
Can I think it ever will pass away?
Let me look up to it as up to heaven
In remembrance of him—over-awed as I am!

Envoys

Because of our lord who has gone
To rule the Heavens above
In what endless longing we live,
Scarce heeding the days and months that pass!

Like the water of the hidden pool[4]
On the bank of the Haniyasu Lake
They know not whither to go—
Sore perplexed are they, the servants of the prince!

---

[1] It would seem that the palace of the prince was situated near the Haniyasu Lake.
[2] In Kita-Kazuraki District, Yamato. It is a plain lying between Kinohé and Asuka District.
[3] The palace stood probably on this hill of Kagu.
[4] A pool confined within a bank—say, of stone.

SINCE in Karu[1] lived my wife,
    I wished to be with her to my heart's content;
But I could not visit her constantly
Because of the many watching eyes—
Men would know of our troth,
Had I sought her too often.
So our love remained secret like a rock-pent pool;
I cherished her in my heart,
Looking to after-time when we should be together,
And lived secure in my trust
As one riding a great ship.
Suddenly there came a messenger
Who told me she was dead—
Was gone like a yellow leaf of autumn.
Dead as the day dies with the setting sun,
Lost as the bright moon is lost behind the cloud,
Alas, she is no more, whose soul
Was bent to mine like the bending seaweed!

When the word was brought to me
I knew not what to do nor what to say;
But restless at the mere news,
And hoping to heal my grief
Even a thousandth part,
I journeyed to Karu and searched the market-place
Where my wife was wont to go!

There I stood and listened,
But no voice of her I heard,
Though the birds sang in the Unebi Mountain;[2]
None passed by, who even looked like my wife.
I could only call her name and wave my sleeve.

---

[1] At that time an extensive district in Yamato, where there was a well-known market-place. The name survives in Ōkaru, in Shirakashi Village, Takaichi District.

[2] Rises to the north-west of Karu.

In the autumn mountains
The yellow leaves are so thick.
Alas, how shall I seek my love
Who has wandered away?—
I know not the mountain track.

I see the messenger come
As the yellow leaves are falling.
Oh, well I remember
How on such a day we used to meet—
My wife and I!

109-11   IN the days when my wife lived,   [II : 210–2]
    We went out to the embankment near by—
We two, hand in hand—
To view the elm-trees[1] standing there
With their outspreading branches
Thick with spring leaves. Abundant as their
    greenery
Was my love. On her leaned my soul.
But who evades mortality?—
One morning she was gone, flown like an early bird.
Clad in a heavenly scarf of white,
To the wide fields where the shimmering *kagerō*[2] rises
She went and vanished like the setting sun.

The little babe—the keepsake
My wife has left me—
Cries and clamours.
I have nothing to give; I pick up the child
And clasp it in my arms.

---

[1] *Tsuki*, a kind of elm, whose yellow leaves are particularly beautiful in autumn.
[2] *Kagerō*, the quivering appearance of the air rising from the hot surface of the ground.

In her chamber, where our two pillows lie,
Where we two used to sleep together,
Days I spend alone, broken-hearted;
Nights I pass, sighing till dawn.

Though I grieve, there is no help;
Vainly I long to see her.
Men tell me that my wife is
In the mountains of Hagai[1]—
Thither I go,
Toiling along the stony path;
But it avails me not,
For of my wife, as she lived in this world,
I find not the faintest shadow.

Envoys

To-night the autumn moon shines—
The moon that shone a year ago,
But my wife and I who watched it then together
Are divided by ever-widening wastes of time.

When leaving my love behind
In the Hikité mountains[2]—
Leaving her there in her grave,
I walk down the mountain path,
I feel not like one living.

112–4   *On the death of an unemé[3] from*   [II : 217–9]
                        Tsu, Kibi Province.

BEAUTY was hers that glowed like autumn moun-
        tains

[1] Unidentified ; but presumably it was a hill near Kasuga.
[2] Also an unidentified range of hills in the vicinity of the Hagai above.
[3] An *unemé* (see note to No. 51) was known by the name of the place and the
province from which she came. Tsu of Kibi Province was situated in Tsu
District of that time—now Tsukubo District, Okayama Prefecture. Since she had
a husband, the lady was evidently a former *unemé*.

And grace as of the swaying bamboo stem.
How was it that she died—she who should have
   lived
A life long as the coil of *taku*[1] rope,
Though the dew falls at morn
To perish at dusk,
Though the mists that rise at eve
Vanish with the daybreak.
On learning her fate I grieve—
I who saw her but casually.
But her husband, tender as young grass,
Who with her soft white arm for pillow
Lay at her side close like a guardian sword—
How lonely must he lie—he in his widowed bed!
What anguish must fill his love-lorn heart,
Yearning for her who all too soon has gone—
Like morning dew—like mists of evening!

Envoys

How sorrowful to see
The road across the river-shallows
By which departed the lady
Of Shigatsu of Sasanami![2]

When we met, I only took—
And how I regret it now!—
A vague careless glance
At the lady of Ōtsu.[3]

---

[1] See note 3 on p. 40.
[2] Situated in the vicinity of the present city of Ōtsu, Shiga Prefecture. Here she presumably lived with her husband.
[3] Presumably another name for Shigatsu.

115–7   *Seeing a dead body lying among the*   [II : 220–2]
stones on the island of Saminé[1]
in the province of Sanuki.

O SANUKI of beautiful seaweed
On which I never tire to look!
So fair is the province
Because of its origin,
And so hallowed the land
For its divinity,[2]
With the very face of a god
Enduring full and perfect
With heaven and earth, with sun and moon.

I, travelling from place to place,
Embarked at Naka's[3] haven
And thence sailed on,
When with the tide the wind arose,
Blowing from the dwelling-place of clouds.
I saw the billows racing on the sea,
And white surges beat upon the shore.
In fear of the whale-haunted sea
We rowed, straining the oars,
And sought, of all the islands thereabout,
Saminé, the island of renown,
And on its rugged coast
We built a hut for shelter.

There I found you, poor man!—
Outstretched on the beach,
On this rough bed of stones,
Amid the busy voices of the waves.

---

[1] Now known as Sami and situated a short distance off the coast of Utatsu, Nakatado District, Sanuki Province: the island still has a fairly large population.

[2] In Japanese mythology a province was sometimes regarded as a deity, and its face as the face of a god.

[3] Said to be the present town of Nakatsu, to the north-east of which lies the island of Sami. In that case, the poet was sailing the Inland Sea from west to east.

If I but knew where was your home,
I would go and tell;
If your wife but knew,
She would come to tend you.
She, knowing not even the way hither,
Must wait, must ever wait,
Restlessly hoping for your return—
Your dear wife—alas!

Envoys

Had your wife been with you,
She would have gathered food for you—
Starworts on Sami's hill-side[1]—
But now is not their season past?

On the rugged beach
Where the waves come surging in from sea
You sleep, O luckless man,
Your head among the stones!

118   *Composed when the Empress[2] climbed the*   [III : 235]
Thunder Hill.[3]

Lo, our great Sovereign, a goddess,
   Tarries on the Thunder
In the clouds of heaven![4]

---

[1] i. e. Saminé Island.
[2] The Empress was the Empress Jitō.
[3] In Yamato Province.
[4] This poem is based on the idea that the Sovereigns are the offspring of Amaterasu Ōmikami, and that their proper sphere is heaven. Here the Thunder Hill is regarded as the actual embodiment of Thunder.

Oᴜʀ noble Prince, child of the Bright One on high,
　　Holds a royal hunt, horses bridle to bridle,
On the field of Kariji, thick with tender reeds,
There the boars and deer crouch and adore him,
And the quails run bending low about him.
Like the boars and stags we fall and adore him,
Like the quails we run bending low about him,
Tendering our loyal service;
And when we look up to him
As we look up to the sunny sky,
His freshness ever increases
Like the grass in spring—
Oh, our mighty lord!

Envoy

Our mighty lord,
Having caught the sky-traversing moon
In his net,
Makes it his silken canopy !³

Pᴀssɪɴɢ the shore of Minumé⁴ where they gather
　　The beautiful seaweed,
My boat has approached
Cape Nujima⁵ of drooping summer grass.⁶

---

¹ Son of the Emperor Temmu.
² In Yamato.
³ The poem must have been composed on the way home from hunting, when the full moon seemed to be following the Prince, as though it were his canopy.
⁴ Seashore to the east of the present city of Kōbé.
⁵ On the north-west of Awaji Island.
⁶ ' Of drooping summer grass ' is a pillow-word for Nujima (now Nojima).

On the seashore at the cape of Nujima in Awaji,
I let the salt-breeze flutter
The riband my wife has bound[1] for me.

Would they by chance take me
For a fisherman
Angling for bass in Fujié Bay[2]—
Me, a lonely voyager?

While I linger, passing Inabi Plain,[3]
The isle of Kako,[4] dear to my heart,
Appears in sight.

The day my boat enters
The noble straits of Akashi,[5]
I shall sail away
And see my home no more.

As I come a long way under distant skies,
Ever pining for home,—
Now through the straits of Akashi
The land of Yamato looms in sight.

The sea must be calm on Kehi Bay,[6]
For I see fishermen's boats
Crowding out
Like so many cut reeds.

---

[1] In olden days the wife used to tie the riband of her husband's clothes on his departure for a journey.

[2] In Harima Province, west of Akashi.

[3] Situated between Akashi and the River Kako.

[4] Supposed to have been the sand-bar at the mouth of the River Kako.

[5] Akashi is in Harima, and the straits lie between Akashi and Awaji Island.

[6] Kehi was formerly supposed to be in the province of Echizen, but, in relation to the preceding poems, the opinion has gained ground that it must have been in the northern part of Awaji. The name survives in Kei-no (Kei Plain) in Matsuho Village.

By the River Uji[1] on his way to the   [III : 264]
          capital from the province of Ōmi.

THE waves lingering about the fish-weir stakes
    In the Uji, the river of eighty clans of warriors[2]—
Whither they are drifting away
Who knows?

129   O PLOVERS flying over the evening   [III : 266]
              waves,
On the lake of Ōmi,
When you cry, my heart grows heavy,
With memories of by-gone days.[3]

130-1   *During the voyage down to Tsukushi.*[4]   [III : 303-4]

BEYOND the waves rearing a thousandfold,
    Far away upon the sea of fair-named Inami,[5]
Is hidden, ah, the land of Yamato![6]

When I behold the straits between the islands,
The passage for travellers
To our Sovereign's distant court,[7]
They remind me of the mighty age of the gods.[8]

---

[1] Rises in Lake Biwa and pours into Ōsaka Bay. Its lower course is called the
Yodo.
    [2] 'The river of eighty clans of warriors' is an introductory verse to the Uji.
    [3] See Nos. 74-6.
    [4] The province of Tsukushi was in the northern part of Kyūshū, where the Da-
zaifu was situated. These two poems were made, perhaps, during the voyage
thither on some official business, but the date is unknown.
    [5] On the edge of the coast between Akashi and the River Kako.
    [6] The capital then was situated in Yamato, where the poet had his home.
    [7] The second and the third lines are construed by some scholars to read:
        'The distant portals for travellers
            To our Sovereign's court,'
    [8] An allusion to the gods, Izanagi and Izanami, who created the islands of Japan.

132   *At the cremation of the Maiden of*   [III : 428]
        Hijikata on the hills of Hatsusé.

THE cloud drifting over the brows
    Of the hills of secluded Hatsusé—
Can it, alas, be she?

133   THOUGH my thoughts of her   [IV : 496]
            Grow a hundredfold in my heart
Like the leaves of the crinum[1]
On the sea-coast of Kumanu,[2]
I do not meet her face to face.

134   DID men living long ago   [IV : 497]
            Pass also sleepless nights like me,
Longing for their beloved?

135   *Lamenting his own fate as he was about*   [II : 223]
            to die in the land of Iwami.

ALL unaware, it may be,
    That I lie in Kamo-yama,
Pillowed on a rock,
She is waiting now—my wife—
Waiting for my return.

Yosami, Wife of Hitomaro

136   *On parting from Hitomaro.*   [II : 140]

THOUGH you say, 'Do not grieve!'
    I know not, alas,

---

[1] A tall bulbous plant with strap-shaped leaves found in southern Japan.
[2] Situated in the province of Kii.

51

When we shall meet again;
How can I but pine after you?

137-8   *On the death of Hitomaro.*   [II . 224-5]

DAY in, day out,
    I wait for my husband—
Alas! he lies buried, men say,
In the ravine of the Stone River.

There can be no meeting
Face to face with him.
Arise, O clouds,
Hover above the Stone River
That I may watch and remember!

From the 'Hitomaro Collection'

139   *On the sky.*   [VII : 1068]

ON the sea of heaven the waves of cloud arise,
    And the moon's ship is seen sailing
To hide in a forest of stars.

140   *On clouds.*   [VII : 1088]

AS the mountain torrents roar and roar again,
    Over Yuzuki's peak[1]
The clouds arise and hover.

---

[1] Rises east of Mount Miwa in the eastern part of Yamato.

141   *Composed on the spot.*   [VII : 1269]

LIKE the bubbles on the water
    That runs echoing by the hill of Makimuku,
Frail human thing, am I.

142   *During the journey.*   [VII : 1271]

I would quickly reach my loved one's dwelling
    That stands far away under the clouds;
Hasten, my black steed!

143   *Presented to Prince Oshikabé on viewing*   [IX : 1682]
            an image of a wizard.

Is it that summer and winter
    Ever come and go in company?
He neither puts away his fan, nor his furs,
This wizard of the mountains!

144   *By the River Uji.*   [IX : 1699]

THE inlet of Ōkura[1] is echoing;
    To the fields of Fushimi
The wild geese are passing.

145   *Presented to Prince Yugé.*   [IX : 1701]

THE night hours have advanced,
    It must be the dead of night:
In the sky where the wild geese call
I see the moon travelling on.

---

[1] i. e. Lake Ōkura (now called Ogura) which is formed by the Uji River. Situated to the north of the Uji, where the town of Fushimi now stands.

146   K<small>AGU</small>-<small>YAMA</small>,   [x : 1812]
          The Heavenly Hill afar,
     Is misted over this evening—
     Spring is here !

147   O<small>VER</small> the branches of the cryptomerias,   [x : 1814]
          Planted, perhaps, by men of old,
     There hangs a trailing mist—
     Spring has come !

148   W<small>HILE</small> I wait and long for you, my   [x : 2015]
          loved one,
     I hear the boat crossing the River of Heaven—
     The sound of the oars
     Echoing over the waters of night.

149   *Love in autumn.*   [x : 2240]

     D<small>EBATE</small> not who I am,
          Say neither this nor that
     Of me who, drenched
     In September's chilling dew,
     Await my dear love's coming !

150   'R<small>EAPER</small> on the Suminoé fields,   [vii : 1275]
          Have you no servants ?'
     'Servants I have ; yet for my love
     I labour on her private ground.'

151   T<small>HIS</small> is the cloth I wove for my lord   [vii : 1281]
          With weary hands ;
     When the spring comes round,
     In what colours shall I print it ?

152   THE lasses dance and tread the ground   [XI : 2352]
      for the new house[1]
And the jewels of their bracelets jingle;
That lad who sparkles as the jewels,
Ask him to come in!

153   O THAT she might rather die   [XI : 2355]
      Whom I cherish in my heart!
Even when she lives,
None says she will be mine.

154   YOU start so early this morning,   [XI : 2357]
      The dewy grass will wet your leg-ties;[2]
I, too, out so early,
Will gladly dip the hem of my skirt.

155   SINCE I left the loving hands of my   [XI : 2368]
      mother,
Never once have I known
Such helplessness in my heart!

156   LET none, born after me,   [XI : 2375]
      Ever, ever meet, as I did,
Such ways of love!

157   I HAVE lost a true man's mettle,   [XI : 2376]
      Day to night and night to day
I waste with thoughts of love.

---

[1] This refers to the ceremony of purifying the building-site, invoking the gods and levelling the ground.
[2] Bands for fastening the hem of the lower garment.

158   PEOPLE throng the sun-lit Palace-road,   [XI : 2382]
        Yet, you—and you alone—
Are my heart's desire!

159   STRONG man as I am,   [XI : 2386]
        Who force my way even through the rocks,
In love I rue in misery.

160   AS if to say that I may die   [XI : 2401]
        If I die of love for her,
That cruel girl now passes
The front-gate of my house.

Poems of love referring to various things.

161   HOW named is the god   [XI : 2418]
        Whom I would entreat with offerings,
That I may meet my love,
If but in dream?

162   SHOULD the time come   [XI : 2419]
        When the names of heaven and earth perish,
Then, then alone we should cease to meet!

163   O THAT the hill, the stony road,   [XI : 2421]
        Were removed from your way hither;
Your horse will stumble,
While I wait for you.

164   OVER Kohata, the hill in Yamashina,   [XI : 2425]
       I can get a horse to ride,
Yet on foot I have come,
Driven by stress of love for you !

165   MY life vanishing   [XI : 2433]
       Like the numbers written on water,[1]
I have appealed to the gods with vows
That I may meet my love.

166   THE great earth itself   [XI : 2442]
       Might be exhausted by digging,
But of love alone in this world
Could we never reach the end !

167   SLEEPLESS with longing for my love,   [XI : 2491]
       Now I see the morning break;
O the mandarin-ducks[2] flying by—
Are they the couriers from my girl ?

168   LIKE the silkworm in the cocoon   [XI : 2495]
       Which her loving mother rears,
That maid so close secluded in her home—
O for the means of seeing her !

169   AS the *yū*-cloth is dyed fast and deep   [XI : 2496]
       Which ties the forelock of the men
In the land of Hi,[3]

[1] Quoted from the *Nirvana Sutra*, a Buddhist scripture.
[2] A pair of mandarin-ducks is a symbol of affectionate love.
[3] The south-western portion of Kyūshū. It is possible that the native customs there may have differed from those of the central provinces.

So is my heart coloured with love;
How can I forget?

170   Now that I have uttered my name[1]   [XI : 2497]
      Clear as the famous call
Of a Hayahito[2] on his night-watch round,
Trust me as your wife, my lord!

171   I will tread the sharpness of the   [XI : 2498]
      double-edged sword
And die with a good heart,
If it be for your sake.

172   How plainly one may see   [XII : 2855]
      The new road now they make!
So plainly have I heard
Everything about you, dear girl.

173-4   *Dialogue poems.*   [XI : 2513-4]

If the thunder rolls for a while
    And the sky is clouded, bringing rain,
Then you will stay beside me.

Even when no thunder sounds
    And no rain falls, if you but ask me,
Then I will stay beside you.

---

    [1] It was the custom in old days for a woman to tell her name to a man, when she accepted his proposal of marriage.
    [2] Natives of the south of Kyūshū. They were called to the Imperial Palace to serve as guards, and were noted for their stentorian voices at ceremonies.

175-6 THE Rice-abounding Land of Reed   [XIII : 3253-4]
        Plains
Is a land where things fall out
As will the gods, without lifted words of men,[1]
Yet must I lift up words :
' Be fortunate, and travel safe and sound ! '
If you be free from evils,
Then shall we meet once more ;
So I lift up words over and over again
As the waves roll a hundredfold,
A thousandfold !

Envoy

The Land of Yamato is a land
Where the word-soul[2] gives us aid ;
Be happy, fare you well !

Lady Ishikawa

177   *Addressed to Ōtomo Sukunamaro.*   [II : 129]

OLD, old woman that I am,
    How could I have sunk so deep in love,
Like a helpless child !

Lady Ishikawa and Ōtomo Tanushi

178   I HEARD that you were   [II : 126]
        A gallant courtier,
Yet you refused me shelter and sent me away—
How boorish of the gallant courtier ! —*By Ishikawa.*

---

[1] *Kotoagé* : it was believed that in Japan things happened according to the will of the gods and that men therefore needed not offer prayers.

[2] *Kotodama* : the uttered words were believed to possess spirits of their own and the wishes would therefore bring forth what were requested in them.

59

Ōtomo Tanushi was known by the name of Chūrō. He was very good-looking, and his manners were courtly beyond comparison, wherefore he was admired by all who saw, or heard of him. There was a certain young woman, named Ishikawa, who, wishing to live with him, was ever lamenting her solitude. She desired to write him a note, but there was no favourable opportunity to send it. Thereupon, she devised a plan. Disguising herself as a humble old woman, and carrying a pail with her, she went near his bed-chamber, where she squatted and rapped on the door, and said in a hoarse voice that she was a poor woman of the neighbourhood who had come to beg for fire. Chūrō in the darkness did not discover the fraud. The girl, disappointed at the failure of her artifice, took all the fire she wanted, and thereafter went away. Next morning, ashamed of her own misbehaviour but indignant at the frustration of her heart's desire, she indited this poem, which she sent him in order to mock at him.

179 A GALLANT courtier,   [II : 127]
   I am, indeed;
A gallant courtier am I,
Who refused you shelter and sent you away!
           —*By Ōtomo Tanushi.*

Ōtomo Miyuki

180   *Written after the War of Jinshin*[1]   [XIX : 4260]
                    was ended.

O UR Sovereign, a god,
   Has made his Imperial City[2]
Out of the stretch of swamps,
Where chestnut horses sank
To their bellies.

[1] The civil war of 672.
[2] The Emperor Temmu built his capital on the plain of Kiyomihara of Asuka.

Furu Tamuké

181   *Leaving the province of Tsukushi.*   [IX : 1766]

WOULD my love were a bracelet!
Tying her to my left arm,
I would start on my journey!

Naga Okimaro

182   *Composed in obedience to the Sovereign's*   [III : 238]
command.

HARK! even here, into the chambers of the Palace,[1]
Come the voices of the fishermen,
Who are arranging the seiners
To drag the net.

183   HOW sorely the rain besets me!   [III : 265]
Neither at the cape of Miwa, nor by the ferry
of Sanu[2]
Is there a cottage in sight.

---

[1] The Palace is supposed to have been that of Naniwa in the province of Settsu. The *Shoku-nihongi* mentions that the Emperor Mommu visited the Palace of Naniwa in the 1st month of the 3rd year of his reign. Also in the *Manyōshū*, Book I, it is written that the Empress Jitō, as ex-Empress, visited Naniwa. It is most likely that the Emperor Mommu in his visit in the 3rd year of his reign was accompanied by the Empress Jitō, then ex-Empress, and that the poem was composed on the occasion. To those who had lived only in Yamato, which commanded no sea-view, and had then come to the Palace by the seashore, the doings of the fishermen must have been curious and interesting.

[2] Miwa and Sanu were both in the province of Kii, now included in the town of Shingū.

184   **B**OIL water, my lads,   [XVI : 3824]
         In the kettle with a spout!
We will dash it on the fox,
Coming from the Ichihi Ford
Over the log-bridge of cypress.

Once there was a large feasting party. In the middle of
the night the company heard the barking of a fox. They
invited Okimaro to make a poem with reference to some
utensil used at the banquet, the barking fox, and a bridge
over a river, whereupon he instantly composed this poem.

Takechi Furuhito

185-6   Poems of sorrow at the old capital of Ōmi.   [I : 32-3]

AM I a man of the days gone by,
         That, when I see, in Sasanami,
The ruined Imperial City,
My heart grows heavy?

Desolate is the shrine of the god[1]
Of the land of Sasanami,
And I am bowed down with grief
To see the capital in ruin!

Takechi Kurohito

Poems of travel.

187   **W**HEN on my travels I pine for home,   [III : 270]
         I see a vermilion ship[2] sailing

---

[1] 'The shrine of the god' is often construed as 'the spirit of the god.'

[2] Ships in government employ were painted red. The poet, an official, felt
homesick at the sight of a red-painted ship.

Far out on the waters.

188   CRANES fly calling towards Sakurada¹   [III : 271]
          Fields ;
       The tide, it seems, has ebbed from Ayuchi Lagoon ;
       Look where the cranes fly calling.

189   AS we row round the jutting beaches,   [III : 273]
          Cranes call in flocks at every inlet²
       Of the many-harboured lake of Ōmi.

190   OUR boat shall harbour at the port of   [III : 274]
          Hira ;³
       Row not far from shore,—
       It is night and late !

191   WHERE shall I seek shelter,   [III : 275]
          If, in Takashima,⁴ on the plain of Kachinu,
       This day is spent ?

192   *In the old capital of Ōmi.⁵*   [III : 305]

       SO I refused to see them :
          Yet you show me over the ruins
       Of the Imperial City of Sasanami,
       Saddening me in vain !

----

¹ In the province of Owari, facing Ayuchi Beach, which is near Atsuta in Aichi
District.
² An inlet or a river-mouth, which naturally gave moorings.
³ Situated on the west side of the lake.
⁴ A district on the west side of Lake Biwa.
⁵ See Hitomaro's poems Nos. 74-6.

Okisomé Azumabito

193-4 *On the death of Prince Yugé.* [II : 204-5]

OUR lord and prince, ruling in peace,
    Child of the Bright One above,
God as he is, has taken
His divine seat in the Heavenly Palace
Far above. We, awe-stricken,
Lie prostrate and weep
Day after day, and night after night,
And to our weeping there is no end.

Envoy

Our lord and prince,
Because he is a god,
Has gone to dwell unseen
In the five-hundredfold clouds of heaven.

Osakabé Otomaro

195 *Composed during the visit of the Emperor* [I : 71]
Mommu¹ to Naniwa.

WHEN I lie sleepless, longing for Yamato,
    Must you be so heartless, O cranes,
Crying around the end of the sand-bar?

---

¹ The Emperor Mommu visited the Palace of Naniwa twice, in the 3rd year
(699) after his accession and in the 3rd year of Keiun (706).   It is not clear on
which occasion this poem was composed.

Mikata Shami

196–7 TREAD not the snow   [XIX : 4227–8]
    Around the palace;
It is not a fall
We often see;
Only on the mountains
We have such snow.
Away, away, away—
Tread not the snow.

Envoy

Our lord will view it later
Where it lies;
Tread not the snow
Around the palace.

The above verses were sung by Mikata Shami, in compliance with the order of Fujiwara Fusasaki, Minister of the Left by posthumous appointment.

Mikata Shami and his Wife

*Composed during an illness of Mikata shortly after
his marriage to a daughter of Sono Ikuha.*

198 IF tied, it would slip off;   [II : 123]
    And untied, it was too long,—
Ah, that hair of yours!—
Is it all disarranged
Now while I see you not?—*By Mikata.*

199 'DO it up!'   [II : 124]
    'It is now so long!'
So say they all.

But as you saw it, I will keep
This hair of mine, dishevelled though it be.
                                        —*By his wife.*

200   IN the city square   [II : 125]
           Men come and go, treading
       On the orange-tree shadows;
       My thoughts turn a thousand ways
       When I see you not, beloved.—*By Mikata.*

Wife of Go Dan-ochi

201   *Composed during her husband's journey*   [IV : 500]
                        to Isé.

       BREAKING and spreading for a bed
           The shore reeds of Isé of the Divine Wind,
       Does he, my husband, sleep a traveller's sleep—
       On that lonely rugged sea-coast?

Lady Fuki

202   *Looking at the rocks of the hill-range of Yoko-*   [I : 22]
           yama of Hata when Princess Toochi went
                to worship at the Isé Shrine.[1]

       FIVE hundred rocks by the river
           Allow no weedy growth,
       May our princess so flourish,
       Youthful for ever!

       [1] The *Nihonshoki* records that, in spring, in the 2nd month of the 4th year of
the Emperor Temmu's reign (676), Princess Toochi and Princess Ahé went to
worship at the Isé Shrine.—Original Note.

*On the occasion of the progress[1] to the province of
Mikawa of the ex-Empress Jitō in the
second year of Daihō (702).*

203   PUSHING freely through the bush-clovers[2]   [1 : 57]
    Flowering on Hikuma Plain,
Let your clothes take on their colours
In remembrance of your travels.
                            —By Naga Okimaro.

204   WHERE will that boat find harbour   [1 : 58]
    Which coasted round the cape of Aré?—
Ah, that little *tana*-less boat![3]—*By Takechi Kurohito.*

205   HOW distinct is Matokata,[4] the Target Bay,   [1 : 61]
    That tells of the warrior shooting,
Standing up, arrow in hand![5]
                    —By an attendant maiden Toneri.

Anonymous

206   *Composed by one of the workmen engaged in*   [1 : 50]
     the building of the Palace of Fujiwara.[6]

OUR great Sovereign who rules in peace,
    Offspring of the Bright One on high,

---

[1] She started on her journey on the 10th of the 10th month and returned to the capital on the 25th.

[2] Originally *hari* (alder, *Alnus japonica*), but it is believed that it was probably mis-written for *hagi* (bush-clover, *Lespedeza*).

[3] A boat of some sort of a very simple structure.

[4] Believed to have been in Také District, Isé.

[5] The second and third lines are an introductory verse to Matokata.

[6] The Palace of Fujiwara was the seat of the court since the time of the Empress Jitō. Its site now forms part of Kamokimi Village, in Takaichi District, Yamato.

Wills, as a goddess, to rule her dominion
And to decree her towering Palace
On the plain of Fujiwara.
Then the gods of heaven and earth,
Gracious to serve,
Float the cypress timbers
From Mount Tanakami[1] of Ōmi
Down the stream of Uji;
We people throng into the river—
Splashing in the water like so many mallards,
Never thinking of our homes,
And forgetful of ourselves—
To gather and turn those timbers
Into the river of Izumi;[2] which reminds us
That the mystic tortoise, as it is told,
Will appear, in celebration of the new era,
With an auspicious figure on its shell,
Presaging the eternal happiness of our Land,
From the pass of Kosé;[3] which reminds us also
That alien powers will come that way,
To swear fealty to the Palace that we build.
And there the logs are roped into rafts
Which we vie in poling
Against Izumi's stream;
Looking on these labours well we know,
All is done by her divinity!

It is recorded in the 'Nihonshoki' that the Empress paid a visit to the site of the Palace of Fujiwara, in autumn, in the eighth month of the seventh year of Shuchō (693), and she again visited the Palace, in spring, in the first month of the eighth year. Then, in winter, on the sixth day of the twelfth month of the same year she removed there.

---

[1] In Kurimoto District, Ōmi Province.
[2] i. e. River Kizu: it runs through Sōraku District, Yamashiro Province.
[3] In Minami-Kazuraki District, Yamato, reached by the road over to Kii Province.

OUR great Sovereign who rules in peace,
    Offspring of the Bright One on high,
Has begun to build her Palace
On the plain of Fujii;[1]
And standing on the dyke of Lake Haniyasu
She looks around her:
The green hill of Kagu of Yamato
Stands at the eastern gate,
A luxuriant spring-time hill;
Unebi, with its fragrant slopes,
Rises at the western gate,
Ever fresh and flourishing;
Miminashi, the green sedgy mount,
Rears at the northern gate
Its form divine;
And the mountains of Yoshinu, of lovely name,
Soar into the sky,
Far from the southern gate.
At this towering Palace,
The shelter from the sun,
The shelter from the sky,
The waters will be everlasting,
These clear waters of the sacred well!

Envoy

The bevies of maidens who will be born
And come in succession into service
At the mightly Palace of Fujiwara,
How I envy their happy lot!

---

[1] Fujii-ga-hara (Plain of Wistaria Well) may have been an earlier name for Fuji-wara (Wistaria Plain).

209   ALAS, the Garden Palace of my prince,   [II : 171]
      Child of the Bright One above,
Who was to rule the land
Through ten thousand ages !

210   I HAVE waited on my lord,   [II : 176]
      Wishing the days to endure
With heaven and earth—
That hope is now broken !

211   ON the hill slope of Sada[2]   [II : 177]
      Bright in the morning sun,
We gather and weep;
Our tears fall endlessly.

212   ON the desolate stony shore   [II : 181]
      Of the garden-lake, where once he walked,
There grow—alas ! weeds,
That grew not there before.

213   I AM at my post   [II : 184]
      At the Cascade Gate[3] on the east-side.
Never—yesterday nor to-day—
Does my prince bid me come in.

---

  [1] The *Manyōshū* contains a group of 23 such poems. The regulation number of palace-guards for the Crown Prince was 600.

  [2] The name of the hill where the prince was buried.

  [3] At the eastern gate of the palace there was an outlet for the water of the garden-lake, which flowed forth like a cascade.

214   THAT path through the azaleas   [II : 185]
        Blooming thick on the rocky margin
Of the meandering stream—
Shall I ever see it again?

215   A THOUSAND times a day   [II : 186]
        I used to enter by the east gate.
How hard it is now to pass through
That wide gate of the Palace!

216   THE morning sky was overcast,   [II : 188]
        Hiding the sun.
I went down to the Palace garden,
And how I wept where once he walked!

217   IN the Garden Palace,   [II : 189]
        Bright in the morning sun,
There is no human sound,
Nought but gloom that bows me down.

218   *Composed during the Sovereign's stay*   [IX : 1714]
            at the Palace of Yoshinu.

    THE tumbling water breaks upon the rocks
        And rushes to its pool—
There, in the water stilled
I see a shining moon.

219-20   WITH reverence I compose these   [XIII : 3324-5]
        words—
Amid this busy crowd,
Among the many princes,

Overflowing the Imperial City
Of Fujiwara,
I trusted to our noble prince,
Awe-stricken as I was,
Gazing up toward the Palace
As to heaven,
Where I had served for many a year,
Hoping he would come to manhood
And flourish like the full-orbed moon.

He looked upon the land
When spring came round,
Climbing the brow of Uétsuki
Along the pine-wood path;
In autumn, in the showery month,
He loved the blooming bush-clovers,
Heavy with dew,
Waving about the drip-stones
In the palace-court;
And in the morning of snowy winter
He took his strong birchwood bow
To fondle in his hands.

I never tired of seeing him
Like a shining mirror
For all the long spring day,
And I wished that this would last for ages,
Trusting in my noble prince
As a sailor in his ship.

When, lo! I looked up to the Palace;
Was it a trick? Were my eyes deluded?—
I saw it draped in snow-white cloth,
And the servitors of the sun-lit Palace
All in hempen mourning dressed.

While I, as one wandering in a clouded night,
Doubted: Was I dreaming or awake?

The bearers climbed the path of Kinohé
Overlooking Iwaré,
And there entombed my prince
With holy rites.

I knew not whither
I might betake myself,
My grieving naught availed,
No hope came to my heart.

I will ever lift up my tearful eyes
Towards that dumb pine towering in the sky,
Which in passing
His august sleeve once brushed,
Remembering my prince,
Month after month,
Bending my head in awe.

Envoy

The white cloud hovering
Above the hill of Iwaré—
Is that, alas, my prince?

221-2 THE steeds the prince of Minu   [XIII : 3327-8]
         keeps
In his western stables,
The steeds our noble prince keeps
In his eastern stables—
Though they are fed with grass in plenty,
Though they are given fresh-drawn water,
Why do these grey steeds neigh and whinny so?

Envoy

His grey steeds neighing so—
What says their cry?
It is strange to me!

Once upon a time there lived an old man. He was called 'Old Bamboo-Cutter' (Taketori no Oji). In the last month of spring he went up a hill to view the country-side. Suddenly he discovered nine girls who were cooking soup, and who were all possessed of an unrivalled beauty and charm. One of the damsels called to the old man, laughed and said : 'Uncle, come blow up the fire under the kettle!' 'Very well, very well,' he replied. Hobbling slowly, he reached the spot where the girls were, and seated himself among them. After a while, all the girls, with smiles on their faces, began to question one another, saying, 'Who called this old man?' Thereupon the Bamboo-Cutter apologized and said, 'Most unexpectedly I have met you fairy maidens. My mind is perplexed beyond endurance. Let me redeem with a poem the offence of having intruded myself upon your company!' So saying, he made the following poem and envoys.

WHEN I was a new-born babe
    My mother carried me in her arms ;
When an infant still tied with a band
To the back of my nurse, I wore
A sleeveless gown with lining sewed in ;
When a boy with hair trimmed at the neck
I was clad in a dappled robe with sleeves.
At the age of you dear maidens
My hair was black as the bowels of a mud-snail.[1]
I would comb it down to the shoulders,
Or have it bound up in knots
Or sometimes let it hang loose like a boy.

I had a vest of thin silk with large woven figures
Of purple matching well with its reddish tint,
And a robe of a fabric dyed with the *hagi*-flower
Of Tōzato Onu in Suminoé,

---

[1] *Mina*, a small shell-fish found in a pond or river.

74

To which was attached a cord of *Koma*[1] brocade—
These I wore one over the other.

There was the cloth of *tahé*[2] tissue
And the hand-woven cloth of sun-dried hemp,
Made with rare skill by girl hemp-spinners
And by girls who were treasured like precious
    robes ;
When I put these on together like a double skirt,
Many a country lass from her lowly cottage
Would come, asking me to marry her.

The double-patterned stockings from a far country,
And the shoes fashioned by the men of Asuka,
Shunning the damp of the rainy season,—
I would put them on and stand under the eaves ;
Then maidens who had heard of me somewhere,
Would come to me, bidding me not to walk away.

I would arrange my silken girdle of azure
In the manner of a *Kara* girdle like a pendant sash,
And so bedeck my waist slim as a wasp
Flying above the tiled roof of the Sea God's Tem-
    ple ;
Then would I hang up clear mirrors side by side,
And turn back to them again and again
To see my face therein.
When in spring I sauntered forth afield,
The pheasants of the moor, delighting in me,
Came flying and crowing merrily.
When I went to the hills in autumn
The enamoured clouds of heaven hovered low above
    me.
When I started for home, all along the way
The gay ladies of the palace and the court gallants
Would all look back on me in admiration,

[1] Same as ' Kara ' below, i. e. Korea.
[2] Same as *taku*, paper mulberry, from the inner bark of which cloth was made.
See note to No. 103.

75

And ask one another, saying, 'Who is he?'
So did I do and live in days gone by.

Though to-day you dear damsels may wonder
Who I am and say: 'We don't know the man,'
I was once the talk of the town—
Thus did I do and live in days gone by.

Did not the wise man of ancient times
Bring back, to set an example for after ages,
The cart in which the old man was sent away?[1]

Envoys

Can it be that grey hair
Will never grow on you maidens
If you live long, unless death
Spares you from seeing it?

When grey hair has grown
On you, may it not be then
That you too will be mocked
By young folk as I am now?

Replies by the maidens.

THE dear old man's verse   [XVI : 3794]
    Has stunned us,
We fairy maidens nine—
Are we humbled by his word?

---

[1] The last three lines allude to the old Chinese story of a man by the name of Yuan Ku. When he was fifteen years old his parents, in spite of his tearful protests, took his aged grandfather to the mountains in a cart, and there abandoned him. The boy went and brought back the cart. Being questioned by his father why he had done so, Yuan Ku replied: 'You may not be able to make a cart by yourself when you are old.' The father, much ashamed of his misdeed, brought back the old parent and took good care of him thereafter.

76

M^Y shame I will bear,　　　　　[XVI : 3795]
　　My shame I will ignore;
And before he speaks another word,
To his counsel mutely will I yield.

SHALL I be false to friends　　　　[XVI : 3797]
　　To whose hearts mine is bound
In life and death?
To his counsel I also will yield.

229–30　FROM Mount Kamunabi[1] of　　[XIII : 3268–9]
　　Mimoro[1]
Clouds overshadow the sky,
Bringing heavy rain;
The rain is swept in spray
And the storm gathers.

Has he reached home,
He who went back
Across the great-mouthed Wolf's Moor,[2]
Deep in thoughts of me?

Envoy

Troubled with thoughts of him,
Who had gone from me,
I, too, could not sleep
The whole night through.

[1] In Asuka District in Yamato. Both Mimoro and Kamunabi mean the grove
or forest as an abode of the gods.
[2] Orig. the Moor of Makami; Makami means 'wolf.'

NARA PERIOD

Empress Gemmyō and Princess Minabé

231   *Composed by the Empress in the first*   [1 : 76]
year of Wadō (708).

Listen to the sounds of the warriors' elbow-guards;[1]
    Our captain must be ranging the shields
To drill the troops.[2]

232   *Reply by the Princess.*   [1 : 77]

Be not concerned, O my Sovereign;
    Am I not here,
I, whom the ancestral gods endowed with life,
Next of kin to yourself?

Empress Genshō

233   *On the occasion of her visit to Yamamura.*   [xx : 4293]

*The Empress said to those attending upon her, 'Princes
and noblemen, make poems to match this one of mine!' She
then recited the following:*

This is the mountain souvenir
    That a wizard of the mountain
Gave me as I went
To Yama, the mountain village.

---

[1] Made of leather and worn on the left arm, to prevent the bow-string from springing back and hurting the elbow. The string struck the elbow-guard with a loud sound.

[2] This poem probably alludes to the expeditionary force that was sent against the Ainus in northern Japan.

Emperor Shōmu

234-5   On giving saké to the Inspectors-General.[1]   [VI : 973-4]

WHEN you are thus gone
　　To the far courts of my realm,
I shall rest tranquil,
And wait with folded arms.
To requite your loyal service,
I, your emperor,
With my sovereign hand
Stroke you tenderly and caress you.
This wine we will drink again together
On the day of your return—this bounteous wine.

Envoy

You go the way of men of valour;
Go not with light minds,
You valiant men!

236   On granting to Prince Kazuraki the surname   [VI : 1009]
　　　of Tachibana, in winter, in the eleventh
　　　　　month of the eighth year of
　　　　　　　Tempyō (736).

THINE is a happy name:
　　' Tachibana '[2]—abundant in fruit,
In bloom and in foliage;
A tree of evergreen leaves that thrives
Though the hoar-frost falls on its branches.

*Prince Kazuraki petitioned the Throne to be allowed to
renounce his status as a member of the imperial family and*

---

[1] The Inspectors-General were Fujiwara Umakai sent to Saikaidō, Fujiwara Fusa-maé sent to Tōkaidō and Tōsandō, and Tajihi Agatamori sent to San-indō.
[2] i. e. the orange-tree.

to take the rank of subject by assuming the surname of Ta-
chibana. The Emperor, consenting, gave in his honour a
banquet, on which occasion the above poem was composed by
His Majesty.

Empress Kōken

237-8   A poem and envoy granted to Fujiwara   [XIX : 4264-5]
Kiyokawa,[1] ambassador to China, to-
gether with food and drink, by her mes-
senger, Koma Fukushin, of the
Lower Fourth Rank Senior, whom
she sent down to Naniwa.

THE spacious Land of Yamato
  Is a land guarded by the gods;
You go upon the waters
As upon the land;
You sit in the ship
As on the floor at home.

In your four ships,[2] prow by prow,
You travel in safety,
Return in haste,
Then make your reports;
On that day we will take this wine—
This bounteous wine.

Envoy

That your four ships may soon come back
I pray to the gods,
Tying white hemp
To my skirt.[3]

---

[1] Despatched in the 4th year of Tempyō-Shōhō (752).
[2] The entire embassy was carried in a fleet of four ships.
[3] A woman's skirt (Jap. *mo*) was believed in ancient times to have magic power.

Emperor Junnin

239   *At the palace banquet*[1] *on the eighteenth day*   [xx : 4486]
of the eleventh month of the first year of
Tempyō-Hōji[2] *(757).*

SINCE thy reign is to endure
   With the sun and the moon
That illumine heaven and earth,
What could ever trouble our hearts ?

Empress Kōmyō

240   *To the Emperor Shōmu.*   [viii : 1658]

How gladdening would be this falling snow,
   Could I but watch with you, my husband !

241   *A poem which the Empress Dowager of*   [xix : 4240]
Fujiwara[3] *composed at the supplication*
ceremony[4] *at the Kasuga Shrine,*[5] *and*
gave to Fujiwara Kiyokawa,
ambassador to China.

IN the great ship, full-oared,
   I speed this child of mine[6] to the Land of Kara;
Bless him, O gods !

---

[1] The annual feast of *Toyo-no-akari* given by the Emperor to princes and officials on the day following the Harvest Festival (*Niinamé-sai*).

[2] The Emperor was then still Crown Prince. The poem probably alludes to the rebellion of Tachibana Naramaro and his followers, which occurred during the year, but which was quickly subdued.

[3] i. e. the Empress Kōmyō.

[4] At this perhaps they prayed for the safety of the embassy.

[5] The shrine is in the present city of Nara.

[6] i. e. Fujiwara Kiyokawa, nephew of the Empress Dowager.

Prince Toneri and a Maiden

242   'SHAME it is,' I say and sigh,   [II : 117]
      'For a strong man to love unloved!'
    Yet so do I love—wretched that I am.
                               —*By the Prince.*

243   NOW I know—   [II : 118]
      For a strong man
    Loveth and sigheth—
    Why my hair-cord is wet.—*By the Maiden.*

Prince Hozumi

244   AH, that rascal love   [XVI : 3816]
      I have put away at home,
    Locked in a coffer—
    Here he comes, pouncing on me!

The above was a favourite poem of Prince Hozumi, who used always to recite it at banquets when the merry-making was at its height.

Princess Ki

245   EVEN the wild-ducks skimming   [III : 390]
      By the shore of the pond of Karu[1]
    Do not sleep alone
    On the dainty water-weeds!

---

[1] The pond of Karu was dug in the 11th year of the reign of the Emperor Ōjin (280). The name still remains in Takaichi District, Yamato.

Prince Yuhara

246   *At Yoshinu.*   [III : 375]

ON the pool of the River of Natsumi[1]
    That flows through Yoshinu
The wild-ducks are crying,—
In the shade of the mountains.

247   *At a banquet.*   [III : 377]

LIKE the white cloud on the green hill,
    Although I see him every day,
Our host is ever new to me !

248   *Addressed to a young woman.*   [IV : 632]

WHAT can I do with you—
    You who so resemble
The laurel[2] in the moon
That I see with my eyes
But cannot touch with my hands?

249   *On the moon.*   [VI : 985]

O MOON God seated high in heaven,
    Offerings I will gratefully bring—
Make this night last as long, I pray,
As five hundred nights in one !

---

[1] The River Yoshino was called the Natsumi at Natsumi, to the east of Miyataki.
[2] The legend of a laurel growing in the moon was of Chinese origin.

Wɪᴛʜ the bounteous wine the doughty warrior
   blesses,
Striking¹ at it with the point of tempered steel,
Drunk am I now—I!

Tʜᴇ evening moon shines—
   Here in the garden white with dew
The crickets sing, alas!
Burthening my weary heart.

Prince Yuhara and an Anonymous Person

252   Bʏ the light of the Moon God   [IV : 670]
      Come to me, dear heart!
   No mountain walls divide us—
   The way is not long.—*By the Prince.*

Reply.

253   Tʜᴏᴜɢʜ clear and bright   [IV : 671]
      The Moon God lights the way,
   So blind am I with love,
   I feel I cannot reach you.

¹ Presumably the drinker, in order to drive away evil spirits, made a gesture to
strike the vessel filled with wine with his sword.

Prince Aki

254 *On an imperial visit*[1] *to the province* [III : 306]
of Isé.

WOULD that they were flowers,
The white surges far upon the sea of Isé—
I would wrap and bring them home
As a souvenir for my beloved wife.

255–6 OH, my dear love far away![2] [IV : 534–5]
Because you are not here,
And the way is distant,
Restless is my heart with longing;
My grieving heart knows no respite.
Oh, were I the cloud that sails the sky!
Oh, were I a high-flying bird!
To-morrow I would go and speak to you.
Then you, my love, untroubled for my sake,
And for your sake I myself untroubled,
We would live together even now
A happy pair as ever.

Envoy

No longer do I sleep
With your dainty arm for pillow.
Meantime a year has passed away—
To think of it, alas!—
Without my seeing you.

---

[1] The visit is said to have taken place in the 2nd year of Yōrō (718), in the reign of the Empress Genshō.

[2] According to the Original Note, Prince Aki married, against court regulations, an *unemé* (see note to No. 51) from Yagami, Inaba Province, for which he was punished and the lady sent back to her native province.

Prince Ichihara

257   PEERLESS are the gems   [III : 412]
     That I wear on my locks;
Such are you to me,
And my heart moves at your will.

258   *Composed at a banquet, wishing his* [VI : 988]
        father, Prince Aki, a long life.

THE flowering herbs of spring
    Fade all too soon.
Be like a rock,
Changeless ever,
O noble father mine!

259   *On the occasion of men ascending the hill of* [VI : 1042]
       Ikuji to drink under a pine-tree.

O SOLITARY pine, how many
    Generations of man have you known?
Is it because of your great age
That the passing winds sing in so clear a tone?

Prince Nagaya

260   *Composed when the Emperor Mommu visited* [I : 75]
       the Pleasure-Palace of Yoshinu.

THE morning air is cold on Mount Ujima,[1]
    Now that I travel far from my beloved
Who would offer me clothing.

[1] Said to be the mountain north of the town of Kamiichi in Yoshino District.
It was on the route from the Palace of Fujiwara to that of Yoshino.

Prince Funado

261   *At a banquet in the residence of Isonokami* [XIX : 4284]
       Yakatsugu, on the fourth of the first month
       of the fifth year of Tempyō-Shōhō (753).

A T the coming of the New Year
    All our trusted friends are gathered together :
My heart is light with gladness !

Prince Kadobé

262   *Viewing the trees in the streets at the*   [III : 310]
            Eastern Market.[1]

I HAVE not met her for so long
    That the street-trees at the Eastern Market
Let droop their branches low—
Well may I languish for love of her !

263   *Thinking of the capital, while he stayed in*   [III : 371]
           Izumo[2] *as Governor.*

O H, plovers on the river-shore,
    On the water flowing into the sea of Ou,[3]
When you cry, dearly I remember
Saho,[4] the stream of my native town.

[1] In those days there were two markets in the capital called respectively the Eastern and the Western.
[2] A province, now part of Shimané Prefecture.
[3] A district in Izumo.
[4] A river flowing through Nara, the capital.

Prince Atsumi

264   Mirrored in the waters of the   [VIII : 1435]
        Kamunabi River,[1]
Where the song-frogs call,
Do they bloom now—those flowers of the yellow
    rose?[2]

Prince Odai

265   I saw this house   [XVI : 3820]
        Standing on the river-bank
Where shone the setting sun.
I came hither, powerless indeed
To resist the charm of its shape.

Prince Odai was in the habit of reciting the above poem whenever he took up his koto[3] at banquets.

Prince Takamiya

266   *On sundry objects.*   [XVI : 3856]

A crow[4] that feeds on the rice
    Of the Brahmin's[5] field
Is, with eyelids swollen,
Perched on a lance-head streamer.

---

[1] Sometimes called the Asuka River, or the Tatsuta River. It is in Yamato Province, and famous for the song-frogs (Mod. Jap. *kajika*) and the yellow rose on its banks.

[2] *Yamabuki* (*Kerria japonica*), a shrub, with yellow flowers which open in spring.

[3] A kind of lute.

[4] Some scholars believe that the crow was simply a figure shown on the streamer.

[5] A priest representing himself to be a Brahmin prelate arrived in Japan from India in the Nara Period.

Princess Takata

267   *To Prince Imaki.*   [IV : 541]

THIS world is so full
   Of men with slanderous tongues.
May we not meet in the life to come—
If we may not now, my dearest ?

268   ALL over the meadow,   [VII : 1444]
   Where the yellow roses bloom,
Multitudes of violets have opened
With this spring rain.

Princess Hirokawa

269   THE sheaves of my love-thoughts   [IV : 694]
   Would fill seven carts—
Carts huge and heavy-wheeled.
Such a burden I bear
Of my own choice.

270   I THOUGHT there could be   [IV : 695]
   No more love left anywhere.
Whence then is come this love,
That has caught me now
And holds me in its grasp ?

Tajihi Kunihito

271-2   *Climbing Mount Tsukuba.*[1]   [III : 382-3]

THOUGH many are the lofty mountains
    In the cock-crowing[2] Eastland of Azuma,
Fame has told of Mount Tsukuba,
Since the age of the gods,
As the noble mountain throning god and goddess,
The beautiful mountain with two peaks,
For men to climb to overlook the land.
So, if I do not climb it now—
Though winter's close
Is not the time for climbing—
I shall miss it greatly;
So, labouring up the thawing paths,
I have reached the summit.

Envoy

IMPATIENT of its sight from afar,
    I have climbed Mount Tsukuba,
Labouring up the thawing paths!

Tajihi Kasamaro

273-4   *On his journey to Tsukushi.*[3]   [IV : 509-10]

BY the sea-shore of Mitsu,[4] that reminds one
    Of the mirror standing on a girl's comb-case,
I linger, longing for my wife, and sleep alone,
My scarlet sash untied.

---

[1] Situated 70 miles to the north-east of Tokyo, in Ibaraki Prefecture.
[2] A pillow-word for Azuma, the Eastland.
[3] Composed probably during his journey to the Dazaifu on an official errand.
[4] i. e. Naniwazu, the original name of the present port of Ōsaka.

I can but weep aloud like the crane crying
In the morning mist at the twilight hour of dawn.
Seeking to relieve me of my sorrow,
If only by a thousandth part,
I go out to gaze toward my home,
Which is—alas!—lost in the white clouds,
That trail across the green mountain of Kazuraki.[1]

I journey on to the far-off land—
Passing Awaji Island now lying before,
And leaving behind me the island of Awashima.[2]
I hear the shouts of sailors in the morning calm,
And in the calm of evening the plash of oars.
Labouring over the waves,
Circling about amid the rocks,
And past the beach of Inabizuma,[3]
I wander on like a bird
Till Ié-no-shima,[4] the 'Home Island,' comes into
    sight,
Where thick and swaying on the stony shore
Grows the weed men call ' Speak-not '[5]—
Ah, why have I come away from my wife
Without a word of farewell?

Envoy

Would that my wife and I,
Unfastening our girdles for each other
And with our snow-white sleeves overlapping,
Had reckoned the day of my return
Before I came away upon my journey!

[1] A mountain rising between the provinces of Yamato and Settsu.
[2] Unidentified. Probably an islet adjacent to Awaji.
[3] Presumably a small island at the mouth of the Kako River.
[4] In the Harima Channel. It is now pronounced 'Ejima.'
[5] Orig. *nanoriso*, now known as *hondawara* (*Sargassum*). The word may be translated literally as ' Speak-not.'

Tajihi Yanushi

275 HER husband is gone towards Naniwa; [VIII : 1442]
     Pity it is to see a young wife,
Left gathering spring herbs!

Tajihi —

276-7   *An old threnody*   [XV : 3625-6]

THE mallards call with evening from the reeds
    And float with dawn midway on the water;
They sleep with their mates, it is said,
With white wings overlapping and tails a-sweep
Lest the frost should fall upon them.

As the stream that flows never returns,
And as the wind that blows is never seen,
My wife, of this world, has left me,
Gone I know not whither!
So here, on the sleeves of these clothes
She used to have me wear,
I sleep now all alone!

Envoy

Cranes call flying to the reedy shore;
How desolate I remain
As I sleep alone!

   *This poem was composed in grief at the death of his
wife.*

Tajihi Takanushi

*At the farewell banquet in honour of Ōtomo Komaro,
vice-ambassador to China, in the residence of Ōtomo Kojihi,
in the third month intercalary of the fourth year of Tempyō-
Shōhō (752).*

278   TO you, brave warrior, starting for the   [XIX : 4262]
           Land of Kara,
       That you may fulfil your duties,
       And come home safely,
       I offer you a cup of wine.

Ishikawa Kimiko

279   THE fisher-maids at Shika,[1]   [III : 278]
           So scanty is their leisure-time,
       Gathering sea-weed, burning salt,
       They seldom take the little combs
       Out of their toilet-cases.

Taguchi Masuhito

*Composed at Cape Kiyomi in the province of Suruga,[2] on
the way to his new post, when he was appointed Governor of
the province of Kamitsukenu.[3]*

280   RESTING my eyes on the bay of Miho   [III : 296]
           On the boundless calm of the sea,
       Near Cape Kiyomi of Iohara,[4]

---

[1] In the province of Chikuzen in Kyūshū.
[2] Part of Shizuoka Prefecture at present.
[3] It was in the 1st year of Wadō (708), in the reign of the Empress Genshō
Kamitsukenu, later called Kōzuké, is now Gumma Prefecture.
[4] A district in Suruga.

I am free from all my cares!

281   THE whole day's light is not enough   [III : 297]
      To view the Bay of Tago,[1]
   Which at night I saw, hasting
   At our awful Sovereign's word.

Ono Oyu

282   THE Imperial City of fairest Nara   [III : 328]
      Glows now at the height of beauty,
   Like brilliant flowers in bloom!

Kasa Kanamura

283   *Composed on Mount Shiotsu.*[2]   [III : 364]

   THIS is the arrow which I, a warrior, shot,
      Lifting up the bow-end:
   Let it remind those who find it
   To talk of me for ever.

284   AS I pass over Mount Shiotsu,   [III : 365]
      My horse stumbles;[3]
   Perhaps my dear ones at home
   May be thinking of me.

---

[1] The name Tago-no-ura is now used to denote to the bay east of the River Fuji, but formerly it was also applied to the bay westward as far as the town of Kambara.

[2] In the northern part of Ōmi Province.

[3] The ancients believed that the thoughts of those left at home were made manifest to their dear ones on their journeys.

sending to a member of the Emperor's retinue
on a journey to Ki, in winter, in the tenth
month of the first year of Jinki (724).[1]

Yɴᴏᴜ, dear husband, who have gone forth
   With the many men of eighty clans
Accompanying the Emperor on his journey—

You who went by the highway of Karu,
Admiring the view of the Unebi Mountain,
And now having entered the province of Ki
Are crossing, perhaps, the mountain of Matsuchi[2]—

You may find your journey a pleasant thing,
As you watch the autumn leaves fly and scatter,
Yet never a tender thought give to me.
Though this may be an empty fear,
I cannot stay at peace at all.
A thousand times over I wish
To follow you on your track.
And yet, young and helpless girl that I am,
I should not know what answer to give,
If a road-guard should challenge me—
So here I stand, faltering.

Envoys

Rather than remain behind
To pine after you,
I would we were the Imo-Sé Mountains of Ki—
The 'Man and Wife' for ever.

If I go seeking after you,
Following your footmarks,
Will the guard of the pass
In Ki bid me halt?

---

  [1] The 1st year of the Emperor Shōmu's reign.
  [2] A mountain in Kii lying just over the border from Yamato and to the north of the Ki River.

288-90   *On winning the love of a maiden during the*   [IV : 546-8]
         Emperor's visit to the Detached Palace at
         Mika-no-hara,¹ in spring, in the third
         month of the second year of Jinki (725).

A SOJOURNER in Mika's plains,
    I saw you on the road,
A stranger to me like a cloud of heaven:
The words I could not speak to you,
Quite choked my heart.
Yet we two, by the mercy of the gods,
Are now wedded in love and trust,
Lying upon each other's sleeve.
Ah, to-night!   Would it were as long
As a hundred autumn nights together!

                Envoys

I have leaned, body and soul,
Towards you, beloved,
From the moment I saw you—
A stranger like a cloud of heaven.

Unable to bear the thought
That to-night will quickly pass,
Oh, how I pray that it might be
Long as a hundred autumn nights!

291-3   *On the occasion of the Sovereign's² journey to*   [VI : 907-9]
        Yoshinu, in summer, in the fifth month
            of the seventh year of Yōrō (723).

ON the mountain of Mifuné
    That hangs over the cascading waters³

---

¹ In Yamato.   A village of the same name is still in existence.
² The Empress Genshō.
³ The Yoshino River.

There grow the *toga*[1]-trees in luxuriance,
Spreading out their verdant branches—

O the Akitsu Palace of Yoshinu!
Where in endless succession—
So spells the name of those trees—
Will endure as now for ten thousand ages
The court of our Sovereigns!
Is it so sublime because of the god presiding?
Is it so alluring to look upon
Because of the pristine excellence of the province?
Well was here established the Pleasure-Palace
From the age of the gods
Amid these clear streams and immaculate hills.

Envoys

Oh, would I could thus feast my eyes
Year after year on the beautiful scene—
The clean dale of Yoshinu
With its cascades breaking into white spray!

How I gaze, unwearied, upon the dale
Where the river, because of the towering hills,
Flowing, falls in cascades
White as the flowers of mulberry-cloth!

294–6   *On the occasion of the Sovereign's*[2] *visit to*   [VI : 920–2]
the Detached Palace at Yoshinu, in
summer, in the fifth month of the
second year of Jinki (725).

Lo! the unsullied stream of the Yoshinu,
        Thundering through the mountains,
Rushes down in cascades.

---

[1] A kind of fir-tree (*Tsuga Sieboldi*).   The name was often used as an introductory word to 'successively.'
[2] The Emperor Shōmu.

In the upper reach the plovers cry incessantly,
In the lower reach the song-frogs call to their mates,
While here and there the palace lords and ladies
Gaily throng the banks;
Enchanted am I beyond words
Whenever I watch the scene.
May it ever be thus—continuous
As the fair creeping vine—for ten thousand ages!
So in awe I pray to the gods of heaven and earth.

Envoys

Shall I ever weary of gazing
Even for ten thousand ages
Upon these imperial palace grounds
On the bank of the Yoshinu rapids?

Would that the lives of my fellow-men,
And mine as well, were everlasting
As the rocks that bed
The rapids of the Yoshinu River!

297–9　*On the occasion of the Sovereign's[1] visit*　　[VI : 928–30]
　　　to the Palace of Naniwa in the tenth
　　　month [of the same year].

THOUGH the land of wave-bright Naniwa,
　　Regarded by all men as a ruined place
No better than an old reed-fence,
Was left all forgotten and unfriended—

Now that our Sovereign is pleased to dwell
Here at the Palace of Nagara,
Pillared stout and high,
Thence to rule his wide domain,
And the courtiers of eighty clans

---

[1] The Emperor Shōmu.

Have built their cottages on Ajifu Field,
This place has become an Imperial City,
If but for the time of their sojourn.

Envoys

Desolate like a moorland
Though this place has been,
When here our Sovereign dwells,
Lo! it blooms forth in the splendour
Of an Imperial City.

The fisher-maids
In their little *tana*-less[1] boats
Are rowing out to sea—
Lying in my wayfarer's bed,
I hear the sound of the oars.

300–2 On the occasion of the Sovereign's journey to [VI: 935–7]
Inami District, Harima Province, in autumn,
on the fifteenth of the ninth month of the
third year of Jinki (726).

ON Matsuho's shore of Awaji Island,
    Seen yonder from Funasé of Nakisumi,
There are fisher-maids, I am told,
Who cut the dainty seaweed in the morning calm,
And in the evening calm burn salt-fires.
But I, knowing not how to reach them,
And deprived of my manly courage,
Am maid-like distraught with sorrow,
And wander about yearning for the far beach—
Helpless without boat and oar!

Envoys

O that I had boat and oar

---

[1] See note to No. 204.

That I might visit those fisher-maids
Cutting the dainty seaweed!—
I would go, however high the waves might be.

Could I ever weary of watching,
Walking back and forth interminably,
The white waves that ceaselessly break
On Funasé's beach of Nakisumi?

303-5   *Addressed to an envoy departing for*   [VIII : 1453-5]
       China, in spring, in the third month
         intercalary of the fifth year of
                Tempyō (733).

YOU who are constantly on my mind,
     And dear to me as the breath of life—
You depart in obedience to the imperial command,
From the cape of Mitsu in Naniwa Bay,
Where in the evening the cranes call to their mates.
You will board a great ship, full-oared,
And sail away past many an island
On the ocean of high white waves.
Then, I, who remain, will see you go,
Making offerings and prayers to the gods.
Come back soon, O friend!

Envoys

Beyond the waves in the clouds
Is lost a small island—
Even so, when you are gone,
Oh, the choking grief!

Would I could be
The shaft of your ship's oar
Rather than thus remain
Disconsolate even unto death!

103

Isonokami (Otomaro[1]) and Kasa Kanamura

306   IN the great ship, full-oared,   [III : 368]
      I sail along the coast,
  Obedient to our Sovereign's word.
                   —*By Isonokami.*[1]

307   A BRAVE liegeman like you   [III : 369]
      Should do his service
  As our mighty Sovereign wills.
                   —*By Kasa Kanamura.*

From the 'Kasa Kanamura Collection'

308–10   *On the occasion of the death of Prince Shiki,* [II : 230–2]
          in autumn, in the ninth month of the
          first year of Reiki[2] (715).

THE warriors go forth
    With birchwood bows in their hands
And hunting arrows under their arms—
On the hill slope of Takamado ;[3]
There flamed up fires
That seemed like moorland fires
Burning in the spring.
I wondered and asked
A wayfarer upon the road.
Lo, he wept; his tears fell like rain,
Drenching the hempen cloak.
He stops to say :

[1] According to the Original Note Isonokami might be Isonokami Otomaro, as the latter was appointed Governor of Echizen. But concerning his appointment nothing is found in the historical records.

[2] The era of Reiki began with the 9th month of the year.

[3] The preceding three lines are introductory to 'Takamado' which may be taken to mean 'high target.'

' Oh, what a woeful question you ask !
To hear it is to weep;
To answer is to break the heart.
They are the torch-fires
Of the funeral train
Of our dear imperial prince—
Child of the gods—
That all so brightly shine !'

Envoys

Can it be that the bush-clovers
Of Takamado blow—
Blow in vain and fade
Upon the autumn plain
Where none comes now to see ?

That road through the brake
On Mikasa's hill-side[1]—
How desolate it is,
And overgrown with weed,
So soon !

311-2   *Upon the departure of an official for his*   [IX : 1785-6]
            new post in the land of Koshi,[2] in
            autumn, in the eighth month of the
            fifth year of Jinki (728).

SINCE I came by chance into this life
    Where it is rare to be born a man,
I have trusted you through life and death.
But now, obedient to our mighty Sovereign's word,
—As is our human lot—
To govern the land far-off as the skies,
You set out early as the morning bird,

---

[1] Forms part of the Kasuga Hill at the foot of which, it seems, the palace of the Prince stood.
[2] i. e. the provinces of Echizen, Etchū and Echigo, all facing the Japan Sea.

With all your followers like a flock of fowl.
And I remaining shall miss you deeply,
Seeing not your face for many a day!

Envoy

The day you cross the mountains in Kọshi,
Where the snow is falling,
O think of one who remains behind.

Lady Kasa

313　　　　　　*To Ōtomo Yakamochi.*　　　　　[III : 396]

Fᴀʀ off as the reed-plain of Manu[1]
　　Lies in 'Road's End,'[2]
Yet in vision, they say,
It comes near.

To Ōtomo Yakamochi.

314　Iɴ the loneliness of my heart　　　　　[IV : 594]
　　I feel as if I should perish
　Like the pale dew-drop
　Upon the grass of my garden
　In the gathering shades of twilight.

315　Eᴠᴇɴ the sands uncounted of a long　　　[IV : 596]
　　beach
　That takes eight hundred days to travel—
　Could they at all outnumber
　My thoughts of love,
　O guardian of the isle on the sea?

---

[1] There still remains a place so called in Sōma District, Fukushima Prefecture.
[2] i. e. Michinoku; an old name for the north-eastern region of Japan.

316   OH how steadily I love you—   [IV : 600]
      You who awe me
  Like the thunderous waves
  That lash the sea-coast of Isé!

317   MORE sad thoughts crowd into my   [IV : 602]
      mind
  When evening comes; for then
  Appears your phantom shape—
  Speaking as I have known you speak.

318   IF it were death to love,   [IV : 603]
      I should have died—
  And died again
  One thousand times over.

319   I DREAMED I was holding   [IV : 604]
      A double-edged sword close to my body—
  What does it foretell?   It tells
  That I shall meet you soon.

320   IF the gods of heaven and earth   [IV : 605]
      Were bereft of reason,
  I might die
  Without seeing you
  Whom I love so well.

321   THE bells are tolling,   [IV : 607]
      Bidding all to rest.
  But you being for ever on my mind,
  I cannot sleep.

322 To love you who love me not   [IV : 608]
    Is like going to a great temple
To bow in adoration
Behind the back of the famished devil.[1]

Takahashi —

323-5   *An elegy on the death of his wife.*   [III : 481-3]

TILL my black hair be white,
    We shall be together, I and my darling,
Sleeping, our sleeves overlapped,
She nestling by my side,
Bound in never-ending love,
Through this new age of our Sovereign;
So I vowed, but my word proved false,
My hopes were vain.
She has gone from me and our loved home,
Leaving a crying child,
And faded like a morning mist,
Vanished among the Sagaraka Hills[2]
Of Yamashiro.
I know not what to say, nor what to do.
But out of the room we slept in
I come at morn, thinking of my wife,
With evening I go back and grieve.
When my precious child cries,
Helpless man as I am—
I bear him on my back or in my arms;
And ceaselessly I weep, as sings the morning bird,

---

[1] It was believed by old commentators, though without sufficient evidence, that the images of a demon were kept in Buddhist temples merely as a warning to show what state of existence a man might be transmuted into in after-life through disbelief and evil conduct. To worship these images was, of course, absurd and useless.

[2] In Sōraku District, Yamashiro.

Longing for her in vain;
And, though dumb the hills that bind her,
I gaze upon them as my heart's resort!

Envoys

Changing is this world of ours;
Those hills, cold to my heart,
I now must gaze upon
As my heart's resort!

I cannot but weep aloud
And ceaselessly, as sings the morning bird,
Since no way remains to me
To regain my love!

Kuramochi Chitosé

326-7 As one but hears the rumbling   [VI : 913-4]
      thunder,
So had I only heard of fair Yoshinu—
And how that name rang in my wistful ears!
There on the mountain with trees overgrown
I stand to gaze below.
The morning mist rises everywhere
From the river shallows as day breaks,
And there the song-frogs chirp in the evening.
O what a pity that, being on a journey
And even obliged to sleep in my clothes,
I must alone without you, love,
Look on this clean and beautiful river-beach!

Envoy

Mount Mifuné above the cascades
Overawes me by its grandeur,
Yet never for a day, nor for a moment,
Do I forget you, my love!

THE beach is beautiful; and there   [VI : 931–2]
   grow
The sea-tangles swaying,
Lapped by a thousand waves
In the calm of morning,
And by five hundred waves
In the evening calm.
O Suminoé Beach,
Where white-crested waves are racing around!
Could I weary of watching, not only now,
But day in, day out, over and over again,
As those waves break on the shore?

Envoy

Let me go, with my clothes stained
For remembrance with the yellow clay
Of Suminoé's shore, which white-crested waves
Visit, ceaselessly lapping!

Wife of Kuramochi —

330-2   *To a long absent husband.*   [XVI : 3811–13]

I AM sick body and soul
  Because not even a messenger comes
To bring me word of you,
My husband ruddy-cheeked.
Pray not to the gods,
Nor call in the diviner
To burn the tortoise-shell!
It is love that torments me:
The pain pierces me to the bone,
And grief has broken my heart.
My life is fast ebbing towards its end.
Who calls me now?—

Is it you, sweet husband of mine,
Or is it my dear mother?
In vain you seek at the cross-roads
The oracle of evening and of the way
For the sake of me who must die!

Envoys

Though they ask the diviner,
And seek oracles at the cross-roads,
There is no finding
The means to see you.

Not that I cared for my life—
But just because of you,
Sweet husband of mine,
Have I wished to live on.[1]

*It is said that there was a young woman (her surname
was Kuramochi), whose husband had deserted her for many
years. Pining after him, she was taken ill. Growing
weaker and more wasted every day, she suddenly faced death.
Thereupon, she sent for her husband; she then recited the
above poems with sobs and tears. She died shortly after.*

Kosé Sukunamaro

333   *At a feast of court nobles gathered at*   [VI : 1016]
       *his residence, in spring, in the second
          month [of the ninth year of
            Tempyō] (737).*

OVER the far ocean plains
   I made hither my toilsome way—
I, a fairy maiden—
To watch the gallant lords make merry.

[1] Given in a certain book as an envoy.—Original Note.

The above poem, which was written on a piece of white paper and hung upon the wall, bore a preface reading: 'This is a garland made by a fairy maid of Peng-lai, which the vulgar may in no wise behold.'

Fujiwara Hirotsugu and a Young Lady

334 *Poem sent with cherry-flowers to a young*   [VIII : 1456]
 lady by Fujiwara Hirotsugu.

SLIGHT not these flowers!
 Each single petal contains
A hundred words of mine.

335 *Reply by the young lady.*   [VIII : 1457]

WERE these flowers broken off,
 Unable to hold in each petal
A hundred words of yours?

Abé Okina

336 *Poem of sorrow addressed to his mother*   [XIX : 4247]
 when he was despatched to China.[1]

MY love for you, O mother,
 Is endless like the bounds of heaven
Where the clouds drift on and on,
But the day I must leave you
Now draws near!

---

[1] This poem was handed down by Takayasu Tanemori of Etchū, an official of the Fourth Rank.—Original Note.

Ikeda — and Ōmiwa Okimori

337   *Poem of ridicule by Ikeda addressed to*   [XVI : 3840]
                   Ōmiwa Okimori.

THUS say the famished she-devils
   In the temples far and near:
'Grant me Ōmiwa, the he-devil,
That I may bear him
A litter of baby devils!'

338   *Reply by Ōmiwa Okimori.*   [XVI : 3841]

IF you lack, makers of Buddhas,
   The vermeil clay
For your idols,
Go dig the nose-top
Of my Lord of 'Pond-field'![1]

Nakatomi Yakamori and a Maiden Sanu Chigami

        Poems exchanged while Yakamori
                lived in exile.

339   O FOR a fire from heaven   [XV : 3724]
     To haul, fold and burn up
The long-stretched road you go!—
              By the Maiden, on parting.

340   WERE it not for the dresses   [XV : 3733]
     You gave me as a keepsake,
How, beloved, could I
Live the days of my life?—*By Yakamori.*

[1] i. e. a literal translation of *Ikeda*.

341   A STRANGE land is hard to live in,   [xv : 3748]
            men say;
        Come quickly home,
        Before I die of love for you !—*By the Maiden.*

342   WITHIN the bounds of heaven and   [xv : 3750]
            earth
        None, none you can find
        Who loves you as I !—*By the Maiden.*

343   THESE are the clothes your dainty girl,   [xv : 3753]
            Bowed in thought, has sewn—
        A keepsake for the day
        When we shall meet again.—*By the Maiden.*

344   DO the courtiers even now   [xv : 3758]
            Delight in nothing
        But teasing and mockery ?—*By Yakamori.*

345   THOUGH I try to calm down my soul[1]   [xv : 3767]
            By prayers night and morning,
        My heart aches
        With overwhelming love.—*By the Maiden.*

346   'A LORD returning home   [xv : 3772]
            Has come,' said they—
        And I well-nigh swooned,
        Thinking it was you.—*By the Maiden.*

[1] A religious function observed lest the soul should depart from the body.

347   FOR the time that you return,   [XV : 3774]
        I will guard my life, my lord;
O forget me not!—*By the Maiden.*

348   EVEN to-day, were I in the City,   [XV : 3776]
        I would be standing
Outside the western royal stables,
Breathless to see you.—*By Yakamori.*

Lady Abé

349–50   I SHALL think of nothing more now.   [IV : 505–6]
        To you I have yielded, my dear;
Upon you my soul leans.

Think not of things, my beloved!
Have you not me—who would go,
If need be, through fire and flood for you?

351   MY very soul, it seems,   [IV : 514]
        Has stolen into every stitch
Of the robe you wear.

Lady Heguri

*Sent to Ōtomo Yakamochi, Governor of Etchū, by
occasional posts.*

352   GAZING at the hand you squeezed   [XVII : 3940]
        When we were heart to heart,
Pledging the love of a myriad years,
I am overwhelmed with longing.

353   THE pine bloom, though you   [XVII : 3942]
        overlook it
    Among the mass of blossoms,
    Blows now in vain.

Ōtomo Tabito

354-5 Composed at the imperial command during   [III : 315-6]
      the Emperor's stay at the Detached Palace
      of Yoshinu, in the third month.[1]

    O THE Palace of Yoshinu,
      Beautiful Yoshinu—
    Noble for its mountains,
    Bright for its rivers !
    As long as heaven and earth shall last,
    For a myriad ages,
    It will flourish unchanging—
    This Pleasure-Palace !

Envoy

    The rivulet of Kisa[2] that I saw long ago—
    When I see it now,
    How much more limpid are its waters !

356   CAN the prime of youth come back to   [III : 331]
        me ?
    I fear that I may die
    Without seeing the City of Nara once again ![3]

---

  [1] Probably in the first year of Jinki (724) in the reign of the Emperor Shōmu.
  [2] Runs through the Kisa valley and falls into the Yoshino.
  [3] This poem was composed when Tabito was sixty-three or four years old and at the time when he was Governor-General of the Dazaifu. In spite of the pessimism expressed in the poem he returned to the capital as Grand Councillor of State (730). He died in the 7th month of the following year at the age of sixty-seven.

INSTEAD of wasting thoughts on unavailing things,
    It would seem wiser
To drink a cup of raw saké.

How true is his saying,
That great sage of old who gave saké
The name of ' sage.'[1]

Even with the seven wise men[2] of the days of old,
Saké was, it seems,
The crown of their desire.

Far better, it seems, than uttering pompous words
And looking wise,
To drink saké and weep drunken tears.

I know not how to name it, how to define it,
Ten thousand times precious
Is saké to me !

Ceasing to live this wretched life of man,
O that I were a saké-jar ;
Then should I be soaked with saké !

Grotesque !   When I look upon a man
Who drinks no saké, looking wise,
How like an ape he is !

Even a treasure priceless in the world—
How could it surpass
A cup of raw saké ?

---

[1] In ancient China, the Emperor Taitsung of Wei prohibited the use of saké, but those who drank it secretly called white saké ' wise man ' and pure saké ' sage.'
[2] The so-called ' seven wise men of the bamboo wood ' who lived under the Chin dynasty were all good drinkers.

If there were a gem shining in the darkness of night,
How could it excel
Saké that kills all care?

Among the countless ways of pleasure
What refreshes most
Is weeping drunken tears![1]

If I could but be happy in this life,
What should I care if in the next
I became a bird or a worm![2]

All living things die in the end:
So long as I live here
I want the cup of pleasure.

Silence with the airs of wisdom
Is far worse
Than weeping drunken tears!

Remembering his deceased wife: composed in the fifth year of Jinki (728), when he was Governor-General of the Dazaifu.

370   *Some weeks after her death.*   [III : 438]

MY dear wife loved my arm,
     Her pillow, to sleep on;
Now I have none like her,
To sleep upon it.

---

[1] The second and third lines are alternatively construed, i. e.
     'And when we are melancholy,
       Better take to weeping drunken tears.'
[2] This poem alludes to the Buddhist idea of the transmigration of the soul.

WHEN I sleep alone, in the Imperial City,
  In my long forsaken house,
How much more painful that will be
Than ever on my journey!

*Composed during his journey from the Dazaifu to the
capital, in winter, in the twelfth month of the second year of
Tempyō (730).*

Passing the shore of Tomo.[1]

372   MY darling gazed[2] at the juniper   [III : 446]
  On the shore of Tomo;
It stands, flourishing as ever,
But she who saw it is dead.

373   O JUNIPER, that grasps the rocks of the   [III : 448]
    beach
With ancient roots,
If I ask where she is, she who saw you,
Can you answer me?

Passing the cape of Minumé.

374   TOGETHER with my wife I passed   [III : 449]
  This lovely cape Minumé;
Now on my lonely voyage home
I see it and I weep.

[1] In Bingo Province.
[2] i. e. when they journeyed to the Dazaifu.

375   WHEN last I journeyed down,   [III : 450]
            We two admired this cape;
        Now I am filled with sadness,
        Passing it all alone.

376–8   *On reaching his residence.*   [III : 451–3]

        MY house forsaken by my love,
            And so desolate—
        How much more it pains my heart
        Than did my travels, grass for pillow!

        This garden which I, together with my darling,
        Laid out and planted,
        Has now grown waste and rife
        With tall and wild-boughed trees!

        Each time I see this plum-tree,
        Which my darling planted,
        My heart swells with sadness
        And tears fill my eyes.

379   *Addressed to Lord Tajihi Agatamori, an*   [IV : 555]
        official of the Dazaifu, on the occasion
                of his departure for Nara.

        THIS wine I have brewed for you
            And laid aside for your company—
        Must I drink it, O friend, without you,
        And alone on the plain of Yasu![1]

---

[1] The plain, situated several miles south-east of the Dazaifu, provided perhaps a convenient hunting ground for the officials.

In reply to condolences he had received   [v : 793]
                 on his wife's death.

Calamity after calamity has befallen me, and many sad tidings gather around.   Overwhelmed by grief, and all alone, I shed tears with a breaking heart.   Your kind consolations narrowly hold back my fast-declining life.   My pen cannot express what I wish to say.   But all ages have had this same regret.

Now that I am brought to know
      The vanity of human life,
Sadness bows me down
Deeper than ever.

381   *In reply[1] to Ishikawa Taruhito, an official of   [vi : 956]*
                 the Dazaifu.

THIS being a place over which
      Our great Sovereign rules in peace,
Whether in Yamato, or here in this far province,
I feel ever the same.

382   *In reply[2] to a young woman named Kojima on   [vi : 968]*
                 the occasion of his departure for
                       the capital.

THAT I who thought myself a strong man
      Should now, on Mizuki's embankment,[3]
Shed tears in bidding you farewell!

---

[1] Ishikawa Taruhito sent a poem to Tabito, the Governor-General, asking him, if he did not long for his home at Nara.

[2] When Ōtomo Tabito set forth for the capital, he stopped his horse at Mizuki to look back at his residence in the Dazaifu.   The young woman, one of those who were there to see him off, presented him with a poem expressing her grief at separation.   Tabito replied with the above, reciprocating her sentiments.—Original Note.

[3] This embankment was constructed for the defence of the Dazaifu.   Traces of it may still be seen in the neighbourhood of Mizuki Station, on the main railway line to Kagoshima.

Manzei and Ōtomo Tabito

383   *Addressed by Manzei, the monk, to Lord*   [IV : 573]
         Ōtomo, Governor-General of the Da-
         zaifu, after his return to the
         capital.

EVEN after my locks,
    Black as the berries of pardanthus,[1]
Have all turned white,
There comes a time when I must nurse
Heart-aching love, alas!

384   *By Ōtomo Tabito.*   [IV : 574]

HERE in the capital I wonder
    Where may be your land of Tsukushi—
It must lie, alas! my friend,
Far beyond the mountains
Where white clouds hover.

Ōtomo Sukunamaro

385   SHE goes to the sun-bright palace;   [IV : 532]
            Yet so dear to me is the maiden,
         It is heart-ache to keep her,
         But despair to let her go.

---

[1] *Nubatama*, used as a pillow-word for 'black,' are berries of an iridaceous plant called *hiōgi* (*Belamacanda* or *Pardanthus chinensis*).

Lady Ōtomo of Sakanoé

386-7   *Chanted at a religious service to her*   [III : 379-80]
ancestral god.

Oh, our heaven-born god,
    Descended[1] from the heavenly plains—
With the *sakaki* branch[2]
Fresh from the inmost hill,
Tied with white paper and mulberry cloth,
With a wine-jar set in the purified earth,
With a cord of many bamboo-rings
Hanging from my neck,
With my knees bent like the deer's,
With my maiden's scarf flung over me,—
Thus I entreat thee, our god,
Yet can I not meet him?

Envoy

With folded mulberry cloth in my hands,
Thus I entreat thee, our god,
Yet can I not meet him?

388-9   *An elegy on the death of Rigan,[3] a nun,*   [III : 460-1]
in the seventh year of Tempyō (735).

She came from distant Shiragi,
    Hearing praises of our Land,
Though there was no kith nor kin
With whom to talk her cares away;

---

[1] It alludes to the legend that her ancestral god descended from heaven together with Ninigi-no-Mikoto.

[2] An evergreen broad-leaved tree, found in the mountains of southern Japan, and also cultivated in gardens and in the precincts of Shinto shrines; it is considered sacred and used as an offering to the gods.

[3] Rigan, a Korean nun, was naturalized and lived for some years at the house of the father of the poetess. When she died, the poetess's mother was away at the hot springs of Arima, so that the lady herself attended to the nun's burial services.

And, with choice of homes in plenty
In the prosperous Imperial City,
In the Land where rules our Sovereign,
Though what she wished I know not,
Eagerly she sought, like a crying child,
This alien hill of Saho;[1]
There she built herself a cottage,
Which she kept for many a year;
And, while her trusted friends were all away
On their journey, grass for pillow,
Since none could elude
The fate of all that live,
She crossed Saho's stream at morning,
And going to the mountain-side,
With Kasuga Field[2] behind her,
Hid herself as in the shades of evening.
I know no word, I know not what to do,
But lingering all alone in grief,
Endlessly I weep upon my sleeves;
Do not my tears rise in clouds
And fall in rain on Mount Arima?[3]

Envoy

Life one cannot hold fast—
She left her dwelling
And hid herself among the clouds.

390   *Reply to Fujiwara Maro.*   [IV : 527]

Even if you say, ' I come,'
     At times you will not come.
Now you say : ' I will not come.'
Why should I look for your coming—

---

1 The hill rises to the north-west of the present Nara, on which stood the residence of Yasumaro, her father.
2 An open tract at the foot of Mount Kasuga.
3 Near the hot springs of Arima, Settsu Province.

When you say you will not come!

At wave-bright Naniwa
    The sedges grow, firm-rooted—
Firm were the words you spoke,
And tender, pledging me your love,
That it would endure through all the years;
And to you I yielded my heart,
Spotless as a polished mirror.
Never, from that day, like the sea-weed
That sways to and fro with the waves,
Have I faltered in my fidelity,
But have trusted in you as in a great ship.
Is it the gods who have divided us?
Is it mortal men who intervene?
You come no more, who came so often,
Nor yet arrives a messenger with your letter.
There is—alas!—nothing I can do.
Though I sorrow the black night through
And all day till the red sun sinks,
It avails me nothing.   Though I pine,
I know not how to soothe my heart's pain.
Truly men call us ' weak women.'
Crying like an infant,
And lingering around, I must still wait,
Wait impatiently for a message from you!

Envoy

If from the beginning
You had not made me trust you,
Speaking of long, long years,
Should I have known now
Such sorrow as this?

393   THE cold dew of heaven has fallen,   [IV : 651]
        And so arrives another season.
    Ah! my children staying far away at home—
    You, too, must long and wait for me![1]

394   I DELIVER the jewel[2]   [IV : 652]
        To the jewel-keeper.
    Then, oh, my pillow and I!—
    Let us two sleep together!

395   DO you desire our love to endure?   [IV : 661]
        Then, if only while I see you
    After days of longing and yearning,
    Pray, speak to me
    Sweet words—all you can!

396   AS if a cloud were sailing   [IV : 688]
        Across the green mountain-side,
    Do not smile to yourself too frankly,
    Lest others should know of our love!

397-8   *Sent from her country estate[3] of Tomi to*   [IV : 723-4]
        her eldest daughter remaining
            at home.

    DEAR child, my daughter, who stood
        Sadly musing by the gate

---

[1] The poem was composed by Lady Ōtomo of Sakanoé, presumably during her sojourn at the Dazaifu, where she had gone to visit her elder brother, Ōtomo Tabito, the Governor-General, leaving her two daughters at home in Nara.

[2] The jewel alludes to Lady Ōtomo of Sakanoé's second daughter, and the jewel-keeper to the latter's husband Ōtomo Surugamaro.

[3] The estate was the hereditary property of the Ōtomo family, who had a villa there. The place was situated to the east of the present town of Sakurai in Yamato. The poems were sent in reply to a poem from the daughter.

Though I was leaving for no foreign land,
I think of you day and night
And my body is become lean;
My sleeves, too, are tear-soaked with weeping.
If I must long for you so wretchedly,
I fear I cannot stay these many months
Here at this dreary old farm.

Envoy

Because you long for me so much—
Your sad thoughts all confused
Like the tangles of your morning hair—
I see you, dear child, in dream.[1]

399   *Given to her nephew, Yakamochi, as he left*   [VI : 979]
           her house at Saho for his Western Residence.

THE garment is thin
    That my loved one wears—
O Saho wind, blow not too hard
Until he reaches his home!

400   *Feasting with her kinsfolk.*   [VI : 995]

THUS let us drink and be merry!
    Even the grass and the tree thrive in spring
Only to fade and fall with autumn.

401   OH, the pain of my love that you   [VIII : 1500]
          know not—
A love like the maiden-lily
Blooming in the thicket of the summer moor!

---

[1] It was popularly believed that a person would appear in the dream of the one
for whom he yearned.

I CHERISHED you, my darling,
    As the Sea God the pearls
He treasures in his comb-box.
But you, led by your lord husband—
Such is the way of the world—
And torn from me like a vine,
Left for distant Koshi;
Since then, your lovely eyebrows
Curving like the far-off waves,
Ever linger in my eyes,
My heart unsteady as a rocking boat;
Under such a longing
I, now weak with age,
Come near to breaking.

Envoy

If I had foreknown such longing,
I would have lived with you,
Gazing on you every hour of the day
As in a shining mirror.

Lady Ōtomo of Sakanoé and an Anonymous Person

404   A FTER we, dear friends, have drunk   [VIII : 1656]
            together,
Setting plum-blossoms afloat in our wine-cups,
I care not if those on the tree be gone.
                              —*By the Lady.*

¹ Composed in the second year of Tempyō-Shōhō (750).

405   T<small>HE</small> law allows our feasting;[1]   [VIII : 1657]
      Are we to drink the wine this one night only?
Do not fall, O blossoms, fall not away!
                       —*Anonymous.*

Lady Ōtomo of Sakanoé and Ōtomo Yakamochi, her Nephew

406   I<small>F</small> I sent my forlorn love   [XVIII : 4081]
      On a pack-horse—a stout horse—
To your land of Koshi,
Would anyone be tempted,
I wonder, to cajole it away?—*By the Lady.*

407   S<small>HOULD</small> a horse-load of love   [XVIII : 4083]
      Arrive from the Imperial City
When my love's daily stock
Is by no means exhausted,
I could not carry it, I fear.—*By Yakamochi.*

Lady Ōtomo of Tamura

408   *To her sister, Lady Ōtomo of Sakanoé's* [VIII : 1622]
         Elder Daughter.

A<small>T</small> home the *hagi* flowers of autumn
      Are abloom in the evening glow—
Would that this moment
I could see your radiant form!

---

[1] In those days—according to the Original Note—a decree had been issued, reading: 'There shall be within the confines of the capital no banqueting save private feastings of a few individuals, which are permitted.' Hence the first line of the above poem.

Ōtomo Yakamochi

Elegies[1] on the death of his mistress, in summer,
in the sixth month of the eleventh year of
Tempyō (739).

409   FROM this time on   [III : 462]
          The autumn wind will chill me;
How shall I sleep alone
The long nights through?

410   *Seeing the fringed pink by the stone-paving*   [III : 464]
               under the eaves.

    THE fringed pink in my garden
          Which my beloved planted
For her remembrance in autumn-tide,
Has all come out in bloom.

411   *In sorrow at the autumn wind in the*   [III : 465]
              following month.

    WELL do I know that human life is passing;
          Yet this autumn[2] wind chills me,
Reminding me of my lost love.

412-5   THE flowers have blossomed in my   [III : 466-9]
          garden,
    Yet do not soothe my sorrow;
If only my love were living,
Side by side could we be
Like a pair of mallards;

---

[1] These poems were probably composed in his 21st year.
[2] According to the lunar calendar autumn begins in the 7th month.

And I would pick them for her sake!
Brief is our lease of life,
She vanished like a drop of dew;
Seeking the mountain-side,
Like the setting sun she hid herself;
Remembrance wrings my heart.
Past speech the world is vain—
What can I do?

Envoys

Could she not have chosen another time?
To my grief she died, my love,
Leaving me a babe.

Had I but known the way she left our world,
I would have built a barrier
Between my dying love and death.

In the garden which my darling loved
The flowers still bloom;
And a long time has passed,
Yet my tears are not dry.

Still depressed in his sorrow.

416   SUCH a fleeting life though we shared   [III : 470]
      together,
We both had trusted that our love
Would last a thousand years.

417   ONCE I saw it with uncaring eyes;   [III : 474]
      Now that it is her sepulchre,
How dear it is, this hill of Saho!

418-20   MY thought and my tongue   [III : 475-7]
     Are held with awe—
Now that the spring has come
In the Imperial City of Kuni[3]
In great Yamato,
Which my lord and prince
Was to rule for a myriad ages,
The hills are burthened with blossoms,
And the *ayu*[4] sport in the river-shallows.

When thus the city prospers day by day,
Is it some trick or rumour
That, followed by his servitors in white,
He stayed his royal palanquin
On the mountain of Wazuka[5]
And thence rose up to heaven?
Alas! we writhe upon the ground
And shed endless tears;
But all is vain.

Envoys

I had not thought that thence
My prince would rise to heaven;
With careless eyes I'd looked
Upon this wooded mountain of Wazuka.

The blossoms made all the mountain glow,
But now are scattered down;
Such was he, my noble prince!

---

   [1] Composed on the 3rd of the 2nd month in the 16th year of Tempyō (744).

   [2] Son of the Emperor Shōmu. He died at the age of seventeen on the 13th of the 1st month intercalary, in the 16th year of Tempyō (744).

   [3] Kuni was the site of the court of the Emperor Shōmu from the 12th month of the 12th year of Tempyō till the 26th of the 2nd month in the 16th year of Tempyō. The site is located in Mika-no-hara Village, Sōraku District, Yamashiro.

   [4] A fresh-water fish (*Plecoglossus altivelis*), several inches long, resembling the brook trout.

   [5] Situated to the east of Kuni.

421-31 MY thought is held with awe—   [III : 478-80]
  My lord and prince, leading
All the captains of eighty clans,
Would rouse deer in the morning chase,
And start birds in the evening hunt;
Then halting his horse by the bit,
Joyously he would gaze far
From the hill of Ikuji.²

But now on this hill the blossoms
That filled the leafy trees
All are scattered away.
So is it with the world;
His servitors who, warrior-hearted,
Gathered at the prince's palace,
Noisy as the flies of May,
With swords at their waists,
Birchwood bows in hand,
And full quivers on their backs,
Trusting their service would last
Long as heaven and earth endured,
For a myriad ages,
Now go in doleful white;
And daily fade their wonted smiles
And their ways grow less gay;
Which rends my heart!

Envoys

The path he traced, my dear prince,
The path to Ikuji where he admired the view,
Lies wild and desolate!

My heart, that bears the fame of Ōtomo,
My trust to serve, quiver on back,
For a myriad ages,
Where shall I take it now?

¹ Composed on the 24th of the 3rd month (in 744).
² One of the Wazuka Hills.

133

OVER the river ferry of Saho,   [IV : 715]
     Where the sanderlings cry—
When can I come to you,
Crossing on horseback
The crystal-clear shallows?

HAVING seen your smile   [IV : 718]
     In a dream by chance,
I keep now burning in my heart
Love's inextinguishable flame.

HOW I waste and waste away   [IV : 719]
     With love forlorn—
I who have thought myself
A strong man!

427   RATHER than that I should thus pine   [IV : 722]
     for you,
Would I had been transmuted
Into a tree or a stone,
Nevermore to feel the pangs of love.

428   *To Lady Ōtomo of Sakanoé's*   [IV : 728]
         Elder Daughter.

WOULD there were a land
     Uninhabited by man!
Thither I'd take my love,
And happily we twain would live.

429   *To the same.*   [IV : 741]

WHAT pain and distress
        A dream tryst brings!
I start and wake,
And grope in vain for you,
Beyond the reach of my hand.

430   *On the new moon.*   [VI : 994]

WHEN I look up and gaze
        At the young moon afar
I remember the painted eyebrows
Of her whom only once I saw.

431   *On the cicadas.*[1]   [VIII : 1479]

TIRED of sitting indoors all day long,
        I seek the garden for solace, only to hear
The shrill chirps of the cicadas.

432   *On the cuckoo.*[2]   [VIII : 1491]

IN the leafy tree-tops
        Of the summer mountain
The cuckoo calls—
Oh, how far off his echoing voice!

---

[1] i. e. *higurashi*, a kind of cicada which chirps in a shrill tone early in the evening, as though to hasten the nightfall.
[2] i. e. *hototogisu* (*Cuculus poliocephalus*): a bird which resembles the English cuckoo. It is said to lay its eggs in the nest of the *uguisu*. (Cf. No. 664)

WHILE I waited and wondered,
    The orange-tree that grows in my garden,
Spreading out a hundred branches,
Has burst into bloom, as the fifth month
For garland-making draws near.
Every morning and every day I go out
To see the flowers and keep close guard,
Lest they should fall off
Before you, whom I love as the breath of life,
Have seen them once on a night when the moon
Is clear as a shining mirror.
But the wicked cuckoo,
Though I chase him again and again,
Comes crying in the sad hours of dawn
And wantonly scatters the blooms on the ground.
Knowing not what to do,
I have reached and broken off these with my hand,
Pray, see them, my lady!

Envoys

These are the orange-blossoms of my garden
I had intended you to see
Some time after mid-month
On a clear moonlight night.

The cuckoo has scattered
My orange-blooms on the ground.
Oh, had he only come
After you had seen the flowers!

ON the miscanthus[1] of my garden
  White dew-drops lie;
Would I could pierce them without breaking
And make a string of gems!

So loud the deer cries, calling to his mate,
  That the answering echo resounds
Through the mountains,
Where I am alone.

THINKING sad thoughts over and over,
  I know not what to say,
I know not what to do.

You and I went out hand in hand
Into the garden in the morning,
While in the evening we brushed our bed
And lay together, our white sleeves overlapped.
Those nights—did they last for ever?
Though the copper-pheasant woos his mate,
They say, from an opposite mountain peak,
I, man that I am, if separated
Even for a single day or a single night,
Must long for you and grieve—ah, why?
I dwell on it, and my heart aches.

So, for healing I go forth
To Takamado and wander over hill and dale;
But there I find only the fair-blooming flowers

---

[1] i. e. *susuki.* See note to No. 83.

That remind me ever the more of you.
What can I do to forget this thing called Love?

Envoy

Ah, I cannot forget you—
In the *kao-bana*[1] that blooms
In the fields of Takamado
I see your phantom face.

440-1   *To a lean man.*   [XVI : 3853-4]

IWAMARO, I tell you,
   Catch and eat eels!
They are good, they say,
For summer loss of flesh.

Yet, no matter how lean you are,
It is better to be alive.
So drown not yourself in the river
Trying to catch an eel!

There was a man called Yoshida Oyu, otherwise known as Iwamaro, who was a son of Ninkyō. He was extremely lean; and though he ate and drank much, he always had a famished look. Ōtomo Yakamochi composed the above poems to deride him.

442-4   *Poems of lamentation composed when he*   [XVII : 3962-4]
              was afflicted with a sudden illness
                 and death threatened him.[2]

OBEDIENT to our Sovereign's orders
   And mustering up a warrior's heart,
I crossed the hills and mountains

---

[1] Lit. 'face-flower,' not identified ; perhaps 'convolvulus.'
[2] Composed at his governor's mansion on the 21st of the 2nd month of the 19th year of Tempyō (747).—Original Note.

To these frontiers far-off as the skies;[1]
But before many months have passed
And before I can yet breathe at leisure,
—Mortal creature that I am—
I roll on a bed of illness,
My pain increasing with the days.
My loving mother, uneasy as a ship
Tossed on the waves,
Must long for me in her heart
And wait for my return—
To think of her grieves me.
And my beloved wife must await me,
Leaning against the gate at break of day,
With her sleeves turned back,[2]
At evening she must brush the bed,
And, with her black hair spread thereon,
Sigh, 'When will he come to me?'
And my boys and girls all cry
Here and there about the house.
But far is the way—no messenger is here
To take my heart-felt words.
My soul is well-nigh burning
With homeward thoughts.
Though clinging to my life,
I know not what to do,
And stricken with grief, I, a man,
Lie in bed.

Envoys

How brief is this lease of life,
To think my days will end,
Lost in those falling flowers of spring!

Over the rivers and mountains,
At this farthest reach,

[1] i. e. Etchū where he was sent as Governor.
[2] This act was intended as a charm to bring back a person away on a journey.

And without seeing my beloved,
Must I thus grieve!

445-6   Two poems of sorrow which were sent [XVII : 3965-6]
to his secretary, Ōtomo Ikenushi.

Unexpectedly seized with a serious illness, I have been suffering pain for some weeks. I petitioned a hundred gods and have now obtained some relief. Yet I am still weak and emaciated, and not strong enough to visit you to express my thanks. And so I long to see you the more. Now, in the morning, the spring flowers give forth their sweet fragrance in the garden, and in the evening the spring uguisu warble in the forest. In this genial season we should play the koto and make merry over saké. I am tempted to such pleasure, yet I cannot bear even the labour of walking with a staff. Confined alone within the curtain-screens, I have composed some little verses, which I send herewith for you to laugh at. They are as follows:

FLOWERS of spring must now
    Be blooming in full glory;
Would that I had the strength
To break a spray for my hair.

Now the *uguisu*[1] must be warbling
And scattering the flowers of spring;
O when can I, together with you,
Pick them to adorn our heads?

447-50   Also sent to Ikenushi.[2]   [XVII : 3969-72]

Your all-embracing virtue gave blessings to this poor

[1] *Homochlamys cantans*, a song-bird, which is often called ' Japanese nightingale.' The bird, however, sings in the daytime in a cheerful manner.

[2] Yakamochi wrote this to Ikenushi, in answer to the latter's reply to his first letter dated the 29th of the 2nd month. This letter, written in classical Chinese, contains four poems at the end.

creature and your unmeasurable sympathy gave comfort to my
starved heart, in favouring me with your answer; which I
value above all compare. As I did not in my younger
days cultivate the garden of the literary arts, I have no skill
in letters. Nor could I find the way through the gates of
Yamabé and Kakinomoto; and I cannot use happy words.
You put it in your letter ' to patch brocade with wistaria
cloth';[1] *I have composed verses in response to yours, which is,*
as it were, mingling pearls with pebbles.[2] *And as my*
nature makes me incapable of keeping them to myself, I send
them to you for you to laugh at. They are as follows:

OBEDIENT to our Sovereign's command,
 I, a man, travelled all the way
To rule distant Koshi;
But changing is the world of men,
I lie on a bed of illness,
My pain increasing with the days,
Now thinking of the saddest things,
Now haunted by cruel thoughts,
I am troubled with grief,
I am tortured with fears.
Yet, as the mountains rise between
And the way is stretching far,
I know no means to send a messenger,
Nor can I speed my heart-felt words,
And struggle as I may for my life,
I know not what to do.
So in my room I bewail,
And nothing eases my heart.
Now at the height of spring
I cannot break the flowering sprays
With my friends, to deck our heads;
I cannot hear the voices of the warblers[3]

---

[1] A euphemism signifying that to answer another's beautiful poems with clumsy
verses is like patching a piece of brocade with crude cloth woven of wistaria fibre.
[2] Practically the same as the above.
[3] i. e. *uguisu.* See note above.

Flitting through the thickets of the spring field;
Vainly have I passed the best of the month
When maidens come and go
Gathering the herbs of spring,
With their bright scarlet skirts
Wet with gentle rain.
Gladdened by your sympathy,
Sleepless all the night
And all the day, I long for you!

Envoys

If I could share but a glimpse with you
Of those mountain cherry-blossoms,
Should I thus pine for you?

You may listen to the warblers
Flitting through the thickets of yellow roses;
How I envy you!

With no strength to stir abroad
And confined within,
Hardly am I myself
When I think of you!

451-5   *Love poems.*[1]   [XVII : 3978-82]

MY wife and I are one in heart:
  However long we are side by side,
She is charming all the more;
Though face to face we sit,
She, my cherished love,
Is ever fresh as a new flower,
Never annoying, nor vexing.
I, obedient to our Sovereign's word,
To rule the frontiers far-off as the skies,

---

[1] Composed in a paroxysm of love for his wife, which seized him on the evening of the 20th of the 3rd month (in 747).—Original Note.

Crossed the mountains and the plains,
Parting from my wife.[1]
Since then the year has changed,
The spring flowers have fallen,
Yet never have I seen her.
So, forlorn and comfortless,
I sleep with my sleeves turned back;
And I meet her each night in my dream,
But as I cannot waking see her,
My longing grows a thousandfold.
Were I near enough, I would go
Even for a day's visit,
Lying in each other's arms;
But the way is all too far
And the barrier[2] stands between.
Though that is so, yet I may hope—
Would that the month[3] might quickly come
When the cuckoo cries!
And I might seek the Ōmi road,
And set sail upon the lake,[4]
Gazing far upon the hills
Dotted with *unohana* bloom.[5]
And there in Nara, at my home—
While, like the 'night-thrush,' she grieves,
Forlorn in her heart,
Asking the evening oracle at the gate,
And in sleep awaiting me—
I would hasten to my wife again.

[1] Yakamochi set out for his new post in the 7th month of the 18th year of Tempyō.

[2] On the way from Etchū to Nara there was the barrier of Arachi.

[3] Yakamochi went up to the capital with the reports on the state taxes in the 5th month of this year. This phrase presumably refers to his anticipated journey to Nara.

[4] i. e. Lake Biwa, which travellers from northern Japan used to cross on their way to Nara.

[5] i. e. *Deutzia crenata*; a bush plant, with graceful white flowers that bloom in May.

Though a year has passed
I have not seen her,
And my heart is heavy
With thoughts of my love.

Vainly I meet her in my dream,
But, waking, cannot see her face to face,
My longing but increases.

Though she is far away
Beyond the hills I crossed,
My thoughts reaching out to her,
Bring her to me in dream.

Though the spring flowers are gone,
I have not seen my love;
And she must wait for me,
Counting the days and months.

456–8　　　*In praise of Mount Futagami.*[1]　　[XVII : 3985–7]

MOUNT Futagami,[2] round which flow
　　The waters of Imizu,[3]
When I come out and gaze upon it
In the rich and blossomed spring,
Or in the glorious leaf of autumn—
How sublime it soars
Because of its divinity,[4]
And how beautiful it stands,

---

[1] Composed on the spur of the moment on the 30th of the 3rd month (in 747).
—Original Note.

[2] Situated in Imizu District, in the province of Etchū in Toyama Prefecture, to the north-west of the then provincial capital, the present town of Fushiki.

[3] The river of Imizu rises in the province of Hida, south of Etchū, and runs to the north through the Etchū plain, skirting Mount Futagami at the north-eastern base.

[4] A mountain or a peak was believed to be a god.

With its shapely peaks![1]

Ceaselessly as the white waves break
At morning calm,
And increasing as the flood-tide swells
At evening lull,
About the rocky cape of Shibutani,[2]
The godlike skirting ridge,
All who gaze upon it
Give admiration to this mountain
From old times to this day!

Envoys

Continuously as break the waves
About the rocky cape of Shibutani,
My thoughts turn to the days of old.

The time has come now
When I long to listen
To the wistful voices of the birds[3]
On Mount Futagami.

459–60   *On the sorrow of separation when his*   [XVII : 4006–7]
departure[4] for the capital drew near.

UNCHANGING as the *tsuga*-trees,[5]
    That divinely grow,
Green in bole and branch,[6]
On Mount Futagami,
You are dear and fresh to me;
We meet and talk each morning,
With evening, hand in hand,

[1] Mount Futagami has twin peaks.
[2] The mountain runs up towards the north, thus forming the cape of Shibutani.
[3] Probably cuckoos.
[4] i. e. as revenue-officer.
[5] Same as the *toga*-tree (see note to No. 291).
[6] ' The bole and branch of the *tsuga*-tree ' alludes to the descent of Yakamochi and Ikenushi from the same stock, the Ōtomo family.

Walk out to the clear valley
Of Imizu's stream,
And there look on the waters;
Then, in the fresh wind from the east,
The river-mouth is white with waves,
Water-fowls are noisy on the bar,
Calling to their mates,
And the inlet sounds with the oars
Plied by the fishermen cutting reeds.
Gladdened by the sight,
We are at the height of pleasure,
But, at our Sovereign's word,
—Since he rules this land—
I must depart.
It is well for you, left behind,
But I must journey far away,
Treading the rocky paths
Over the cloud-wreathed mountains;
Many will be the days
When I shall long for you;
To think of it pains my heart.
O that you were beads,
Strung on the cuckoo's call!
Then I would wear you on my arm,
Gazing on you morning and evening;
With sorrow now I leave you!

Envoy

O that you were beads, my friend,
Which I would string
With the cuckoo's call,
And wear upon my arm!

THIS is our Sovereign's distant court;
    It is a land far away as are the skies,
Known as snowy Koshi;
Lofty are the mountains
And large the rivers;
Wide are the plains
And rich the grasses.
At midsummer when the *ayu*[1] abound,
The cormorant-fishers[2] labour up,
Carrying fishing-torches
Everywhere over the purling shallows.
When autumn comes with dew and frost,
Flocks of birds gather in the brakes,
Then I, together with my noble friends,
Would bring my arrow-tailed Great Black,
With his silver-coated bells,
Choosing him from many hawks.
I put five hundred birds to flight
In my morning chase;
In the evening hunt, a thousand.
Never did he miss the bird he followed,
And in his coming and going
He was matchless.
While thus I passed the days,
Smiling in my heart
And proud of my peerless hawk,
That dullard of an old servant of mine
Went hawking, without my leave,
Telling but his name,
When the sky was clouded
And the rain was falling!
Returning he said, coughing as he spoke,

---

[1] The *ayu* swim up-stream in shoals early in summer.
[2] Cormorants are used in fishing in the river.

'He left Mishima Field behind him
Soared over Mount Futagami,
And flew into the clouds.'
Unable to reach my hawk,
I was at a loss what to do;
Fire burned within my heart.
My sighs and longing knew no end;
I set watchmen, I spread nets
On this side and the other of the hill,
That, with luck, I might regain him.
At the shrine of the gods
I offered twill bands and a shining mirror,
And prayed and prayed, and waited.
Then, in dream, a girl said to me:
'That beautiful hawk which you miss
Was benighted flying over the beach at Matsudaé,[1]
He crossed Himi's creek where they fish for sprats,
And wandered about the isle of Tako;
I saw him the day before yesterday
At Furué where the mallards flock,
Yesterday I saw him there again.
In two days at soonest,
At latest within seven days,
He will come again to you.
Put away your sighs.'—
Thus she spoke in my dream.

Envoys

Perching on my hand that arrow-tailed hawk,
I have not hawked on Mishima
For many a day—a month.

On Futagami I spread nets
On this side and on that,
Then a maid told me of that hawk in dream
That I await impatiently!

---

[1] Lies between Cape Shibutani and Himi, west of the town of Fushiki.

A dullard he was, that old Yamada![1]
He searched for him that day
And could not bring him back.

Heart-sick still,
I long for him helplessly,
As suggests the name of the hill of Suga.[2]

In the village of Furué, Imizu District, a hawk was caught.
It was perfect in form and matchless in ferocity. Yamada
Kimimaro, the hawker, lacked proper care in training it, and
used it out of season. It soared up and flew away and could
by no means be brought back. With nets spread out it was
watched for, many prayers were made, with offerings, and
I trusted to chance. A girl appeared in a dream and said :—
' Good Sir, do not be distressed, nor let your heart so pine !
The stray hawk will be caught before long.' I awoke and
joy revived in me. Therefore in response to the dream I com-
posed a poem to put away my sorrows.

466   *Gazing on the moon while staying in the bay*   [XVII : 4029]
of Nagahama during his voyage from
Suzu to Ōnu.

STARTING in the morning from the sea of Suzu,
I have sailed along
To see, above the bay of Nagahama,
The shining moon.

The above is one of the poems which he composed[3] at various
places on his tour of inspection for the spring distribution of
seed rice.[4]

---

[1] i. e. Yamada Kimimaro.
[2] ' The hill of Suga ' is an introductory phrase to ' helplessly ' (=*suganaku*).
[3] In the 20th year of Tempyō (748).
[4] The authorities supplied the poor with seed rice, of which the amount borrowed
plus interest was paid back in kind after harvest.

On the ninth day of the fifth month of the first year of Tem-
pyō-Kampō (749) the officials banqueted together at the res-
idence of Hata Iwataké, on which occasion the host made
three garlands of lilies, placed them on a stand one over
another, and presented them to the guests, each of whom com-
posed a poem on the garlands.

467   How winsome are the lilies of my   [XVIII : 4086]
            garland,
        Seen in the blaze of the burning cressets !

468-71   *Congratulatory poem and envoys on the* [XVIII : 4094-7]
              issuance of the Imperial Rescript[1]
                regarding the production of
                    gold in Michinoku.[2]

Succeeding to the Celestial Throne
    Of the Imperial Ancestor divine,[3]
Who came down from heaven to rule
The Rice-abounding Land of Reed Plains,
A long line of Emperors has reigned
From age to age over these provinces,
Which with their deep mountains and wide rivers
Yield countless tribute and inexhaustible treasures.
However, our great Lord and Sovereign,
On convoking the people and inaugurating
His auspicious work,[4] was sorely troubled
For fear lest there should not be gold enough.
It was then reported to the Throne

---

[1] The Emperor Shōmu, at the time of building the great bronze statue of Buddha Lochana (the Daibutsu of Nara), was temporarily embarrassed because of an insufficient supply of gold. In 749 the metal was presented to the court for the first time from Michinoku. The Emperor, greatly pleased therewith, issued a rescript in the 4th month of that year, granting honours and gifts to officials and members of their families, and also bounties to the people.

[2] An ancient province which roughly covered the present north-eastern prefectures of the Main Island. Translated ' Road's End ' in l. 15.

[3] i. e. Ninigi-no-Mikoto.

[4] The construction of the Great Buddha.

That gold had been found in the Eastland[1]—
In the hills of Oda[2] of 'Road's End'—
Setting the mind of our Sovereign at rest.
'The gods of heaven and earth,' thought he—
Himself a god—'have approved
My enterprise, and the spirits of my ancestors
Have given aid that such a marvel
As might have been in the ancient days
Should be revealed under my reign,
Auguring prosperity for my realm.'
So now he exhorts his vassals of many clans
To loyalty and devotion,
Extending at the same time his benevolence
To the old and to women and children
Till their hearts' desires are satisfied.[3]

This overcomes me with awe and joy.
I ponder more deeply than ever
How to the Ōtomo clan belongs a great office
In which served our far-off divine ancestor[4]
Who bore the title of Ōkumé-nushi.
We are the sons of the fathers who sang,
　'At sea be my body water-soaked,
　On land be it with grass overgrown,
　Let me die by the side of my Sovereign!
　Never will I look back;'
And who to this day from olden times
Have kept their warrior's name for ever clean.
Verily Ōtomo and Saheki[5] are the clans
Pledged to the maxim, as pronounced
By their ancestors: 'Extinguish not, sons,
The name of your fathers! Serve your Sovereign!'

1 i. e. the territory comprising the eastern part of the Main Island.
2 An ancient district, now part of Tōda District, Miyagi Prefecture.
3 Alludes to the grant of gifts and honours.
4 i. e. Amé-no-Oshihi-no-Mikoto, who led as vanguard the troops of Kumebe when Ninigi-no-Mikoto first descended to the earth.
5 A branch of the Ōtomo family. The two clans served as hereditary guards of the Imperial Palace.

O let us grip birchwood bows in our hands,
Wear on our loins double-edged swords,
And stand guard morning and evening!
There are no men but we to defend the imperial
    gate—
I exclaim with a fervent heart
When I hear His Majesty's gracious words,
That overwhelm me with awe.

Envoys

I feel within me a warrior's heart
When I hear my Sovereign's gracious words
That overcome me with awe.

Set a mark plainly over the grave
Of Ōtomo's far-off divine ancestor
To make it known to the world!

Among the hills of Michinoku in the Eastland
Gold has bloomed forth—an augury
That His Imperial Majesty's reign shall prosper.

472–6   *Wishing for pearls to send to his home* [XVIII : 4101–5]
                 in the capital.

OF those abalone pearls
    That Suzu's fisher-maids dive for,
Crossing over, I hear,
To the holy isle of the sea,
Would I had many—even five hundred!
To my dear loving wife,
Who ever since we parted sleeves,
Must be sighing after me,
Counting the weary days and months
Passing the nights in a half-empty bed,
And forbearing to comb her morning hair—
To her I'd pack and send them,

Saying: ' Just to comfort you, darling,
Make a garland of these pearls,
Threading them together with orange-blossoms
And the sweet flag flowers of June,
When the cuckoo comes to sing ! '

Envoys

How I wish to send home to my love
A package of those lucent pearls,
That she might string them together
With orange-blossoms and sweet flag flowers !

O for the abalone pearls
They dive for, I hear,
Crossing over to the holy isle of the sea !
I would pack and send them home.

O for the lucent pearls
From the holy isle of the sea,
That I might send them to my love
To comfort her heart !

How happy should I be,
Were there a fisher-maid to give me
Those shining pearls by the hundred,
Scooping them up in her hands !

*477–80   Admonition¹ to Owari Okuhi, a shishō² [XVIII : 4106–9]
of Etchū Province.*

*Under the Seven Causes³ permitting Divorce the law says :
For any one of these causes the husband may divorce his*

---

¹ Composed on the 15th of the 5th month (in 749).—Original Note.

² Official of the lowest rank in a provincial office.

³ The Seven Causes were : 1, childlessness ; 2, adultery ; 3, disobedience to the
husband's parents ; 4, loquacity ; 5, theft ; 6, jealousy ; 7, foul disease.   The
old marriage code permitted the husband to divorce his wife for any one of these
causes.

wife. But he, who in the absence of any of the Seven Causes wantonly casts his wife away, shall be liable to penal servitude for one year and a half.

Under the Three Cases[1] prohibiting Divorce it says:

In these cases the wife may not be divorced even if guilty of the offences under the Seven Causes.

A violation of this provision is punishable by one hundred strokes. Only in the case of adultery, or foul disease, may she be cast away.

Under Bigamy the law says:

A man who, having a wife, marries another woman, shall be liable to penal servitude for one year. The woman shall after one hundred strokes be separated from him.

The Imperial Rescript says:

Righteous husbands and faithful wives shall be accorded benevolence and bounties.

In my humble opinion the things cited above constitute the foundation of law and source of morality. Thus, the way of a righteous husband lies in constancy of heart. Man and wife live under one roof and share a common property. How can it be allowed that a husband should forget the old bond of love and form a new one? I have therefore indited the following short poem in order to make you repent of having forsaken your old ties.

SINCE the time of the gods
    Of Ōnamuchi[2] and Sukunahikona[3]
It has been said from age to age:
'To see one's parents is to revere them,
To see one's wife and children is to love them:
This is the law of the world of man.'

---

[1] The Three Cases were: 1, when the wife had observed the mourning period of three years for her parents-in-law; 2, when the husband had risen to a high rank after having married in a humble station; 3, when the wife had no near relative.

[2] The deity who ruled over Izumo, and who offered his land to Ninigi-no-Mikoto upon the latter's descent from heaven.

[3] The deity who assisted Ōnamuchi in governing the land of Izumo.

And so has it been told unto these days.
You who are a man of this world—
Have you not declared—did you not sighing say
In that full-flowering time of the *chisa*-trees,[1]
While talking with your dear wife,
Morning and evening, 'mid smiles and tears :
' It will not be thus for ever.
The gods of heaven and earth helping us,
Some day we may prosper like spring flowers.' ?
.Now that prosperity has come which you longed
   for,[2]
Your wife far away[3] is waiting
In sorrow and in solitude,
Wondering when you will send for her.
Yet to that Saburu[4] girl, who drifts
With no place to settle in like the foam
That floats on the swelling stream of the Imizu[5]
When the south wind blows and melts the snow,
You cling inseparably like tangled twine.
Paired with her like the grebes,
You plunge into the depths of folly
Deep as the gulf of Nago,[6] hopeless man !

Envoys

How deeply your wife must feel,
Who in the distant city of Nara
Is waiting—is it not so ?—
Waiting on tiptoe for your messenger !

The townsfolk watch you from behind
When you go to the Government Hall—

[1] A tall tree now called *chisha-no-ki* (*Ehretia thyrsiflora*), found principally in southern Japan. Its small white flowers appear in July and August.
[2] The line refers to the appointment of Okuhi to the office of *shishō*.
[3] The wife was living in Nara.
[4] The name of a wandering woman of pleasure.
[5] A river flowing by the provincial capital.
[6] Part of Etchū Bay lying to the east of Fushiki, which was then the capital of the province.

What a shameless figure of a man
Infatuated with the Saburu girl!

Pink fades so quickly.
Better far, beyond comparison,
Are the long-accustomed clothes
Dyed in the grey of *tsurubami*.[1]

481   *On the arrival of the wife, who came by herself* [XVIII : 4110]
without waiting for a messenger
from her husband.[2]

AT the house where the Saburu girl
    Worships her lover,
There has arrived a post-horse without bells,[3]
Upsetting the whole town.

482–3   *On the tachibana-tree.*[4]   [XVIII : 4111–2]

IN the glorious age of the Emperor, a god
    Awesome beyond speech,
Tajimamori went to the Land of Eternity[5]
And brought back saplings thence, eight in number,
Of the tree of 'Timeless Fragrant Fruit,'[6]
Which were graciously bequeathed[7] to the nation.
Our land is now full of the trees
Which grow everywhere in profusion,

---

[1] A kind of oak (*Quercus acutissima*).   The dye was obtained from the acorns.
[2] Composed on the 17th of the 5th month (in 749).—Original Note.
[3] Government post-horses had bells.   The horse without bells indicated that the wife came privately on her own account.
[4] Composed on the 23rd of the 5th month intercalary (in 749).—Original Note.
[5] In the reign of the Emperor Suijin (29B.C.–A.D.70) Tajimamori was despatched to Tokoyo to obtain *tachibana*-trees.   Tokoyo is a land inhabited by superhuman beings.
[6] The old name for *tachibana*, a variety of citrus bearing small fruit.
[7] So described because the tree was imported by imperial order.

Spreading their young shoots in spring.
In the *Satsuki* month when the cuckoo sings
We may pluck the first flowers with the branches,
To give to young girls as presents,
Or pick them to carry in our sleeves,
Or leave them to dry for their perfume.
The fallen fruits[1] may be strung like beads
And wound about the arm for endless admiration.
When autumn approaches with its cold showers,
The mountain tree-tops turn red and soon go bare,
But the *tachibana* fruits glow and gleam upon the
     tree,
The more alluring to look upon.
And when at last the snowy winter arrives,
Their foliage, though frost-laden, does not wither
But thrives lustily, green as ever.
Well has it been called, this *tachibana*,
Since the age of the God-Emperor[2]
' The Timeless Fragrant Fruit.'

Envoy

The *tachibana* I have seen
In flower and in fruit ;
Still I would see the tree
All the seasons round.

484–6   *Looking at the flowers in the garden.*[3]   [XVIII : 4113–5]

Since by the imperial order to serve
    At my Sovereign's distant court
I came to Koshi, the land of snow,
For five long years[4] I have not laid

---

[1] The tree sheds a large number of small unripe fruits in May, the *Satsuki* month.
[2] The Emperor Suijin.
[3] Composed on the 23rd of the 5th month intercalary (in 749).—Original Note.
[4] A poetic exaggeration. Actually three years.

My head on your dainty arm,
But have slept in my clothes
With my girdle about me.
To console my sad weary heart
I have sown in the garden the fringed pink
And transplanted the lilies[1]
Plucked from the summer plain.
Ah, but for the comforting thought they awaken
Every time I go out to see them in bloom—
The pink that so resembles you, my dear,
And the lily which spells 'afterwards'—
The thought that afterwards I shall see you again,
How could I ever live a single day
In this far provincial town?

Envoys

Every time I see the pink flower
I remember, dear girl,
The beauty of your radiant smile.

But for the hope of seeing you
'Afterwards,' as tells the lily,
How could I live through this one day to-day?

Owing to a drought of some severity that had set in begin-
ning with the sixth day of the fifth month intercalary of the
first year of Tempyō-Kampō (749), the crops began to show
signs of wilting. Suddenly, on the first day of the sixth month,
a rain cloud was sighted. Thereupon the writer composed
the following poem.

487-8 BY all the routes under heaven,   [XVII : 4122-3]
       And from all places in the imperial domain—
       From the land's end where horse's hooves can reach,

---

[1] The Japanese words meaning ' lily ' and ' afterwards ' are both pronounced
yuri. The word-play in the original verse can be only suggested in translation.

And the farthest waters where ship's prow may
  rest—
Myriads of tributes are rendered,
And, as the greatest of them all, men have grown
The rice from ancient times to these.

Now, because no rain has fallen for days on days,
The crops planted in the lowland fields
And those sown in the upland fields
Begin to wilt and wither away
More and more with each morning.
My heart aches at seeing it;
And with my eyes turned upwards,
I long and wait for heaven's water
Eagerly like an infant craving milk—
When lo! from yonder mountain hollow
There appears a drift of grey cloud.
May it spread ever oceanwards,
Even to the Sea God's palace,
Darken all the heavens, and give us rain!

Envoy

May the cloud seen yonder spread,
Darken the skies, and send down rain
To our hearts' satisfaction![1]

489   *Congratulatory poem on a fall of rain.*   [XVIII : 4124]

THE long-wished-for rain has fallen.
    So then, without our lifting of words
The rice-crop will flourish.

[1] These two poems were composed on the evening of the 1st of the 6th month
(in 749).—Original Note.

490–1   Seeing the blossoms of the peach and [XIX : 4139–40]
         damson trees in the garden in spring,
          on the evening of the first day of the
             third month of the second year
                  of Tempyō-Shōhō (750).

IN the garden of spring
   The peach-blossoms rosily glow,
And on the flower-lit path beneath
Lo ! a maiden walking !

Are these the blossoms fallen
From the damsons of my garden ?
Or patches of the snow
That fell within my garden-walls ?

492   Hearing the song of a boatman rowing up the [XIX : 4150]
             river, on the second day.[1]

IN my morning bed I listen—
   Afar on Imizu's stream[2]
Sings a boatman,
Plying his morning oars.

493   *At a banquet in his mansion, on*   [XIX : 4153]
                      the third day.

TO-DAY, when people in China,[3] it is said,
   Float their rafts[4] for pleasure,

---

  [1] Composed in the same month as the above.
  [2] The mansion of Yakamochi, Governor of Etchū, probably stood on the
hill near the river of Imizu.
  [3] On the 3rd of the 3rd month the Chinese made it a custom to purify
themselves in the stream, and to make merry, drinking saké and floating the cups
on the water. The ancient Japanese followed this custom, from which the Dolls'
Festival of later days was evolved.
  [4] Some scholars interpret this word as ' boats.'

Make merry, my friends,
With flower-wreaths upon your brows.

494–5   *On his great white hawk, on*   [XIX : 4154–5]
                     the eighth day.

OVER the hills and mountains I came,
    And have lived through many a changing year
Here in this land of Koshi.
Believing as I do in my mind,
That in the realm where rules our Sovereign,
City and country are the same,
My heart is heavy with sorrows,
So seldom do I see my friends
To talk my cares away.

And, for solace, when autumn comes,
Giving rein to my horse I will go
To the fields of Iwasé,[1]
Blooming with bush-clovers,
Near and far set wild fowl up in flight,
And let my hawk pursue them,
Its silver bells[2] tinkling.
Watching it far in the sky
My burdened heart will be eased.
Glad at such a thought,
I make a place in my bed-chamber,
And there keep this white and mottled hawk.

Envoy

Keeping in my chamber
My arrow-tailed white hawk,
I pat and stroke its back—
O the pleasure of it !

---

[1] Situated probably to the east of the city of Takaoka.
[2] Bells, presumably coated with silver, were tied to hunting hawks.

WHEN, at our Sovereign's command,[2]
     I started on my travels
To rule the province far-off as the skies,
My brother followed me across the hills of Nara
As far as Izumi's[3] shining bed;
There we stayed our horses,
And in parting, said I:
'In safety I shall go and come back home,
Be happy, pray to the gods and wait.'
Ever since, I have sorely missed him,
With the road stretching far
And rivers and mountains between us;
While thus eager for a sight of him,
A courier came—how gladly I received him!
I asked!—With what strange, wild words he an-
     swered me!
My dearest brother—of all times of the year,
In autumn when the waving *susuki* blooms,
At his home where blow the bush-clovers,[4]
Neither walking in his court at morn,
Nor treading the ground at eve,
He passed through the village of his native Saho,[5]
And rose into white clouds[6] trailing
Over the tree-tops of the hill:
So the courier said.

---

[1] Composed on the 25th of the 9th month of the 18th year of Tempyō (746).
—Original Note.

[2] i. e. his appointment to the Governor of Etchū.

[3] i. e. a river in Yamashiro, the upper reach of the present Kizu.

[4] He had a great liking for flowering plants, which he had planted in profusion in front of his presence-chamber.—Original Note.

[5] The north-eastern part of the capital of Nara, where the Ōtomo families had their mansions.

[6] He was cremated on the hill of Saho.—Original Note.

Although I wished him health,
He rose into white-trailing clouds,
How sad I am to hear!

Had I known him destined thus,
I had shown him the breakers on the jutting rocks
Of the sea of Koshi!

499-501   *On the uncertainty of life.*   [XIX : 4160-2]

SINCE the far beginning of heaven and earth
    It has been said from mouth to mouth
That life is uncertain;
When we look up to the plains of heaven
The bright moon waxes and wanes;
On the tree-tops of the mountains,
Flowers bloom with spring,
In autumn, with dew and frost,
The coloured leaves are scattered in the blast.
So is it with the life of a man:
The rosy colour fades from the cheek,
The black hair turns white,
The morning smile is nowhere found at eve.
Looking at our life's changes,
Unseen as the passing wind,
Ceaseless as the flowing water,
I cannot stop my tears streaming
Like floods on the rain-beaten ground.

Envoys

Even the dumb trees flower in spring,
And with autumn shed their yellow leaves,
Because of this world,
So changeable.

When I see this changing life,
Many are my weary days
And less and less I cling
To human things!

502-3   *A wish to make a name as a warrior.*[1]   [xix : 4164-5]

A<small>M</small> I the son my father and mother cherish
     With common love and care?
Can it be well that I, a man,
Live but an idle life?
Lifting up the bow-end,
Shooting arrows a thousand fathoms far,
Bearing my sword by my side,
Scaling the many-peaked mountains—
Betraying not our Sovereign's trust—
I ought to win a name
To echo from age to age!

Envoy

A worthy man should win such fame
That those who hear it told in after years
May echo it again.

504-6[2]   *On the cuckoo and the flowers of*   [xix : 4166-8]
                the seasons.[2]

A<small>S</small> the seasons change,
     Ever new are the flowers which bloom
On plants and trees past number,
And various are the songs of birds.
When I hear their altered notes
And see those changes,

---

[1] Composed to match the poem of Yamanoé Okura (No. 641).—Original Note.
[2] Composed on the 20th, on the spur of the moment, although it was before the season of the cuckoo.—Original Note.

With sighs my heart is bowed;
And while I long to hear the cuckoo,
Then, with the fourth month,
When all's in heavy leaf,
The cuckoo calls ere dawn.
Is he truly an offspring of the *uguisu*,[1]
As has been said since days of old?
Until the time when maidens wreathe their garlands
With flags and orange-flowers,
He flies across the eightfold hills
All the livelong day,
And we see him darting to and fro against the moon
Through the night till dawn,
His voice starting echo after echo,
How can I ever weary of his song!

Envoys

As the seasons change
Ever new are the flowers that bloom,
Whether in our hands or not,
To our eyes a constant joy.

Though every year the cuckoo comes and cries,
Still my heart rejoices at his song,
For many are the weary days
When I see him not.

507–8   *On being asked by his wife*[2] *for a poem* [xix : 4169–70]
*which she could send to her mother
at the capital.*

LIKE the orange-flowers that blow
    With the fifth month when the cuckoo calls,

---

[1] The cuckoo lays its eggs in the nest of the *uguisu*, and the latter hatches and rears them as its own.

[2] Yakamochi's wife, Lady Ōtomo of Sakanoé's Elder Daughter, was probably in the province of Etchū with her husband.

Your voice is sweet to me, O mother.
But as many are the lonely days
I have lived in the country distant as the skies,
Where morning and evening I hear you not,
And as I look far towards the clouds
Arising from between the mountains,
I do not cease from grieving,
Nor do I cease from thoughts of you.
So, until I see your loving face
That I long to look upon,
Like the pearls the fisher-maids
Dive for in Nago Bay,[1]
Flourish, my noble mother,
Like the pines and junipers.

Envoy

So long have I not seen you
Whom I long to see like the white pearls:
I scarcely feel alive,
Remaining in this distant land.

509   *Viewing the wistaria at Tako[2] where he landed,* [XIX : 4199]
after boating on the lake of Fusé[3] on the
twelfth day.

CLEAR is the bottom of the lake,
    That mirrors the wistaria bloom;
And there in those sunken pebbles
I see countless gems.

[1] Probably situated to the east of the provincial office.
[2] Perhaps Tago in Miyata Village.
[3] Situated to the north of Mount Futagami, where, however, we now find nothing
but fields.

510   *Gazing up at the moon on the shore while*   [XIX : 4206]
             he journeyed home.

UPON this shore which I follow to Shibutani,
     Fully would I enjoy the moonlight;
Stay my horse a while.

511–2   *Composed[1] after older poems on the tomb*   [XIX : 4211–2]
              of the Maiden Unai.[2]

TOLD from age to age,
     It is a tale of long ago,
Wonderful as sad to hear,
That the young men, Chinu and Unai,
With their lives at stake
For the sake of their dear names,
Met in deadly strife
For the love of the Maiden Unai.
Then at the very bloom of her life,
Beautiful as flowers of spring,
Bright as the autumn leaf,
In pity for her lovers' suits,
Bidding farewell to her parents,
And away from home, at the seashore,—
When life is precious, even for so short a space
As the joint of the seaweed swaying in the eightfold
     waves
That flood with morn and eve—
She died,[3] as vanish dew and frost.

So, here her tomb was built,
And for those who hear the story told,
That they may remember it for ever,
Her boxwood comb was planted

---

[1] Composed on the 6th of the 5th month of the 2nd year of Tempyō-Shōhō
(750).—Original Note.
[2] i. e. Takahashi Mushimaro's poems (Nos. 674–6).
[3] She plunged into the sea and was drowned.

Which struck root and grew,
Ever, as now, thus sideways leaning ![1]

Envoy

Her little boxwood comb, the maiden's memory,
Grows now as a tree,
Throwing shoot after shoot,
Ever sideways leaning.

513-5   *An elegy*   [XIX : 4214-6]

SINCE the beginning of heaven and earth,
   Men of eighty clans have been set in office
Under our Sovereign's sway.
So, obedient to his word,
I crossed the hills and rivers
To rule the distant land.
Though wind and cloud may come and go
As couriers of my heart,
Many are the days
Since I saw you face to face,
And I long and sigh for you.
Then a traveller brought me word :—
That lately you have been sad at heart,
And you pass your days in grief.
The world is full of pain and sorrow,
The blooming flowers fade with time,
Inconstant is the life of man.
So your loving mother, at her age,
In the ripeness of her womanhood,
Alluring to the eye like a mirror—
As fades the mist that rises
And breaks the fresh-formed dew—

---

[1] Hearing of her death, the young men killed themselves. Their graves were built, with that of the maiden in between them. The comb planted on her grave struck root and grew into a tree, its branches bending towards the grave of Chinu, whom she had loved.

Drooped, like the swaying seaweed,
And is gone as goes the stemless stream.
Was it to deceive me?
Was it a trick?
But since I have heard it told,
Though faint as the distant twanging
Of the nail-flipped bowstring,
Sadness fills my heart,
And I cannot check my streaming tears
Like floods on the rain-beaten ground.

Envoys

When I hear, though from far away,
That you are bowed in grief,
I can but weep aloud,
I, your bosom friend.

You who know so well
How fleeting is our human life,
Do not wear out your heart,
You, a brave warrior!

Yakamochi wrote the above verses on the twenty-seventh of the fifth month of the second year of Tempyō-Shōhō (750), when his son-in-law, the second son of Fujiwara Toyonari, lost his mother.

516-7   *Composed during his journey[1] to the*   [XIX : 4254-5]
*capital, there intended to be delivered
as a banquet recitation in compliance
with the imperial order.*

SINCE our ancestral gods
Surveyed the Land of Yamato,

---

[1] In the 7th month of the 3rd year of Tempyō-Shōhō (751), Yakamochi was appointed Councillor of State, and in the next month, he left Etchū for the capital.

As they rowed the rock-built boat,
Full-oared on stem and stern,
Through the clouds of heaven,
And, alighting, pacified the land,
All the successors to the Throne
Have ruled our land reign after reign ;
Now our great Sovereign, a goddess,
Our Lady, successor to the Celestial Throne,
Holds her sway under heaven,
Loves her courtiers of eighty clans,
And has established order, blessed her subjects
Everywhere within her realm.
So, good omens, one after another,
Unheard-of since of old,
Have been reported to the Throne.
Then the record of her peaceful rule,
Her arm-folded rule,
Shall be left for ever,
As long as last heaven and earth,
Sun and moon.
Lo ! our Sovereign, who rules in peace,
Looks at the autumn flowers,
Delights in each kind,
And pleasures in her royal feast ;
How glorious this day !

Envoy

Though many are the flowers in autumn,
She sees them and delights in each ;
How glorious this day !

LASTING as tell the *tsuga²*-trees,
 Green on many a mountain,
And endless as the pine-tree's roots,
Our Sovereign, our goddess—
That she may rule the land for ages
In the Imperial City of Nara—
This day holds a royal banquet,
Out of her godlike will;
And courtiers of eighty clans,
Their locks bedecked with *tachibana*,
Ripened in the garden,
And their ribands loosened,
Wish her a life of a thousand years,
And rejoice and revel in her presence;
At this I revere her all the more.

Envoy

Through a myriad ages
Of our Sovereign's sway,
She will thus take her pleasure
When comes the New Year in.

520   *At a banquet³ in the residence of Tachibana*   [XIX : 4272]
*Moroé, Minister of the Right, on the eighth
of the eleventh month of the fourth year
of Tempyō-Shōhō (752).⁴*

IS it because our mighty Sovereign stays,
 Her glory overflowing heaven and earth,
That joy lifts up this little village?

---

¹ In the 4th year of Tempyō-Shōhō (752).
² See note to No. 291.
³ The banquet was attended by the ex-Emperor (the Emperor Shōmu).
⁴ This poem had not yet been reported to the Throne.—Original Note.

Composed extempore, on the twenty-third [XIX : 4290–1]
of the second month of the fifth year
of Tempyō-Shōhō (753).

OVER the spring field trails the mist,
 And lonely is my heart;
Then in this fading light of evening
A warbler sings.

Through the little bamboo bush
Close to my chamber,
The wind blows faintly rustling
In this evening dusk.

523   *Composed on the twenty-fifth day.* [XIX : 4292]

IN the tranquil sun of spring
 A lark soars singing;
Sad is my burdened heart,
Thoughtful and alone.

In the languid rays of the spring sun, a lark is singing.
This mood of melancholy cannot be removed except by poetry:
hence I have composed this poem in order to dispel my gloom.

524-6 *Composed[1] at a later date to express his* [XX : 4331–3]
sympathy with a frontier-guard
leaving home.

OUR Sovereign's far-off court
 Is Tsukushi, the isle of unknown fires;[2]
It is the citadel defending

---

[1] On the 8th of the 2nd month of the 7th year of Tempyō-Shōhō (755).—Original Note.

[2] The surface of the sea off the coast of the province of Chikugo sometimes appears as though illuminated at night—a phenomenon which remains still unexplained. Hence, *shiranuhi* (unknown fires) is used as a pillow-word for Tsukushi, of which the province forms a part.

Her empire against the foreign enemy.
Therefore, though all the provinces she rules
Are full of men without number,
Those of the Eastland, as fierce fighters
Who, going forth to battle, never turn back,
Are for their valour rewarded;
To them the imperial word is given.—

Upon which you go, counting the weary days,
Away from the sight of your mother,
Away from your young wife's embrace.
From Port Naniwa of wind-blown reeds
Your stately ship, many-oared,
With her crew ranged in the morning calm
And with her oars bent against the evening tide,
Sails column-wise with others.

May you, ploughing your way through the waves,
Arrive safely in good time;
And in obedience to the imperial command
Serve with a manly heart,
Passing from garrison to garrison;[1]
And when your duty is done, may you return
In happiness and health!—
                    So she prays,
Putting the sacred wine-jar at her bedside.
Pining and waiting for you these long days,
She will sleep with her sleeves turned back,[2]
And her black hair spread out—
Your sweet young wife!

Envoys

When the soldier-husband went forth
Carrying a quiver on his shoulder,
How bitterly she must have wailed—

---

[1] The frontier-guards posted at one garrison were shifted to another at the end of each season.
[2] A form of magic to insure the safe return of an absent person.

His wife so loath to part!

How sad was the parting
Of the Eastlander from his wife—
He brooding on the long years
Of separation!

527-9   Expressing his humble thoughts.[1]   [xx : 4360-2]

ONCE in the long-gone age—
   So has it ever been told to this day—
An Emperor[2] ruled the under-heaven
From his court in the land of wave-bright Naniwa.
Here our august Sovereign,[3] a very goddess,
Of whom I dread to speak,
Deigns to dwell, now that in early spring
A thousand flowers have burst into bloom;
The mountains are wondrous fair to see
And clear run the rivers;
And all things prospering
Please the eye and gladden the heart.
O the imperial palace of Naniwa!
Hither from all the provinces of the realm
The tribute-bearing ships come—
A noisy throng like a flight of teal—
Piloted through the canal,
Bending their oars up-stream
In the calm of morning,
Or plying their poles down-stream
On the evening's flood-tide.
Out beyond the beach there are seen
The fishermen's boats, dotting the sea-plain
Amid the white waves breaking one upon another.

---

[1] Composed on the 13th of the 2nd month of the 7th year of Tempyō-Shōhō (755).
—Original Note.
[2] The Emperor Nintoku.
[3] The Empress Kōken.

They are fishing to provide for the august table.
O how spacious is the view!
How free and open!
Well was here established the imperial abode
From the age of the gods.

Envoys

The cherry-trees are in full bloom
Now, while at the palace by the sea
Of wave-bright Naniwa
Reigns our gracious Empress.

Here in Naniwa of wind-blown reeds
I feel I might forget my home
And pass years upon years,
Gazing on the spacious sea.

530-21 IN obedience to the imperial   [xx : 4398-400]
       command,
   Though sad is the parting from my wife,
   I summon up the courage of a man,
   And dressed for journey, take my leave.
   My mother strokes me gently;[2]
   My young wife clings to me, saying:
   'I will pray to the gods for your safe-keeping.
   Go unharmed and come back soon!'
   As she speaks, she wipes with her sleeves
   The tears that choke her.
   Hard as it is, I start on my way,
   Pausing and looking back time after time;
   Ever farther I travel from my home,
   Ever higher the mountains I climb and cross,
   Till at last I arrive at Naniwa of wind-blown reeds.
   Here I stop and wait for good weather,

[1] Composed on the 19th of the 2nd month of the 7th year of Tempyō-Shōhō(755).
—Original Note.
[2] Perhaps signified a prayer for the son's safety.

175

To launch the ship upon the evening tide,
To set the prow seawards,
And to row out in the calm of morning.
The spring mists rise round the isles,
And the cranes cry in a plaintive tone.
Then I think of my far-off home—
Sorely do I grieve that with my sobs
I shake the war-arrows I carry
Till they rattle in my ears.

Envoys

On an evening when the spring mists
Trail over the wide sea,
And sad is the voice of the cranes,
I think of my far-off home.

Thinking of home,
Sleepless I sit,
The cranes call amid the shore reeds,
Lost in the mists of spring.

533-7   *Parting sorrows of a frontier-guard.*   [xx : 4408–12]

At the bidding of my great Sovereign[1]
I set out as a defender of the isle.[2]

My mother picking up the hem of her skirt,
Stroked me with it[3] and caressed me.
My father said regretfully with tears streaming
Down his beard white as the *taku*[4] rope :
'My fawn, my only son—how sad
Your parting in the morning, dear child !

[1] i. e. the Empress Kōken.
[2] A frontier-guard, the ' isle ' being Kyūshū.
[3] The skirt of a woman's garment was believed to possess magic power. Hence, the custom that apparently existed of a woman stroking a person with her skirt in wishing him a safe journey. Cf. note to No. 238.
[4] Made from the bark of *kōzo*, i. e. paper-mulberry (*Broussonetia papyrifera*). Because such rope was white, the *taku* rope became a pillow-word for ' white.'

I shall miss you when I see you not
For such long years. Let me talk to you
If only for to-day.' He sighed and moaned.
My wife and children gathering about here and
    there,
Wailed like the birds of spring,
Their sleeves all wet with weeping.
They tugged me by the hand to retain me;
And loath to part, they followed after me.

But in dread obedience to the imperial command
I started out on the road,
Looking back many times from the corner of each
    hill.
Having left my dear ones far behind,
My mind knew no rest
While the pain of longing wrung my heart.
Mortal creature as I am,
How could I be sure of my life?
Until the time when I reach my post,
Sailing the fearful sea-path from island to island,
And after the round of service come back again,
May all be well with my parents!
May my wife in sound health wait for me!

Oh, tell my people at home
That thus to our Gods of Suminoé[1]
I prayed making offerings;
And that launching the ship at Port Naniwa,
Fitting her with many oars and ranging the crew,
I rowed out at daybreak!

Envoys

Oh, tell my parents
That I have set sail; and all is well
Because, I think, my folks are praying for me!

---

[1] Later known as Sumiyoshi, where there is still the shrine of Sumiyoshi, dedicated
from early times to patron gods of seafarers.

Though men say that the cloud
Travelling the sky is a messenger,
I know no means to send home my presents.

I have gathered sea-shells
To take home as presents,
Though ever higher the waves beat on the shore.

Though the ship stops at an island haven,
There is none by whom I may send word home—
So must I sail on, longing in vain!

538-40   *Admonition to his clansmen.*[1]   [xx : 4465-7]

IN the remote age of the gods
    When the Imperial Ancestor,[2] opening heaven's
        gate,
Descended upon the Peak of Takachiho,
It was the founder of our clan,
Who, gripping in his hand a wax-tree[3] bow
And grasping withal arrows for the deer hunt,
Made advance the brave troops
Of Ōkumé with quivers on their backs ;
Forced his way across mountains and rivers,
Trampling under foot rocks and stones ;
And who, seeking for a good habitable land,
Subdued the fierce gods
And pacified the unruly tribes—
Sweeping and cleansing thus the country,
He rendered a loyal service to his lord.

Thereafter, under the successive reigns
Of the sovereigns on the Celestial Throne,

---

[1] Composed on the occasion of the dismissal from office of Ōtomo Kojihi, Governor of Izumo, through false accusations made to the court by Ōmi Mifuné (in 756).—Original Note.
[2] i. e. Hikohohoninigi-no-Mikoto.
[3] i. e. *hazé* (*Rhus succedanea*).

178

Descended from that First Emperor[1]
Who, raising the stout-pillared Unebi Palace
Of Kashihara[2] in the land of Yamato,
Ruled the under-heaven,
Our forefathers served the Imperial House
With all their hearts faithful and true.

Ours is the ancestral office of the clan,
So proclaimed and bestowed upon us,
To be handed down from father to son,
Generation after generation—
Those who see will tell of it from mouth to mouth;
Those who hear will hold it up as a mirror.

So cherished and clean is the name of our clan.
Neglect it never, lest even a false word
Should destroy this proud name of our fathers,
You clansmen all, who bear the name of Ōtomo.

Envoys

Beware, you leaders of our clan
Which bears a most illustrious name
In this wide land of Yamato!

Polish it like a double-edged sword,
Make it ever bright—the name
Borne through ages, clean and without spot!

*541–2 Desiring to pursue the Way of Buddha[3] [xx : 4468–9]
while lying in his sick-bed and lament-
ing the transience of life.*

BRIEF is this mortal life—
   Let me go and seek the Way,

---

[1] The Emperor Jimmu.
[2] Now usually pronounced *Kashiwara*.
[3] Buddhism teaches that the Way of Buddha cannot be attained save for special and excellent causes. The pursuit of the Way in this life will, however, enable one to find it in the life to come.

Contemplating the hills and streams undefiled!

O let me seek the Pure Way,
Striving against the light of the heaven-coursing
sun,
That I may find it again in after-life!

543   *Wishing for a long life.*[1]   [xx : 4470]

I KNOW well this body of mine
   Is insubstantial as foam;[2]
Even so, how I wish
For a life of a thousand years!

544   *At the farewell banquet in honour of Onu* [xx : 4514]
Tamori, ambassador to Po-hai,[3] and others at
the residence of the Prime Minister[4] on the
tenth day of the second month of the second
year of Tempyō-Hōji (758).

THE wind and waves sinking low
   Over the blue plains of the sea,
Swift will be your ship
Without hindrance,
As you go and as you come home.

---

[1] Composed on the 17th of the 6th month in the 8th year of Tempyō-Shōhō (756).
—Original Note.
  [2] According to Buddhist philosophy, the human body is but a temporary union of the four elements, viz. earth, water, fire and wind.
  [3] Then a large independent state in North Manchuria.
  [4] Fujiwara Nakamaro.

545   *At the banquet on New Year's Day of the*   [XX : 4516]
           third year of Tempyō-Hōji (759).

EVEN as the snow falls to-day
   At the commencement of the New Year
And with the new-born spring,
Ever thick come, good things!

Lady Ki and Ōtomo Yakamochi

546-7 FOR your sake, O slave,   [VIII : 1460-1]
     I plucked with busy hands
These sedge-buds[1] from the spring meadow.
Eat them and grow fat!

The silk-tree[2] that blooms in daytime
And sleeps the love-sleep at night,
Your lady should not see alone—
Look on this well, my slave!—*By Lady Ki.*

548-9 WITH his lady your slave must be   [VIII : 1462-3]
     in love,
For however much he devours
The sedge-buds so graciously given,
He wastes and wastes.

The silk-tree, my lady's precious keepsake—
Is it not, alas, a tree
That brings forth only the flower,
And bears not fruit?—*By Ōtomo Yakamochi.*

---

[1] The budding ears of the sedge are often eaten.
[2] A mimosa-like tree (*Albizzia Julibrissin*) whose leaves fold up in the evening.
The flowers have long silky reddish stamens.

Ōtomo Yakamochi and Ōtomo Ikenushi

In praise of Mount Tachi.[1]   [XVII : 4000-2]

IN the land of Koshi
  Famous among the distant regions,
Many are the mountains
And countless rivers run,
But on Mount Tachi of Niikawa[2]
Because of its divinity,[3]
Snow lies throughout summer.[4]
Unlike the mists that form and lift
Each morning and evening
Over the limpid shallows
Of the engirdling Katakai,[5]
The mountain will not leave our memory.

Each year I will come
And gaze upon this mountain afar,
Then speak of it to those
Yet strangers to its beauty,
Spreading its fame to future years,
That all who hear but its name
May long to see it.

Envoys

The snows on Mount Tachi
Refresh me all through summer,
Thanks to its divinity!

---

[1] Composed on the 27th of the 4th month (of the 19th year of Tempyō, 747).
—Original Note. 'Mount Tachi stands in Niikawa District' (Original Note), in Etchū, i. e. in the south-eastern part of Toyama Prefecture, where it borders on Nagano Prefecture. Tateyama, as it is now called, has several peaks, the highest of which, the Male Peak, is 2,912 metres above sea level.
[2] A district in Etchū.
[3] It was believed that the mountain was a deity.
[4] Mount Tachi was covered with snow even in summer, which interested Yakamochi, who had seen no such mountain in Nara.
[5] It flows at the foot of Tateyama, pouring into the sea east of the town of Uozu.

Unfailing as the limpid water
On Katakai's shallows,
Will I come and gaze upon the mountain.

553-5   *Responding to Yakamochi's poems on*   [XVII : 4003-5]
                    Mount Tachi.[1]

LOFTY beyond the mountains,
    Bright in the rising sun,
Mount Tachi, a god standing,
As tells its sacred name,
Soars in majesty to heaven
Through thousandfold white clouds.

Crowned with snow it stands
Through summer and winter,
Ever since the days of old,
Rugged with its antique rocks,
Through ages numberless.

Mysterious, however I look upon it,
Steep are its peaks, deep its gorges,
The rapid waters wash the vales,
Whereover rise the mists each morning,
And at evening trail the clouds.

Then, grave as are the clouds,
Constant as never are the mists,
Clear as the sound of the rushing water,
Will I speak of it for ever,
Long as runs its river.

Envoys

The snows on Mount Tachi lie
Unmelted all through summer,
Thanks, indeed, to its divinity.

Unfailing as Katakai's waters

[1] Composed on the 28th of the 4th month (in 747).

That fall and rush along,
Will you who see the mountain
Come and gaze upon it.

Ōtomo Azumabito

556   *Composed during the Emperor's sojourn*   [VI : 1034]
                at Tagi in Mino Province.

Hᴇʀᴇ is the water by which—
     So men have told from ancient times—
The old are made young again :
This rushing stream deserving well
The name Tagi, the 'Rapids.'

Lady Ōtomo of Sakanoé's Elder Daughter

557   *To Ōtomo Yakamochi.*   [IV : 731]

Wʜᴀᴛ do I care if my name
     Be on the tongues
Of five hundred, or a thousand, men !
Only should your name get abroad
I would regret it and weep.

Ōtomo Yotsuna

558-9 Iɴ the Land where our Sovereign   [III : 329-30]
          rules
The Imperial City dwells
Most dearly in my heart.

The waving wistarias are in full bloom;
Do they not remind you, my lord,
Of the Imperial City of Nara?[1]

560   *Composed when bidding farewell at the post town* [IV : 571]
of Ashiki, Chikuzen, to Lord Ōtomo, Governor-
General of the Dazaifu, who was appointed
Grand Councillor of State and departed
for the capital.

BEAUTIFUL is the moon-lit night,
   And clear the voice of the river.
Here let all of us make merry—
You who go and we who remain!

Ōtomo Minaka

561–3   *On the suicide of his clerk, Hasetsukabé* [III : 443–5]
Tatsumaro, in the first year of Tempyō
(729), when he was chief controller of
the rice-fields[2] *in Settsu.*

EVER since the day he started,
   Telling his mother and father,
His wife and children,
That, as he was called a warrior
Of a far-off land where bend the clouds of heaven,
He would give himself to service
In or out of the Imperial Gates,
Thereby ensuring the ancestral fame,
Long as vines reach out.

---

[1] Nara abounded, as it still does, in wistarias. Probably addressed to Ōtomo
Tabito, Governor-General of the Dazaifu.

[2] Every man and woman of six years and upwards was allotted a certain tract of
land every six years. The affairs were transacted in the Home Provinces by officials
specially appointed for the purpose.

His loving mother would sit praying
To the gods of heaven and earth,
With the wine-jar before her,
With mulberry cloth in one hand
And fine silk in the other,
For his safety and well-being;
She waited, standing or sitting,
Wondering on which day, in which month and year,
That son, beauteous as the azalea,
Would come to her again
Back from the toil of travels,
As comes a black mallard through the waves,
But, while obedient to the Sovereign's word,
Night and morning he remained in wave-bright
   Naniwa,
Until the year had passed
Without leisure even to dry his sleeves,
How thought he of his life?
He left this dear and precious world
As vanishes a drop of dew,
Long enough before his time!

Envoys

Yesterday he lived here,
But unexpectedly
He hovers now in clouds
Above the sea-beach pines.

Sending no word to his loved wife
Who waits for his return,
He has left this world, alas!

Ōtomo Momoyo

564–5   *Love poems.*   [IV : 559–60]

I HAVE lived my life
    In peace and quiet—
Ah, that I should encounter
Now in my declining years
Love such as this!

When I shall have died of love—
What can avail me then?
I crave again to see you
While I live, dear lady.

Ōtomo Miyori

566   *On again meeting a lady.*   [IV : 650]

YOU seem to have lived, my lady,
    In the Land of Eternity.
You have grown younger
Than when so many years ago
I saw you last.

Yamabé Akahito

567–8   *On a distant view of Mount Fuji.*[1]   [III : 317–8]

EVER since heaven and earth were parted,[2]
    It has towered lofty, noble, divine,

---

[1] Mount Fuji towers over the provinces of Suruga and Kai.
[2] According to legend, heaven and earth gradually came to be separated out of chaos.

187

Mount Fuji in Suruga![1]

When we look up to the plains of heaven,
The light of the sky-traversing sun is shaded,
The gleam of the shining moon is not seen,
White clouds dare not cross it,
And for ever it snows.

We shall tell of it from mouth to mouth,
O the lofty mountain of Fuji!

Envoy

When going forth I look far from the shore of Tago,
How white and glittering is
The lofty Peak of Fuji,
Crowned with snows!

569-70   *At the hot springs[2] in Iyo.*   [III : 322-3]

THOUGH many were the hot springs
   Everywhere in the dominion
Ruled by the Sovereigns of the imperial line,
They loved the land of Iyo
For the beauty of its island-hills,
And standing on the hill of Isaniwa,
At the base of the steep mountains,
Meditated poems,
And mused upon the words.
Now when I look at the growth of trees
Above the hot springs,
The old firs are flourishing,
Succeeded by their offshoots,
And the twitter of the birds
Is not changed.

[1] Part of Shizuoka Prefecture.
[2] The spa of Dōgo of to-day. Visits were paid here, it is said, by the Emperor Keikō, the Emperor Chūai, Prince Shōtoku, the Emperor Jomei, and the Empress Saimei.

This will remain as venerable
Throughout endless ages,
This site of imperial visits.

Envoy

The gay courtiers set out to sea
At Nigitazu;
But how far away in time,
Who knows?

571-2 *Climbing the hill of Kami.*[1] [III : 324-5]

CONTINUOUSLY, as their name tells,—
  The *tsuga*-trees that grow in luxuriance
With five hundred boughs outbranching,
On Mount Kamunabi of Mimoro—
And as endlessly as the creeping vine,
I would visit these ruins
Of the Palace of Asuka.[2]
Here the hill[3] is high, the river long;
On a spring day the hill is sweetest,
The stream is limpid of an autumn night,
The cranes wing the morning clouds in flocks,
The frogs call in the evening mists;
Whenever I gaze upon them
I am bowed in tears,
Remembering the days of old.

Envoy

Like the mists that ever rise
Over Asuka's quiet pools,
My longing is such
As will not easily die.

[1] Identified by some as the hill of Ikazuchi (Thunder Hill), and by others as Mount Kannabi.
[2] Asuka was the site of the capital established by the Emperor Temmu.
[3] The hill is the hill of Kami and the river is the Asuka flowing at its base.

ON Mikasa, a peak of Mount Kasuga,
    Clouds hover every morning,
Kao-birds[1] are for ever crying.
Like the clouds my heart is wavering;
And like the endless calling of the birds,
I long for love requited;
Every moment of the day,
Every moment of the night,
Standing or sitting,
I pine with thoughts of love
For the girl who will not heed me.

Envoy

Like the birds that call and call again,
On the height of Mikasa,
I only cease from weeping
To fall into tears.

THOUGH they say her tomb is here,
    The tomb of Tekona at Mama
Of Katsushika,
Whom a man of old had courted,
Building a cottage for her sake,
There to talk with the maiden,
Unbinding their sashes of twill—
Nowhere can I see it;
Is it because of the leafy cypresses?
Or of the ancient pines
With roots out-reaching far?

---

[1] Not identified.
[2] The present town of Ichikawa, Katsushika District, Shimōsa Province.

Yet the story and her name will never
Leave my memory.

Envoys

I saw it; I will tell my friends
The place of Tekona's tomb
At Mama of Katsushika.

She would gather swaying seaweed
In the inlet of Mama of Katsushika;
Well do I imagine that Tekona!

*578–80   On the occasion of the Sovereign's[1] journey to   [VI : 917–9]
the province of Ki, in winter, on the fifth
day of the tenth month of the first year
of Jinki (724).*

FROM Saiga's plain, where we serve
     At the palace everlasting
Of our august Sovereign reigning in peace,
The island lies athwart in the sea.
White waves gambol along its clean shore
When the wind arises.
Men gather the dainty seaweed
When the tide is low—
So precious since the age of the gods,
This Tamatsu-shima, Island of Jewels!

Envoys

Shall I not miss the dainty seaweed
On the rugged island beach
When it is hidden under the flood-tide?

As the tide flows into Waka Bay,
The cranes, with the lagoons lost in flood,
Go crying towards the reedy shore.

[1] i. e. the Emperor Shōmu.

581-3 HERE in a beautiful dell where the   [vi : 923-5]
    river runs,
The Yoshinu Palace, the high abode
Of our Sovereign reigning in peace,
Stands engirdled, fold on fold,
By green mountain walls.
In spring the flowers bend the boughs;
With autumn's coming the mist rises and floats over
    all.

Ever prosperous like those mountains
And continuously as this river flows,
Will the lords and ladies of the court
Come hither.

Envoys

Oh, the voices of the birds
That sing so noisily in the tree-tops
Of the Kisa Mountain of Yoshinu,
Breaking the silence of the vale!

Now the jet-black night deepens;
And on the beautiful river beach,
Where grow the *hisagi*-trees,[1]
The sanderlings cry ceaselessly.

584-5 IN the Akitsu Dale of Yoshinu   [vi : 926-7]
    Our great Lord and Sovereign,
Placing game-trackers in the fields,
And posting bow-men upon the hills,
Rouses the beasts for the morning hunt,
Rouses the wild fowl for the evening chase;
So he hunts—he and his men
Riding their horses side by side
Over the lush dale of spring.

[1] i. e. *Mallotus japonicus.*

Lo! His Majesty's huntsmen
With hunting arrows under their arms—
I see them scattering far and wide
Over fields and over craggy hills.

586-7   OUR Sovereign has come to dwell   [VI : 933-4]
      At the Palace of wave-bright Naniwa,
Where he rules his realm
Eternally as endure the heaven and earth
And ever long as shine the sun and moon.
As a daily tribute from Awaji,
The Land of Imperial Purveyance,
Nujima's fisher-folk dive for abalone pearls
Deep to the bottom of the sea,
And gather many from amid the ocean rocks,
And carry them in boats rowed abreast,
So rendering service to His Majesty—
What a noble scene to watch!

In the calm of morning
The sound of oars is heard—
It must be the boats of Nujima's fisher-folk
From the Land of Imperial Purveyance.

588-91   THE Field of Ōmi in Inami Plain,   [VI : 938-41]
      Where our Sovereign, ruling in peace,
Has reared high a palace,
Befitting the god that he is,
Adjoins Fujii Bay, whose waters
Are thickly dotted with fishermen's boats
Angling for albacore, and whose shore
Is thronged by men burning salt-fires.
They may well fish on so fine a bay,

And burn salt-fires on so fine a beach.
It is well that oft His Majesty
Is pleased to come hither to view
This fair beach of white sands.

Envoys

The waves being still
On the far waters, and by the shore,
Boats are out to fish,
Swarming over Fujié[1] Bay.

Now that many are the nights
I have slept on Inami Plain,
Pressing down the scanty sedge
For a bed—how I long for home!

From to-morrow I shall travel
By the road of the tide-dry shore
Along the Straits of Akashi,
Smiling in my heart as I near my home.

Passing Karani Island.

Away from the sight of my dear wife
    I journey, sleeping without even a pillow;
And fitting with oars a birch-bark boat,
I come rowing on,
Past Nujima off the shore of Awaji.
From between the isles of Inamizuma
And Karani I look back homeward
Only to see the blue mountains,
But nowhere my house, which is lost
Beyond thousandfold white clouds.
Every time my ship skirts round a bay,

---

[1] Evidently to be identified with the bay in the preceding poem, of which the name is written 'Fujii.' It is not known which version is correct.

Every time an island point disappears from view,
And at each and every turn—
Ever thinking of home, I have come
Throughout the long and weary days of travel.

Envoys

O that I were a cormorant
Circling round Karani Island,
Where men cut dainty seaweed!
Then should I feel no such longing for home.

As we come rowing on
Under the island lee,
Lo! there goes a *Kumanu* ship—
How I envy it!—heading for Yamato.

When the wind began to blow,
For fear of a high sea
We made for Tsuta's narrow cove.
Now sheltered in the bay, our ship lies waiting.

596   *Composed during the Emperor's visit to the*   [VI : 1001]
Palace of Naniwa in the third month of
the sixth year of Tempyō (734).

THE men of the court go forth
   To join in the royal hunt,
While the maidens promenade,
Trailing their pink skirts,
Along the clean waterside.

597-8 *Composed by the imperial command during* [VI : 1005-6]
the Emperor's sojourn at the Palace of
Yoshinu, in summer, in the sixth month
of the eighth year of Tempyō (736).

HERE where stands the Palace of Yoshinu,
 Which our great Sovereign ruling in peace
Is pleased to behold,
High rise the mountains wreathed in clouds ;
Swift runs the river, its shallows singing clearly.
O hallowed peaks, how sublime to watch !
O fair stream, how refreshing to the eyes !
Not till these mountains crumble,
And this river run dry,
Shall the stately palace ever cease to be.

Envoy

Our Sovereigns from the age of the gods
Have often come to hold court
Here at the Palace of Yoshinu—
Because of the beauty of the mountains and river.

599   FORTH to the field of spring   [VIII : 1424]
 I went to gather violets—
Enamoured of the field
I slept there all night through.

600   IT snowed yesterday—   [VIII : 1427]
 And to-day it snows
On the meadow I have marked
For gathering spring herbs to-morrow.

Hanishi Mitōshi

601   *Composed at sea during his voyage from*   [IV : 557]
                       Tsukushi to the capital.

As we go fast, rowing the huge ship,
   Should she hit the rocks and overturn—
Oh, let her overturn! I shall not mind
Since it is for my dear wife's sake.

Ama-no-Inukai Okamaro

602   *In reply to an Imperial Rescript in the sixth*   [VI : 996]
                   year of Tempyō (734).

I, thy humble subject,
   Live not in vain, having seen
Both heaven and earth prosper
In this glorious age of thine.

Yamanoé Okura

603   *Thinking, while in China,[1] of his*   [I : 63]
                   homeland.

Come, my men, let us hasten to Yamato!
   The shore pines on Mitsu[2] of Ōtomo[3]
Must wait and long for us.

---

  [1] Okura was a member of the embassy to China, which left Japan in the 2nd year of Daihō (702) and returned home in the 1st year of Keiun (704).
  [2] An old name for the port of Ōsaka.
  [3] The general name for what is now Ōsaka and its vicinity.

I, Okura, will leave now;
  My children may be crying,
And that mother of theirs, too,
May be waiting for me!

605–10   *An elegy[1] on the death of his wife.[2]*   [V : 794–9]

To this land of Tsukushi,
  Our Sovereign's distant court,
She followed me, my wife,
As a crying child its mother.
But before she gained her breath,
Ere many months had flown,
She sickened and lay dead,
When least I feared.
Now I know not what to do or say,
Vainly I seek soothing words
From trees and stones.
Had she remained at home,
Her form would still exist;
What means my heartless wife,
Breaking the vows we made
Side by side like grebes,
To wander from her home?

Envoys

When back at home, what shall I do?
How desolate I shall find
Her vacant bower!

Poor beloved!

---

[1] Composed on the 21st of the 7th month of the 5th year of Jinki (728).—
Original Note.
[2] According to some commentators Okura wrote this poem on the death of
Ōtomo Tabito's wife.

Destined thus, she travelled far to me,
I cannot tell my grief!

How it fills me with regret!
Had I foreknown it, I would have shown her
All in this beautiful land!

The bead-tree's flowers my darling saw
Will be scattered
While my tears have not dried.

Over Mount Ōnu the fog is rising;
Driven by my sighs of grief,
The fog is rising.

611–2   *An expostulation to a straying mind.*   [V : 800–1]

*I know one who, although he respects his parents, neglects
his filial duties.   He cares for his wife and children no more
than for cast-off shoes.   He calls himself Master Eccentric.
His mind may soar higher than the blue sky, yet his body
remains clinging to the sordid earth.   He seems anything but
a sage of spiritual discipline and enlightenment.   He is such
a man, it seems, as seeks refuge in the mountains or in the
valleys.   Hence, for his serious reflection, I have composed a
poem, referring him to the three great principles[1] and inculcat-
ing the five virtues.[2]*

THE sight of our parents
     Inspires our hearts with reverence;
When we see our wives and children
How lovable they are!

---

[1] The three principles are :—the relations between sovereign and subject, parent
and child, husband and wife.   These constitute the fundamental principles of
morality.
[2] The five virtues are :—righteousness from the father, affection from the mother,
kindness from the elder brother, modesty from the younger brother, and filial piety
from the child.

It is the way of human life;
Fettered we are like the lime-caught bird;
We know not whither to flee.

Were you born of rock or tree,
You who leave these bonds,
Like a pair of worn-out shoes?
Tell me your name.

When you are in heaven,
Do as you please.
While you live on earth,
Our Sovereign rules.
Under the sun and moon that shine,
To the sky's ends where bend the clouds of heaven,
To the earth's bounds whither creeps the toad,[1]
All is his exalted realm.

In everything you behave with wilfulness.
Have I not spoken truly?

Envoy

Far is the way to heaven,
Obediently go home,
And attend you to your work!

613-4 *Thinking of children.* [v : 802-3]

Buddha, from his holy mouth, truly preached, ' I love mankind as I love Rahula.'[2] Again he preached, ' No love exceeds a parent's love.' Even so great a saint loved his child. Should not, then, the common run of men do so all the more?

WHEN I eat melon,
 I remember my children;
When I eat chestnuts,

---

[1] The toad was believed to retire to some region where no human being ever set foot.

[2] Buddha's son before he renounced the world.

Even more do I recall them.
Whence did they come to me?
Before my eyes they will linger,
And I cannot sleep in peace.

Envoy

What use to me
Silver, gold and jewels?
No treasure can surpass children!

615-6   *An elegy on the impermanence of*   [v : 804-5]
human life.[1]

What threaten us and are difficult for us to master are the eight great pains. What are hardly attainable and quickly spent are the pleasures of a hundred years. The ancients grieved over this, as we do to-day. Hence I have composed a poem to drive away the sorrows of my grey-haired age.

WE are helpless before time
   Which ever speeds away.
And pains of a hundred kinds
Pursue us one after another.
Maidens joy in girlish pleasures,
With ship-borne gems on their wrists,
And hand in hand with their friends;
But the bloom of maidenhood,
As it cannot be stopped,
Too swiftly steals away.
When do their ample tresses
Black as a mud-snail's bowels
Turn white with the frost of age?
Whence come those wrinkles
Which furrow their rosy cheeks?
The lusty young men, warrior-like,

[1] Composed in Kama District, on the 21st of the 7th month of the 5th year of Jinki (728).—Original Note.

Bearing their sword-blades at their waists,
In their hands the hunting bows,
And mounting their bay horses,
With saddles dressed with twill,
Ride about in triumph;
But can their prime of youth
Favour them for ever?
Few are the nights they keep,
When, sliding back the plank doors,
They reach their beloved ones
And sleep, arms intertwined,
Before, with staffs at their waists,
They totter along the road,
Laughed at here, and hated there.
This is the way of the world;
And, cling as I may to life,
I know no help!

Envoy

Although I wish I were thus,
Like the rocks that stay for ever,
In this world of humanity
I cannot keep old age away.

617-8   *The Bosom-soothing Stones.*[1]   [v : 813-4]

*On the plain of Kofu, in the village of Fukaé, Ito District,
Chikuzen, there are two stones on the hill which overlooks the
sea. The larger is one shaku*[2] *two sun*[2] *and six bu*[2] *in length,
one shaku eight sun six bu in circumference, and eighteen kin*[3]
five ryō[3] *in weight. The smaller is one shaku one sun in
length, one shaku eight sun in circumference, and weighs sixteen kin ten ryō. Both are egg-shaped. Their beauty is
beyond words. These are truly what are called gems of ' one*

---

1 The authorship is sometimes ascribed to Ōtomo Tabito.
2 *Shaku*=foot; *sun*=$\frac{1}{10}$ *shaku*; *bu*=$\frac{1}{10}$ *sun*.
3 *Kin*=1$\frac{1}{3}$ lb. avoirdupois; *ryō*=$\frac{1}{16}$ *kin*.

foot across.' Placed by the roadside, twenty ri[1] from the stage-house at Fukaé, every traveller, official or not, dismounts and does them reverence. The elders of the village hand down the story that, long ago, when the Empress Jingu was on her expedition to subjugate Shiragi, she kept them one in each sleeve, as a charm to postpone child-birth. Therefore all travellers do them reverence.

M^Y tongue is awed—
    The Empress, to soothe her bosom
And subjugate Shiragi,
Took up two gem-like stones,
And held them in reverence.
Then, on the plain of Kofu by the sea
In far-secluded Fukaé,
She herself placed the stones
Before the eyes of the world,
To leave them honoured by all men
Throughout all time to be.
So, when I see these sacred stones
Still remaining as deities,
Reverence fills my heart.

Envoy

To leave them honoured by all men,
Long as heaven and earth shall last,
She placed these sacred stones.

619   *At the farewell banquet in honour of Ōtomo Tabito,* [v : 880]
      when he was starting for the capital in the twelfth
        month of the second year of Tempyō (730).

A^{FTER} five years passed in the country
    Far away as are the skies,
I have become a stranger
To the graceful manners of the City.

---

[1] *Ri*=0.41 mile; so that ' 20 *ri* ' is about ' 8 miles.'

*Ōtomo Kumagori was a native of Mashiki District, Higo
Province.   At the age of eighteen, in the sixth month of the
third year of Tempyō (731), he started for the capital, having
been appointed attendant to a governor and an official of the
Board of Wrestling.   But, by Heaven's will, he unfortunately
fell ill during his journey, and died at a stage-house at Taka-
niwa in Aki Province.   On his death-bed he sighed and said,
' Man's body, being a chance combination of the elements, easily
perishes, and life does not endure longer than a bubble, so I
am told.   Hence many sages have died, and many wise men
have not lived long.   Then how can such as I, mean and
humble, elude the grasp of death?   My parents are both alive
at home.   Anxiety will seize them, waiting for me so long.
When their longing has proved vain at last, they will weep
themselves blind.   That is my grief.   O poor father!   O
poor mother!   I grieve not so much for my death as for my
old parents who will be left in lamentation.   If I die to-day,
in what world can I meet them again?'   He then composed
these six poems.*

To go up to the sun-lit Imperial City,
    I left the loving hands of my mother,
Travelled through the far and unknown lands,
And crossed a hundred mountains,
Ever talking with my friends,
Ever thinking, as we talked,
' When can we see the City? '
Then my body sorely pained me,
So, at the turning of the road,
I bent and gathered the weeds and brushwood,
Where I laid myself,
And as I lay in grief, I thought,
If I were in my native land,
My father would take up my hands,
As would my mother nurse me, if I lay at home.
Is this the way of all the world?

Lying by the roadside like a dog,
Must I thus end my life?

Envoys

Far from my loving mother's eyes,
Unsteady and forlorn,
Whither shall I bend my steps
From this world?

On the far-stretching, untravelled road
My heart lost in gloom,
How shall I guide my steps
Without something to nourish me?

If at home my mother nursed me,
Holding my hands in hers,
My heart would be lightened,
Though I should die.

Ah! counting the weary days
Since I set out on my journey,
My father and mother must surely wait for me,
Saying, ' To-day, to-day.'

Leaving my father and mother
Whom I shall not see a second time
In this one life of mine,
Must I now depart for ever?

626–7   *A dialogue on poverty.*   [v : 892–3]

ON the night when the rain beats,
    Driven by the wind,
On the night when the snow-flakes mingle
With the sleety rain,
I feel so helplessly cold.
I nibble at a lump of salt,

Sip the hot, oft-diluted dregs of saké;
And coughing, snuffling,
And stroking my scanty beard,
I say in my pride,
'There's none worthy, save I!'
But I shiver still with cold.
I pull up my hempen bed-clothes,
Wear what few sleeveless clothes I have,
But cold and bitter is the night!
As for those poorer than myself,
Their parents must be cold and hungry,
Their wives and children beg and cry.
Then, how do you struggle through life?

Wide as they call the heaven and earth,
For me they have shrunk quite small;
Bright though they call the sun and moon,
They never shine for me.
Is it the same with all men,
Or for me alone?
By rare chance I was born a man
And no meaner than my fellows,
But, wearing unwadded sleeveless clothes
In tatters, like weeds waving in the sea,
Hanging from my shoulders,
And under the sunken roof,
Within the leaning walls,
Here I lie on straw
Spread on bare earth,
With my parents at my pillow,
My wife and children at my feet,
All huddled in grief and tears.
No fire sends up smoke
At the cooking-place,
And in the cauldron
A spider spins its web.
With not a grain to cook,

We moan like the 'night-thrush.'
Then, ' to cut,' as the saying is,
' The ends of what is already too short,'
The village headman comes,
With rod in hand, to our sleeping-place,
Growling for his dues.
Must it be so hopeless—
The way of this world?

Envoy

Nothing but pain and shame in this world of men,
But I cannot fly away,
Wanting the wings of a bird.

628-30   *A wish for safety at the departure of Tajihi*   [v : 894–6]
*Hironari, ambassador to China, in the
fifth year of Tempyō (733).*

SINCE the age of the gods it has always been said
    That the Land of Yamato is
A land where Sovereign-Gods hold solemn sway,
A land where the word-soul brings us weal;
Not only has it been so told from mouth to mouth,
But all of us see and know it now.

Though many are the worthy men,
Our Sovereign, like the sun of heaven,
Out of his godlike love and favour,
Has chosen you, my lord,
A scion of a minister's house.
Now you go upon your journey
To China, the distant land,
Faithful to his dread commands.

All the gods who rule the shores
And wide seas far away
At the prow will pilot you.
And the gods of heaven and earth

207

And the 'Great-Land-Spirit' of Yamato,
Will look down from the sky,
As they soar through heaven.

When you return, your duties done,
The gods again, with their hands upon the prow,
Will speed your journey home,
Straight as the drawn ink-line,
From Chika's cape to Ōtomo
Where your ships will harbour at Mitsu's shore.

Be safe and well, my lord,
Quickly come back home!

Envoys

I will sweep the pine-wood
At Mitsu of Ōtomo,
And stand there waiting for you;
Quickly come back home!

When I hear of you at anchor
In Naniwa's port,
I will hasten to your side,
Not even tying my riband.

631–7   *Suffering from old age and prolonged*   [v : 897–903]
         illness, and thinking of his children.

So long as lasts the span of life,[1]
    We wish for peace and comfort
With no evil and no mourning,
But life is hard and painful.
As the common saying has it,
Bitter salt is poured into the smarting wound,
Or the burdened horse is packed with an upper load,
Illness shakes my old body with pain.

---

[1] The span of human life was considered to be 120 years.

All day long I breathe in grief
And sigh throughout the night.
For long years my illness lingers,
I grieve and groan month after month,
And though I would rather die,
I cannot, and leave my children
Noisy like the flies of May.
Whenever I watch them
My heart burns within.
And tossed this way and that,
I weep aloud.

Envoys

I find no solace in my heart;
Like the bird flying behind the clouds
I weep aloud.

Helpless and in pain,
I would run out and vanish,
But the thought of my children holds me.

No children to wear them in wealthy homes,
They are thrown away as waste,
Those silks and quilted clothes!

With no sackcloth for my children to wear,
Must I thus grieve,
For ever at a loss!

Though vanishing like a bubble,
I live, praying that my life be long
Like a rope of a thousand fathoms.

Humble as I am,
Like an arm-band of coarse twill,
How I crave a thousand years of life!

WHAT worth to me the seven treasures,
    So prized and desired by all the world?
Furuhi, born of us two,
Our love, our dear white pearl,
With dawn, with the morning-star,
Frolicked about the bed with us, standing or sitting;
When dusk came with the evening-star,
He pulled our hands, urged us to bed,
' Leave me not, father and mother,
Let me sleep between you,
Like *saki-kusa*,[2] the three-stalked plant.'
So spoke that lovely mouth.
Then we trusted, as one trusts in a great ship,
That he would grow up as time passed by,
And we should watch him, both in weal and woe.
But, as of a sudden sweeps the storm,
Illness caught our son.
Helpless and in grief,
I braced my sleeves with white cord,
Grasped my shining mirror,
And gazing up into the sky
I appealed to the gods of heaven;
Dropping my forehead to the ground
Madly I prayed to the gods of earth :
' It is yours to decide his fate,
To cure him or to let him die.'
Nothing availed my prayers,
He languished day by day,
His voice failed each morning,
His mortal life ebbed out.
Wildly I leapt and kicked the floor,
Cried, stared up, stared down,

---

   [1] Though this poem is of uncertain authorship, it is put here because it suggests
Okura in style.—Original Note.
   [2] Not identified.

And beat my breast in grief.
But the child from my arms has flown ;
So goes the world . . . .

Envoys

So young he will not know the way ;
Here is a fee for you,
O courier from the Nether World,
Bear him on your back.

With offerings I beseech you,
Be true and lead him up
Straight along the road to heaven !

641   *Composed on the occasion of his illness.*   [VI : 978]

SHOULD I, a man, die in vain
   With no renown—no name
Spoken of for ten thousand ages ?

*Once Yamanoé Okura fell gravely ill.   Fujiwara Yatsuka
sent a messenger to him to inquire after his condition. Okura,
after making a reply, burst into tears, and recited the above
poem.*

642-4   *A Seventh Night[1] Poem.[2]*   [VIII : 1520-2]

THE Oxherd and the Weaver Maid standing
   Face to face across the River,

---

[1] The 7th night of the 7th month is the only night in the year on which the Oxherd (a star in Aquila) is allowed to visit his sweetheart, the Weaver Maid (the star Vega), living on the other side of the Heavenly River (the Milky Way). The legend, which is of Chinese origin, early found its way into Japan, where the celebration of the 'Seventh Night,' or *Tanabata Matsuri*, as it is called, became, and still remains, one of the most popular festivals throughout the country.

[2] Okura composed these poems on gazing up at the Heavenly River on the night of the 7th day of the 7th month in the 1st year of Tempyō (729).—Original Note.

Since heaven and earth were parted—
Never has he ceased from loving,
Nor has he ceased from grieving.
Because of the blue waves all hopes are lost,
Because of the white clouds many tears have been
  shed.
Must he thus go on sighing?
Must he thus go on longing?
Had he a boat, vermilion-stained,
Had he an oar with a jewelled shaft,
He would ferry across in the calm of morning,
Or row over on the swelling tide of evening.
Then, on the shining beach of the Heavenly River,
The lovers would spread the celestial scarf
And lie, their beautiful arms interlocked,
In many a love-tryst, autumn though it be not.

Envoys

The wind and the cloud go to and fro
Between the banks—but no word comes
From his wife so far away.

Though it seems a stone's throw,
The Heavenly River separates them—
Nay, help there is none.

645–6   *Flowers of the autumn moorlands.*   [VIII : 1537–8]

THE flowers that blow
  In the autumn fields,
When I count them on my fingers,
There they are—
The flowers of seven kinds.

They are the bush-clover,[1]

---

[1] i. e. *Lespedeza.*

The 'tail flower,'[1] the flowers
Of the *kuzu*[2] vine and patrinia,[3]
The fringed pink, and the agrimony,[4]
And last the blithe 'morning face.'[5]

647–8   *Poems of the fisher-folk of Shika, in the*   [XVI : 3861]
province of Chikuzen.

THOUGH, waiting for you to come,
    I put your rice in the bowl
And stand outside by the gate,
You come not home, Arao!

YOU care naught for the living   [XVI : 3865]
    Of your wife and children—
Though I wait these many years,
You come not home, Arao!

In the era of Jinki[6] *the Dazaifu*[7] *appointed Munakatabé
Tsumaro, a citizen of Munakata District, Chikuzen Province,
steersman of the ship carrying provisions to the island of
Tsushima. Tsumaro went to Arao, a fisherman of Shika
Village, Kasuya District, and said to him: 'I have something to ask of you.' Arao replied: 'Though we belong to
different districts, we have long sailed in the same ship. To
my heart you are dearer than a brother, and I am prepared
to share death with you. I will refuse you nothing.' Tsumaro said: 'The Dazaifu authorities have appointed me
steersman of the ship carrying provisions to the island of*

---

[1] *Obana*, otherwise called *susuki*, i. e. *Miscanthus sinensis*. See note to No. 83.
[2] A broad-leaved creeping vine, with reddish-purple flowers(*Pueraria Thunbergiana*).
[3] i. e. *Patrinia scabiosaefolia*, a wild plant, three or four feet in height, with yellow
flowers in small heads.
[4] A kind of 'hemp agrimony' (*Eupatorium japonicum*).
[5] Literal translation of *asagao*, which meant a different flower from what it does
to-day, viz. 'morning glory.'
[6] i. e. 724–9.
[7] The government which administered Kyūshū and the two islands of Tsushima
and Iki.

*Tsushima. But I am too old and weak to go to sea.
Therefore, I have come to you. Will you take my place?'
Arao consented, and went to his work. Setting out from the
headland of Mimiraku,[1] Matsura District, Hizen Province,
he sailed for Tsushima. Then, suddenly the sky grew dark,
and a violent storm broke out, attended with rain. Under
the stress of weather, Arao went down with his ship. His
wife and children, lamenting and longing for him, composed
these poems. It is also said that Yamanoé Okura, then
Governor of Chikuzen Province, who was touched by the
plight of the wife and children, composed these poems in order
to express their sentiments.*

Takahashi Mushimaro

*649-50   To Fujiwara Umakai on his departure as   [VI : 971-2]
            Inspector-General of Saikaidō.*

AT this time of the year when the white-clouded
    Tatsuta Hill
Begins slowly to crimson with dew and frost,
You cross it to go on a journey.
Over five hundred hills you will tramp your way
Till you reach the land of Tsukushi
Where men guard the shore against the alien foes.
There, despatching your subordinates for inspection
To the extremities of hill and plain,
You will survey the land's defences everywhere,
Even in that far place whence Echo makes reply
And at the remotest nook whither creeps the toad.[2]

But with the approach of springtime,
Come back swiftly like a bird on the wing!
Yes, when the red azaleas glow by the wayside
Amid the knolls along the Tatsuta road,

---

[1] Sometimes regarded as a scribal error for *Mineraku.*
[2] See note to No. 611.

And when the cherry-trees are in bloom,
I will come to meet you—to greet you on your
    return.

Envoy

I believe you to be, my lord,
A man who without lifting up words
Will conquer an enemy
Even ten thousand strong, and then return.

From the 'Mushimaro Collection'

651–3   *Mount Fuji.*   [III : 319–21]

Lo! There towers the lofty peak of Fuji
    From between Kai and wave-washed Suruga.
The clouds of heaven dare not cross it,
Nor the birds of the air soar above it.
The snows quench the burning fires,
The fires consume the falling snow.
It baffles the tongue, it cannot be named,
It is a god mysterious.

The lake called Sé[1] is embosomed in it,
The river we cross, the Fuji,[2] is its torrent.

In the Land of Yamato, the Land of the Rising Sun,
It is our treasure, our tutelary god.
It never tires our eyes to look up
To the lofty peak of Fuji!

Envoys

The snows that crown the peak of Fuji
Melt on the mid-June day,
And that night it snows again.

---

[1] Lake Sé was divided by a subsequent eruption into Lake Shōji and Lake Sei-ko.
[2] The Fuji is one of the three most rapid rivers in Japan.

So lofty and awful is the peak of Fuji,
The clouds of heaven dare not cross it,
But linger trailing near!

654-5   *Of the Maiden Tamana at Sué[1] of the*   [IX : 1738-9]
province of Kazusa.

THERE lived a maiden Tamana
    At Sué that bordered on Awa.
Broad of breast was she,
Her waist slender like a wasp's,
And radiant her face.

When she stood smiling like a flower,
Wayfarers, breaking their journey,
Turned to her door, unbeckoned.
A neighbour, abandoning his wife,
Unasked, offered his precious keys to her.

Thus charmed were all men;
And lithely she leaned upon them
With wanton airs and graces.

Envoy

When a man stood by her door,
Out she went and met him
Forgetting all,
Though in the dead of night.

656-7   *Urashima of Mizunoé*   [IX : 1740-1]

WHEN, in spring, the sun is misted,
    And going out on Suminoé's shore[2]
I see rocking fisher-boats,
They remind me of the things

[1] Now Kimitsu District in Chiba Prefecture.
[2] In Yosa District, Tango Province.

216

That happened long ago.

Urashima of Mizunoé
Went a-fishing to the sea;
Proud of his plentiful catch
Of sea-bream and bonito,
He did not come back home
Though seven days came and went;
But beyond the bounds of sea
He rowed out his little boat;
Then it happened that he met
The Sea God's daughter.
They talked, agreed, pledged love,
And hand in hand they reached
The Land Everlasting.

There in the Sea God's palace,
In its sweet and inmost chamber,
They might have lived, both he and she,
Never growing old, nor dying,
Until the end of time.
How foolish of this worldly man:
He said to his beloved:
' Let me go home for a while
And take word to my father and mother;
Then, again, as soon as it is morrow,
I shall come back to you.'
' If you will come again
To this Land of Happiness,
And meet me just as now,
Take this casket, but keep it closed.'
She said to him over and over.

Arriving at the shore of Suminoé
He sought his home, but could find none,
He sought his hamlet, which he could not see.
In wild wonderment he thought:
' In three years since I left,

How could my home be lost,
No trace of fence remaining?
If I open this casket,' he said,
' My old house may appear to me.'
Thereupon he opened it a little.
A white cloud rose out of the casket,
And drifted towards the Land Everlasting.

He ran, shouted, waved his sleeves;
He stamped and writhed upon the ground,
Then swooned upon the beach.
Wrinkles furrowed his youthful skin,
His black hair turned white.
His breath grew fainter and fainter,
At last he died.
That Urashima of Mizunoé,
I see the site of his abode.

Envoy

When he mignt have lived for ever
In the Land Everlasting,
How foolish of that man,
Though of his own choice!

658-9   *Of a maidèn walking alone on the great*   [IX : 1742-3]
bridge of Kawachi.

A MAIDEN walks alone
On the great vermilion bridge
Across the Katashiwa.[1]

She trails her crimson skirt,
Her cloak is dyed blue
With the herbs of the mountain.[2]

[1] A river flowing through the present village of Katashita, and joining the River Yamato in Naka-Kawachi District in Ōsaka Prefecture.
[2] *Yama-ai*, i. e. ' mountain indigo-plant ' (*Mercurialis leiocarpa*). The dye was obtained by boiling its leaves.

Has she a husband young as green grass?
Does she sleep single like an acorn?
I would ask her;
But, oh, not to know her bower!

Envoy

Were my dwelling by the bridge,
I would give her shelter,
So wistful she looks, going alone!

660–1   *Composed*[1] *when the courtiers started on a*   [IX : 1747–8]
journey down to Naniwa, in spring, in
the third month.[2]

ON the peak of Ogura above the rapids[3]
    In the mountains of Tatsuta
Soaring in white clouds,
The cherry-trees are in full bloom,
Every branch bending with loaded blossoms.

But the wind is ceaseless as the peak is lofty,
And day after day falls the spring rain;
The flowers have scattered from the upper sprays.

May the blossoms on the lower branches
Neither fall nor lose their beauty,
Till you, who journey, grass for pillow,
Come home again!

Envoy

Seven days will end our journey;
O Tatsuta, God of the Wind,[4]
Never scatter the blossoms
Before thy breath!

[1] By Takahashi Mushimaro.
[2] Perhaps toward the end of the Jinki era.
[3] The rapids are said to have been the *Kamé-no-sé* (the ' Tortoise Rapids ').
[4] The god enshrined in the mountains of Tatsuta.

219

A^S you, honoured Lord, travelled all the way,
   Wishing to see the twin-peaked Tsukuba
In the land of Hitachi,
I have brought you to the summit to enjoy the view,
Climbing, out of breath, by the roots of trees,
And wiping away beads of sweat in the scorching
   sun.

The god allows us and the goddess gives us favour,
They uncover the peaks of Tsukuba in the sun,
Which were veiled with timeless clouds and rain ;
And bare the beauteous land clear to view,
Which lay dim, obscure.

And in our joy and gratitude,
Unbinding the ribands of our clothes
We sported ourselves as freely as at home.

Though the peaks are rank with summer weeds,
How much more delightful it is to see them to-day
Than in genial spring.

Envoy

To-day, has any day surpassed it ?
Even that day when the ancients climbed
The peaks of Tsukuba !

664-5   *On a cuckoo.*   [IX : 1755-6]

O cuckoo, you were born
   Among the eggs of the *uguisu.*
You do not sing like your father,
Nor do you cry like your mother.

---

[1] Presumably Ōtomo Tabito.
[2] An official whose duty it was to inspect the financial affairs of the provincial
governments.

About the fields where the *unohana*[1] bloom
You fly, uttering your high shrill notes
And scattering the orange-flowers.
You cry the livelong day,
But your voice is ever sweet to hear.
O bird, I will offer you a gift;
Go not far, but dwell near my house,
Among the orange-flowers.

Envoy

At night when, darkening the sky,
The rain falls,
A cuckoo goes crying,
Ah! that bird!

666–7   *On climbing Mount Tsukuba.*   [IX : 1757–8]

CLIMBING the peaks of Tsukuba
        Perchance to ease my heart, sorrow-laden
With travelling, grass for pillow,
I see the wild ducks are come,
Chillily calling in the fields of Shizuku[2]
Where the 'tail flowers' fall,
And the land of Toba[3] in Niihari[4]
Is rippled white in the autumn wind.
And the splendid view from the peaks of Tsukuba
Relieves me of the heavy gloom
Gathered on many a weary day.

Envoy

As a gift for the comely maiden
Reaping in the autumn field,

---

[1] See note to No. 451.
[2] Lies east of the mountain, in Niibari District.
[3] Situated west of the mountain, in Makabé District.
[4] An old district comprising the present districts of Makabé and Nishi-Ibaraki.

Far down the Tsukuba Mountain,
Oh, I will break off a spray of tinted leaves.

668-9　　　*Climbing Mount Tsukuba on the*　　[IX : 1759–60]
　　　　　　　　　day of kagai.[1]

ON Mount Tsukuba where eagles dwell,
　By the founts of Mohakitsu,
Maidens and men, in troops assembling,
Hold a *kagai*, vying in poetry ;
I will seek company with others' wives,
Let others woo my own ;
The gods that dominate this mountain
Have allowed such freedom since of old ;
This day regard us not
With reproachful eyes,
Nor say a word of blame.

Envoy

Though clouds upon the Male Peak rise
And autumn showers drench me through,
How can I leave it !

670-1　　*On parting from Lord Ōtomo*[2] *on the bridge*　[IX : 1780–1]
　　　　　　at Karunu[3] *in Kashima District.*

AT the headland of Kashima
　Opposite Cape Miyaké,
Your vermilion boat[4] is ready
With all its jewelled oars,
And when, at evening flood-tide,

---

[1] A colloquialism for *uta-gaki* which was a popular festival in the eastern provinces, during the course of which men and women danced together, singing amorous ditties.
[2] i. e. Ōtomo Tabito.
[3] Located near the present railway station at Hikawa.
[4] See note to No. 187.

You embark with all your rowers,
Cheering, heartening them,
We whom you leave behind
Will crowd side by side on the shore,
Grieved at your going, stamping our feet,
Crying aloud, contorted with sorrow,
As your boat leaves us
For that harbour of Unakami.

Envoy

It were wiser, my lord, if you crossed it
When the seas calm down;
Never set sail on these rising waters!

672-3   *Of the Maiden of Mama of Katsushika.*   [IX : 1807-8]

IN the cock-crowing land of Azuma
    —As men have handed down to us
The tale of long ago—
It was a maiden Tekona
Who lived at Mama of Katsushika.
She wore blue-collared hemp,
And skirt of plain hemp-cloth that she wove;
She walked unshod, her hair uncombed,
And yet no high-born damsel dressed in rich brocade
Compared with this country girl.
When she stood smiling like a flower,
Her face like the full moon,
Many were the suitors seeking her,
As summer moths the fire,
As ships in haste the harbour.
Why did she wish to die
When life is but a breath?
She laid herself in her grave,
The river-mouth, under the noisy surf.
This is of the days long past,

Yet it seems that I had gazed
Upon her yesterday.

Envoy

When I see the well at Mama of Katsushika,
It reminds me of Tekona
Who stood here oft, drawing water.

674-6   *On seeing the tomb of the Maiden Unai.*   [IX : 1809–11]

THE Maiden Unai of Ashinoya,[1]
    From her half-grown eighth year,
Until her loose-hung hair was done up,
Dwelt in safe seclusion,
Unseen by neighbouring folk.

Then many wooers gathered round,
Eager to see this lovely girl;
But two among them, Chinu and Unai,
Vied with each other for her smile.

They met, grasping their sword-hilts,
And with their quivers and bows of spindle-wood
Slung from their shoulders;
Each swearing in hot rivalry
To plunge through flood and fire.

Helpless, she sought her mother:
' When I see their deadly strife
Because of simple me,
How can I live to marry him I love?
I will wait in Yomi, the Nether World.'
So telling of her secret love for one
She killed herself in grief.

Chinu dreamed of it that night
And followed her in death.

---

[1] Now known as Ashiya ; east of Kōbé.

224

Gallant Unai, left behind,
Cried in grief, looking up to heaven,
Ground his teeth and wept upon the earth;
Then bravely followed her with his sword,
'Never shall he defeat me!'

Their kinsfolk gathered in counsel,
And built the maiden's grave,
A tomb on this side and on that
For each hot youth;
As a token of their love for ever,
And a remembrance till the end of time.
Their history thus learned,
And though it happened long ago,
Moved me to tears
As if but now they had died.

Envoys

Whenever, passing through Ashinoya,
I see the Maiden Unai's tomb,
I weep and weep aloud.

The branches of the tree bend to one side
On the maiden's tomb;
It may be that her heart, some say,
Leaned to young Chinu so.

Owari —

677   WHEN the hills of spring   [VIII : 1421]
            Are overladen with cherry-blossoms,
It is well to see
Young girls in their white sashes
Gathering spring herbs.

Kamo Taruhito

678-80 *Mount Kagu.*[1] [III : 257-9]

A s spring has come when the mist trails
   On the heaven-descended hill of Kagu,[2]
The lake[3] is rippled by the breezes through the
   pines
And cherry-flowers fill the leafy boughs.
The mallards call to their mates
Far off on the water,
And the teal cry and whirr
About the beach.
But the pleasure-barges, which of old
The courtiers retiring from the palace rowed,
Now lie desolate,
Oarless, poleless, and unmanned!

Envoys

It is plain that no one comes boating:
The diving mandarin-ducks and teal
Dwell upon the barges.

How time-worn all has grown, unnoticed!
On the hill of Kagu the moss lies green
At the ancient roots
Of the speary cryptomerias.

---

[1] It is supposed that these poems were composed on viewing the desolation lying about the hill, on which once stood the palace of the then deceased Prince of Takechi. The Prince, son of the Emperor Temmu, was proclaimed Crown Prince to the Empress Jitō, but died in the 10th year of the Empress's reign (696).

[2] See note to No. 2.

[3] i. e. the lake of Haniyasu, which was at the foot of the hill.

Sena Gyōmon

681   *On dishonest persons.*   [XVI : 3836]

Iɴ the hills of Nara
   There grows the *child's-hand* cypress[1]
With leaves double-faced.
On either side of me I see
A swarm of rascals.[2]

Tsuki —

682–6 *An elegy on seeing a dead man on the* [XIII : 3339–43]
      shore of Kamishima, in the province
                of Bingo.

Aꜰᴛᴇʀ his weary travels
   Through the plains and mountains,
Across the flooding rivers,
To the wide-spread sea,
And at the ferry ruled by the fearful god,
Where no soft breeze blows
Nor gentle surges break,
On this shore washed by the ceaseless waves,
The lofty mountain as his screen,
The deep bay as his pillow,
In death he lies.
Perchance he was his parents' love,
He may have had a wife tender as a blade of grass.
Ask his home, he cannot tell you where,
Ask his name, that too he cannot tell.

---

[1] *Konoté-gashiwa*: probably a different tree from that now known by the same name.

[2] The poem permits another construction according to which the last two lines may be rendered to read :
    ' Double-faced rascals I see everywhere
    No matter which way I turn.'

Whose word did he fondly follow
That he dared this perilous voyage,
These raging seas?

Envoys

His parents, wife and children,
Wait for him on tiptoe,
This ill-fated man!

In spite of his dear ones' longing,
He is pillowed on the beach,
On the rugged rocks!

While he lies by the deep sea,
Poor wife, she looks for his return,
'To-day, surely to-day.'

On the shore washed by the surges,
In misery he lies;
But I know not his homeward way!

From the 'Tanabé Sakimaro Collection'

687–9   *Lament for the decay of the old City*   [VI : 1047–9]
                           of Nara.

THE Land of Yamato over which reigns
    Our great Lord and Sovereign in peace,
Being a land governed by the Imperial House
Since the time of the first God-Emperor,
This Imperial City of Nara was here founded,
That hence the heirs born to the Throne
Might rule the under-heaven in endless succession
Down through the myriads of ages.
    Here in spring when the shimmering *kagerō*[1] rises,

---

[1] See note to No. 109.

The cherry-bloom blazes forth in the tree-shade
While the *kao-dori*[1] sings without ceasing
In the Mikasa fields near the hill of Kasuga.
When autumn comes with its dew and frost,
On the Beacon Height of Mount Ikoma
Many a stag, trampling the *hagi*[2] bush,
Calls to his mate with an echoing voice;
Alluring are the hills to look upon,
And pleasant the homes to live in.
The courtiers of eighty clans
Having built their mansions in rows,
I thought its Great Palace would flourish
As long as heaven and earth endured—
O Nara, city of my abiding trust!
But because the times are new,
All have gone—led by their Sovereign—
Even as the spring flowers fade and go,
Or as the birds fly away with daybreak.
On its wide streets where once proudly trod
The lords and ladies of the Great Palace,
No horses pass; nor men.
What desolation—alas!

Envoys

Now that with the change of times
Nara is become
An Imperial City that was,
The grass grows rank in the streets.

Since Nara, the Imperial City,
So long familiar to me,
Is now falling to decay,
Whenever I go outdoors,
Bitterer grows my grief.

---

[1] A bird, not identified.
[2] i. e. *Lespedeza*, elsewhere rendered ' bush-clover.'

IN Ō-Yashima, the dominion under heaven
  Of our Sovereign, a god in living flesh,
Many are the provinces,
And unnumbered the dwelling-places of men.
But as a province of well-ranged mountains,
And a happy place where the rivers meet,
Here in the Kasé Mountains of Yamashiro
Has he planted stout pillars and raised
The Futagi Palace, whence he rules the land.

The rivers being near,
Clear comes the sound of the running waters;
The mountains rising close by,
The clamorous voices of birds are heard.
When the autumn comes,
The stags call loudly to their mates,
Their voices echoing through the mountains.
When the spring comes,
Thick over hill-sides and amid rocks
The flowers bloom bending the sprays.

O happy fields of Futagi!
O noble palace site!
Well did our Sovereign, learning this,
Here establish after his august desire,
The great imperial abode.

Envoys

It must surely be for the unsullied loveliness
Of the Futagi fields on Mika's plain,
That here was established the imperial abode.

Lofty are the mountains,
And clear run the river waters.
Hallowed ever shall remain
The imperial abode for a hundred ages.

O Futagi Palace where is enthroned
   high
Our Lord and Sovereign, the Divine One!
Here the mountains are covered deep with countless
   trees,
And clear-voiced are the tumbling river waters.
In the spring when the warblers come to sing,
The shady mountain slopes glow
With a profusion of flowers that bloom
Like brocade amid the rocks;
In the autumn when the stags call to their mates,
The encrimsoned leaves fall
With the passing showers that darken the sky.

As will the Sovereigns born in succession
Rule hence the under-heaven for thousands of years,
So shall remain the great imperial abode
Immutable for all ages.

Envoys

Should the waters of the Izumi River
Ever cease to flow,
Then the great imperial abode—
Then only—might suffer change.

When I see how pleasingly ranged
Are the Futagi Mountains,
I know this is an imperial abode
That will not change with ages.

The mountain land of Kasé—
The ' reel ' on which the maidens
Wind the hempen yarn they spin—
Is become, as time passes,
An Imperial City!

Because in the Kasé Mountains
The trees stand thick,

231

Every morning the voice is heard
Of the warblers thronging there
In song.

The cuckoo singing yonder
In the mountain of Koma
Will not come here,
Because far is the passage
Across the Izumi River.

699-701   *Composed at the Palace of Naniwa.*   [VI : 1062-4]

THE Palace of Naniwa, whither often comes
      Our Lord and Sovereign ruling in peace,
Stands by the whale-haunted sea—
And so near the beach where men gather shells,
That there is heard the clamour of the waves
Chafing at the morning breeze,
And the plash of oars in the evening calm.
When I listen waking from sleep at dawn—
Hark! with the ebbing of the ocean tide
The plovers are calling to their mates
On the sand bank, while amid the reeds
Re-echo the voices of cranes.

Whoever sees it will praise,
Whoever hears of it will yearn to see—
This Palace of Ajifu I never tire to look on.

Envoys

The Palace of Naniwa, whither often comes
Our Sovereign, stands so near the ocean,
I see the little boats
In which the fisher-maids ride.

As the tide ebbs,
The voice of the cranes

Calling to their mates amid the reeds
Re-echoes through the Palace.

702-4   *On passing the bay of Minumé.*   [vi : 1065–7]

O Minumé Bay, chosen by all Yashima's shipmen
    Since the age of the God of Eight Thousand
        Spears[1]
As the haven for mooring their countless ships,
Here the shore waves clamour in the morning wind,
And the ocean weeds drift in on the evening waves.
O clean beach of white sand!
Unwearied I watch it, walking back and forth.
Well has it been commended by every visitor
To be widely admired.
And admired will it be ages after—
This clean white beach!

Envoys

O Minumé Bay, reminding one
Of a shining mirror!
Never will the countless ships
Pass, unheeding, by its shore.

Clean is the shore, and beautiful the bay.
So has it been since the age of the gods
A calling-place for a thousand ships—
This beach of Ōwada.

705   *On seeing a dead man when crossing the pass*   [ix : 1800]
                    of Ashigara.[2]

He lies unloosened of his white clothes,
    Perhaps of his wife's weaving

---

¹ Yachihoko-no-Kami (Ōkuninushi-no-Kami).
² A mountain-pass between Sagami and Suruga Provinces.

233

From hemp within her garden-fence,
And girdled threefold round
Instead of once.
Perhaps after painful service done
He turned his footsteps home,
To see his parents and his wife;
And now, on this steep and sacred pass
In the eastern land of Azuma,
Chilled in his spare, thin clothes,
His black hair fallen loose—
Telling none his province,
Telling none his home,
Here on his journey he lies dead.

706-8   *On passing the tomb of the Maiden*   [IX : 1801-3]
of Ashinoya.[1]

I STAND and gaze at the tomb
  Of the Maiden Unai of Ashinoya,
For whom two valiant youths
Strove with each other long ago;
It stands by the roadside, built of rocks,
To leave a tale for many an age to come.
And every traveller upon this road,
Even from lands remote as clouds of heaven,
Pauses by the grave,
Some grieving, others weeping loud;
And as I see this maiden's tomb
Of which the people tell from mouth to mouth
And with sighs from heart to heart,
Grief breaks me down,
Thinking of the piteous tale of old.

[1] See Nos. 674-6.

Envoys

She was wooed by gallant Shinuda[1]
In those far days,
The Maiden Unai, and this is her tomb.

This maiden, how lovely even in the tale!
They saw her with their living eyes,
Those young men.

709-11   *An elegy on a younger brother's death.*   [IX : 1804-6]

MY beloved brother, born of my own parents,
    A life fleeting as the morning dew,
Helpless before the gods,
And shelterless,
In this Rice-abounding Land of Reed Plains—
Never will he homeward turn his face again.
He departed, as vines do part,
Led by his spirit,
Far from us as the clouds of heaven,
To *Yomi*, region of the dead.
Bewildered as in the darkest night,
With heart-ache like the arrow-stricken deer,.
Disturbed like the reed-fence in the wind,
Crying loud like birds in spring,
With my heart burning day and night,
I sorrow over him!

Envoys

Parted though we are,
If ever I could hope again to meet him,
I should not thus wildly grieve.

Watching the mourners leave him
In the rugged hills,

---

[1] Another name of Chinu.

My heart is wrung again.

Wakamiya Ayumaro

712   *On the fairy mountain-mulberry branch.*   [III : 387]

HAD not there been the man
    Who set the fish-weir of old,
Here it would still remain,
That mountain-mulberry branch.[1]

Kon Myōgun

713   *At the death of Lord Ōtomo,[2] Grand Councillor* [III : 455]
            of State, in the seventh month of the third
                    year of Tempyō (731).

WHEN so little of his life remained,
    He asked, ' Are the bush-clovers
Yet in flower ? '—Alas, my master !

Tsukan

*When some girls presented Tsukan, a priest, with a packet
of dried abalone, and, for amusement, asked him to perform
incantations, he responded with this poem.*

714   EVEN if you bore them to the deepest sea   [III : 327]
            And cast them into the water,
        How could these come to life again ?

---

[1] According to legend, a man called Umashiné, in Yoshino, built a fish-weir in
the River Yoshino, and caught a spray of a ' mountain-mulberry tree ' (*Morus
bombycis*). He brought it home, when it turned into a beautiful girl. They became
man and wife.
[2] i. e. Ōtomo Tabito.

Manzei

715   *On quilted silk.*   [III : 336]

THE quilted silk from Tsukushi,
    The land of unknown fires,[1]
Although I have not worn it,
Looks comfortable and warm.

716   To what shall I liken this life?   [III : 351]
    It is like a boat,
Which, unmoored at morn,
Drops out of sight
And leaves no trace behind.

A Monk of the Gango-ji Temple

717   *A poem of self-lamentation.*   [VI : 1018]

A WHITE gem unknown of men—
    Be it so if no one knows!
Since I myself know its worth
Although no other—
Be it so if no one knows!

*The Monk of the Gango-ji temple, having attained en-
lightenment, was possessed of much wisdom, but the world
knew little of him and treated him with contempt. So he
composed the above poem bewailing the ignorance concerning
his talent.*

---

[1] See note to No. 524.

Kojima, a Young Woman of Tsukushi

718   *To a traveller.*   [III : 381]

BE not hasty,
    However much you long for home;
Go, watching well the winds,
For rough is your way.

Ōyakemé, a Young Woman of Buzen

719   IN the twilight darkness   [IV : 709]
    Indistinguishable is the road.
Wait till the moon-rise, and go,
That I may see you, my dearest,
Even for that while!

Ato Tobira, a Young Woman

720   ONCE—only once,   [IV : 710]
    I saw him in the light
Of the sky-wandering moon;
Now I see him in my dreams.

Taniha Ōmé, a Young Woman

721   HERE where the wild ducks   [IV : 711]
    Sport in the pond,
The leaves fall from the trees
And float—but no floating heart
Have I who love you true.

A Young Woman of Hitachi

722   To Fujiwara Umakai¹ when he left the province   [IV : 521]
for the capital upon his transfer to a new post.

FORGET not, I pray, your Eastland girl
   Who will be thinking of you always,
As she cuts the hemp-stalks standing in the yard
And spreads them out to dry.

A Young Woman of Harima

723   To the steward Ishikawa² when he left for   [IX : 1777]
his new post in the capital.

WHEN you are away, wherefore should I adorn
   myself?
Never shall I think of taking even the boxwood
   comb
Out of my toilet-case!

724-5   Composed on the occasion of an imperial   [III : 287-8]
visit³ to Shiga.

NOW that I am here,
   I wonder where is my home:
We have come over the ranging mountains
Wreathed with white trailing clouds!
                              *—By Lord Isonokami.*⁴

---

¹ Son of Fujiwara Fubito. He was appointed Inspector-General of the three
provinces of Awa, Kazusa and Shimōsa in 719.
² i. e. Ishikawa Kimiko.
³ Probably refers to the visit of the Empress Genshō in the 1st year of Yōrō (717).
⁴ Isonokami Otomaro.

Should I be favoured with a happy lease of life,
Again I will see the breaking waves
White on the shore of Ōtsu in Shiga.
                              —*By Hozumi Oyu.*[1]

726-9   *Composed at a snow-viewing court banquet.*

*In the first month of the eighteenth year of Tempyō (746)
snow fell some inches deep.*[2] *Tachibana Moroé, Minister
of the Left, went, together with princes and courtiers, to the
Palace of the ex-Empress,*[3] *and swept it away. The ex-
Empress called the party into the Palace, gave a feast,
awarded saké, and ordered each to compose a poem.*

TILL my hair is white[4] like the falling   [XVII : 3922]
    snow,
I enjoy our Sovereign's grace;
My heart overflows with gratitude!
                              —*By Tachibana Moroé.*

WHILE I behold the brightness of the   [XVII : 3923]
    fallen snow
That has covered all under heaven,
Veneration fills my heart!—*By Ki Kiyohito.*

ON this New Year's Day,   [XVII : 3925]
    The beginning of the year,
It promises a fruitful autumn,
This snow that lies so deep.—*By Fujii Moroai.*

[1] Hozumi Oyu served at court in the two reigns of the Empress Genshō and the
Emperor Shōmu.   He was exiled to the Isle of Sado for some offence in the 6th year
of Yōrō (722) in the reign of the Empress Genshō, and was called back to court
under the Amnesty, proclaimed in the 12th year of Tempyō (740) in the reign of
the Emperor Shōmu.   This poem was perhaps made on the way to Sado.
[2] At Nara, the then capital, little snow fell and very seldom lay many inches
deep.
[3] i. e. the Empress Genshō.
[4] Moroé was then fifty-eight years of age.   Thirty-five years had passed since
his promotion to the Junior Grade of the Fifth Rank.

THE white snow which lies so deep   [XVII : 3926]
   that it glistens
Within and without the palace-court
Never wearies my eyes !—*By Ōtomo Yakamochi.*

730–1 *Poems composed in obedience to the imperial* [XIX : 4273–4]
      order at the banquet after the Harvest
      Festival,[1]* on the twenty-fifth of the eleventh*
      month of the fourth year of Tempyō-
      Shōhō (752).

IN building the great sanctuary[2]
   That she may flourish long
As last heaven and earth,
Awe and gladness fill my heart.
              —*By Kosé Natemaro.*

HIGH in the sanctuary
   Five hundred ropes are stretched out ;
That her reign may last for a myriad ages,
Five hundred ropes are stretched out.
            —*By Ishikawa Toshitari.*

732–7 *Poems composed at the plum-blossom viewing banquet*
      which was held at the residence of Ōtomo Tabito,
      Governor-General of the Dazaifu, in the first
      month in the second year of Tempyō (730).

WHEN with the first month comes the   [V : 815]
   spring,
Thus breaking sprays of plum-blossoms,
We'll taste pleasure to the full.
            —*By Ki, the secretary.*

---

[1] The Harvest Festival is a ceremony held at court every autumn, at which new rice is offered to the gods.   It is followed by a banquet at the Palace.
[2] A new sanctuary was built every year in which to worship the gods.

IN my garden fall the plum-blossoms—   [v : 822]
  Are they indeed snow-flakes
Whirling from the sky?—*By the host.*

WHEN the plum-blossoms are gone,   [v : 829]
  Are not the cherry-flowers
Ready to bloom in their place?
                    —*By Sakiko, the physician.*

THE prime of my life has far declined;   [v : 847]
  Even if I drank an elixir
To wing me to the clouds,
How could I regain my youth?—*By the host.*

IF I could see the capital,   [v : 848]
  Rather than drink an elixir
To wing me to the clouds,
Youth would bud in me again,
Humble though I am.—*By the host.*

On plum-blossoms (composed later by Tabito).   [v : 852]

IN my dream said a plum-blossom:
  A gallant flower I count myself,
Float me in your cup of saké.

Embassy to Shiragi.

Poems exchanged between the embassy despatched to Shiragi and those who were left at home, expressing their sorrow at separation, in the eighth year of Tempyō (736), and poems on the hardships and solitude of the voyage.

738   WHEN I am parted from you, my   [xv : 3578]
        dearest,
      Who fold me as with wings,

As a water-bird its chick on Muko Bay,[1]
On the sand-bar of the inlet—
O I shall die of yearning after you.

739   COULD my great ship take you in,   [xv : 3579]
        I would keep you, beloved,
Folding you as with wings!

740   WHEN mist rises on the seashore   [xv : 3580]
        Where you put in,
Consider it the breathing
Of my sighs at home.

741   WHEN autumn comes we shall meet   [xv : 3581]
        again;
Then how should you raise such sighs
That they would mist the shore!

742   WEAR yourself not out   [xv : 3586]
        With yearning after me,
In the month when the autumn wind blows
We shall meet again.

743   FOR you, who journey to Shiragi,   [xv : 3587]
        I will, in purification,[2] wait,
Longing to see your eyes again,
To-day or to-morrow.

744   UNAWARE that the ships must wait   [xv : 3594]
        For high tide,
I have parted, to my grief,
From my love so soon.

---

[1] Muko was a general name for Kōbé and vicinity.
[2] When any one of the family was on a journey, those left at home lived in purification, worshipping the gods. They believed that if anything evil happened at
home the same would befall the one on his journey.

745   *On the evening when they harboured at the*   [xv : 3613]
shore of Nagai, in Mizuki District,
Bingo Province.

ALTHOUGH across the plains of the sea I came,
    Passing through eighty islands,
Not once has the City of Nara
Left my heart.

746   *On the evening when they stopped at the*   [xv : 3615]
shore of Kazahaya.[1]

MY love must sigh after me—
    Far off from the shore of Kazahaya
A mist is trailing.

747-8   *On looking up at the moon when embarking* [xv : 3623-4]
from the shore of Nagato.[2]

AS the moon sinks on the mountain-edge
    The fishermen's lights flicker
Far out on the dark wide sea.

When we think that we alone
Are steering our ships at midnight,
We hear the splash of oars
Far beyond us.

749--51   *Referring to various things.*   [xv : 3627-9]

FROM Mitsu, dearest shore to me,
    As to my wife her mirror in the morning,
We started at the flood-tide

[1] In the province of Aki.
[2] Also in Aki.

244

In our stately full-oared ships
For the Land of Kara,
Steering straight ahead to Minumé
Piloted through the waves.

But the sea ran high with white surges
And we coasted shore after shore;
As evening drew on, clouds arose
And veiled the island of Awaji,
That made me long to see my love.

At dead of night, with our bearings lost,
We harboured in the bay of Akashi
And passed the night upon the water;
When far out at sea we saw
Fisher-maids row their little boats,
Floating them side by side.

As daylight came and the flood-tide reached us,
Cranes called flying to the reedy coast;
To leave the shore with morning calm,
Both our boatmen and rowers,
Laboured with loud cheers;
And like the grebes we pushed our way
To see the dim, far isle of ‘ Home.’

If the isle was faithful to its name,
It would relieve our weary hearts;
We strained and rowed our stately ships
To come to port the sooner,
But the sea rose up between.

We left the islet far away
And anchored ship at Tama;
Like a crying child we wept
To see the shore and the beach.

Here I have gathered for my wife
The gems that deck the Sea God’s arms

And put them in my sleeves;
But what use are they
When I have no messenger
To take them home?
So I drop them down again.

Envoys

At Tama Bay I have gathered
The white pearls of the ocean,
But I drop them down again,
To no one can I show them.

When autumn comes
Our ships will harbour here;
Bear and leave shells of forgetfulness,[1]
You, white surges of the ocean.

752   *By Tanabé Akiniwa, two nights after they*   [xv : 3638]
              passed Naruto[2] at Ōshima.

A RE these truly the fisher-maids
        Who are said to gather the beautiful weeds
In the whirling tide of famed Naruto?

753   *They encountered a sudden contrary storm and*   [xv : 3644]
        rough sea off Saba and drifted. On the next day,
        with a favourable wind they reached the shore
        of Wakuma, in Shimotsuké District, Buzen
        Province. Here, reflecting on the hardships,
              Yuki Yakamaro composed a poem.

A T our dread Sovereign's word,
        Whither his royal ships take us,

---

[1] i. e. *wasure-gai*; *wasure* means ' forget,' and *kai* means ' shell.' By reason of its
name it was believed to make all sorrows forgotten.

[2] The straits where the swift current, forming whirlpools, passes with a resounding noise.

There we find our harbour.

7J4 THE fishing fires far away   [xv : 3648]
       On the plain of the sea—
    Oh, make them brighter
    That I may see the Island of Yamato.

7JJ   *Gazing on the moon by the seashore.*   [xv : 3666]

    As evening falls the autumn wind is cold;
        Would that I were at home, wearing the sweet
        clothes
    My wife unstitched and washed for me!

7J6 *Three days after they had landed at Karadomari*[1] [xv : 3669]
    in Shima District, Chikuzen Province, they look-
    ed at an unusually beautiful moon, and, moved
    by the scene, each composed a poem on the tedium
    of the journey. This poem, one of six, was
    composed by Mibu Utamaro, the Daihangan.[2]

    ALTHOUGH I am on a journey,
        I pass the evening by the blazing fire,
    While my wife at home
    Must long for me in the dark.

7J7   *At the port of Hikitsu.*[3]   [xv : 3676]

    O FOR my couriers,
        Yon heaven-traversing wild-geese,

---

[1] Derived from *Kara* (Korea) and *tomari* (stopping-place); so named because the port then occupied an important place in the communication between Japan and Korea.
[2] i. e. title for an official, third in rank, in the embassy to Shiragi.
[3] An old seaport in the north of Kyūshū.

That I might send my words
To the City of Nara!

758-60   *On the death of Yuki Yakamaro from a* [xv : 3688–90]
        sudden attack of the plague when he
           arrived at the isle of Iki.

O YOU, who were voyaging to the Land of Kara,
  Our Sovereign's distant court—
Since you told her that had suckled you,
' I shall return when autumn comes,'
Weary months of time have passed.

And your housefolk wait and long,
' He may be home to-day,
He will surely come to-morrow.'

But, have your kinsmen failed
In purifications due?
Or have you failed in your duties?

Before you reach the distant land,
And far away from Yamato,
You lie for ever here
On this isle of rugged rocks.

Envoys

O you, who lie at Iwata Field,
If your housefolk ask me where you are,
How shall I answer them?

You have parted from us, as if to say,
' This is the way of the world,'
While I go upon my voyage
With vain abiding love for you!

248

WHEN you well might have wished to live
    Eternal as heaven and earth,
You left your long-beloved home,
To furrow the surging waves,
And days and months have come and passed.
As the wild-geese in succession come and cry,
Your wife and mother leave the door and wait,
Skirts drenched with the morning dew,
Garments wet with the evening mist,
As if you lived and flourished still.

But now you reck not of the grief
That wrings a beating heart;
And on the field strewn with flowering bush-clovers,
Under the roofs thatched with early *susuki*,[1]
You lie for ever in your resting-place,
Beside the mountain cold with dew and frost,
In regions far as clouds from home.

Envoys

Are you hidden behind the isle,
You for whom your beloved wife and children
Patiently on tiptoe wait?

Poor wretched creatures they,
Who must wait in vain for you,
For you who lie upon this mountain
Where soon the yellow leaves will fall.

---

[1] A kind of feathery pampas grass. See note to No. 83.

Poems by the frontier-guards despatched from various prov-
inces to Tsukushi as a relief contingent in the second month
of the seventh year of Tempyō-Shōhō (755).

Presented to the court by the Military Commissioner,[1]
Sakamoto Hitogami, an official of Tōtōmi Province,
on the sixth day of the second month.

764   THE dread imperial command   [xx : 4321]
     I have received : from to-morrow
I will sleep with the grass,
No wife being by me.
    —By Mononobé Akimochi, Lower Naga District ;[2]
    a guard from a Kuni-no-miyatsuko[3] family.

765   MY wife thinks of me much, I know ;   [xx : 4322]
     Her shadow shows in the water
Of the well-pool from which I drink—
For the world I can't forget her !
    —By Wakayamatobé Mumaro, Aratama District ;[4]
    a guard who was a district official.

766   EVEN in a strange land I see   [xx : 4323]
     The flowers of each season bloom—
The flowers I have known at home.
Why is it that there grows
No flower called ' Mother ' ?
     —By Hasetsukabé Mamaro, Yamana District ;[5]
     a guard.

---

[1] An officer appointed for each province to take its newly enlisted men as far as the port of Naniwa.

[2] An ancient district, now part of Hamana District, Shizuoka Prefecture.

[3] A local chief.

[4] An ancient district, now part of Iwata District, Shizuoka Prefecture.

[5] An ancient district, now part of Inasa District, Shizuoka Prefecture.

767　O THAT my father and my mother were　[xx : 4325]
　　　flowers!
　　Then, even if I must travel, grass for pillow,
　　I would take them with me,
　　Holding them reverently in my hands.
　　　　　　—*By Hasetsukabé Kuromasa, Saya District.*[1]

768　I WISH I had the leisure　　　　　[xx : 4327]
　　　To draw a picture of my wife
　　That I might look on it and think of her
　　As I go on my journey!
　　　　　　—*By Mononobé Komaro, Lower Naga District.*

*Presented to the court by the Military Commissioner
of Sagamu Province, Fujiwara Sukunamaro,
the Governor.*

769　I LEAVE my father and mother behind　[xx : 4328]
　　　In obedience to the imperial command,
　　And sail the perilous sea
　　Where my ship sweeps against the rocks.
　　　　　　—*By Hasetsukabé Hitomaro, a guard.*

770　WITH the ships all in trim　　　　[xx : 4330]
　　　At the port of Naniwa,
　　To-day is the day I leave—
　　Without my mother to see me go.
　　—*By Mariko Ōmaro, Kamakura District ;*[2] *a guard.*

[1] An ancient district, now part of Ogasa District, Shizuoka Prefecture.
[2] Now, Kamakura District, Kanagawa Prefecture.

*Presented to the court by the Military Commissioner
of Suruga Province, Fusé Hitonushi, on the
seventh day of the second month.*[1]

771   How I regret it now—   [xx : 4337]
         In the flurry of departure,
As of the waterfowl taking to flight,
I came away without speaking a word
To my father and my mother.
                              —*By Udobé Ushimaro, a guard.*

772   Be strong like a mansion built   [xx : 4342]
         With blessings on its true-wood pillars—
May the years bring no change,
O mother, to your lovely look!
                              —*By Sakatabé Obitomaro.*

773   As for me, I can take   [xx : 4343]
         Travels as they come;
But my poor wife with the children—
She must be falling thin with care!
                              —*By Tamatsukuribé Hiromé.*

774   Though I tried to forget, as I came   [xx : 4344]
         Trudging over moors and over mountains,
I cannot forget them—
My father and my mother!
                              —*By Akino Osamaro.*

775   Never can I forget the words   [xx : 4346]
         My father and mother spoke—
Patting me on the head, and saying:

  [1] The actual presentation of this group of poems took place on the 9th of the 2nd
month.—Original Note.

' My son, good fortune be with you ! '
                    —*By Hasetsukabé Inamaro.*

*Presented to the court by the Military Commissioner of
Kazusa Province, Mamuta Samimaro, on the ninth day of
the second month.*

776　RATHER than that I should remain at　[xx : 4347]
　　　home,
　　Longing for you,
　　I would be the sword that you wear
　　And pray the gods to keep you from harm.
　　　　　—*By the father of Kusakabé Minaka, a guard.*

777　AH, must I leave you, dear—　[xx : 4352]
　　　You, who clasp me,
　　Even as the creeping bean-vine clings
　　To the wild rose-bush by the wayside !
　　　—*By Hasetsukabé Tori, Amaha District ;*[1] *a guard.*

778　WELL do I remember how she wept,　[xx : 4357]
　　　Standing in the reed-fence corner—
　　That dear girl of mine—
　　Her sleeves all wet with tears !
　　　—*By Osakabé Chikuni, Ichihara District ;*[2] *a guard.*

779　WHEN I started out from home　[xx : 4358]
　　　In obedience to the imperial command,
　　How the girl clung to me
　　And moaned her grief!
　　　　　—*By Mononobé Tatsu, Sué District ;*[3] *a guard.*

[1] Now part of Kimitsu District, Chiba Prefecture.
[2] Now part of Ichihara District, Chiba Prefecture.
[3] Now part of Kimitsu District, Chiba Prefecture.

Presented to the court by the Military Commissioner
of Hitachi Province, Okinaga Kunishima, the
Daimoku.

780 A FRONTIER-guard when I set out, [xx : 4364]
  Oh, what turmoil there was!
 Of the work my wife should do
 I said not a word and came away.
   —By Wakatoneribé Hirotari, Ubaraki District.[1]

781 WHAT do I care for life or death— [xx : 4370]
  I who have come praying all the way
 To the god of hail-spattering Kashima[2]
 And joined the imperial host?
   —By Ōtoneribé Chifumi, Naga District;[3] *a guard.*

782 THE steep mountain-road of Ashigara[4] [xx : 4372]
  I will travel, the good god granting,[5]
 And never will turn back homewards;
 The Pass of Fuwa[6] I will cross,
 Where well a reckless man might fear to stand;
 I will go as far as my horse can take me,
 Even to the uttermost point of Tsukushi[7]—
 There I will stop and thus will pray:
 ' May those I love be well till I return! '
   —By Shidoribé Karamaro.

---

 [1] An ancient district, comprising parts of the present districts of Higashi-Ibaraki, Nishi-Ibaraki, and Niibari, Ibaraki Prefecture.
 [2] i. e. Takemikazuchi-no-kami, who is enshrined at Kashima, and who is a patron of warriors.
 [3] Identical with the present district of the same name in Ibaraki Prefecture.
 [4] On the north side of Hakoné. This road, which led from Sagami Province into Suruga, was famous for its steepness.
 [5] It was the custom for travellers crossing a mountain to pray to its god for safety.
 [6] In the western part of Mino Province, and near the border of Ōmi.
 [7] The frontier-guards were garrisoned in the various headlands of Kyūshū.

*Presented to the court by the Military Commissioner of
Shimotsuké Province, Taguchi Ōto, on the fourteenth
day of the second month.*

783   I will not from to-day   [xx : 4373]
      Turn back toward home—
I who have set out to serve
As Her Majesty's humble shield.
        *—By Imamatsuribé Yosofu, a non-commissioned
        officer.*[1]

784   Praying to the gods of heaven and   [xx : 4374]
      earth,
And thrusting hunting arrows in my quiver,
For the far isle of Tsukushi
Now I depart—yes, I !
        —By Ōtabé Aramimi, a non-commissioned officer.

785   Those pines standing in rows—   [xx : 4375]
      How like to my own people !
They stood just so,
As they came out
To bid me farewell.
        —By Mononobé Mashima, a non-commissioned officer.

786   Oh, that my dear mother   [xx : 4377]
      Were a jewel-piece
That I might place in my hair-knot[2]
And always wear above me !
        —By Tsumori Okurusu.

---

[1] A non-commissioned officer in command of ten men.
[2] In old times men wore their hair parted in the middle and done up into a knot
(*mizura*) on each side of the head.

787   O FOR a sight once more   [xx : 4383]
        Of my dear mother now—
When the ships are ready
By the shore of Tsu-no-Kuni,[1]
And I go forth !
    —*By Hasetsukabé Taruhito, Shioya District ; a guard.*

Presented to the court by the Military Commissioner of Shimofusa Province, Inukai Kiyohito, on the sixteenth day of the second month.

788   BEFORE me on my track   [xx : 4385]
        Lie the sounding waves of the sea;
Behind me, my wife and children—
All left at home !
        —*By Kisakibé Isoshima, Katsushika District.*

Presented to the court by the Military Commissioner of Shinanu Province on the twenty-second day of the second month.

789   AT Misaka, the Pass of the Gods,[2]   [xx : 4402]
        I have made offerings,
Praying for the safety of my life—
All for my mother's and father's sake.
        —*By Kamutobé Kooshio, Hanishina District ;[3] a guard.*

[1] The province of Settsu of later times, comprising parts of the present prefectures of Ōsaka and Hyōgo. Naniwa was situated in this province.

[2] The pass leading from Ina District, Shinano Province, to Ena District, Mino Province, was known as ' Misaka ' (Pass of the Gods), because of its exceeding steepness.

[3] The present Hanishina District, Nagano Prefecture.

Presented to the court by the Military Commissioner,
Kamitsukenu Suruga, a provincial official.

790   I WISH there were a man going to my   [xx : 4406]
      home.
By him I would send word and say :
' Hard is travelling, with grass for pillow.'
              —By Ōtomobé Fushimaro.

Presented to the court by the Military Commissioner
of Musashi Province, Azumi Mikuni, on the
twenty-ninth day of the second month.

791   THE red pony cannot be fetched,   [xx : 4417]
      Being let loose on the upland plain.
Must I send my man on foot—alas !
Over the hill range of Tama ?[1]
      —By Ujibé Kuromé, wife of a guard, Kurahashibé
        Aramushi, Toyoshima District.[2]

792   WHILE, sleeping in your clothes,   [xx : 4420]
      You travel, grass for pillow,
Should your sash-string tear off,
Sew it on yourself, using
For my hand—see, this needle !
      —By Kurahashibé Otomé, wife of Mononobé Mané,
      Tachibana District ;[3] *a guard.*

---

[1] The hill-range stretching along the south bank of the Tama River in Musashi.
[2] Now part of Tōkyō Prefecture.
[3] The present Tachibana District, Kanagawa Prefecture.

Preface.

Once I wandered for a while in the district of Matsura. When I visited the abyss of Tamashima, I happened to meet some girls fishing. Their flowery faces and radiant forms were beyond compare. Their eye-brows were like tender willow leaves, and their cheeks were like peach flowers. Their spirits soared above the clouds, and their gracefulness was not of this world. I asked, ' Where do you live ? What is your father's name ? Are you, if I may ask, fairies ? ' They answered, smiling, ' We are a fisherman's daughters. Being of low birth, we live in a grass-thatched cottage. We have neither land nor house of our own. How can we give you our names ? But, by nature we are kin with the water, and love the mountains. So, at one time, at Lopu[2] *we vainly envy the life of the giant fish ; at another, lying at Wuhsia*[2] *vainly do we look up to the banks of trailing mists. Now, by rare chance, we have met with one so noble as you, and we are happy to have revealed ourselves. So, will you pledge yourself to us for life ? ' ' Yes,' I replied, ' gladly I will.' Just then the sun set beyond the western mountains, and my horse was impatient to leave. Therefore I expressed my feeling in verse.*

BUT a fisherman's daughters   [v : 853]
   You say of yourselves,
Yet your looks reveal
That you are girls of noble birth.—*By Tabito.*

On the Tamashima River,   [v : 854]
Here by its upper stream, stands our home.
But from bashfulness
We did not tell you where.—*By the girls.*

In the river of Matsura,   [v : 855]

---

[1] The river of Matsura flowed into the bay of Karatsu through Matsura District, Hizen. It was not the present river of the same name, but the upper reach of the river Tamashima. It is also called the Kuri.

[2] Lopu and Wuhsia are places alluded to in Chinese fairy-tales.

You stand fishing for *ayu*,
Brightening up the shallows;
Your skirts are drenched.—*By Tabito.*

When spring comes round,   [v : 859]
Through the ford near our home,
The little *ayu* will shoot,
Impatient for you.—*By the girls.*

Anonymous

797-8   *On the occasion of the transfer¹ of the court*   [1 : 79-80]
                from Fujiwara to Nara.

OBEDIENT to our mighty Sovereign's word,
    I left my long-loved home,
And paddled my boat down the Hatsusé,²
Many times looking back toward my home,
At each of the eighty windings of the river;
And benighted on the stream I reached
The River Saho³ flowing through Nara;
There from my couch I could see,
Clearly in the bright moonlight of dawn,
The night-frost lying like a sheet of linen
And the river bound with ice as if with rocks.
Often on such a freezing night, loyal to my duties,
I paddled down to build the mansion,
Where I hope my lord will live
For a thousand ages,
And that I too may journey here for as long.

---

¹ The capital was transferred to Nara by the Empress Gemmyō in the 3rd year
of Wadō (710).
² The Hatsusé runs near the town of Hatsusé and at the foot of Mount Miwa,
and, flowing to the north, pours into the Saho.
³ Runs from north to west of the present city of Nara, and through the old
capital of Nara, and, joining the Hatsusé, it thus forms the River Yamato.

I shall come to the mansion of Nara
For a myriad ages;
Think not I shall forget!

799   *An elegy on seeing the dead body of a beautiful*   [III : 434]
       woman in the pine-woods of Himeshima,[1]
       in the fourth year of Wadō (711).

THOUGH I see the white azaleas on the shore
   Of Miho of Kazahaya,
I am sad, remembering the lady
Whose soul is here no more.

800   *An elegy on the death of Prince Kashiwadebé.*[2]   [III : 442]

As if to foreshadow
   That the world will be vain,
This bright moon waxes and wanes!

801   *On bidding farewell at Ashiki, Chikuzen, to*   [IV : 549]
       Ishikawa Taruhito, an official of the Da-
       zaifu, transferred to a new post, in
       the first year of Jinki (724).

MY friend, you are setting out
   On a long, long journey—
May the gods of heaven and earth
Help you till you reach your home!

---

1 Himeshima was at Naniwa, in Settsu Province, whereas Kazahaya in the poem
was in Kii Province, the obvious discrepancy pointing to textual corruption. The
poem probably alludes to the legend of a young noble, called Kumé, said to have
lived in Miho of Kazahaya.

2 Son of Prince Nagaya, Minister of the Left, who was condemned to death in
the 2nd month in the 6th year of Jinki (729), whereupon Prince Kashiwadebé
committed suicide.

Ōtomo Sadehiko[2] *was suddenly despatched on a special*
mission to the Sovereign's tributary.[3]   *His sweetheart, Lady*
Sayo of Matsura, sorrowing at this hasty separation, and in
her fears of never meeting him again, climbed a steep hill, and
watched her lover's ship sail away, her heart breaking with
grief.   At last she took off her scarf and wildly waved it.
At this, those who happened to be near her burst into tears,
and ever after people called the hill the Scarf-Waving Hill.

LADY Sayo of Matsura, as her name tells
   Of one waiting for a lover far away,
Pressed by her longing, waved her scarf;
Hence the name of this hill.

803–4   Composed on the occasion when the princes and [vi : 948–9]
     courtiers were by imperial order confined
        in the Bureau of Palace-Guards.

To the hill of Kasuga where *kuzu* vines creep,
   The spring has come—the lush spring,
With mists hovering over the dale
And warblers singing on Takamado.

Ah, the spring we could scarce wait for—
We, courtiers of eighty clans, hoping
That with such days following one upon another,
When wild geese come flocking together,
We might go out with friends to sport,
And ride our horses side by side in the fields !

Had we foreseen this punishment,
Dreadful beyond speech,

---

   [1] A little hill standing on the eastern skirts of the village of Kagami in Hamasaki,
Matsura District, Hizen.   It borders on Niji-no-Matsubara.
   [2] Ōtomo Sadehiko was sent to Mimana to suppress a rebellion, and to support
Kudara, in the 2nd year of the reign of the Emperor Senka (537).
   [3] i.e. Mimana in Korea.

We would have gone to the Saho River
Where the sanderlings cry,
And purified ourselves
With the root of the sedge growing on the rock,
And cleansed our stains in the running water.

O that we, men of the Great Palace,
Should, in obedience to the imperial command,
Dare not even go out in the streets,
But pass the days—these days of spring—
Longing for the open air.

Envoy

We went to sport in the Saho vale,
Only because we feared to miss
Its plum-bloom and the willows in their prime.
Who then noised it throughout the palace?

In the first month of the fourth year of Jinki (727) several princes and a number of court nobles met in the Kasuga Field to play a ball game. It happened on that day that the skies suddenly grew dark and a rain-storm broke, attended with lightning and thunder. At this moment in the palace there were present neither guards nor attendants. By imperial order all the men were punished for delinquency by being confined in the Bureau of Palace-Guards, from which they were forbidden to go out in the streets. The above poem was composed in sorrow and dismay. The author is unknown.

Isonokami Otomaro and his Wife

805-6   On the banishment to Tosa of Isonokami [VI : 1019-20,1]
Otomaro.[1]

BECAUSE of your errant love for a maid,
Luckless Lord Furu Isonokami,

[1] These two poems are addressed to Otomaro in sympathy with his plight.

Bound with a rope like a horse,
And surrounded with bows and arrows
Like a hunted boar,
You go at the dread imperial command
Down to the province, heaven-distant.
Would from the mountain of Matsuchi
You could return to us who wait behind !

You set out, dear lord and friend,
In obedience to the imperial command,
For that land across the sea,
May the Gods of Suminoé who—
Though too awesome to speak of—
Appear in mortal shape,
Descend upon your ship's prow
To protect you from wind and wave,
At every island point you touch,
And every turn of the coast you pass !
May they keep you free from all ills
And shortly send you back to your homeland !

807–8 **I,** a dear child to my father,   [VI : 1022–3]
       And a dear child to my mother—
Alas ! on the ' Awesome Pass ' of Kashiko
Where men of eighty clans
Returning to the capital
Make offerings with joyful thanks,
I present my *nusa*[1] sadly in prayer,
Going down the long road to Tosa !

Envoy

Off the hallowed strand of Ōsaki,
Though narrow is the sound,
The boatmen thronging the water
Will not pass hastily on,

[1] A wreath of white paper hung up before a deity.

263

As I—alas ! an exile—must.[1]

Anonymous

809   *On the ruins of the City of Nara.*   [VI : 1045]

H ow truly now I understand
   The impermanence of this world,
Seeing Nara, the Imperial City,
Lie thus in ruins.

810–1   *Addressed to a son by his mother when the* [IX : 1790–1]
        ships of the embassy to China were leaving
        the port of Naniwa in the fifth year[2] of
        Tempyō (733).

A DEER that seeks the *hagi* flowers for mate
   Brings forth a single fawn, it is told;
My son, single as that fawn, now starts
Upon his travels, grass for pillow;
And I, purified, hang a string of bamboo-rings
And, setting out the sacred wine-jar
Dressed with mulberry cloth,
Implore the gods,
May he of whom I think
Ever travel safe and sound.

Envoy

When hoar-frost falls on the plain
Where the traveller shelters,
Cover my darling with your wings,
O flock of cranes of heaven !

---

[1] This long poem and envoy are put into the mouth of Otomaro.
[2] Perhaps in April.

812–3   Addressed to an envoy[1] setting out for China [XIX : 4245–6]
in the fifth year of Tempyō (733).

AFTER travelling from the Imperial City
  Of beauteous Nara in Yamato
Down to wave-bright Naniwa,
You are now sent on a voyage
From Mitsu of Suminoé,[2]
Straight to the land
Where the sun sets ;[3]
May our great Gods of Suminoé—
With reverence I speak—
Sitting on the prow of your ship
And standing by the stern,
Guard it from the perilous wind and wave,
At every strand you touch,
At every port you harbour in,
And lead you back in safety
Home to our land.

Envoy

May the surges near and far from shore
Never wash over your ship,
Until it is rowed back
And harbours in this port !

814   SHALLOW is the mountain well-pool   [XVI : 3807]
  That glasses the clean image
Of yonder hill of Asaka[4]—
But no shallow heart
Have I for you, O Prince !

Regarding the above poem it is said :   On the occasion

[1] i. e. Tajihi Hironari.
[2] i. e. the present Sumiyoshi of Ōsaka.
[3] i. e. China, as opposed to Japan, the Land of the Rising Sun.
[4] In Fukushima Prefecture.

when Prince Kazuraki[1] was despatched to the province of Mutsu, the Governor received him in a conspicuously neglect-ful manner. The prince was displeased, and there was anger in his looks. Though wine and food were offered him, he refused to touch them. Now there was in the company a former unemé (a palace attendant), who was an accomplished lady. Holding a wine-cup in her left hand, and wine in her right hand, she tapped the prince on the knee and recited this poem. The prince, appeased and delighted, made merry, drinking all day long.

815　　　　　　　　　*To Prince Niitabé*　　　　　[XVI : 3835]

THE lake of Katsumata
　　Has no lotus, I know,
Just as Your Highness,
Speaking so, has no beard.[2]

A story is told as follows. Once Prince Niitabé went out for a walk in the city, and saw Lake Katsumata, the sight of which delighted his heart. Even after returning to his mansion, he was unable to contain his enthusiasm. So he spoke to a lady, saying : ' I went out to see Lake Katsumata. Pure and limpid was the water, and gorgeous the lotus-bloom —a sight lovely indeed beyond speech ! ' The lady replied by reciting the above satirical poem.

---

[1] i. e. Tachibana Moroé.
[2] The prince had a luxuriant growth of beard.

When the Governor-General of the Dazaifu, Ōtomo Tabito, was appointed Chief Councillor of State, and travelled home to the capital, in winter, in the eleventh month of the second year of Tempyō (730), his followers took a different route, going by sea. On that occasion they composed poems on the sorrows of the journey. The following is one of the ten anonymous poems.

816   STARTING out on my travels,   [XVII : 3897]
  Unknown as the limit of the great sea,
She asked me when I should return,
That lovely girl!

817-8   *A Seventh Night Poem.*   [IX : 1764-5]

OVER the River of Heaven,
  I throw a jewelled bridge
Across its upper shallows,
I float a chain of boats
Across its lower shallows.
Even when the rain is falling
Though the wind is hushed,
Even when the wind is blowing
Though the rain falls not,
That my lord may come over to me,
Failing me never,
Not wetting his skirt,
I throw a jewelled bridge.

Envoy

A mist rises over the River of Heaven;
My lord whom I awaited,
' To-day, surely to-day '—
Poles out his boat at last!

YONDER on the plain of Kasuga
   I see wreaths of smoke arise—
Are the young girls
Boiling the starworts,
Plucked from the fields of spring ?

PERIOD UNKNOWN

Anonymous

820 *Composed during the Sovereign's visit to Isé.*   [VII : 1089]

O<small>N</small> the ocean where no islands are in sight,
   Far out on the surging waves
White clouds arise.

821-2 O<small>UR</small> Sovereign who rules in peace,   [XIII : 3234-5]
   Offspring of the Bright One on high,
Holds in demesne
The land of Isé, of the Divine Wind,
Which provides the august table.[1]

When we survey this realm,
High and noble rise the hills,
Bright and clear run the rivers,
Broad is the sea that gives us harbour,
And famous is the island there we see.

Because he prized these,
—So awful on my lips—
On the plain of Ishi in Yamanobé
His sun-lit palace was reared,
Glorious as the morning sun
And radiant as the evening sun.

As long as heaven and earth shall last,
And as long as sun and moon,
May the courtiers serve him
At the palace prosperous like the spring hills
Loaded with the blossoms,
And alluring as the coloured leaves
On the hills of autumn.

[1] Fishes were caught in Isé for imperial use.

Lo, near the royal well of Ishi
In Yamanobé, rise the mountains
Hung with nature's own brocade !

823–4   *Cherry-Flower Maid.*   [XVI : 3786–7]

*Once there was a young woman of the name of Sakura-ko
(Cherry-Flower Maid). She was courted by two young men,
who in their rivalry cared not for their lives, but contended
bitterly as if eager for death. The girl wept and said to herself : ' From olden times to these days never has it been heard
nor seen, that one woman should go to two houses to marry.
Now there is no way to reconcile the hearts of these young men.
It would be best for me to die so that they may cease for ever
from harming each other.' Then, she sought the wood,
where, hanging herself from a tree, she died. The two young
men could scarce contain their grief. Tears of blood trickled
down their collars. These are the poems they made to express their sentiments :*

I THOUGHT I would wear it
    When the spring came—
Alas, my ' cherry-flower '
Is fallen and gone !

When the cherry-flower blooms—
My dear love's namesake—
I shall long for her
Each year and evermore !

Once there was a young man and a fair maid (their names cannot be ascertained), who were meeting in secret, unknown to their parents. Now the maid, desiring to acquaint the parents with the affair, wrote a poem, and sent it to her lover.

825 LOVE is a torment   [XVI : 3803]
    Whenever we hide it.
  Why not lay it bare
  Like the moon that appears
  From behind the mountain ledge ?

826 IF need be, I'd follow you   [XVI : 3806]
    Even to the rock vault
  In the Ohatsusé Mountains
  And be together with you ;
  Be not troubled, dearest !

It is said that there was a young woman who met a young man in secret without letting the parents know of it. The young man, fearing their rebuke, seemed rather doubtful about continuing the affair. Thereupon, the young woman composed the above poem and sent it to him.

827 IF there be a law that allows   [XVI : 3809]
    The tradesman to break a contract,
  Return to me, then, my under-robe !

It is said that there was once a young woman beloved of a high-born personage. His love waning, he returned to her the keepsake she had given him. Thereupon the girl, aggrieved and resentful, composed the above poem and sent it to her fickle lover.

Loathing both seas of Life and Death,
    How deeply I long
For the upland of Nirvana,
Untouched by the tides of Change !

One of two poems said to have been inscribed on the face of a koto which was found in the Hall of Buddhas of the Kahara Temple.

So to the mud-bed
    Of the Kumaki Sea
You have dropped a hatchet,—
A Shiragi hatchet, ha ha !
Oh, never mind, do not cry !
Let us see if it will
Float up to the top, ha ha !

It is said that a foolish man once dropped a hatchet into the bottom of the sea, but he did not know that a piece of metal, once it sunk under the water, would not rise to the surface. The above poem was composed and recited for purposes of instruction.

At the Table Island
    Of Kashimané
Have you gathered turbo shells
And brought them home ?—
Crushed the meat out with a stone,

---

[1] A province on the northern side of Honshū, jutting out into the Japan Sea.

Washed and cleaned it
In a swift-flowing river,
Rubbed it hard in salt,
Put it in a tall dish,
Set it on a table,—

And so served it to your mother,
Darling little housewife?
And so served it to your father,
Darling little housewife?

Two Beggar Songs.[1]

The Hart.   [XVI : 3885]

O GOOD friend, dear master,
    You are settled snugly at home.
Should you set out on a journey,
Whither would it be?   To the Land of Kara
To capture the monsters called ' tigers '—
Eight head of them all alive—
Bring them back and make mats
Of their skins and pile them eightfold—

To the ' eightfold mat ' mountains
Of Heguri, in the months of April and May,
I go to serve in the medicine hunt.[2]
Once as I stood on the one-slope hill
Under two tall *ichihi*[3]-trees
And waited for deer, grasping eight bows
And grasping eight turnip-head arrows,[4]
Lo, there stood before me a hart—
Says he, wailing : ' Soon must I die.
But still I will serve my lord,

---

[1] These songs or ballads were sung from door to door by mendicant minstrels.
[2] Deer were hunted in this season for their newly grown horns, which were used for medicinal purposes.
[3] A kind of oak (*Quercus gilva*).
[4] Arrows with turnip-shaped heads.

Dedicating humbly to his use
My horns for hat ornaments,
My ears for inkstands,
My eyes for shining mirrors,
My hoofs for bow-ends,
My hair for writing-brushes,
My skin for leather-boxes,
My flesh for mincemeat,
My liver, too, for mincemeat,
And my umbles for salt-pickles.

' Thus, old slave as I am,
This single body of mine
Will put forth a sevenfold bloom,
Will put forth an eightfold bloom—
So sing my praise, sing my praise ! '

*This poem relates on behalf of the hart its hardships
and sufferings.*

832   **The Crab.**   [XVI : 3886]

IN the wave-bright Naniwa Bay
    I make my home and live in hiding.
My lord calls me, I hear, to his mansion—
Me, a humble crab amid the reeds.
Wherefore this lordly summons ?
Am I called as singer
Of the songs I know well ?[1]
Am I called as flute-player ?
Am I called as *koto*-player ?[2]

Anyhow to hear the lordly command

[1] The line is sometimes interpreted as meaning ' I know well the circumstance (the reason for the summons).' In that case, it should precede the line above it, reading :
    ' I know well the circumstance.
      Am I called as a singer of songs ? '
[2] All these questions are, of course, rhetorical, each implying the negative answer.

One day I journey to Asuka;[1]
Come to Okina[1] though I stand;
To Tsukunu[1] though I carry no cane.
And at the inner gate on the east side
I enter the mansion to await the lordly command.

There I am seized and bound,
Though I am no horse to be strapped and haltered,
Though I am no ox to be tied with a nose-cord.

Then, my lord, going to the hill,
Peels an ample measure of elm bark;
Lets it hang and dry in the sun;
Pounds it in a mortar;
Grinds it through a quern standing in the yard.

He fetches salt from Naniwa Bay,
The fine first-dripped salt.
One day he goes to the potter
And brings back on the morrow a jar he made.

My lord, smearing my eyes with salt,
Bestows on me lordly praise—
Lordly praise!

This poem relates on behalf of the crab its hardships and sufferings.

833-4   *An elegy on the death of his wife.*[2]   [XIX : 4236-7]

ARE there no gods of heaven and earth?
    My dearest wife is dead!
Though I wished to live hand in hand
With my love, Hata-otomé—
Her name tells of the god
Who lightens and thunders—

---

[1] *Asu* of *Asuka*, *Oki* of *Okina*, and *Tsuku* of *Tsukunu*, are homophones respectively of the words for *to-morrow*, *lay down*, and *lean on a staff*. In the translation the play on these words is entirely lost.

[2] These verses were recited by Gamō, a courtesan.—Original Note.

All my hopes were vain !
And I am in despair.
With a sash of mulberry cloth on my shoulders,
And in my hands offerings of twill bands,
I prayed, ' Divide us not ! '
Yet those sleeves of hers I slept upon
Now trail among the clouds !

Envoy

O that I could think it real !
No use : I only dream I lie
Pillowed on her sleeves.

Azuma Uta (Eastland Poems)

835–6   *Poems from the province of Hitachi.*   [XIV : 3350–1]

THOUGH I have silks
    Fresh from the new mulberry cocoons,
Of the Tsukuba Mountain,
Oh, how I'd love
To wear that gown of yours.

On the Tsukuba Mountain slope
Has snow fallen ?—or no ?
Has she—my darling girl—
Hung out her clothes to dry ?

837–8   *Poems from the province of Shimofusa.*   [XIV : 3386–7]

THOUGH it be the night when I make
    Offerings of the early rice[1]
Of Katsushika,

---

[1] On the sacred night of rice-offering all the menfolk of the household were obliged to stay outside.

278

I will not keep you, darling,
Standing outside the house.

Would there were a horse
That could travel with silent feet !
Then, over the jointed bridge of Mama
In Katsushika, I'd come to you
Night after night.

839   *A poem from the province of Hitachi.*   [XIV : 3393]

As if with wardens posted
    On this and that side of the Tsukuba Mountain,
My mother watches me ;
But our spirits have met.

840-1   *Poems from the province of Shinanu.* [XIV : 3399-400]

THE highway of Shinanu
    Is a new-cut road.
You may trip on the stubs :
Put on your sandals, dearest !

Even the pebbles on the beach
Of the Chikuma River in Shinanu,
If you walk on them,
I will gather like precious stones.

842-4   *Poems from the province of Kamitsuké.*

LET our love be made as plain   [XIV : 3414]
    As the rainbow that spans
The Yasaka weir of Ikaho,
Could I but sleep and sleep with you !

279

Do not rumble, O Thunder,   [XIV : 3421]
Over the mountains of Ikaho !
Though to me it is no matter,
You frighten this little darling of mine.

The mountain wind of Ikaho—   [XIV : 3422]
There are days when it blows
And there are days when it blows not.
But my love is timeless.

845   *A poem from the province of Shimotsuké.*   [XIV : 3425]

SWIFT over the plains of Shimotsuké
    And across the Aso's river-beach,
My feet scarce touching the pebbles,
I have come as if through air—
Now pray, tell me your mind !

          *   *   *

846   HARK, the bells are ringing   [XIV : 3438]
            Over Tsumuga Fields;
It must be that the younger lord
Of the mansion of Kamushida
Goes hawking on the plains.

847   THE post-horse bells are tinkling,   [XIV : 3439]
            The post-house well is fenced in;
Will you give me water—mind you,
Straight from your own sweet hand ?

848   SEE, neighbour,   [XIV : 3440]
            Washing morning greens in the river,

Your child and mine are well-matched
In years—give me yours !

849   Do not burn the brake—   [XIV : 3452]
            So lovely as it is !
       Let new grass grow there as it will—
       The new grass mingling with the old !

850   My hands so chapped from rice-   [XIV : 3459]
            pounding—
       To-night again, he will hold them, sighing,
       My young lord of the mansion !

851   Away, you who rattle at my door,   [XIV : 3460]
            On this sacred night of new rice-offering,
       When I've sent my man out
       And worship in the house alone.

852   In obedience to the imperial command   [XIV : 3480]
            I set out as a soldier;
       Away from my dear wife I've come,
       And away from her pillowing arm.

853   O that I were the cloud   [XIV : 3510]
            That sails the sky !
       To-day I'd go and talk to my wife;
       To-morrow I'd come back again.

854   The cloud clings   [XIV : 3514]
            To the high mountain peak—
       So would I cling to you, were I a cloud,

And you, a mountain peak!

855   THE mouth of the mare   [XIV : 3532]
      Grazing in the spring meadow
Never stops; nor do her lips at home,
She talks of me—my wife!

856   HERE at the river neck,   [XIV : 3546]
      With green-budding willows overgrown,
Oh, how I wait for you—
No water I draw from the stream,
But stand, ever stamping the ground!

Poems of Frontier-Guards

857-8   IF I leave you behind,   [XIV : 3567-8]
      I shall miss you:
O that you were
The grip of the birchwood bow
I am taking with me!

If I stay behind,
I must suffer
The pain of longing—
Rather I'd be the bow
You carry on your morning hunts.

859   A FRONTIER-guard   [XIV : 3569]
      I set out in the morning;
And at the door—
How she wept, my darling wife,
Unwilling to let go my hand!

860   I WILL think of you, love,   [XIV : 3570]
      On evenings when the grey mist
    Rises above the rushes,
    And chill sounds the voice
    Of the wild ducks crying.

861   WHEN I see a woman   [XX : 4425]
      Indifferently asking,
    Whose husband is going
    As a frontier-guard,
    How I envy her lot,
    So free from all cares ![1]

862   O FOR the body of my darling wife,   [XX : 4431]
      Better far than seven coats
    Worn one over another,
    When on a chilly night of frost
    The bamboo leaves are rustling loud ![1]

Dialogue Poems

863-4   HAD I foreknown my sweet lord's   [XI : 2824-5]
      coming,
    My garden, now so rank with wild weeds,
    I had strewn it with pearls !

    What use to me a house strewn with pearls ?
    The cottage hidden in wild weeds
    Is enough, if I am with you.

[1] These are poems of a previous year, which were copied by Iwaré Moro-gimi, and sent to Ōtomo Yakamochi.—Original Note.

865-6 SINCE I had shut the gate   [XII : 3117-8]
　　　And locked the door,
Whence did you, dear one, enter
To appear in my dream?

Though you had shut the gate
And locked the door,
I must have come to you in your dream
Through the hole cut by a thief.

867-8 I WOULD make my way without a   [XIII : 3305-6]
　　　thought of you,
But when I look up to the green-clad hills,
The azaleas are you, my lovely girl,
And you, my blooming girl, the cherry-flowers.
People would make you mine,
They would make me your own.
Even the rugged hills, if men so wish,
Will draw towards each other;
Keep true your heart!

Envoy

How can I rid my thoughts of love?
I pray to the gods of heaven and earth,
Yet ever does my love increase!

869-70 SO it is, my dearest lover;   [XIII : 3307-8]
　　　As time goes, eight long years,
Beyond the term of childhood
When my tufty hair was clipped,
Beyond the bloom of girlhood
Thriving like the sprays of the orange-tree,
And secret like this stream
That runs beneath the sand,
I wait till I win your heart.

I, too, have prayed to the gods
Of heaven and earth,
Yet love will have its way.

871–4 WHERE others' husbands ride on   [XIII : 3314–7]
            horseback
Along the Yamashiro road,
You, my husband, trudge on foot.

Every time I see you there I weep,
To think of it my heart aches.

My husband, take on your back
My shining mirror, my mother's keepsake,
Together with the scarf thin as the dragon-fly's wing,
And barter them for a horse,
I pray you, my husband.

Envoys

Deep is the ford of the Izumi,
Your travelling clothes, I fear,
Will be drenched, my husband.

What worth to me my shining mirror,
When I see you, my husband,
Trudging on your weary way !

By her husband.

If I get a horse, my beloved,
You must go on foot;
Though we tread the rocks,
Let's walk, the two of us, together !

875–9 TO gather the wave-borne pearls   [XIII : 3318–22]
            On the shores of Ki,

My dearest lord has travelled far,
Crossing the mountains of ' Man and Wife ';
When, standing by the roadside in the evening,
I tried to divine :
' When will he come home ? '
Then came the oracle;
' Lady, your husband whom you await
Does not come to you,
Because he seeks the pearls
Borne by the ocean waves,
Because he gathers the white pearls
Washed by the ripples on the shore;
" Seven days at longest, it will take me,
At soonest, two."
So your husband said;
Do not lose heart, good lady.'

Envoys

With the aid of staff or none
Would I start to meet him,
But alas, I know not
Which way he comes !

Not straight,
But by this road to Kosé,
Treading the stony shore,
I have come,
In love's distress.

He passed the night with me,
And as day dawned
Opened the doors and left for Ki;
When can I have him back at home ?

By her husband.

Though my love, long standing at the gate,
May now have retired within,

Since she so loves me, I return.

.

880-1   *Poem of ridicule addressed to a priest,*   [XVI : 3846-7]
                               and reply.

Do not tether a horse
     To the stubble
Of my new-shaven priest's chin,
And pull too hard !
For, poor priest, he will cry.

Oh, say not that !
Do you not cry—
You too, good parishioner—
When the village master comes
To collect the taxes ?

From the 'Collection of Ancient Poems'

882   TERRIBLE are the ocean billows ;   [VII : 1232]
               Yet, shall we not set sail
        With entreaties to the gods ?

883   THE waves toss high ;   [VII : 1235]
               ' Boatman,' I say—
        ' Should we stay the night here floating like water-
               fowl,
        Or still press on ? '

884   THE night crow calls as if to tell of   [VII : 1263]
               dawn,
        But, on this hill-side,
        Over the tree-tops all is still.

287

885 GOING alone to the western market,[1]   [VII : 1264]
　　　Making no careful choice I bought the silk,
　　But what a costly bargain it was !

886 THESE hemp-clothes which you take—   [VII : 1265]
　　　A frontier-guard enlisted for this year—
　　When they are worn out at the shoulders,
　　Who will mend them for you, my husband ?

887 COME to me, my dearest,   [XI : 2364]
　　　Come in through the bamboo-blinds ![2]
　　Should my mother ask me,
　　I'll say, 'Twas but a gust of wind.

888-9   *On the cuckoo.*   [X : 1937-8]

IN the Kamunabi Mountains—
　My old home,
Whither I, a young man, am bound—
There among the mulberry twigs at dawn,
And in the young pine-trees at eve,
Your voice is heard;
The village-folk fondly listen,
While the mountain echo replies—
Is it for love of your mate,
O cuckoo, that you cry
Through the midnight hours ?

Envoy

Are you, too, O cuckoo,
A wanderer from home

---

　[1] There were two markets, eastern and western, in Nara. The western market
was situated near the present town of Kōriyama.
　[2] *Tamadaré* : screens made of reeds or finely-split bamboo, used to prevent the
entrance of too much light.

And longing for your mate—
You, who in the Kamunabi Mountains
Cry far into the night?

*   *   *

890-1   *A poem of travel.*   [III : 388-9]

WONDERFUL is the Sea;
      Setting the isle of Awaji in the middle,
He girdles with white waves the land of Iyo;[1]
And from the straits of Akashi
He leads the flowing tide at evening,
And lets it ebb at dawn away;
And we, in fear of the brawling waves,
Harbour at the isle of Awaji,
Sleepless, waiting for the break of day;
When on the field of Asanu[2]
Above the waterfall
The pheasants make their shrill cries
To tell us of the dawn;
Come, men, let us row out with a will,
Now, while the sea is calm.

Envoy

As I coast round the cape of Minumé,
Flocks of cranes are crying,
Making me long for Yamato.

892   CLEARLY I see the pebbles in the water,   [VII : 1082]
      So bright the moon is shining,
As the night wears on.

---

[1] By Iyo the poet seems to mean the whole of Shikoku.
[2] The present village of Asano at the north-western shore of the island, where
there is a waterfall of the same name.

893   As if to say the land will prosper   [VII : 1086]
        With its Ōtomos[1]—the mighty clan
   Of warriors bearing quivers—
   The bright moon shines.

894   *On rain.*   [VII : 1091]

   Let no rain fall to drench me through;
      I wear beneath my clothes—
   The keepsake of my loved one.

895   *On a hill.*   [VII : 1096]

   Though not sure of the tale of old,
      It is long years since I myself saw,
   This heaven-descended hill of Kagu.

896   *On grass.*   [VII : 1121]

   Susuki, growing along the way to my beloved,
      When I go to her,
   Bend, O *susuki* on the plain!

897   *On the koto.*[2]   [VII : 1129]

   When I take the *koto*, sobs break forth;
      Can it be that in its hollow space
   The spirit of my wife is hiding?

---

   [1] The text for the second line admits of various interpretations : (1) at the guards' quarters occupied by the Ōtomo family, (2) at Mitsu of Naniwa, the fief of the Ōtomo family, (3) at the mansion of the Ōtomo family.
   [2] A kind of lute. See also No. 265.

       In Yamashiro.   [VII : 1138]

HOWEVER loud I call to the man,
   'Ferry me across Uji's stream,'
My voice, it seems, does not reach him,
I hear no splashing of his oar.

899   *In Settsu.*   [VII : 1154]

THE rain beats on me, I make a shelter—
   Ah, when can I gather pebbles
On the low-tide shore of Ago ?

900   *During the journey.*   [VII : 1161]

THIS evening on my journey far from home,
   In the chilly autumn wind,
The wild-geese go crying.

901   LIKE the sails spread on the fishing-   [VII : 1182]
      boats,
I see the white waves rearing
Along the shore of Tomo.[1]

902   ABOVE the height of Mikasa in Kasuga   [VII : 1295]
      The boat of a moon appears ;
We, revellers, see it,
Reflected in our wine-cups.

[1] The Inland Sea coast of Hiroshima Prefecture.

903   *A love poem referring to the pearl.*   [VII : 1317]

THE white pearl, sunk under the deep sea,
    Though the wind blows and the seas run high,
I will not rest until I make it mine !

904   *Referring to the grass.*   [VII : 1336]

HE who burns the sere weeds
    On the open plain in early spring—
Is it not enough !
Must he burn my heart, too !

905   *Referring to the thunder.*   [VII : 1369]

LIKE the flash and roar near the clouds of heaven,
    To see him awes me,
To see him not saddens me.

906   *Elegy.*   [VII : 1411]

HOW fortunate he is !
    Who, until his raven hair is grey,
Can hear his wife's soft voice !

907   *On the warbler.*   [X : 1821]

WHERE the spring mist slowly drifts,
    The warbler in the green willow-tree
Sings, holding a twig in his beak.

908   WHEN the spring comes,   [X : 1830]
    The sweet spring,—

Brushing the slender bamboo-tops
With his wings and tail,
Warbles the *uguisu*.

909   *On the snow.*   [x : 1840]

YONDER in the plum-tree,
    Fluttering from branch to branch,
The warbler sings;
And white on his wings falls
Airy snow.

910   *On the cherry-flowers.*   [x : 1855]

THOUGH your season is not over,
    Cherry-blossoms, do you fall
Because the love is now at its height
Of those who look on?

911   OH, when will this night end   [x : 1873]
    And the morning break?
I long to see the plum-blossoms
That the songster scatters,
Flitting from branch to branch!

912   *An outing.*   [x : 1883]

THE lords and ladies
    Of the Great Palace
Have leisure enough;
Here they are out together
Bedecked with plum-flowers.

WHEN winter is gone and spring comes,
    New is the year, and new the month;
But man grows old.

All things are best when new;
But perchance with man
He alone is good who is old.

CAN only a spring rain so drench
    Your garments through?
If it rains for seven days,
Will you not come for seven nights?

MY love-thoughts these days
    Come thick like the summer grass
Which soon as cut and raked
Grows wild again.

THAT you like me not
    It may well be—
Yet will you not come
Even to see the orange-tree
Abloom in my door-yard?

EVEN in the heat
 Of the blazing sun of June,
That cracks the earth's green face,
My tear-wet sleeves will not dry
Because I see you not.

Seventh Night Poems.

919   YON white cloud blown   [x : 2041]
 And wafted by the autumn wind—
May it not be the celestial scarf
Of the Weaver, the Star-maid ?

920   THE rain-drops   [x : 2052]
 That fall this evening
Are, perhaps, the spray
From the oars of the Oxherd,
Rowing fast his boat.

921   WITH the jewels of my anklets   [x : 2065]
 And of my armlets all a-swinging,
I weave at the loom.
Would I might sew your robe in time !

922-4 TO-NIGHT he makes his one journey   [x : 2089-91]
 of the year
Over the Heavenly River, passing Yasu Beach—
He, the love-lorn Oxherd longing for his maid,
Whom he can never see but once a year,
Though from the beginning of heaven and earth
They have stood face to face across the Heavenly
 River.

This evening when the autumn wind arises,
Swaying the pennoned reeds, stalk and blade,
He in his red boat, many-oared
And gaily trimmed, bow and stern,
Buffeting the white waves of the Heavenly River
And crossing the swift and swirling waters,
Will come rowing—the lone Star-man—
Certain of the bliss
Of his young love's embrace.
So will he sate his year-long want
To-night, this Seventh Night of the Seventh Moon—
Strangely it thrills my heart !

Envoys

This is the night
When the celestial lovers meet
To undo, the one for the other,
Their girdles of *Koma*[1] brocade—
Ah, that rapture in the skies !

I think of the happy river-quay
Where the Oxherd, rowing on
Across the stream,
Will come at last
To moor his little boat.

925   *On the cricket.*   [x : 2160]

A PASSING shower
    Has fallen on the garden grass ;
And I hear the voice
Of the crickets singing—
Autumn is here.

---

[1] i. e. North Korea.

On the hills.			[x : 2177]

BURGEONING anew in spring,
   All green in summer,
And now in dappled-crimson clad
Oh, gorgeous hills of autumn !

927			*On the moon.*			[x : 2298]

As I sit worn and weary,
   Pining after you,
The autumn wind goes sighing
And low hangs the moon.

928			*Referring to night.*			[x : 2303]

THOUGH men say
   An autumn night is long,
It is all too brief
For unloading my heart
Of all its love.

     *   *   *

929	THE crickets chirp at my bedside—			[x : 2310]
   And how my heart aches !
I sit up, unable to sleep,
Thinking of you all the while.

930			*Referring to frost.*			[x : 2336]

Go not away, dear heart,
   So late in the night !

The hoar-frost is on the leaves
Of the dense bamboo-grass by the lane.

931   *Referring to snow.*   [x : 2342]

HAVING met you as in a dream,
    I feel I would dissolve, body and soul,
Like the snow that falls,
Darkening the heavens.

*   *   *

932   IF you so heed your mother,   [xi : 2517]
    All is lost—never could you and I
Fulfil our love !

933   IF I come to her   [xi : 2526]
    When she waits and waits,
Full of gladness she will beam on me—
I will hasten to that smile.

934   I HAVE determined that my dear lord's   [xi : 2531]
    name
Shall not be revealed,
Even with my life at stake;
Never forget me !

935   IF I come, surprising her,   [xi : 2546]
    Full of gladness she will brighten;
Those eyebrows linger in my eye.

936   WHEN I meet you,   [XI : 2554]
        I cannot but conceal my face,
Yet, ever after, I desire
To see you, dearest lord.

937   YOU had better tell   [XI : 2572]
        A more plausible tale;
Who upon earth, since what age,
Died for a girl he never had seen?

938   HOWEVER much I beat him   [XI : 2574]
        With my clenched fist,
That he may forget her face,
Never chastened is he,
This rascal love!

939   I WILL not comb my morning hair: [XI : 2578]
        Your loving arm, my pillow,
Has lain under it.

940   I WHO have counted me for a strong   [XII : 2875]
    man,
Only a little less than heaven and earth—
How short of manliness now that I love!

941   STANDING or sitting,   [XII : 2887]
        I know not what to do.
Though I tread the earth,
My heart is in the skies.

942   TO-NIGHT I am coming   [XII : 2912]
        To visit you in your dream,
     And none will see and question me—
     Be sure to leave your door unlocked !

943   THE drum that the watchman beats   [XI : 2641]
        Tells the time of our tryst;
     It is strange that he has not yet come.

944   THE vivid smile of my sweetheart,   [XI : 2642]
        That shone in the bright lamp-light,
     Ever haunts my eyes.

945   WERE the Itada bridge to crumble   [XI : 2644]
        At Oharida,[1]
     By the cross-beams I would come to you;
     Be not troubled, my love.

946   UNRESTING, like the people   [XI : 2645]
        Dragging logs for the palace
     In the timber-forest of Izumi,
     I long for you.

947   SOOT-BLACK as she is, like the shed   [XI : 2651]
        Where Naniwa people burn the reeds,
     My wife is ever fresh to me.

948   AT every trotting sound of a horse's   [XI : 2653]
        hoofs,
     I rush out under the pine and look,
     Hoping it may be you.

[1] In Asuka District, Yamato.

949   L EAVE me, O propitious spirits;   [XI : 2661]
        Since my love has come to this,
    What care I for useless life ?

950   WHILE with my sleeves I sweep the bed [XI : 2667]
        And sit up, lonely, awaiting you,
    The moon has sunk.

951   NO ways are left me now to meet my   [XI : 2695]
        love;
    Must I, like the lofty peak of Fuji[1] in Suruga,
    Burn on for ever
    With this fire of love ?

952   TROUBLES are many in the path of a   [XII : 2998]
        little boat
    Making for port through the reeds.
    Think not I have ceased visiting you—
    I who would come this very minute.

953   WHEN the moon[2] that shines   [XII : 3004]
        In the far empyreal sky
    Is no more—then, only then,
    Shall cease this love of mine.

954   NEVER do I doubt your heart,   [XII : 3028]
        From whose depths ocean-deep
    You promised me your love.

[1] Mount Fuji was an active volcano in the Manyo age.
[2] An alternative text gives the ' sun.'

955 Loath to pass by her gate,   [xii : 3056]
  I have bound the grass stalks there.
 Let stay the knot, O wind!
 For I will come to see it there again.

956 Though I am chidden like a horse [xii : 3096]
  That crops the barley grown across the fence,
 I love and love—
 Never can I halt my thoughts of you!

     *   *   *

957 At the upper course of the river [xi : 2838]
  People wash the tender herbs;
 Like a.straying leaf thereof, I would float down,
 And reach the shallows near my love!

958 Well is the hill of Mimoro[1] guarded; [xiii : 3222]
  The staggerbush is in bloom at the foot,
 Camellias are in flower at the top;
 How beautiful she is,
 A mountain that would soothe even a crying child![2]

959-60 With the ninth month when the [xiii : 3223-4]
    thunder
 Rumbles and the sky is overclouded,
 The autumn showers set in
 Before the wild-geese come and call.

---

[1] There are many mountains bearing the name of Mimoro.

[2] The maiden whom the poet loves is likened to Mount Mimoro. She is well guarded by her mother, lest people should approach her; a girl, sweet and tender-hearted, taking care of a crying child.

By the watch-house on the sacred fields of Kamu-
    nabi,
On the pond-dykes in the hedge-bound fields,
Many elm-trees intermingle
With the sprays of autumn tints.

With my little wrist-bells ringing,
Woman though I am,
On tiptoe I bend and break the sprays
And run to deck your locks with them.

Envoy

Sorrowing to see them alone,
The yellow leaves of Kamunabi,
I broke some off to bring to you, beloved.

961-3   As people have told from mouth to   [XIII : 3227-9]
    mouth,
Since the age of the gods when, it is said,
Five million, ten million gods alighted
On this Rice-abounding Land of Fertile Reed Plains,
To pacify the evil gods,—
Mount Mimoro of Kamunabi is misted with spring
And in autumn the leaves are dyed in crimson;
The Asuka that girdles Mimoro of Kamunabi
With its swift stream, allows of no rank moss
On its pillowy boulders;
But, till those rocks grow green with moss,
May every fresh night bring happiness to me—
O let me in my dreams divine the way,
Thou, God, who art a Sword enshrined!

Envoys

Till mosses green the bole
Of the cryptomeria, the sacred tree,
On Mimoro of Kamunabi,
Never shall my longing pass away.

When the priest erects the sacred wand
And offers saké to the gods,
How fair is the berried vine
That adorns his locks!

*   *   *

964-5 WITH my axe I felled the trees   [XIII : 3232-3]
        On the cypress-covered Mount of Niu;
I built a raft of them,
I fixed a pair of oars.
Along the stony beach I row,
By many a jutting rock.
It never tires my eye to see
The white spray and swift water
Roaring through the rapids of Yoshinu.

Envoy

Roaring through the rapids of Yoshinu—
Falls the white-breaking water;
I would show my wife at home
This white-breaking water.

966   EIGHTY are the harbours   [XIII : 3239]
        Around the lake of Ōmi;
And at every jutting
Of eighty islets
Stands an orange-tree.

On the top spray they spread bird-lime,
On the middle twig they tie a grosbeak,
And on the lower bough a hawfinch.

But in frolic sport the birds,
Luring innocently their mothers,

Snaring innocently their fathers;
Grosbeak and hawfinch, alas![1]

967-8 AT our awful Sovereign's word,   [XIII : 3240-1]
    I crossed the hills of Nara
That never tire our eyes,
I poled across the rapids of the Izumi,
With its timber-piled shore,
I crossed the Uji gazing at the torrents,
I prayed, making offerings to the god
On Mount Ōsaka, the pass to Ōmi;
And I journeyed over to Karasaki
Of Shiga in Sasanami,
Which, if fortune favours me, I shall see again
When I turn homeward.
Thus, as I travelled on, with many a sigh,
At each of the eighty turnings of the road,
Farther and farther receded my home,
Steeper and steeper the mountains I crossed;
And now on Mount Ikago,[2] terrifying
Like an unsheathed blade,
I stand bewildered,
Knowing not what may lie before me.

Envoy[3]

I sigh and implore
The gods of heaven and earth :
If fortune favours me,
On my journey home I shall see again
The headland Karasaki of Shiga.

[1] This poem is supposed to allude to some political event of the day.
[2] Stands on the north side of Lake Biwa.
[3] According to a book the envoy was composed by Hozumi Oyu when he was banished to the Isle of Sado.—Original Note.

969   A⊤ the palace of Kukuri   [XIII : 3242]
         At Takakita in Minu,¹
     I learn that eastward lies²
     Another palace it were well to see,
     But they bar my way,
     The Okiso, the mountains in Minu !

     Howsoever people
     Tread them to the plain,
     Howsoever people
     Thrust them to one side,
     Heartless they are,
     The Okiso, the mountains in Minu !

970-1   O THAT the bridge to heaven were   [XIII : 3245-6]
         longer,
     And the lofty mountain loftier !
     Then I would fetch and offer to him
     The magical elixir
     Which the Moon God treasures,
     And give him back the ardour of his youth.

Envoy

     How grievous it is to see
     Old age upon him stealing day by day,
     —On him, whom I cherish
     As the moon and the sun of heaven.

972-3   THOUGH there are men without   [XIII : 3248-9]
         number
     In this fair Land of Yamato,
     My mind ever clings to you
     Like a wistaria-vine,

¹ Minu (i. e. Mino) is a province in the middle of Honshū.
² Scholars differ in reading and interpreting the text of this and the preceding lines.

My heart ever holds to you
Like a tender blade of grass,
And I shall pass this tedious night
Longing for a sight of you !

Envoy

Could I but think
There breathed another like you
In this fair Land of Yamato,
How should I so languish ?

974-6   THE Land of Yamato is a land   [XIII : 3250-2]
      Where matters fall as will the gods
Without lifted words[1] of men.
It is so, yet I do lift up words :
Do not the gods of heaven and earth
Know my love-lorn heart ?
As days and months have passed,
With loving my mind is troubled,
With longing my heart aches.
If never I meet him,
I shall languish
Till I die.
When I see him face to face,
Only then my pain will cease.

Envoys

Since I trust you as a sailor
His stately ship at sea,
However much I spend myself for your sake,
Regret I shall not know.

Now you leave the Imperial City
On your journey, grass for pillow,
When can I have you home again ?

[1] See note to No. 175.

307

977-8   SINCE days of old it has been said :   [XIII : 3255-6]
     ' Love brings trouble to our hearts.'
So it is said from mouth to mouth.
And, not sure of my maiden's mind,
Nor of the means whereby to learn it,
Pouring all my mind and soul out
Till my heart withers like cut rushes,
In secret and unknown
I shall feed my helpless love for her
While I have breath.

Envoy

Though she may not think of me like this,
Alas, I cannot forget her
Even for a moment !

979-80   THE water at Ayuchi in Oharida[1]—   [XIII : 3260-1]
     People draw it ceaselessly,
They drink it constantly;
Ceaselessly as they draw it,
Constantly as they drink it,
I love you, lady, with a love
Which will never cease.

Envoy

To cast away my love-thoughts
I know not how;
So long it is since I met you !

981-2   IN that most wretched hovel   [XIII : 3270-1]
     Only fit for burning,
On the foul and ragged matting
Ready for the rubbish heap,

---

[1] Identified variously as in Nara and Aichi Prefectures by different scholars.

He sleeps, his own arm intertwined
With the vilest of vile arms
Which I would tear awry.
Yet, for him,
Each moment of the whole long day,
Each moment of the darkest night,
I weep and wail
Until the flooring creaks.

Envoy

It is I that burn my heart out,
My heart
That yearns for him !

983-4   THAT meadow¹ which my heart   [XIII : 3272-3]
     loved
Was fenced in by a villager;
Since when I heard that it was done
I know not how to stand,
I know not where to sit ;
Even in my own house,
As if on a journey,
My heart is seared with longing,
Nor can I cease from grieving;
And wavering as clouds of heaven,
Disturbed as the fence of reed,
Disordered as entangled hemp,
Without a thousandth part of my great love
Being known and understood,
I languish till I die !

Envoy

Peerless is the love I make,
And so lean I waste,
I must wear my girdle threefold round.

¹ The girl he loves is likened to the meadow where she lives.

985   HOWEVER long I wait for him,   [XIII : 3280]
       My lord does not come,
When I look up to the plains of heaven,
The night hours have advanced.
Late at night, the storm beats,
And the snow-flakes falling on my sleeves
Are frozen while I wait and linger.
Now never will he come to me,
But I will meet my loved one later,
As vine meets vine.
So comforting my lonely heart,
With my sleeves I sweep our bed,
And as I cannot waking meet him,
May I meet him in my dream,
On this heavenly-perfect night!

986-7   THROUGH the plain of Miyaké   [XIII : 3295-6]
       Treading the earth with your bare feet,
Breasting your way through the summer grass,
What sort of girl do you visit, my son?[1]

But, Mother, you don't know her,
But you don't know her, Father.
Her tresses black as a mud-snail's bowels,
The way she wears those fluttering *yū*-ribbons,
The way she wears her Yamato boxwood comb,
That beauteous maid,—my love.

Envoy

To her, kept secret from my parents,
Pushing by the summer grass I hasten,
Through the plain of Miyaké.

---

[1] This is a dialogue poem.   But the question is asked by the son himself.

988   MY love stands in my sight   [XIII : 3299]
        Across the stream,
And on this side stand I.
I do not cease from longing,
Nor do I cease from grieving.

O for a little vermilion boat,
And a pair of little jewelled oars,
That I might row across
And talk and talk with her !

989–90   THE village-folk told me, saying :   [XIII : 3303–4]
      Your sweet husband whom you miss
Came from the hill of Kamunabi,
Now strewn with yellow leaves ;
He rode a jet-black horse
And crossed the shallows seven ;
Yes, lonely and wan he met us—
This they told me.

Envoy

Would that I had passed them,
Untold, unspeaking !
Oh ! why did they tell me
Of my husband's plight ?

991   IN the land where white clouds hover,   [XIII : 3329]
      In the land where blue skies bend,
Among all the people under the clouds of heaven,
Is it I alone that long for him ?
Since I alone thus miss my lord,
Filling heaven and earth with words of longing,
Is it with pining that my heart sickens ?
Is it with thinking that my heart aches ?
My love increases with the days ;

311

Ceaselessly I languish for my husband,
Yet, this ninth month which he told me
To keep as our never-to-be-forgotten month—
To recall for a thousand ages,
And talk of through eternity—
This ninth month, when our love began,
Fast races to its close;
How can I bear an agony so great?
For me the month is dying
To leave me in despair.
So, on the steep and rocky path,
To the rock-bound doorway
With morning I go out in grief,
With evening I come in, weeping;
And spreading out my jet-black hair I lie;
Not for me the soothing sleep of others,
Uneasy as a boat tossing on the waves,
With sorrowful thoughts I pass
Dreary nights numberless!

992   THE hill of secluded Hatsusé,   [XIII : 3331]
     And the hill of green-bannered Osaka,
Are graceful where they slope down,
Are beautiful where they rise up.
A pity that these dear hills
Should grow desolate!

993   THE lofty mountains and the seas,   [XIII : 3332]
     Being mountains, being seas,
Both exist and are real.
But frail as flowers are the lives of men,
Passing phantoms of this world.

994-5 WHEN I trusted as one trusts in a [XIII : 3344-5]
     great ship,
That he would come to me this month,
And I waited for the day,
A courier brought me word—
Though vague as a fire-fly's light—
That he was gone like the autumn leaf.
Now I tread the earth as flames,
Standing or sitting I know not where to go;
Bewildered like the morning mists,
Vainly I breathe out eight-foot sighs.
I would, to find him where he lies,
Wander as a cloud of heaven,
And die as the stricken deer,
But, as I do not know the way to him,
Thus I remain alone and miss him,
And weep aloud.

Envoy[1]

When I see the wings of the wild-geese
Skimming the reedy shore,
They remind me of the arrows
He carried on his back.

996 LET only your soul dwell [XVI : 3851]
     In the Realm of Nothingness,[2]
You shall see not far off
Hakoya's transcendent hills.

[1] It is said that this envoy was written by the wife of a frontier-guard. If so, it is probable that she also wrote the long poem.—Original Note.

[2] 'Realm of Nothingness' is mentioned in the book of Chuang-tse, a Chinese philosopher. *Hakoya* (a Japanese reading of the Chinese *Mokuyeh*), mentioned also in the book, is an imaginary region inhabited by superhuman beings. The meaning of the poem is that supreme felicity can be attained only through the emancipation of the mind from worldly preoccupations.

997   Do the vast oceans die?   [XVI : 3852]
          Do the mountains die?
       Verily they do—for lo,
       The waters vanish from the seas;
       The green mountain becomes bare and barren.

998-9 My love's labours of these days,   [XVI : 3858-9]
          If reported and recommended
       For the grant of honours,
       Would win a cap of the Fifth Rank.

       Should no grant be made
       For my love's labours of these days,
       I would go and appeal
       To the metropolitan magistrate.

1000   *A fearful thing.*   [XVI : 3889]

       I REMEMBER ever so long
          That rainy night, when all alone
       I met you with your face ghastly pale
       Like a spectral fire.[1]

---

[1] *Hitodama*, here rendered as 'spectral fire,' is a luminous manifestation in the form of a ball of phosphorescent fire. It is supposed to emanate from a dead body.

TEXT IN ROMAJI

1

Ko moyo miko mochi fugushi moyo mifugushi mochi
kono oka ni na tsumasu ko   ie kikana na norasane
soramitsu Yamato no kuni wa   oshinabete ware koso ore
shikinabete ware koso mase   ware kosowa se towa norame
ie womo na womo

2

Yamato niwa murayama aredo   toriyorou Ame-no-Kaguyama
noboritachi kunimi wo sureba   kunibara wa keburi tachitatsu
unabara wa kamame tachitatsu   umashikuni zo Akitsushima
Yamato no kuni wa

3

Yū sareba Ogura no yama ni   naku shika wa koyoi wa nakazu
inenikerashimo

4-5

Yasumishishi waga Ōkimi no   ashita niwa torinadetamai
yūbe niwa iyoritatashishi   mitorashi no azusa no yumi no
nakahazu no oto sunari   asagari ni ima tatasurashi
yūgari ni ima tatasurashi   mitorashi no azusa no yumi no
nakahazu no oto sunari

Tamakiharu Uchi no ōnu ni   uma namete asa fumasuran
sono kusafukanu

6-8

Kamiyo yori aretsugikureba   hito sawani kuni niwa michite
ajimura no kayoi wa yukedo   waga kouru kimi nishi araneba
hiru wa hi no kururumade   yoru wa yo no akuru kiwami

omoitsutsu i mo negatenito   akashitsurakumo nagaki kono yo wo

Yama no ha ni ajimura sawagi   yukunaredo ware wa sabushie
kimi nishi araneba

Ōmiji no Toko no yama naru   Isayagawa ke no korogoro wa
koitsutsumo aran

9–11

Kaguyama wa Unebi wo oshito   Miminashi to aiarasoiki
kamiyo yori kaku narurashi   inishie mo shika narekoso
utsusemi mo tsuma wo   arasourashiki

Kaguyama to Miminashiyama to   aishi toki tachite mi ni koshi
Inami-kunibara

Watatsumi no toyohatagumo ni   irihi sashi koyoi no tsukuyo
akirakekukoso

12–5

Kimi ga yuki kenagaku narinu   yama tazune mukae ka yukan
machi nika matan

Kakubakari koitsutsu arazuwa   takayama no iwane shi makite
shinamashimonowo

Aritsutsumo kimi woba matan   uchinabiku waga kurokami ni
shimo no okumadeni

Aki no ta no ho no e ni kirau   asagasumi izuhe no kata ni
waga koi yaman

16

Amanohara furisakemireba   Ōkimi no miinochi wa nagaku
amatarashitari

318

Aohata no Kohata no ue wo   kayoutowa me niwa miredomo
tadani awanukamo

Hito wa yoshi omoiyamutomo   tamakazura kage ni mietsutsu
wasuraenukamo

Isanatori Ōmi no umi wo   oki sakete kogikuru fune
he tsukite kogikuru fune   okitsukai itaku na-haneso
hetsukai itaku na-haneso   wakakusa no tsuma no
omou tori tatsu

Ie naraba imo ga te makan   kusamakura tabi ni koyaseru
kono tabito aware

Iwashiro no hamamatsu ga e wo   hikimusubi masakiku araba
mata kaeri min

Ie ni areba ke ni moru ii wo   kusamakura tabi nishi areba
shii no ha ni moru

Kasumi tatsu nagaki harubi no   kurenikeru wazuki mo shirazu
murakimo no kokoro wo itami   nuekodori uranagekioreba
tamadasuki kake no yoroshiku   tōtsukami waga Ōkimi no
idemashi no yama kosu kaze no   hitori oru waga koromode ni
asa yoi ni kaerainureba   masurao to omoeru ware mo
kusamakura tabi nishi areba   omoiyaru tazuki wo shirani
Ami no ura no amaotomera ga   yaku shio no omoi zo yakuru
waga shitagokoro

Yamagoshi no kaze wo tokijimi   nuru yo ochizu ie naru imo wo
kakete shinubitsu

25

Nigitazu ni funanori sento   tsuki mateba shio mo kanainu
ima wa kogiidena

26

Fuyugomori haru sarikureba   nakazarishi tori mo kinakinu
sakazarishi hana mo sakeredo   yama wo shigemi iritemo torazu
kusa fukami toritemo mizu   akiyama no konoha wo mitewa
momiji woba toritezo shinubu   aoki woba okitezo nageku
soko shi urameshi akiyama ware wa

27-8

Umasake Miwa no yama   aoniyoshi Nara no yama no
yama no ma ni ikakurumade   michi no kuma itsumorumadeni
tsubarani mo mitsutsu yukanwo   shibashiba mo misaken yama wo
kokoro naku kumo no kakusaubeshiya

Miwayama wo shika mo kakusuka   kumo danimo kokoro aranamo
kakusaubeshiya

29

Kimi matsuto waga koioreba   waga yado no sudare ugokashi
aki no kaze fuku

30

Yasumishishi wago Ōkimi no   kashikokiya mihaka tsukauru
Yamashina no Kagami no yama ni   yoru wamo yo no kotogoto
hiru wamo hi no kotogoto   ne nomiwo nakitsutsu ariteya
momoshiki no ōmiyabito wa   yukiwakarenan

Kaze wodani kouruwa tomoshi   kaze wodani kontoshi mataba
nani ka nagekan

Ware wamoya Yasumiko etari   minahito no egateni su tou
Yasumiko etari

Imo ga tame ware tama hiriu   okibe naru tama yosemochiko
okitsushiranami

Asagiri ni nurenishi koromo   hosazushite hitori ya kimi ga
yamaji koyuran

Kakaranto kanete shiriseba   ōmifune hateshi tomari ni
shime yuwamashiwo

Yasumishishi wago Ōkimi no   ōmifune machi ka kouran
Shiga no Karasaki

Utsusemi shi kami ni taeneba   hanareite asa nageku kimi
sakariite waga kouru kimi   tama naraba te ni makimochite
kinu naraba nugu toki mo naku   waga kouru kimi zo kizo no yo
ime ni mietsuru

*   *   *

Mi-Yoshinu no Mimiga no mine ni   toki nakuzo yuki wa furikeru
ma nakuzo ame wa furikeru   sono yuki no toki nakiga goto
sono ame no ma nakiga goto   kuma mo ochizu omoitsutsuzo kuru
sono yamamichi wo

Waga sato ni ōyuki fureri   Ōhara no furinishi sato ni
furamakuwa nochi

Waga oka no okami ni iite   furashimeshi yuki no kudake shi
soko ni chiriken

Haru sugite natsu kitarurashi   shirotae no koromo hoshitari
Ame-no-Kaguyama

Yasumishishi waga Ōkimi no   yū sareba meshitamaurashi
akekureba toitamaurashi   Kamioka no yama no momiji wo
kyō mokamo toitamawamashi   asu mokamo meshitamawamashi
sono yama wo furisakemitsutsu   yū sareba ayani kanashimi
akekureba urasabikurashi   aratae no koromo no sode wa
hiru toki mo nashi

Moyuru hi mo torite tsutsumite   fukuro niwa iruto iwazuyamo
shiruto iwanakumo

Kitayama ni tanabiku kumo no   aogumo no hoshi sakariyuku
tsuki mo sakarite

Ina to iedo shiuru Shihi noga   shiigatari konogoro kikazute
ware koinikeri

Ina to iedo katare katareto   norasekoso Shihi iwa mōse
shiigatari to noru

Momozutau Iware no ike ni   naku kamo wo kyō nomi miteya

kumogakurinan

48–9

Ashihiki no yama no shizuku ni   imo matsuto ware tachinurenu
yama no shizuku ni

A wo matsuto kimi ga nureken   ashihiki no yama no shizuku ni
naramashimonowo

50

Taki no ue no Mifune no yama ni   iru kumo no tsuneni aranto
waga mowanakuni

51

Uneme no sode fukikaesu   Asukakaze miyako wo tōmi
itazurani fuku

52

Ashibe yuku kamo no hagai ni   shimo furite samuki yūbe wa
Yamato shi omohoyu

53

Iwabashiru Tarumi no ue no   sawarabi no moeizuru haru ni
narinikerukamo

54–5

Waga seko wo Yamato e yaruto   sayo fukete akatokitsuyu ni
waga tachinureshi

Futari yukedo yukisugigataki   akiyama wo ikani ka kimi ga
hitori koyuran

56–7

Kamukaze no Ise no kuni nimo   aramashiwo nani shika kiken
kimi mo aranakuni

323

Mimaku hori waga suru kimi mo   aranakuni nani shika kiken
uma tsukaruruni

58–9

Utsusomi no hito naru ware ya   asu yoriwa Futagami yama wo
irose to waga min

Iso no ue ni ouru ashibi wo   taoramedo misubeki kimi ga
arito iwanakuni

60

Okureite koitsutsu arazuwa   oishikan michi no kumami ni
shime yue waga se

61

Hitogoto wo shigemi kochitami   ono ga yo ni imada wataranu
asakawa wataru

62–3

Utsuso wo Omi no ōkimi   ama nareya Irago ga shima no
tamamo karimasu

Utsusemi no inochi wo oshimi   nami ni nure Irago no shima no
tamamo kariosu

64–6

Tsunusahafu Iware no michi wo   asa sarazu yukiken hito no
omoitsutsu kayoikemakuwa   hototogisu naku satsuki niwa
ayamegusa hanatachibana wo   tama ni nuki kazura ni sento
nagatsuki no shigure no toki wa   momijiba wo orikazasanto
hau kuzu no iya tōnagaku   yorozuyo ni taejito omoite
kayoiken kimi woba asu yu   yoso nikamo min

Komoriku no Hatsuseotome ga   te ni makeru tama wa midarete
arito iwazuyamo

Kawakaze no samuki Hatsuse wo   nagekitsutsu kimi ga arukuni
niru hito mo aeya

67-9

Nayutake no tooyoru Miko   sanitsurau waga ōkimi wa
komoriku no Hatsuse no yama ni   kamusabi ni itsukiimasuto
tamazusa no hito zo iitsuru   oyozure ka waga kikitsuru
tawakoto ka waga kikitsurumo   ametsuchi ni kuyashiki koto no
yononaka no kuyashiki koto wa   amagumo no sokue no kiwami
ametsuchi no itarerumadeni   tsue tsukimo tsukazumo yukite
yūke toi ishiura mochite   waga yado ni mimoro wo tatete
makurabe ni iwaibe wo sue   takatama wo ma naku nukitare
yūdasuki kaina ni kakete   ame naru Sasara no onu no
nanafusuge te ni torimochite   hisakata no Amanokawara ni
idetachite misogitemashiwo   takayama no iwao no ue ni
imasetsurukamo

Oyozure no tawakoto tokamo   takayama no iwao no ue ni
kimi ga koyaseru

Isonokami Furu no yama naru   sugimura no omoisugubeki
kimi naranakuni

70-2

Ōkimi no mutsutama aeya   Toyokuni no Kagami no yama wo
miya to sadamuru

Toyokuni no Kagami no yama no   iwato tate komorinikerashi
matedo kimasazu

Iwato waru tajikara mogamo   tayowaki omina nishi areba
sube no shiranaku

73

Waga seko wa izuku yukuran   okitsumo no Nabari no yama wo
kyō ka koyuran

Tamadasuki Unebi no yama no   Kashihara no hijiri no miyo yu
aremashishi Kami no kotogoto   tsuga no ki no iya tsugitsugini
amenoshita shirashimeshishiwo   sora ni mitsu Yamato wo okite
aoniyoshi Narayama wo koe   ikasamani omohoshimeseka
amazakaru hina niwa aredo   iwabashiru Ōmi no kuni no
Sasanami no Ōtsu no miya ni   amenoshita shirashimeshiken
Sumerogi no Kami no Mikoto no   ōmiya wa koko to kikedomo
ōtono wa kokoto iedomo   harukusa no shigeku oitaru
kasumi tatsu harubi no kireru   momoshiki no ōmiyadokoro
mireba kanashimo

Sasanami no Shiga no Karasaki   sakiku aredo ōmiyabito no
fune machikanetsu

Sasanami no Shiga no ōwada   yodomutomo mukashi no hito ni
mata mo awameyamo

Yasumishishi waga Ōkimi no   kikoshiosu amenoshita ni
kuni washimo sawani aredomo   yama kawa no kiyoki kōchi to
mikokoro wo Yoshinu no kuni no   hana chirau Akitsu no nube ni
miyabashira futoshikimaseba   momoshiki no ōmiyabito wa
fune namete asakawa watari   funagioi yūkawa wataru
kono kawa no tayuru koto naku   kono yama no iya takashirasu
mizu hashiru taki no miyako wa   miredo akanukamo

Miredo akanu Yoshinu no kawa no   tokoname no tayuru koto naku
mata kaeri min

Yasumishishi waga Ōkimi   kamunagara kamusabi sesuto
Yoshinugawa tagitsu kōchi ni   takadono wo takashirimashite
noboritachi kunimi wo sureba   tatanaharu aogakiyama
yamatsumi no matsuru mitsuki to   harube wa hana kazashimochi
aki tateba momiji kazaseri   Yūkawa no kami mo

ōmike ni tsukaematsuruto   kamitsuse ni ukawa wo tate
shimotsuse ni sade sashiwatasu   yama kawa mo yorite tsukauru
kami no miyo kamo

Yama kawa mo yorite tsukauru   kamunagara tagitsu kōchi ni
funade sesukamo

81–2

Ago no ura ni funanori suran   otomera ga tamamo no suso ni
shio mitsuranka

Shiosai ni Irago no shimabe   kogu fune ni imo noruranka
araki shimami wo

83–7

Yasumishishi waga ōkimi   takaterasu Hi no Miko
kamunagara kamusabi sesuto   futoshikasu miyako wo okite
komoriku no Hatsuse no yama wa   maki tatsu arayamamichi wo
iwagane no shimoto oshinabe   sakatori no asa koemashite
tamakagiru yū sarikureba   miyuki furu Aki no ōnu ni
hatasusuki shino wo oshinabe   kusamakura tabiyadori sesu
inishie omoite

Aki no nu ni yadoru tabibito   uchinabiki i mo nurameyamo
inishie omouni

Makusa karu aranu niwa aredo   momijiba no suginishi kimi ga
katami tozo koshi

Himukashi no nu ni kagiroi no   tatsu miete kaerimi sureba
tsuki katabukinu

Hinamishi no Miko no Mikoto no   uma namete mikari tatashishi
toki wa kimukau

88–90

Iwami no umi Tsunu no urami wo   ura nashito hito koso mirame

kata nashito hito koso mirame   yoshieyashi ura wa nakutomo
yoshieyashi kata wa nakutomo   isanatori umibe wo sashite
Watazu no ariso no ue ni   kaaonaru tamamo okitsumo
asa hafuru kaze koso yorame   yoi hafuru nami koso kiyore
nami no muta ka yori kaku yori   tamamo nasu yorineshi imo wo
tsuyujimo no okiteshi kureba   kono michi no yasokuma gotoni
yorozutabi kaerimi suredo   iya tōni sato wa sakarinu
iya takani yama mo koekinu   natsukusa no omoishinaete
shinuburan imo ga kado min   nabike kono yama

Iwami no ya Takatsunuyama no   ko no ma yori waga furu sode wo
imo mitsuranka

Sasa no ha wa miyama mo sayani   sayagedomo ware wa imo omou
wakarekinureba

91–3

Tsunusahafu Iwami no umi no   kotosaegu Kara no saki naru
ikuri nizo fukamiru ouru   ariso nizo tamamo wa ouru
tamamo nasu nabikineshi ko wo   fukamiru no fukamete moedo
saneshi yo wa ikura mo arazu   hau tsuta no wakare shi kureba
kimo mukau kokoro wo itami   omoitsutsu kaerimi suredo
ōbune no Watari no yama no   momijiba no chiri no magai ni
imo ga sode sayani mo miezu   tsumagomoru Yakami no yama no
kumoma yori watarau tsuki no   oshikedomo kakuroikureba
amazutau irihi sashinure   masurao to omoeru ware mo
shikitae no koromo no sode wa   tōrite nurenu

Aogoma no agaki wo hayami   kumoi nizo imo ga atari wo
sugite kinikeru

Akiyama ni otsuru momijiba   shimaraku wa na-chirimidareso
imo ga atari min

94–6

Ametsuchi no hajime no toki no   hisakata no Amanokawara ni
yaoyorozu chiyorozu kami no   kamutsudoi tsudoiimashite

328

kamuhakari hakarishi toki ni　amaterasu Hirume no Mikoto
ame woba shirashimesuto　Ashihara no Mizuho no Kuni wo
ametsuchi no yoriai no kiwami　shirashimesu Kami no Mikoto to
amagumo no yae kakiwakite　kamukudashi imasematsurishi
takaterasu Hi no Miko wa　Asuka no Kiyomi no miya ni
kamunagara futoshikimashite　Sumerogi no shikimasu kuni to
Amanohara iwato wo hiraki　kamuagari agariimashinu
waga ōkimi Miko no Mikoto no　amenoshita shirashimeshiseba
harubana no tōtokaranto　mochizuki no tatawashikento
amenoshita yomo no hito no　ōbune no omoitanomite
amatsumizu aogite matsuni　ikasamani omohoshimeseka
tsure mo naki Mayumi no oka ni　miyabashira futoshikiimashi
miaraka wo takashirimashite　asa gotoni mikoto towasazu
hitsuki no maneku narinuru　soko yueni Miko no miyabito
yukue shirazumo

Hisakata no ame mirugotoku　aogimishi Miko no mikado no
aremaku oshimo

Akanesasu hi wa teraseredo　nubatama no yowataru tsuki no
kakuraku oshimo

97

Shima no miya Magari no ike no　hanachidori hitome ni koite
ike ni kazukazu

98–9

Tobu tori no Asuka no kawa no　kamitsuse ni ouru tamamo wa
shimotsuse ni nagare furifuru　tamamo nasu ka yori kaku yori
nabikaishi tsuma no mikoto no　tatanazuku nigihada surawo
tsurugitachi mi ni soe neneba　nubatama no yodoko mo aruran
soko yueni nagusamekanete　kedashikumo auyato moite
tamadare no Ochi no ōnu no　asatsuyu ni tamamo wa hizuchi
yūgiri ni koromo wa nurete　kusamakura tabine kamo suru
awanu kimi yue

Shikitae no sode kaeshi kimi　tamadare no Ochinu ni suginu
mata mo awameyamo

Tobu tori no Asuka no kawa no　kamitsuse ni iwahashi watashi
shimotsuse ni uchihashi watasu　iwahashi ni oinabikeru
tamamo zo tayureba ouru　uchihashi ni oiooreru
kawamo mozo karureba hayuru　nani shikamo waga ōkimi no
tataseba tamamo no mokoro　koyaseba kawamo no gotoku
nabikaishi yoroshiki kimi ga　asamiya wo wasuretamauya
yūmiya wo somukitamauya　utsusomi to omoishi toki
harube wa hana orikazashi　aki tateba momijiba kazashi
shikitae no sode tazusawari　kagami nasu miredomo akazu
mochizuki no iya mezurashimi　omohoshishi kimi to tokidoki
idemashite asobitamaishi　mikemukau Kinohe no miya wo
tokomiya to sadametamaite　ajisahafu megoto mo taenu
shikarekamo ayani kanashimi　nuedori no katakoizuma
asatori no kayowasu kimi ga　natsukusa no omoishinaete
yūzutsu no ka yuki kaku yuki　ōbune no tayutau mireba
nagusamuru kokoro mo arazu　soko yueni sen sube shireya
oto nomimo na nomimo taezu　ametsuchi no iya tōnagaku
shinubiyukan mina ni kakaseru　Asukagawa yorozuyo madeni
hashikiyashi waga ōkimi no　katami ni koko wo

Asukagawa shigarami watashi　sekamaseba nagaruru mizu mo
nodoni ka aramashi

Asukagawa asu dani minto　omoeyamo waga ōkimi no
mina wasure senu

Kakemakumo yuyushikikamo　iwamakumo ayani kashikoki
Asuka no Makami no hara ni　hisakata no Amatsumikado wo
kashikokumo sadametamaite　kamusabuto iwagakurimasu
yasumishishi waga ōkimi no　kikoshimesu sotomo no kuni no
maki tatsu Fuwayama koete　komatsurugi Wazami ga hara no

karimiya ni amorimashite   amenoshita osametamai
osukuni wo sadametamauto   tori ga naku Azuma no kuni no
miikusa wo meshitamaite   chihayaburu hito wo yawaseto
matsurowanu kuni wo osameto   Miko nagara yosashitamaeba
ōmimi ni tachi torihakashi   ōmite ni yumi torimotashi
miikusa wo adomoitamai   totonouru tsuzumi no oto wa
ikazuchi no koe to kikumade   fukinaseru kuda no oto mo
atamitaru tora ka hoyuruto   morobito no obiyurumadeni
sasagetaru hata no nabiki wa   fuyugomori haru sarikureba
nu gotoni tsukite aru hi no   kaze no muta nabikuga gotoku
torimoteru yuhazu no sawagi   miyuki furu fuyu no hayashi ni
tsumuji kamo imakiwataruto   omoumade kiki no kashikoku
hikihanatsu ya no shigekeku   ōyuki no midarete kitare
matsurowazu tachimukaishimo   tsuyujimo no kenaba kenubeku
yuku tori no arasou hashi ni   Watarai no Itsuki no miya yu
kamukaze ni ifukimadowashi   amagumo wo hi no me mo misezu
tokoyami ni ooitamaite   sadameteshi mizuho no Kuni wo
kamunagara futoshikimashite   yasumishishi waga ōkimi no
amenoshita mōshitamaeba   yorozuyo ni shika shimo aranto
yūbana no sakayuru toki ni   waga ōkimi Miko no mikado wo
kamumiya ni yosoimatsurite   tsukawashishi mikado no hito mo
shirotae no asagoromo kite   Haniyasu no mikado no hara ni
akanesasu hi no kotogoto   shishijimono ihaifushitsutsu
nubatama no yūbe ni nareba   ōtono wo furisakemitsutsu
uzura nasu ihaimotohori   samoraedo samoraieneba
harutori no samayoinureba   nageki mo imada suginuni
omoi mo imada tsukineba   kotosaegu Kudara no hara yu
kamuhafuri hafuriimashite   asamoyoshi Kinohe no miya wo
tokomiya to takaku shimatsurite   kamunagara shizumarimashinu
shikaredomo waga ōkimi no   yorozuyo to omohoshimeshite
tsukurashishi Kaguyama no miya   yorozuyo ni suginto moeya
ame no goto furisakemitsutsu   tamadasuki kakete shinuban
kashikokaredomo

Hisakata no ame shirashinuru   kimi yueni hitsuki mo shirazu
koiwatarukamo

Haniyasu no ike no tsutsumi no   komorinu no yukue wo shirani
toneri wa madou

Amatobuya Karu no michi wa   wagimoko ga sato nishi areba
nemokoroni mimaku hoshikedo   yamazu yukaba hitome wo ōmi
maneku yukaba hito shirinubemi   sanekazura nochi mo awanto
ōbune no omoitanomite   tamakagiru iwagakifuchi no
komori nomi koitsutsu aruni   wataru hi no kureyukuga goto
teru tsuki no kumogakuru goto   okitsumo no nabikishi imo wa
momijiba no sugite inikito   tamazusa no tsukai no ieba
azusayumi oto ni kikite   iwan sube sen sube shirani
oto nomiwo kikite arieneba   waga kouru chie no hitoe mo
nagusamoru kokoro mo ariyato   wagimoko ga yamazu idemishi
Karu no ichi ni waga tachikikeba   tamadasuki Unebi no yama ni
naku tori no koe mo kikoezu   tamahoko no michi yuku hito mo
hitori dani niteshi yukaneba   sube wo nami imo ga na yobite
sode zo furitsuru

Akiyama no momiji wo shigemi   madoinuru imo wo motomen
yamaji shirazumo

Momijiba no chiriyuku nabeni   tamazusa no tsukai wo mireba
aishi hi omohoyu

Utsusemi to omoishi toki ni   torimochite waga futari mishi
hashiride no tsutsumi ni tateru   tsuki no ki no kochigochi no e no
haru no ha no shigekiga gotoku   omoerishi imo niwa aredo
tanomerishi kora niwa aredo   yononaka wo somuki shi eneba
kagiroi no moyuru aranu ni   shirotae no amahiregakuri
torijimono asadachiimashite   irihi nasu kakurinishikaba
wagimoko ga katami ni okeru   midorigo no koinaku gotoni
toriatau mono shi nakereba   otokojimono wakibasamimochi
wagimoko to futari waga neshi   makurazuku tsumaya no uchi ni
hiru wamo urasabikurashi   yoru wamo ikizukiakashi

nagekedomo sen sube shirani kouredomo au yoshi wo nami
ōtori no Hagai no yama ni waga kouru imo wa imasuto
hito no ieba iwane sakumite nazumikoshi yokekumozo naki
utsusemi to omoishi imo ga tamakagiru honokani danimo
mienu omoeba

Kozo miteshi aki no tsukuyo wa terasedomo aimishi imo wa
iya toshi sakaru

Fusumaji wo Hikite no yama ni imo wo okite yamaji wo yukeba
ikeritomo nashi

112–4

Akiyama no shitaburu imo nayutake no tooyoru kora wa
ikasamani omoioreka takunawa no nagaki inochi wo
tsuyu kosowa ashita ni okite yūbe niwa kiyuto ie
kiri kosowa yūbe niwa tachite ashita niwa usuto ie
azusayumi oto kiku ware mo ohoni mishi koto kuyashikiwo
shikitae no tamakura makite tsurugitachi mi ni soe neken
wakakusa no sono tsuma no ko wa sabushimika omoite nuran
kuyashimika omoikouran toki narazu suginishi kora ga
asatsuyu no goto yūgiri no goto

Sasanami no Shigatsu no kora ga makariji no kawase no michi wo
mireba sabushimo

Amakazou Ōtsu no ko ga aishi hi ni ohoni mishikaba
ima zo kuyashiki

115–7

Tamamoyoshi Sanuki no kuni wa kunikara ka miredomo akanu
kamukara ka kokoda tōtoki ametsuchi hitsuki to tomoni
tariyukan kami no miomo to tsugite kuru Naka no minato yu
fune ukete waga kogikureba tokitsukaze kumoi ni fukuni
oki mireba shikinami tachi he mireba shiranami sawagu
isanatori umi wo kashikomi yuku fune no kaji hikiorite
ochikochi no shima wa ōkedo naguwashi Samine no shima no

arisomo ni iori shite mireba   nami no to no shigeki hamabe wo
shikitae no makura ni nashite   aradoko to yorifusu kimi ga
ie shiraba yukitemo tsugen   tsuma shiraba ki mo towamashiwo
tamahoko no michi dani shirazu   obohoshìku machi ka kouran
hashiki tsumara wa

Tsuma mo araba tsumite tagemashi   Sami no yama nu no he no uhagi
suginikerazuya

Okitsunami kiyoru ariso wo   shikitae no makura to makite
naseru kimi kamo

118

Ōkimi wa kami nishi maseba   amagumo no Ikazuchi no ue ni
iori serukamo

119–20

Yasumishishi waga ōkimi   takahikaru waga Hi no Miko no
uma namete mikari tataseru   wakagomo wo Kariji no onu ni
shishi kosowa ihaiorogame   uzura koso ihaimotohore
shishijimono ihaiorogami   uzura nasu ihaimotohori
kashikomito tsukaematsurite   hisakata no ame mirugotoku
masokagami aogite miredo   harukusa no iya mezurashiki
waga ōkimi kamo

Hisakata no amayuku tsuki wo   ami ni sashi waga ōkimi wa
kinugasa ni seri

121–7

Tamamo karu Minume wo sugite   natsukusa no Nujima no saki ni
fune chikazukinu

Awaji no Nujima no saki no   hamakaze ni imo ga musubishi
himo fukikaesu

Aratae no Fujie no ura ni   suzuki tsuru ama toka miran
tabi yuku ware wo

Inabinu mo yukisugigateni　omoereba kokoro kohoshiki
Kako no shima miyu

Tomoshibi no Akashi-ōto ni　iran hi ya kogiwakarenan
ie no atari mizu

Amazakaru hina no nagaji yu　koikureba Akashi no to yori
Yamatoshima miyu

Kehi no umi no niwa yoku arashi　karigomo no midareizu miyu
ama no tsuribune

128

Mononofu no yaso-Ujigawa no　ajirogi ni isayou nami no
yukue shirazumo

129

Ōmi no mi yūnamichidori　naga nakeba kokoro mo shinuni
inishie omohoyu

130–1

Naguwashiki Inami no umi no　okitsunami chie ni kakurinu
Yamatoshimane wa

Ōkimi no tō no mikado to　arigayou shimato wo mireba
kamiyo shi omohoyu

132

Komoriku no Hatsuse no yama no　yama no ma ni isayou kumo wa
imo nikamo aran

133

Mi-Kumanu no ura no hamayū　momoe nasu kokoro wa moedo
tadani awanukamo

134

Inishie ni ariken hito mo   waga goto ka imo ni koitsutsu
inekaneteken

135

Kamoyama no iwane shi makeru   ware wokamo shiranito imo ga
machitsutsu aran

136

Na-omoito kimi wa iedomo   awan toki itsu to shiriteka
waga koizaran

137–8

Kyō kyō to waga matsu kimi wa   Ishikawa no kai ni majirite
arito iwazuyamo

Tadano ai wa aigatsumashiji   Ishikawa ni kumo tachiwatare
mitsutsu shinuban

139

Ame no umi ni kumo no nami tachi   tsuki no fune hoshi no hayashi ni
kogikakuru miyu

140

Ashihiki no yamagawa no se no   naru nabeni Yuzuki ga take ni
kumo tachiwataru

141

Makimuku no yamabe toyomite   yuku mizu no minawa no gotoshi
yo no hito ware wa

142

Tōku arite kumoi ni miyuru   imo ga ie ni hayaku itaran
ayume kurogoma

143

Tokoshieni natsu fuyu yukeya   kawagoromo ōgi hanatanu
yama ni sumu hito

144

Ōkura no irie toyomunari   imebito no Fushimi ga tai ni
kari watarurashi

145

Sayonaka to yo wa fukenurashi   karigane no kikoyuru sora ni
tsuki wataru miyu

146

Hisakata no Ame-no-Kaguyama   kono yūbe kasumi tanabiku
haru tatsurashimo

147

Inishie no hito no ueken   sugi ga e ni kasumi tanabiku
haru wa kinurashi

148

Waga seko ni urakoioreba   Amanogawa yofune kogitoyomu
kaji no to kikoyu

149

Ta so kare to ware wo na-toiso   nagatsuki no tsuyu ni nuretsutsu
kimi matsu ware wo

150

Suminoe no oda wo karasu ko   yatsuko kamo naki
yatsuko aredo imo ga mitame to   watakushida karu

151

Kimi ga tame tajikara tsukare   oritaru kinu zo
haru saraba ikanaru iro ni   suriteba yoken

152

Niimuro wo fumishizumu ko shi   tadama narasumo
tama no goto teritaru kimi wo   uchi e to mōse

153

Megushito waga mou imo wa   haya mo shineyamo
ikeritomo ware ni yorubeshito   hito no iwanakuni

154

Asatode no kimi ga ayui wo   nurasu tsuyuhara
hayaku okiidetsutsu ware mo   mosuso nurasana

155

Tarachine no haha ga te hanare   kakubakari subenaki koto wa
imada senakuni

156

Ware yu nochi umaren hito wa   waga gotoku koi suru michi ni
aikosuna yume

157

Masurao no utsushigokoro mo   ware wa nashi yoru hiru to iwazu
koi shi watareba

158

Uchihisasu miyaji wo hito wa   michiyukedo waga mou kimi wa
tada hitori nomi

Iwao sura yukitōrubeki   masurao mo koi tou koto wa
nochi kuinikeri

Koishinaba koi mo shinetoya   wagimoko ga wagie no kado wo
sugite yukuran

Ikanaran na wo ou kami ni   tamuke seba waga mou imo wo
ime nidani min

Ametsuchi to iu na no taete   arabakoso imashi to ware to
au koto yamame

Kuru michi wa iwa fumu yama no   nakumogamo waga matsu kimi ga
uma tsumazukuni

Yamashina no Kohata no yama wo   uma wa aredo kachi yu waga koshi
na wo omoikane

Mizu no ue ni kazu kakugotoki   waga inochi imo ni awanto
ukehitsurukamo

Ōtsuchi mo toraba tsukimedo   yononaka ni tsukisenu mono wa
koi nishi arikeri

Imo ni koi inenu asake ni   oshidori no koko yu wataruwa
imo ga tsukai ka

Tarachine no haha ga kau ko no   mayogomori komoreru imo wo
min yoshi mogamo

Hihito no nukagami yueru   shimeyū no shiminishi kokoro
ware wasuremeya

Hayahito no na ni ou yogoe   ichijiroku waga na wa noritsu
tsuma to tanomase

Tsurugitachi moroha no toki ni   ashi fumite shini nishi shinan
kimi ni yoritewa

Niihari no ima tsukuru michi   sayakani mo kikitekerukamo
imo ga ue no koto wo

Narukami no shimashi toyomite   sashikumori ame mo furabaya
kimi ga tomaran

Narukami no shimashi toyomite   furazutomo ware wa tomaran
imo shi todomeba

Ashihara no Mizuho no Kuni wa   kamunagara kotoage senu kuni
shikaredomo kotoage zo waga suru   koto sakiku masakiku maseto

tsutsumi naku sakiku imasaba   arisonami aritemo minto
ioenami chienami ni shiki   kotoage su ware wa kotoage su ware wa

Shikishima no Yamato no kuni wa   kotodama no tasukuru kuni zo
masakiku arikoso

177

Furinishi omina nishiteya   kakubakari koi ni shizuman
tawarawa no goto

178-9

Miyabio to ware wa kikeruwo   yado kasazu ware wo kaeseri
oso no miyabio

Miyabio ni ware wa arikeri   yado kasazu kaeshishi ware zo
miyabio niwa aru

180

Ōkimi wa kami nishi maseba   akagoma no harabau tai wo
miyako to nashitsu

181

Wagimoko wa kushiro ni aranan   hidarite no waga oku no te ni
makite inamashiwo

182

Ōmiya no uchi made kikoyu   abiki suto ago totonouru
ama no yobigoe

183

Kurushikumo furikuru ame ka   Miwa ga saki Sanu no watari ni
ie mo aranakuni

Sashinabe ni yu wakase kodomo   Ichihizu no hibashi yori kon
kitsu ni amusan

Inishie no hito ni ware areya   Sasanami no furuki miyako wo
mireba kanashiki

Sasanami no kunitsumikami no   urasabite aretaru miyako
mireba kanashimo

Tabi nishite monokohoshikini   yamashita no ake no sohofune
oki ni kogu miyu

Sakurada e tazu nakiwataru   Ayuchigata shio hinikerashi
tazu nakiwataru

Iso no saki kogitamiyukeba   Ōmi no mi yaso no minato ni
tazu sawani naku

Waga fune wa Hira no minato ni   kogihaten oki e na-sakari
sayo fukenikeri

Izuku nika ware wa yadoran   Takashima no Kachinu no hara ni
kono hi kurenaba

Kaku yueni mijito iumonowo   Sasanami no furuki miyako wo
misetsutsu motona

Yasumishishi waga ōkimi   takahikaru Hi no Miko
hisakata no Amatsumiya ni   kamunagara kami to imaseba
soko woshimo ayani kashikomi   hiru wamo hi no kotogoto
yoru wamo yo no kotogoto   fushi i nagekedo akitaranukamo

Ōkimi wa kami nishi maseba   amagumo no ioe ga shita ni
kakuritamainu

Yamato koi i no neraenuni   kokoro naku kono su no saki ni
tazu nakubeshiya

Ōtono no kono motohori no   yuki na-fumisone
shibashiba mo furazaru yuki zo   yama nomini furishi yuki zo
yume yoruna hito ya   na-fumisone yuki wa

Aritsutsumo meshitamawanzo   ōtono no kono motohori no
yuki na-fumisone

Takeba nure takaneba nagaki   imo ga kami konogoro minuni
midaritsuranka

Hito wa mina ima wa nagashito   taketo iedo kimi ga mishi kami
midaretaritomo

Tachibana no kage fumu michi no   yachimata ni mono wozo omou
imo ni awazute

Kamukaze no Ise no hamaogi   orifusete tabine ya suran
araki hamabe ni

202

Kawakami no yutsuiwamura ni   kusa musazu tsunenimogamona
tokootome nite

203

Hikumanu ni niou hagiwara   irimidari koromo niowase
tabi no shirushi ni

204

Izuku nika funahate suran   Are no saki kogitamiyukishi
tananashiobune

205

Masurao ga satsuya tabasami   tachimukai iru Matokata wa
miruni sayakeshi

206

Yasumishishi waga Ōkimi   takaterasu Hi no Miko
aratae no Fujiwara ga ue ni   osukuni wo meshitamawanto
miaraka wa takashirasanto   kamunagara omohosu nabeni
ametsuchi mo yorite arekoso   iwabashiru Ōmi no kuni no
koromode no Tanakamiyama no   makisaku hi no tsumade wo
mononofu no yaso-Ujigawa ni   tamamo nasu ukabe nagasere
sowo toruto sawagu mitami mo   ie wasure mi mo tanashirazu
kamojimono mizu ni ukiite   waga tsukuru Hi no mikado ni
shiranu kuni yori-Koseji yori   waga kuni wa tokoyo ni naran
fumi oeru ayashiki kame mo   aratayo to Izumi no kawa ni
mochikoseru maki no tsumade wo   momotarazu ikada ni tsukuri
nobosuran isohaku mireba   kamunagara narashi

207-8

Yasumishishi wago Ōkimi   takaterasu Hi no Miko
aratae no Fujii ga hara ni   ōmikado hajimetamaite
Haniyasu no tsutsumi no ue ni   aritatashi meshitamaeba

Yamato no Ao-Kaguyama wa   hi no tate no ōmikado ni
haruyama to shimisabi tateri   Unebi no kono mizuyama wa
hi no yoko no ōmikado ni   mizuyama to yamasabi imasu
Miminashi no aosugayama wa   sotomo no ōmikado ni
yoroshinabe kamusabi tateri   naguwashi Yoshinu no yama wa
kagetomo no ōmikado yu   kumoi nizo tōku arikeru
takashiruya ame no mikage   ameshiruya hi no mikage no
mizu kosowa tokoshienarame   mii no mashimizu

Fujiwara no ōmiyatsukae   aretsugan otome ga tomo wa
tomoshikirokamo

209

Takahikaru waga Hi no Miko no   yorozuyo ni kuni shirasamashi
Shima no miya wamo

210

Ametsuchi to tomoni oento   omoitsutsu tsukaematsurishi
kokoro tagainu

211

Asahi teru Sada no okabe ni   mureitsutsu waga naku namida
yamu toki mo nashi

212

Mitatashi no shima no ariso wo   ima mireba oizarishi kusa
oinikerukamo

213

Himukashi no taki no mikado ni   samoraedo kinō mo kyō mo
mesu koto mo nashi

214

Mizu tsutau iso no urami no   iwatsutsuji moku saku michi wo
mata minankamo

345

Hitohi niwa chitabi mairishi   himukashi no ōki mikado wo
irigatenukamo

Asagumori hi no irinureba   mitatashi no shima ni oriite
nagekitsurukamo

Asahi teru Shima no mikado ni   obohoshiku hitooto mo seneba
mauraganashimo

Ochitagichi nagaruru mizu no   iwa ni furi yodomeru yodo ni
tsuki no kage miyu

Kakemakumo ayani kashikoshi   Fujiwara no miyako shimimini
hito washimo michite aredomo   kimi washimo ōku imasedo
yukimukau toshinoo nagaku   tsukaekoshi kimi no mikado wo
ame no goto aogite mitsutsu   kashikokedo omoitanomite
itsu shikamo hitarashimashite   mochizuki no tatawashikento
waga omou Miko no Mikoto wa   haru sareba Uetsuki ga ue no
tōtsuhito matsu no shitaji yu   noborashite kunimi asobashi
nagatsuki no shigure no aki wa   ōtono no migiri shimimini
tsuyu oite nabikeru hagi wo   tamadasuki kakete shinubashi
miyuki furu fuyu no ashita wa   sashiyanagi nehariazusa wo
mite ni torashitamaite   asobashishi waga ōkimi wo
kasumi tatsu haru no higurashi   masokagami miredo akaneba
yorozuyo ni kaku shimogamoto   ōbune no tanomeru toki ni
oyozure ni me kamo madoeru   ōtono wo furisakemireba
shirotae ni kazarimatsurite   uchihisasu miya no toneri mo
tae no ho no asaginu keruwa   ime kamo utsutsu kamoto
kumoriyo no madoeru hodo ni   asamoyoshi Kinohe no michi yu
tsunusahafu Iware wo mitsutsu   kamuhafuri hafurimatsureba

yuku michi no tazuki wo shirani   omoedomo shirushi wo nami
nagekedomo okuka wo nami   ōmisode yuki furishi matsu wo
koto towanu ki niwa aredomo   aratama no tatsu tsuki gotoni
Amanohara furisakemitsutsu   tamadasuki kakete shinubana
kashikokaredomo

Tsunusahafu Iware no yama ni   shirotae ni kakareru kumo wa
waga ōkimi kamo

Momoshinu no Minu no Ōkimi   nishi no umaya tatete kau koma
himukashi no umaya tatete kau koma   kusa kosowa torite kau gani
mizu kosowa kumite kau gani   nani shikamo ashige no uma no
ibaetachitsuru

Koromode wo ashige no uma no   ibayu koe kokoro arekamo
tsune yu keni naku

Midorigo no wakugo ga mi niwa   tarachishi haha ni udakae
suki kakuru hau ko ga mi niwa   yūkataginu hitsura ni nui ki
unatsuki no warawa ga mi niwa   yuihata no sodetsukegoromo
kishi ware wo nioiyoru kora ga   yochi niwa
minanowata kaguroshi kami wo   magushi mochi koko ni kakitare
toritsukane agetemo maki mi   tokimidari warawa ni nashimi
usumono no nitsukau iro ni   murasaki no ōaya no kinu
Suminoe no Tōzato-Onu no   mahari mochi nioshishi kinu ni
Komanishiki himo ni nuitsuke   sasae kasanae nami kasaneki
utsusoyashi omi no kora   ariginu no takara no kora ga
utsutae wa hete oru nuno   hizarashi no asatezukuri wo
shikimo nasu wa shikini torishiki   shikiya furu inakiotome ga
tsumatouto ware nizo koshi   ochikata no futaya shitagutsu
tobu tori no Asukaotoko ga   nagame imi nuishi kurogutsu
sashihakite niwa ni tatazumi   makari na-tachito sauru otome ga
honokikite ware nizo koshi   mihanada no kinu no obi wo
hikobi nasu Karobi ni torashi   Watatsumi no tono no iraka ni

347

tobikakeru sugaru no gotoki   koshiboso ni torikazarai
masokagami toriname kakete   onoga kao kaerai mitsutsu
haru sarite nube wo megureba   omoshiromi ware wo omoeka
sanutsutori kinaki kakerau   aki sarite yamabe wo yukeba
natsukashito ware wo omoeka   amagumo mo yukitanabiku
kaeritachi michi wo kureba   uchihisasu miyaomina
sasutake no toneriotoko mo   shinuburai kaerai mitsutsu
taga ko zotoya omohaete aru   kaku zoshi koshi
inishie sasakishi ware ya   hashikiyashi kyō yamo kora ni
isa nitoya omohaete aru   kaku zoshi koshi
inishie no sakashiki hito mo   nochi no yo no katami ni sento
oibito wo okurishi kuruma   mochikaerikoshi

Shinabakoso aimizu arame   ikite araba shirokami kora ni
oizarameyamo

Shirokami shi kora mo oinaba   kaku no goto wakaken kora ni
noraekanemeya

Hashikiyashi okina no uta ni   obohoshiki kokono no kora ya
kamakete oran

Haji wo shinubi haji wo modashite   koto mo naku mono iwanu saki ni
ware wa yorinan

Shini mo iki mo onaji kokoro to   musubiteshi tomo ya tagawan
ware mo yorinan

229–30

Mimoro no Kamunabiyama yu   tonogumori ame wa furikinu
amagirai kaze sae fukinu   ōkuchi no Makami no hara yu
omoitsutsu kaerinishi hito   ie ni itarikiya

Kaerinishi hito wo omouto   nubatama no sono yo wa ware mo
i mo nekaneteki

*   *   *

348

Masurao no tomo no oto sunari   mononofu no ōmaetsugimi
tate tatsurashimo

Waga Ōkimi mono na-omohoshi   Sumegami no tsugite tamaeru
ware nakenakuni

Ashihiki no yama yukishikaba   yamabito no ware ni eshimeshi
yamazuto zo kore

Osukuni no tō no mikado ni   imashira shi kaku makarinaba
tairakeku ware wa asoban   tamudakite ware wa imasan
Sumera waga uzu no mite mochi   kakinadezo negitamau
uchinadezo negitamau   kaerikon hi ainoman ki zo
kono toyomiki wa

Masurao no yuku tou michi zo   ohorokani omoite yukuna
masurao no tomo

Tachibana wa mi sae hana sae   sono ha sae e ni shimo furedo
iya tokoha no ki

Soramitsu Yamato no kuni wa   mizu no ue wa tsuchi yukugotoku
fune no ue wa toko ni orugoto   ōkami no iwaeru kuni zo
yotsu no fune funanohe narabe   tairakeku haya watarikite
kaerigoto mōsan hi ni   ainoman ki zo kono toyomiki wa

Yotsu no fune haya kaerikoto   shiraka tsuke waga mo no suso ni
iwaite matan

Ametsuchi wo terasu hitsuki no   kiwami naku arubekimonowo
nani woka omowan

240

Waga seko to futari mimaseba   ikubaku ka kono furu yuki no
ureshikaramashi

241

Ōbune ni makaji shiji nuki   kono ago wo Karakuni e yaru
iwae kamitachi

242-3

Masurao ya katakoi sento   nagekedomo shiko no masurao
nao koinikeri

Nagekitsutsu masuraonoko no   kourekoso waga motoyui no
hijite nurekere

244

Ie ni arishi hitsu ni kugi sashi   osameteshi koi no yatsuko no
tsukamikakarite

245

Karu no ike no urami yukimeguru   kamo surani tamamo no ue ni
hitori nenakuni

246

Yoshinu naru Natsumi no kawa no   kawayodo ni kamo zo nakunaru
yamakage nishite

247

Aoyama no mine no shirakumo   asanikeni tsuneni miredomo
mezurashi waga kimi

Me niwa mite te niwa toraenu tsuki no uchi no katsura no gotoki
imo wo ikani sen

Ame ni masu Tsukuyomiotoko mai wa sen koyoi no nagasa
ioyo tsugikoso

Yakidachi no kado uchihanachi masurao no hogu toyomiki ni
ware einikeri

Yūzukuyo kokoro mo shinuni shiratsuyu no oku kono niwa ni
kōrogi nakumo

Tsukuyomi no hikari ni kimase ashihiki no yama wo hedatete
tōkaranakuni

Tsukuyomi no hikari wa kiyoku teraseredo madoeru kokoro
taezu omohoyu

Ise no umi no okitsushiranami hana nimoga tsutsumite imo ga
iezuto ni sen

Tōzuma no koko ni araneba tamahoko no michi wo tadōmi
omou sora yasukaranakuni nageku sora yasukaranumonowo
misora yuku kumo nimogamo takatobu tori nimogamo
asu yukite imo ni kotodoi waga tame ni imo mo koto naku
imo ga tame ware mo koto naku ima mo mishi goto taguitemogamo

Shikitae no tamakura makazu   aida okite toshi zo henikeru
awanaku moeba

257

Inadaki ni kisumeru tama wa   futatsu nashi konatakanata mo
kimi ga manimani

258

Harukusa wa nochi wa chiriyasushi   iwao nasu tokiwa ni imase
tōtoki waga kimi

259

Hitotsumatsu ikuyo ka henuru   fuku kaze no koe no sumeruwa
toshi fukamikamo

260

Ujimayama asakaze samushi   tabi nishite koromo kasubeki
imo mo aranakuni

261

Aratashiki toshi no hajime ni   omou dochi imurete oreba
ureshikumo aruka

262

Himukashi no ichi no ueki no   kodarumade awazu hisashimi
ube koinikeri

263

Ou no umi no kawara no chidori   naga nakeba waga Sahogawa no
omohoyurakuni

264

Kawazu naku Kamunabigawa ni   kage miete ima ka sakuran
yamabuki no hana

Yūzuku hi sasuya kawabe ni   tsukuru ya no kata wo yoroshimi
ube yosorikeri

Baramon no tsukureru oda wo   hamu karasu manabuta harete
hatahoko ni ori

Kono yo niwa hitogoto shigeshi   kon yo nimo awan waga seko
imanarazutomo

Yamabuki no sakitaru nube no   tsubosumire kono haru no ame ni
sakari narikeri

Koikusa wo chikaraguruma ni   nanakuruma tsumite kouraku
waga kokoro kara

Koi wa ima wa arajito ware wa   omoeruwo izuku no koi zo
tsukamikakareru

Tori ga naku Azuma no kuni ni   takayama wa sawani aredomo
futagami no tōtoki yama no   namitachi no migahoshi yama to
kamiyo yori hito no iitsugi   kunimi suru Tsukuba no yama wo
fuyugomori tokijiki toki to   mizute yukaba mashite koishimi
yukige suru yamamichi surawo   nazumi zo waga koshi

Tsukubane wo yoso nomi mitsutsu   arikanete yukige no michi wo
nazumikerukamo

Tawayame no kushige ni noreru   kagami nasu Mitsu no hamabe ni
sanitsurau himo tokisakezu   wagimoko ni koitsutsu oreba
akegure no asagirigakuri   naku tazu no ne nomishi nakayu
waga kouru chie no hitoe mo   nagusamoru kokoro mo ariyato
ie no atari waga tachimireba   aohata no Kazurakiyama ni
tanabikeru shirakumogakuri   amazakaru hina no kunibe ni
tada mukau Awaji wo sugi   Awashima wo sogai ni mitsutsu
asanagi ni kako no koe yobi   yūnagi ni kaji no to shitsutsu
nami no e wo iyukisagukumi   iwa no ma wo iyukimotohori
Inabizuma urami wo sugite   torijimono nazusaiyukeba
Ie no shima ariso no ue ni   uchinabiki shijini oitaru
nanoriso ga nado kamo imo ni   norazu kiniken

Shirotae no sode tokikaete   kaerikon tsukihi wo yomite
yukite komashiwo

Naniwabe ni hito no yukereba   okureite haruna tsumu ko wo
miruga kanashisa

Yū sareba ashibe ni sawagi   akekureba oki ni nazusau
kamo suramo tsuma to taguite   waga o niwa shimo na-furisoto
shirotae no hane sashikaete   uchiharai sanu toumonowo
yuku mizu no kaeranugotoku   fuku kaze no mienuga gotoku
ato mo naki yo no hito nishite   wakarenishi imo ga kiseteshi
naregoromo sode katashikite   hitori kamo nen

Tazu ga naki ashibe wo sashite   tobiwataru ana tazutazushi
hitori sanureba

Karakuni ni yukitarawashite   kaerikon masuratakeo ni
miki tatematsuru

Shika no ama wa me kari shio yaki itoma nami kushige no ogushi
tori mo minakuni

Iohara no Kiyomi ga saki no Miho no ura no yutakeki mitsutsu
monomoi mo nashi

Hiru miredo akanu Tago no ura Ōkimi no mikoto kashikomi
yoru mitsurukamo

Aoniyoshi Nara no miyako wa saku hana no niouga gotoku
ima sakari nari

Masurao no yuzue furiokoshi itsuru ya wo nochi min hito wa
kataritsugu gane

Shiotsuyama uchikoeyukeba waga noreru uma zo tsumazuku
ie kourashimo

Ōkimi no idemashi no mani mononofu no yasotomonoo to
ideyukishi uruwashizuma wa amatobuya Karu no michi yori
tamadasuki Unebi wo mitsutsu asamoyoshi Kiji ni iritachi
Matsuchiyama koyuran kimi wa momijiba no chiritobu mitsutsu
mutsumajiku wa woba omowazu kusamakura tabi wo yoroshito
omoitsutsu kimi wa aranto asoso niwa katsu wa shiredomo
shikasugani moda mo earaneba waga seko ga yuki no manimani
owantowa chitabi omoedo tawayame no waga mi nishi areba
michimori no towan kotae wo iiyaran sube wo shiranito
tachite tsumazuku

Okureite koitsutsu arazuwa Ki no kuni no Imose no yama ni
aramashimonowo

Waga seko ga ato fumimotome   oiyukaba Ki no sekimori i
todomenankamo

288–90

Mikanohara tabi no yadori ni   tamahoko no michi no yukiai ni
amagumo no yoso nomi mitsutsu   kototowan yoshi no nakereba
kokoro nomi musetsutsu aruni   ametsuchi no kami kotoyosete
shikitae no koromode kaete   onozuma to tanomeru koyoi
aki no yo no momoyo no nagasa   arikosenukamo

Amagumo no yoso ni mishi yori   wagimoko ni kokoro mo mi sae
yorinishimonowo

Koyoi no hayaku akenaba   sube wo nami aki no momoyo wo
negaitsurukamo

291–3

Taki no ue no Mifune no yama ni   mizue sashi shijini oitaru
toga no ki no iya tsugitsugini   yorozuyo ni kaku shi shirasan
Mi-Yoshinu no Akitsu no miya wa   kamukara ka tōtokaruran
kunikara ka migahoshikaran   yama kawa wo kiyomi sayakemi
ube shi kamiyo yu sadamekerashimo

Toshinoha ni kaku mo miteshiga   Mi-Yoshinu no kiyoki kōchi no
tagitsu shiranami

Yama takami shirayūbana ni   ochitagitsu taki no kōchi wa
miredo akánukamo

294–6

Ashihiki no miyama mo sayani   ochitagitsu Yoshinu no kawa no
kawa no se no kiyoki wo mireba   kamibe wa chidori shiba naki
shimobe wa kawazu tsuma yobu   momoshiki no ōmiyabito mo
ochikochi ni shijini shi areba   miru gotoni ayani tomoshimi
tamakazura tayuru koto naku   yorozuyo ni kaku shimogamoto
ametsuchi no kami wozo inoru   kashikokaredomo

356

Yorozuyo ni mitomo akameya   Mi-Yoshinu no tagitsu kōchi no
ōmiyadokoro

Minahito no inochi mo ware mo   Mi-Yoshinu no taki no tokoha no
tsunenaranukamo

297–9

Oshiteru Naniwa no kuni wa   ashigaki no furinishi sato to
hito mina no omoiyasumite   tsure mo naku arishi aida ni
umio nasu Nagara no miya ni   makibashira futotakashikite
osukuni wo osametamaeba   okitsutori Ajifu no hara ni
mononofu no yasotomonoo wa   iori shite miyako nashitari
tabi niwa aredomo

Aranura ni sato wa aredomo   Ōkimi no shikimasu toki wa
miyako to narinu

Amaotome tananashiobune   kogizurashi tabi no yadori ni
kaji no to kikoyu

300–2

Nakisumi no Funase yu miyuru   Awajishima Matsuho no ura ni
asanagi ni tamamo karitsutsu   yūnagi ni moshio yakitsutsu
amaotome aritowa kikedo   mi ni yukan yoshi no nakereba
masurao no kokoro wa nashini   tawayame no omoitawamite
tamotohori ware wazo kouru   funekaji wo nami

Tamamo karu amaotomedomo   mi ni yukan funekaji mogamo
nami takakutomo

Yukimeguri mitomo akameya   Nakisumi no Funase no hama ni
shikiru shiranami

303–5

Tamadasuki kakenu toki naku   ikinoo ni waga mou kimi wa
utsusemi no mikoto kashikomi   yū sareba tazu ga tsuma yobu

357

Naniwagata Mitsu no saki yori   ōbune ni makaji shiji nuki
shiranami no takaki arumi wo   shimazutai iwakareyukaba
todomareru ware wa nusa tori   iwaitsutsu kimi woba yaran
haya kaerimase

Nami no ue yu miyuru kojima no   kumogakuri ana ikizukashi
aiwakarenaba

Tamakiharu inochi ni mukai   koin-yuwa kimi ga mifune no
kajitsuka nimoga

306-7

Ōbune ni makaji shiji nuki   Ōkimi no mikoto kashikomi
isomi surukamo

Mononofu no omi no otoko wa   Ōkimi no make no manimani
kiku toumono zo

308-10

Azusayumi te ni torimochite   masurao no satsuya tabasami
tachimukau Takamadoyama ni   harunu yaku nubi to mirumade
moyuru hi wo ikani to toeba   tamahoko no michi kuru hito no
naku namida kosame ni fureba   shirotae no koromo hizuchite
tachitomari ware ni kataraku   nani shikamo motona ieru
kikeba ne nomishi nakayu   katareba kokoro zo itaki
Sumerogi no Kami no Miko no   idemashi no tabi no hikari zo
kokoda teritaru

Takamado no nube no akihagi   itazurani saki ka chiruran
miru hito nashini

Mikasayama nube yuku michi wa   kokidaku mo shigeku aretaruka
hisani aranakuni

311-2

Hito to naru koto wa katakiwo   wakurabani nareru waga mi wa

shini mo iki mo kimi ga manima to   omoitsutsu arishi aida ni
utsusemi no yo no hito nareba   Ōkimi no mikoto kashikomi
amazakaru hina osame nito   asatori no asadachi shitsutsu
muratori no muradachiyukeba   tomariite ware wa koinna
mizu hisanaraba

Mi-Koshiji no yuki furu yama wo   koen hi wa tomareru ware wo
kakete shinubase

313

Michinoku no Manu no kayahara   tōkedomo omokage nishite
miyu toumonowo

314

Waga yado no yūkagegusa no   shiratsuyu no kenu gani motona
omohoyurukamo

315

Yaoka yuku hama no masago mo   waga koi ni ani masarajika
okitsushimamori

316

Ise no umi no iso mo todoroni   yosuru nami kashikoki hito ni
koiwatarukamo

317

Yū sareba monomoi masaru   mishi hito no kototou sugata
omokage nishite

318

Omounishi shinisuru mono ni   aramaseba chitabi zo ware wa
shinikaeramashi

Tsurugitachi mi ni torisouto　ime ni mitsu nani no satoshi zomo
kimi ni awan tame

Ametsuchi no kami shi kotowari　nakubakoso waga mou kimi ni
awazu shini seme

Minahito wo neyotono kane wa　utsunaredo kimi woshi moeba
inegatenukamo

Aiomowanu hito wo omouwa　ōdera no gaki no shirie ni
nukazukugotoshi

Shirotae no sode sashikaete　nabikineshi waga kurokami no
mashiraga ni naran kiwami　aratayo ni tomoni aranto
tamanoo no taejii imo to　musubiteshi koto wa hatasazu
omoerishi kokoro wa togezu　shirotae no tamoto wo wakare
nikibinishi ie yumo idete　midorigo no nakuwomo okite
asagiri no ohoni naritsutsu　Yamashiro no　Sagarakayama no
yama no ma wo yukisuginureba　iwan sube sen sube shirani
wagimoko to saneshi tsumaya ni　ashita niwa idetachi shinubi
yūbe niwa irii nagekai　wakibasamu ko no naku gotoni
otokojimono oimi idakimi　asatori no ne nomi nakitsutsu
kouredomo shirushi wo namito　kototowanu mono niwa aredo
wagimoko ga irinishi yama wo　yosuga tozo omou

Utsusemi no yo no koto nareba　yoso ni mishi yama woya ima wa
yosuga to omowan

Asatori no ne nomiwo nakan　wagimoko ni ima mata sarani
au yoshi wo nami

326–7

Umagori ayani tomoshiku   narukami no oto nomi kikishi
Mi-Yoshinu no maki tatsu yama yu   mioroseba kawa no se gotoni
akekureba asagiri tachi   yū sareba kawazu naku nabe
himo tokanu tabi nishi areba   a nomishite kiyoki kawara wo
mirakushi oshimo

Taki no ue no Mifune no yama wa   kashikokedo omoiwasururu
toki mo hi mo nashi

328–9

Isanatori hamabe wo kiyomi   uchinabiki ouru tamamo ni
asanagi ni chienami yori   yūnagi ni ioenami yoru
hetsunami no iya shikushikuni   tsukini keni hibi ni mirutomo
ima nomini akitarameyamo   shiranami no isakimegureru
Suminoe no hama

Shiranami no chie ni kiyosuru   Suminoe no kishi no haniu ni
nioite yukana

330–2

Sanitsurau kimi ga mikoto to   tamazusa no tsukai mo koneba
omoiyamu waga mi hitotsu zo   chihayaburu kami nimo na-ōse
urabe sue kame mo na-yakiso   koishikuni itaki waga mi zo
ichijiroku mi ni shimitōri   murakimo no kokoro kudakete
shinan inochi niwakani narinu   imasarani kimi ka wa wo yobu
tarachine no haha no mikoto ka   momotarazu yaso no chimata ni
yūke nimo ura nimozo tou   shinubeki waga yue

Urabe womo yaso no chimata mo   uratoedo kimi wo aimin
tadoki shirazumo

Waga inochi wa oshikumo arazu   sanitsurau kimi ni yoritezo
nagaku horiseshi

361

Unabara no tōki watari wo   miyabio no asobu wo minto
nazusai zo koshi

Kono hana no hitoyo no uchi ni   momokusa no koto zo komoreru
ohorokani suna

Kono hana no hitoyo no uchi wa   momokusa no koto mochikanete
oraekerazuya

Amagumo no sokie no kiwami   waga moeru kimi ni wakaren
hi chikaku narinu

Teradera no megaki mōsaku   Ōmiwa no ogaki tabarite
sono ko umawan

Hotoke tsukuru masoho tarazuba   mizu tamaru Ikeda no aso ga
hana no e wo hore

Kimi ga yuku michi no nagate wo   kuritatane yakihorobosan
ame no hi mogamo

Wagimoko ga katami no koromo   nakariseba nanimono moteka
inochi tsugamashi

Hitoguni wa sumiashitozo iu   sumuyakeku haya kaerimase
koishinanu to ni

Ametsuchi no sokohi no ura ni   aga gotoku kimi ni kouran
hito wa sane araji

Awan hi no katami ni seyoto   tawayame no omoimidarete

nueru koromo zo

Sasutake no ōmiyabito wa   ima mokamo hitonaburi nomi
konomitaruran

Tamashii wa ashita yūbe ni   tamafuredo aga mune itashi
koi no shigekini

Kaerikeru hito kitarerito   iishikaba hotohoto shiniki
kimi kato omoite

Waga seko ga kaerikimasan   toki no tame inochi nokosan
wasuretamauna

Kyō mokamo miyako nariseba   mimaku hori nishi no mimaya no
to ni tateramashi

349–50

Imasarani nani woka omowan   uchinabiki kokoro wa kimi ni
yorinishimonowo

Waga seko wa mono na-omohoshi   koto shi araba hi nimo mizu nimo
waga nakenakuni

351

Waga seko ga keseru koromo no   harime ochizu irinikerashi
waga kokoro sae

352–3

Yorozuyo ni kokoro wa tokete   waga seko ga tsumishi te mitsutsu
shinobikanetsumo

Matsu no hana hanakazu nishimo   waga seko ga omoeranakuni
motona sakitsutsu

Mi-Yoshinu no Yoshinu no miya wa   yamakara shi tōtoku arashi
kawakara shi sayakeku arashi   ametsuchi to nagaku hisashiku
yorozuyo ni kawarazu aran   idemashi no miya

Mukashi mishi Kisa no ogawa wo   ima mireba iyoyo sayakeku
narinikerukamo

Waga sakari mata ochimeyamo   hotohotoni Nara no miyako wo
mizuka narinan

Shirushi naki inono wo mowazuwa   hitotsuki no nigoreru sake wo
nomubeku arurashi

Sake no na wo hijiri to ōseshi   inishie no ōki hijiri no
koto no yoroshisa

Inishie no nana no sakashiki   hitodomo mo horiseshi mono wa
sake nishi arurashi

Sakashimito mono iuyoriwa   sake nomite einaki surushi
masaritarurashi

Iwan sube sen sube shirani   kiwamarite tōtoki mono wa
sake nishi arurashi

Nakanakani hito to arazuwa   sakatsubo ni nariteshigamo
sake ni shiminan

Ana miniku sakashira wo suto   sake nomanu hito wo yoku mireba
saru nikamo niru

Atai naki takara to iutomo   hitotsuki no nigoreru sake ni
ani masarameya

Yoru hikaru tama to iutomo   sake nomite kokoro wo yaruni
ani shikameyamo

Yononaka no asobi no michi ni   suzushikiwa einaki suruni
arinubekarashi

Kono yo nishi tanushiku araba   kon yo niwa mushi ni tori nimo
ware wa narinan

Ikeru mono tsuini mo shinuru   mono ni areba kono yo naru ma wa
tanushikuwo arana

Moda orite sakashira suruwa   sake nomite einaki suruni
nao shikazukeri

370

Uruwashiki hito no makiteshi   shikitae no waga tamakura wo
maku hito arameya

371

Miyako naru aretaru ie ni   hitori neba tabi ni masarite
kurushikarubeshi

372-5

Wagimoko ga mishi Tomo no ura no   muro no ki wa tokoyo ni aredo
mishi hito zo naki

Iso no ue ni nebau muro no ki   mishi hito wo izura to towaba
kataritsugenka

Imo to koshi Minume no saki wo   kaerusa ni hitori shite mireba
namidagumashimo

Yukusa niwa futari waga mishi   kono saki wo hitori sugureba
kokoroganashimo

Hito mo naki munashiki ie wa   kusamakura tabi ni masarite
kurushikarikeri

Imo to shite futari tsukurishi   waga shima wa kodakaku shigeku
narinikerukamo

Wagimoko ga ueshi ume no ki   miru gotoni kokoro musetsutsu
namida shi nagaru

Kimi ga tame kamishi machizake   Yasu no nu ni hitori ya noman
tomo nashinishite

Yononaka wa munashiki mono to   shiru toki shi iyoyo masumasu
kanashikarikeri

Yasumishishi waga Ōkimi no   osukuni wa Yamato mo koko mo
onajitozo omou

Masurao to omoeru ware ya   mizuguki no Mizuki no ue ni
namida nogowan

Nubatama no kurokami shiroku   kawaritemo itaki koi niwa
au toki arikeri

Koko ni arite Tsukushi ya izuku   shirakumo no tanabiku yama no
kata nishi arurashi

Uchihisasu miya ni yuku ko wo   maganashimi tomureba kurushi yaruwa sube nashi

386–7

Hisakata no Amanohara yori   arekitaru Kami no Mikoto
okuyama no sakaki no eda ni   shiraka tsuke yū toritsukete
iwaibe wo iwai horisue   takatama wo shijini nukitare
shishijimono hiza orifuse   tawayame no osuhi torikake
kaku danimo ware wa koinan   kimi ni awajikamo

Yūdatami te ni torimochite   kaku danimo ware wa koinan
kimi ni awajikamo

388–9

Takuzunu no Shiragi no kuni yu   hitogoto wo yoshito kikashite
toisakuru ukara harakara   naki kuni ni watarikimashite
Ōkimi no shikimasu kuni ni   uchihisasu miyako shimimini
sato ie wa sawani aredomo   ikasamani omoikemekamo
tsure mo naki Saho no yamabe ni   naku ko nasu shitaikimashite
shikitae no ie womo tsukuri   aratama no toshinoo nagaku
sumaitsutsu imashishimonowo   ikeru mono shinu tou koto ni
manukarenu mono nishi areba   tanomerishi hito no kotogoto
kusamakura tabi naru hodo ni   Sahogawa wo asakawa watari
Kasuganu wo sogai ni mitsutsu   ashihiki no yamabe wo sashite
yūyami to kakurimashinure   iwan sube sen sube shirani
tamotohori tada hitori shite   shirotae no koromode hosazu
nagekitsutsu waga naku namida   Arimayama kumoi tanabiki
ame ni furikiya

Todomeenu inochi nishi areba   shikitae no ie yuwa idete
kumogakuriniki

390

Konto iumo konu toki aruwo   kojito iuwo kontowa mataji
kojito iumonowo

Oshiteru Naniwa no suge no nemokoroni kimi ga kikoshite
toshi fukaku nagakushi ieba masokagami togishi kokoro wo
yurushiteshi sono hi no kiwami nami no muta nabiku tamamo no
kanikakuni kokoro wa motazu ōbune no tanomeru toki ni
chihayaburu kami ya sakeken utsusemi no hito ka sauran
kayowashishi kimi mo kimasazu tamazusa no tsukai mo miezu
narinureba ita mo sube nami nubatama no yoru wa sugarani
akarahiku hi mo kururumade nagekedomo shirushi wonami
omoedomo tazuki wo shirani tawayame to iwakumo shiruku
tawarawa no ne nomi nakitsutsu tamotohori kimi ga tsukai wo
machi ya kaneten

Hajime yori nagaku iitsutsu tanomezuba kakaru omoi ni
awamashi mono ka

393

Hisakata no ame no tsuyujimo okinikeri ie naru hito mo
machikoinuran

394

Tamamori ni tama wa sazukete katsugatsu mo makura to ware wa
iza futari nen

395

Koikoite aeru toki dani uruwashiki koto tsukushiteyo
nagakuto mowaba

396

Aoyama wo yokogiru kumo no ichijiroku ware to emashite
hito ni shirayuna

397-8

Tokoyo nito waga yukanakuni okanato ni monoganashirani

368

omoerishi waga ko no toji wo   nubatama no yoru hiru to iwazu
omounishi waga mi wa yasenu   nagekunishi sode sae nurenu
kakubakari motona shi koiba   furusato ni kono tsukigoro mo
arigatsumashiji

Asakami no omoimidarete   kakubakari nane ga kourezo
ime ni miekeru

399

Waga seko ga keru kinu usushi   Sahokaze wa itaku na-fukiso
ie ni itarumade

400

Kaku shitsutsu asobi nomikoso   kusaki sura haru wa oitsutsu
aki wa chiriyuku

401

Natsu no nu no shigemi ni sakeru   himeyuri no shiraenu koi wa
kurushikimonowo

402–3

Watatsumi no kami no mikoto no   mikushige ni takuwai okite
itsuku tou tama ni masarite   omoerishi aga ko nishi aredo
utsusemi no yo no kotowari to   masurao no hiki no manimani
shinazakaru Koshiji wo sashite   hau tsuta no wakare nishi yori
okitsunami toomu mayobiki   ōbune no yukurayukurani
omokage ni motona mietsutsu   kaku koiba oizuku aga mi
kedashi aenkamo

Kakubakari koishikushi araba   masokagami minu hi toki naku
aramashimonowo

404–5

Sakazuki ni ume no hana ukabe   omou dochi nomiteno nochi wa
chirinutomo yoshi

Tsukasa nimo yurushitamaeri   koyoi nomi noman sake kamo
chirikosuna yume

406–7

Kataomoi wo uma ni futsuma ni   ōse mote Koshibe ni yaraba
hito katawankamo

Tsuneno koi imada yamanuni   miyako yori uma ni koikoba
ninaiaenkamo

408

Waga yado no aki no hagi saku   yūkage ni ima mo miteshiga
imo ga sugata wo

409

Ima yoriwa akikaze samuku   fukinanwo ikani ka hitori
nagaki yo wo nen

410

Aki saraba mitsutsu shinubeto   imo ga ueshi yado no nadeshiko
sakinikerukamo

411

Utsusemi no yo wa tsune nashito   shirumonowo akikaze samumi
shinubitsurukamo

412–5

Waga yado ni hana zo sakitaru   sowo miredo kokoro mo yukazu
hashikiyashi imo ga ariseba   mikamo nasu futari narabii
taoritemo misemashimonowo   utsusemi no kareru mi nareba
tsuyujimo no kenuruga gotoku   ashihiki no yamaji wo sashite
irihi nasu kakurinishikaba   soko mouni mune koso itame
ii mo ezu nazuke mo shirazu   ato mo naki yononaka nareba
sen sube mo nashi

Toki washimo itsu mo aranwo   kokoro itaku iyuku wagimo ka
midorigo wo okite

Idete yuku michi shiramaseba   arakajime imo wo todomen
seki mo okamashiwo

Imo ga mishi yado ni hana saki   toki wa henu waga naku namida
imada hinakuni

416

Kaku nomini arikerumonowo   imo mo ware mo chitose no gotoku
tanomitarikeru

417

Mukashi koso yoso nimo mishika   wagimoko ga okutsuki to moeba
hashiki Sahoyama

418-20

Kakemakumo ayani kashikoshi   iwamakumo yuyushikikamo
waga ōkimi Miko no Mikoto   yorozuyo ni meshitamawamashi
Ō-Yamato Kuni no miyako wa   uchinabiku haru sarinureba
yamabe niwa hana sakioori   kawase niwa ayuko sabashiri
iya hi keni sakayuru toki ni   oyozure no tawakoto tokamo
shirotae ni toneri yosoite   Wazukayama mikoshi tatashite
hisakata no ame shirashinure   koimarobi hizuchinakedomo
sen sube mo nashi

Waga ōkimi ame shirasanto   omowaneba ohoni zo mikeru
Wazukasomayama

Ashihiki no yama sae hikari   saku hana no chirinurugotoki
waga ōkimi kamo

421-3

Kakemakumo ayani kashikoshi   waga ōkimi Miko no Mikoto
mononofu no yasotomonoo wo   meshitsudoe adomoitamai

asagari ni shishi fumiokoshi   yūgari ni tori fumitate
ōmima no kuchi osaetome   mikokoro wo meshiakirameshi
Ikujiyama kodachi no shige ni   saku hana mo utsuroinikeri
yononaka wa kaku nomi narashi   masurao no kokoro furiokoshi
tsurugitachi koshi ni torihaki   azusayumi yugi torioite
ametsuchi to iya tōnagani   yorozuyo ni kaku shimogamoto
tanomerishi Miko no mikado no   sabae nasu sawagu toneri wa
shirotae ni koromo torikite   tsunenarishi emai furumai
iya hi keni kawarau mireba   kanashikirokamo

Hashikikamo Miko no Mikoto no   arigayoi meshishi Ikuji no
michi wa arenikeri

Ōtomo no na ni ou yugi obite   yorozuyo ni tanomishi kokoro
izuku ka yosen

424–6

Chidori naku Saho no kawato no   kiyoki se wo uma uchiwatashi
itsu ka kayowan

Omowanuni imo ga emai wo   ime ni mite kokoro no uchi ni
moetsutsuzo oru

Masurao to omoeru ware wo   kakubakari mitsure ni mitsure
katamoi wo sen

427

Kakubakari koitsutsu arazuwa   iwaki nimo naramashimonowo
mono mowazushite

428

Hito mo naki kuni mo aranuka   wagimoko to tazusaiyukite
taguite oran

429

Ime no ai wa kurushikarikeri   odorokite kakisaguredomo
te nimo fureneba

Furisakete mikazuki mireba   hitome mishi hito no mayobiki
omohoyurukamo

Komori nomi oreba ibusemi   nagusamuto idetachi kikeba
kinaku higurashi

Natsuyama no konure no shiji ni   hototogisu nakitoyomunaru
koe no harukesa

Ika to ika to aru waga niwa ni   momoe sashi ouru tachibana
tama ni nuku satsuki wo chikami   aenu gani hana sakinikeri
asanikeni idemiru gotoni   ikinoo ni waga mou imo ni
masokagami kiyoki tsukuyo ni   tada hitome misenmadeniwa
chirikosuna yume to iitsutsu   kokodaku mo waga morumonowo
uretakiya shikohototogisu   akatoki no uraganashikini
oedo oedo nao shi kinakite   itazurani tsuchi ni chiraseba
sube wo nami yojite taoritsu   mimase wagimoko

Mochi kudachi kiyoki tsukuyo ni   wagimoko ni misento moishi
niwa no tachibana

Imo ga mite nochi mo nakanan   hototogisu hanatachibana wo
tsuchi ni chirashitsu

Waga yado no obana ga ue no   shiratsuyu wo ketazute tama ni
nuku mono nimoga

Yamabiko no aitoyomumade   tsumagoi ni ka naku yamabe ni
hitori nomishite

Nemokoroni mono wo omoeba   iwan sube sen sube mo nashi
imo to ware te tazusawarite   ashita niwa niwa ni idetachi
yūbe niwa toko uchiharai   shirotae no sode sashikaete
saneshi yo ya tsuneni arikeru   ashihiki no yamadori kosowa
omukai ni tsumadoi suto ie   utsusemi no hito naru ware ya
nani sutoka hitohi hitoyo mo   sakariite nagekikouran
koko moeba mune koso itame   soko yueni kokoro naguyato
Takamado no yama nimo nu nimo   uchiyukite asobiarukedo
hana nomi nioite areba   miru gotoni mashite omohoyu
ikani shite wasuren monozo   kou toumonowo

Takamado no nube no kaobana   omokage ni mietsutsu imo wa
wasurekanetsumo

Iwamaro ni ware mono mōsu   natsuyase ni yoshito iu mono zo
munagi torimese

Yasuyasu mo ikeraba aranwo   hata ya hata munagi wo toruto
kawa ni nagaruna

Ōkimi no make no manimani   masurao no kokoro furiokoshi
ashihiki no yama saka koete   amazakaru hina ni kudariki
iki danimo imada yasumezu   toshitsuki mo ikura mo aranuni
utsusemi no yo no hito nareba   uchinabiki toko ni koifushi
itakekuno hi ni keni masaru   tarachine no haha no mikoto no
ōbune no yukurayukurani   shitagoi ni itsu kamo konto
matasuran kokoro sabushiku   hashikiyoshi tsuma no mikoto mo
akekureba kado ni yoritachi   koromode wo orikaeshitsutsu
yū sareba toko uchiharai   nubatama no kurokami shikite
itsu shikato nagekasuranzo   imo mo se mo wakaki kodomo wa
ochikochi ni sawaginakuran   tamahoko no michi wo tadōmi
mazukai mo yaru yoshi mo nashi   omohoshiki koto tsuteyarazu
kourunishi kokoro wa moenu   tamakiharu inochi oshikedo

sen sube no tadoki wo shirani   kaku shiteya arashio surani
nagekifuseran

Yononaka wa kazu naki mono ka   harubana no chiri no magai ni
shinubeki omoeba

Yama kawa no sokie wo tōmi   hashikiyoshi imo wo aimizu
kaku ya nagekan

445-6

Haru no hana ima wa sakari ni   niouran orite kazasan
tajikara mogamo

Uguisu no nakichirasuran   haru no hana itsu shika kimi to
taorikazasan

447-50

Ōkimi no make no manimani   shinazakaru Koshi wo osame ni
idete koshi masura ware sura   yononaka no tsune shi nakereba
uchinabiki toko ni koifushi   itakekuno hi ni keni maseba
kanashikeku koko ni omoide   iranakeku soko ni omoide
nageku sora yasukenakuni   omou sora kurushikimonowo
ashihiki no yama kihenarite   tamahoko no michi no tōkeba
mazukai mo yaru yoshi mo nami   omohoshiki koto mo kayowazu
tamakiharu inochi oshikedo   sen sube no tadoki wo shirani
komoriite omoinagekai   nagusamuru kokoro wa nashini
harubana no sakeru sakari ni   omou dochi taorikazasazu
haru no nu no shigemi tobikuku   uguisu no koe dani kikazu
otomera ga haruna tsumasuto   kurenai no akamo no suso no
harusame ni nioihizuchite   kayouran toki no sakari wo
itazurani sugushiyaritsure   shinubaseru kimi ga kokoro wo
uruwashimi kono yo sugarani   i mo nezuni kyō mo shimerani
koitsutsuzo oru

Ashihiki no yamasakurabana   hitome dani kimi toshi miteba
are koimeyamo

Yamabuki no shigemi tobikuku   uguisu no koe wo kikuran
kimi wa tomoshimo

Idetatan chikara wo namito   komoriite kimi ni kouruni
kokorodo mo nashi

451–5

Imo mo ware mo kokoro wa oyaji   tagueredo iya natsukashiku
aimireba tokohatsuhana ni   kokorogushi megushi mo nashini
hashikeyashi aga okuzuma   Ōkimi no mikoto kashikomi
ashihiki no yama koe nu yuki   amazakaru hina osame nito
wakarekoshi sono hi no kiwami   aratama no toshi yukigaeri
harubana no utsuroumadeni   aimineba ita mo sube nami
shikitae no sode kaeshitsutsu   nuru yo ochizu ime niwa miredo
utsutsu nishi tadani araneba   koishikeku chie ni tsumorinu
chikakaraba kaeri nidanimo   uchiyukite imo ga tamakura
sashikaete netemo komashiwo   tamahoko no michi washi tōku
seki saeni henarite arekoso   yoshieyashi yoshi wa aranzo
hototogisu kinakan tsuki ni   itsu shikamo hayaku narinan
unohana no nioeru yama wo   yoso nomimo furisakemitsutsu
Ōmiji ni iyuki noritachi   aoniyoshi Nara no wagie ni
nuedori no uranake shitsutsu   shitagoi ni omoiurabure
kado ni tachi yūke toitsutsu   a wo matsuto nasuran imo wo
aite haya min

Aratama no toshi kaerumade   aimineba kokoro mo shinuni
omohoyurukamo

Nubatama no ime niwa motona   aimiredo tadani araneba
koi yamazukeri

Ashihiki no yama kihenarite   tōkedomo kokoro shi yukeba
ime ni miekeri

Harubana no utsuroumadeni   aimineba tsukihi yomitsutsu
imo matsuranzo

Imizugawa iyukimegureru   tamakushige Futagamiyama wa
harubana no sakeru sakari ni   aki no ha no nioeru toki ni
idetachite furisakemireba   kamukara ya sokoba tōtoki
yamakara ya migahoshikaran   sumegami no susomi no yama no
Shibutani no saki no ariso ni   asanagi ni yosuru shiranami
yūnagi ni michikuru shio no   iyamashini tayuru koto naku
inishie yu ima no otsutsu ni   kaku shikoso miru hito gotoni
kakete shinubame

Shibutani no saki no ariso ni   yosuru nami iya shikushikuni
inishie omohoyu

Tamakushige Futagamiyama ni   naku tori no koe no koishiki
toki wa kinikeri

Kakikazou Futagamiyama ni   kamusabite tateru tsuga no ki
moto mo e mo oyaji tokiwa ni   hashikiyoshi waga se no kimi wo
asa sarazu aite kotodoi   yū sareba te tazusawarite
Imizugawa kiyoki kōchi ni   idetachite waga tachimireba
ayu no kaze itaku shi fukeba   minato niwa shiranami takami
tsuma yobuto sudori wa sawagu   ashi karuto ama no obune wa
irie kogu kaji no oto takashi   soko woshimo ayani tomoshimi
shinubitsutsu asobu sakari wo   Sumerogi no osukuni nareba
mikoto mochi tachiwakarenaba   okuretaru kimi wa aredomo
tamahoko no michi yuku ware wa   shirakumo no tanabiku yama wo
iwane fumi koehenarinaba   koishikeku ke no nagakenzo
soko moeba kokoro shi itashi   hototogisu koe ni aenuku
tama nimoga te ni makimochite   asa yoi ni mitsutsu yukanwo
okite ikaba oshi

Waga seko wa tama nimogamona   hototogisu koe ni aenuki
te ni makite yukan

Ōkimi no tō no mikado zo   miyuki furu Koshi to na ni oeru
amazakaru hina nishi areba   yama takami kawa tōshiroshi
nu wo hiromi kusa koso shigeki   ayu hashiru natsu no sakari to
shimatsutori ukai ga tomo wa   yuku kawa no kiyoki se gotoni
kagari sashi nazusainoboru   tsuyujimo no aki ni itareba
nu mo sawani tori sudakerito   masurao no tomo izanaite
taka washimo amata aredomo   yagatao no aga Ōkuro ni
shiranuri no suzu toritsukete   asagari ni iotsutori tate
yūgari ni chidori fumitate   ou gotoni yurusu koto naku
tabanare mo ochi moka yasuki   kore wo okite mata wa arigatashi
sanaraberu taka wa nakento   kokoro niwa omoihokorite
emaitsutsu wataru aida ni   taburetaru shikotsuokina no
koto danimo ware niwa tsugezu   tonogumori ame no furu hi wo
togari suto na nomiwo norite   Mishimanu wo sogai ni mitsutsu
Futagami no yama tobikoete   kumogakuri kakeriinikito
kaerikite shiwabure tsugure   oku yoshi no soko ni nakereba
iu sube no tadoki wo shirani   kokoro niwa hi sae moetsutsu
omoikoi ikizukiamari   kedashiku mo au koto ariyato
ashihiki no otemokonomo ni   tonami hari moribe wo suete
chihayaburu kami no yashiro ni   teru kagami shizu ni torisoe
koinomite aga matsu toki ni   otomera ga ime ni tsuguraku
na ga kouru sono hotsutaka wa   Matsudae no hama yukigurashi
tsunashi toru Himi no e sugite   Tako no shima tobitamotohori
ashigamo no sudaku Furue ni   ototsui mo kinō mo aritsu
chikaku araba ima futsuka dami   tōku araba nanuka no uchi wa
sugimeyamo kinan waga seko   nemokoroni na-koisoyotozo
ime ni tsugetsuru

Yakatao no taka wo te ni sue   Mishimanu ni karanu hi maneku
tsuki zo henikeru

Futagami no otemokonomo ni   ami sashite aga matsu taka wo
ime ni tsugetsumo

Matsugaeri shii nite arekamo   Sa-Yamada no oji ga sono hi ni
motome awazuken

378

Kokoro niwa yurubu koto naku   Suga no yama suga naku nomiya
koiwatarinan

466

Suzu no umi ni asabiraki shite   kogikureba Nagahama no ura ni
tsuki terinikeri

467

Aburahi no hikari ni miyuru   waga kazura sayuri no hana no
emawashikikamo

468–71

Ashihara no Mizuho no Kuni wo   amakudari shirashimeshikeru
Sumerogi no Kami no Mikoto no   miyo kasane Ama no Hitsugi to
shirashikuru Kimi no miyo miyo   shikimaseru yomo no kuni niwa
yama kawa wo hiromi atsumito   tatematsuru mitsuki takara wa
kazoeezu tsukushi mo kanetsu   shikaredomo waga Ōkimi no
morobito wo izanaitamai   yoki koto wo hajimetamaite
kugane kamo tashikeku aranto   omohoshite shitanayamasuni
tori ga naku Azuma no kuni no   Michinoku no Oda naru yama ni
kugane arito mōshitamaere   mikokoro wo akirametamai
ametsuchi no kami aiuzunai   Sumerogi no mitama tasukete
tōki yo ni kakarishi koto wo   aga miyo ni arawashite areba
osukuni wa sakaen mono to   kamunagara omohoshimeshite
mononofu no yasotomonoo wo   matsuroe no muke no manimani
oibito mo omina warawa mo   shiga negau kokorodarai ni
nadetamai osametamaeba   koko woshimo ayani tōtomi
ureshikeku iyoyo omoite   Ōtomo no tōtsukamuoya no
sono na woba Ōkumenushi to   oimochite tsukaeshi tsukasa
umi yukaba mizuku kabane   yama yukaba kusamusu kabane
Ōkimi no he nikoso shiname   kaerimi wa sejito kotodate
masurao no kiyoki sono na wo   inishie yo ima no otsutsu ni
nagasaeru oya no kodomo zo   Ōtomo to Saheki no uji wa
hito no oya no tatsuru kotodate   hito no ko wa oya no na tatazu
Ōkimi ni matsurou mono to   iitsugeru koto no tsukasa zo

379

azusayumi te ni torimochite tsurugitachi koshi ni torihaki
asamamori yū no mamori ni Ōkimi no mikado no mamori
ware wo okite mata hito wa arajito iya tate omoi shi masaru
Ōkimi no mikoto no saki no kikeba tōtomi

Masurao no kokoro omohoyu Ōkimi no mikoto no saki wo
kikeba tōtomi

Ōtomo no tōtsukamuoya no okutsuki wa shiruku shime tate
hito no shirubeku

Sumerogi no miyo sakaento Azuma naru Michinoku-yama ni
kugane hana saku

472–6

Suzu no ama no okitsumikami ni iwatarite kazukitoruto iu
awabitama iochi mogamo hashikiyoshi tsuma no mikoto no
koromode no wakareshi toki yo nubatama no yodoko katasari
asanegami kaki mo kezurazu idete koshi tsukihi yomitsutsu
nagekuran kokoronagusa ni hototogisu kinaku satsuki no
ayamegusa hanatachibana ni nukimajie kazura ni seyoto
tsutsumite yaran

Shiratama wo tsutsumite yaraba ayamegusa hanatachibana ni
ae mo nuku gane

Okitsushima iyukiwatarite kazuku chiu awabitama moga
tsutsumite yaran

Wagimoko ga kokoronagusa ni yaran tame okitsushima naru
shiratama mogamo

Shiratama no iotsutsudoi wo te ni musubi okosen ama wa
mukashikumo aruka

477–80

Ōnamuchi Sukunahikona no kamiyo yori iitsugikerashi

chichihaha wo mireba tōtoku   meko mireba kanashiku megushi
utsusemi no yo no kotowari to   kakusamani iikerumonowo
yo no hito no tatsuru kotodate   chisa no hana sakeru sakari ni
hashikiyoshi sono tsuma no ko to   asa yoi ni emimi emazumo
uchinageki katarikemakuwa   tokoshieni kaku shimo arameya
ametsuchi no kami kotoyosete   harubana no sakari mo aranto
matashiken toki no sakari zo   hanareite nagekasu imo ga
itsu shikamo tsukai no konto   matasuran kokoro sabushiku
minami fuki yukige masarite   Imizugawa nagaru minawa no
yorube nami Saburu sono ko ni   himo no o no itsugariaite
niodori no futari narabii   Nago no umi no oki wo fukamete
sadowaseru kimi ga kokoro no   sube mo sube nasa

Aoniyoshi Nara ni aru imo ga   takadakani matsuran kokoro
shika niwa arajika

Satobito no miru me hazukashi   Saburu ko ni sadowasu kimi ga
miyadeshiriburi

Kurenai wa utsurou mono zo   tsurubami no narenishi kinu ni
nao shikameyamo

481

Saburu ko ga itsukishi tono ni   suzu kakenu hayuma kudareri
sato mo todoroni

482-3

Kakemakumo ayani kashikoshi   Sumerogi no Kami no ōmiyo ni
Tajimamori Tokoyo ni watari   yahoko mochi maidekoshi
tokijiku no kagu no konomi wo   kashikokumo nokoshitamaere
kuni mo se ni oitachi sakae   haru sareba hikoe moitsutsu
hototogisu naku satsuki niwa   hatsuhana wo eda ni taorite
otomera ni tsuto nimo yarimi   shirotae no sode nimo kokire
kaguwashimi okite karashimi   ayuru mi wa tama ni nukitsutsu
te ni makite miredomo akazu   akizukeba shigure no ame furi
ashihiki no yama no konure wa   kurenai ni nioi chiredomo

381

tachibana no nareru sono mi wa   hitateri ni iya migahoshiku
miyuki furu fuyu ni itareba   shimo okedomo sono ha mo karezu
tokiwa nasu iya sakabaeni   shikarekoso kami no miyo yori
yoroshinabe kono tachibana wo   tokijikuno kagu no konomi to
nazukekerashimo

Tachibana wa hana nimo mi nimo   mitsuredomo iya tokijikuni
nao shi migahoshi

484-6

Ōkimi no tō no mikado to   makitamau tsukasa no manima
miyuki furu Koshi ni kudariki   aratama no toshi no itsutose
shikitae no tamakura makazu   himo tokazu marone wo sureba
ibusemito kokoronagusa ni   nadeshiko wo yado ni makiōshi
natsu no no no sayuri hikiuete   saku hana wo idemiru gotoni
nadeshiko ga sono hanazuma ni   sayuribana yuri mo awanto
nagusamuru kokoro shi nakuba   amazakaru hina ni hitohi mo
arubekumo areya

Nadeshiko ga hana miru gotoni   otomera ga emai no nioi
omohoyurukamo

Sayuribana yuri mo awanto   shitabauru kokoro shi nakuba
kyō mo hemeyamo

487-8

Sumerogi no shikimasu kuni no   amenoshita yomo no michi niwa
uma no tsume itsukusu kiwami   funanohe no ihatsurumadeni
inishie yo ima no otsutsu ni   yorozutsuki matsuru tsukasa to
tsukuritaru sono nariwai wo   ame furazu hi no kasanareba
ueshi ta mo makishi hatake mo   asa gotoni shibomi kareyuku
sowo mireba kokoro wo itami   midorigo no chi kouga gotoku
amatsumizu aogitezo matsu   ashihiki no yama no taori ni
kono miyuru ama no shirakumo   Watatsumi no okitsumiyabe ni
tachiwatari tonogumoriaite   ame mo tamawane

Kono miyuru kumo hobikorite   tonogumori ame mo furanuka

kokorodarai ni

489

Waga horishi ame wa furikinu   kaku shi araba kotoage sezutomo
toshi wa sakaen

490–1

Haru no sono kurenai niou   momo no hana shitateru michi ni
idetatsu otome

Waga sono no sumomo no hana ka   niwa ni chiru hadare no imada
nokoritarukamo

492

Asadoko ni kikeba harukeshi   Imizugawa asakogi shitsutsu
utau funabito

493

Karabito mo ikada ukabete   asobu tou kyō zo waga seko
hanakazura seyo

494–5

Ashihiki no yama saka koete   yukikawaru toshinoo nagaku
shinazakaru Koshi nishi sumeba   Ōkimi no shikimasu kuni wa
miyako womo koko mo oyajito   kokoro niwa omou monokara
katarisake misakuru hitome   tomoshimito omoi shi shigeshi
soko yueni kokoro naguyato   akizukeba hagi sakiniou
Iwasenu ni umadakiyukite   ochikochi ni tori fumitatete
shiranuri no osuzu mo yurani   awaseyari furisakemitsutsu
ikidōru kokoro no uchi wo   omoinobe ureshibi nagara
makurazuku tsumaya no uchi ni   tokura yui suetezo waga kau
mashirafu no taka

Yakatao no mashiro no taka wo   yado ni sue kakinade mitsutsu
kawakushi yoshimo

Amazakaru hina osame nito   Ōkimi no make no manimani
idete koshi ware wo okuruto   aoniyoshi Narayama sugite
Izumigawa kiyoki kawara ni   uma todome wakareshi toki ni
masakikute are kaerikon   tairakeku iwaite mateto
kataraite koshi hi no kiwami   tamahoko no michi wo tadōmi
yama kawa no henarite areba   koishikeku kenagakimonowo
mimaku hori omou aida ni   tamazusa no tsukai no kereba
ureshimito aga machi touni   oyozure no tawakoto tokamo
hashikiyoshi naoto no mikoto   nani shikamo toki shiwa aranwo
hatasusuki ho ni zuru aki no   hagi no hana nioeru yado wo
asaniwa ni idetachi narashi   yūniwa ni fumitairagezu
Saho no uchi no sato wo yukisugi   ashihiki no yama no konure ni
shirakumo ni tachitanabikuto   are ni tsugetsuru

Masakikuto iiteshimonowo   shirakumo ni tachitanabikuto
kikeba kanashimo

Kakaranto kanete shiriseba   Koshi no umi no ariso no nami mo
misemashimonowo

Ametsuchi no tōki hajime yo   yononaka wa tsune naki mono to
kataritsugi nagaraekitare   Amanohara furisakemireba
teru tsuki mo michikake shikeri   ashihiki no yama no konure mo
haru sareba hana sakinioi   akizukeba tsuyujimo oite
kaze majiri momiji chirikeri   utsusemi mo kaku nomi narashi
kurenai no iro mo utsuroi   nubatama no kurokami kawari
asa no emi yūbe kawarai   fuku kaze no mienuga gotoku
yuku mizu no tomaranugotoku   tsune mo naku utsurou mireba
niwatazumi nagaruru namida   todomekanetsumo

Koto towanu ki sura haru saki   akizukeba momiji chirakuwa
tsune wo namikoso

Utsusemi no tsune naki mireba   yononaka ni kokoro tsukezute
omou hi zo ōki

Chichinomi no chichi no mikoto   hahasoba no haha no mikoto
ohorokani kokoro tsukushite   omouran sono ko nareyamo
masurao ya munashiku arubeki   azusayumi sue furiokoshi
naguya mochi chihiro iwatashi   tsurugitachi koshi ni torihaki
ashihiki no yatsuo fumikoe   sashimakuru kokoro sayarazu
nochi no yo no kataritsugubeku   na wo tatsubeshimo

Masurao wa na woshi tatsubeshi   nochi no yo ni kikitsugu hito mo
kataritsugu gane

Toki gotoni iya mezurashiku   yachikusa ni kusaki hana saki
naku tori no koe mo kawarau   mimi ni kiki me ni miru gotoni
uchinageki shinae urabure   shinubitsutsu arikuru hashi ni
konokure no uzuki shi tateba   yogomori ni naku hototogisu
inishie yu kataritsugitsuru   uguisu no utsushimako kamo
ayamegusa hanatachibana wo   otomera ga tama nukumadeni
akanesasu hiru wa shimerani   ashihiki no yatsuo tobikoe
nubatama no yoru wa sugarani   akatoki no tsuki ni mukaite
yukigaeri nakitoyomuredo   nani ka akitaran

Toki gotoni iya mezurashiku   saku hana wo ori mo orazumo
mirakushi yoshimo

Toshinoha ni kinaku monoyue   hototogisu kikeba shinubaku
awanu hi wo ōmi

Hototogisu kinaku satsuki ni   sakiniou hanatachibana no
kaguwashiki oya no mikoto   asa yoi ni kikanu hi maneku
amazakaru hina nishi oreba   ashihiki no yama no taori ni
tatsu kumo wo yoso nomi mitsutsu   nageku sora yasukenakuni
omou sora kurushikimonowo   Nago no ama no kazukitoru tou
shiratama no migahoshi miomowa   tada mukai min toki madewa
matsu kae no sakaeimasane   tōtoki aga kimi

Shiratama no migahoshi kimi wo   mizu hisani hina nishi oreba
ikerutomo nashi

509

Fujinami no kage naru umi no   soko kiyomi shizuku ishi womo
tama tozo waga miru

510

Shibutani wo sashite waga yuku   kono hama ni tsukuyo akiten
uma shimashi tome

511–2

Inishie ni arikeru waza no   kusuwashiki koto to iitsugu
Chinuotoko Unaiotoko no   utsusemi no na wo arasouto
tamakiharu inochi mo sutete   arasoi ni tsumadoi shikeru
otomera ga kikeba kanashisa   harubana no nioesakaete
aki no ha no nioi ni tereru   atarashiki mi no sakari sura
masurao no koto itawashimi   chichihaha ni mōshiwakarete
ie sakari umibe ni idetachi   asa yoi ni michikuru shio no
yaenami ni nabiku tamamo no   fushi no ma mo oshiki inochi wo
tsuyujimo no sugimashinikere   okutsuki wo koko to sadamete
nochi no yo no kikitsugu hito mo   iya tōni shinubi ni seyoto
tsugeogushi shika sashikerashi   oite nabikeri

Otomera ga nochi no shirushi to   tsugeogushi oikawari oite
nabikikerashimo

513–5

Ametsuchi no hajime no toki yu   utsusemi no yasotomonoo wa
Ōkimi ni matsurou mono to   sadamareru tsukasa nishi areba
Ōkimi no mikoto kashikomi   hinazakaru kuni wo osamuto
ashihiki no yama kawa hedate   kaze kumo ni koto wa kayoedo
tadani awazu hi no kasanareba   omoikoi ikizukioruni
tamahoko no michi kuru hito no   tsutegoto ni ware ni kataraku
hashikiyoshi kimi wa konogoro   urasabite nagekaiimasu

386

yononaka no ukeku tsurakeku saku hana mo toki ni utsurou
utsusemi mo tsune naku arikeri tarachine no mihaha no mikoto
nani shikamo toki shiwa aranwo masokagami miredomo akazu
tamanoo no oshiki sakari ni tatsu kiri no usenurugotoku
oku tsuyu no kenuruga gotoku tamamo nasu nabiki koifushi
yuku mizu no todomekanetsuto tawakoto ya hito no iitsuru
oyozure ka hito no tsugetsuru azusayumi tsumahiku yoto no
tōto nimo kikeba kanashimi niwatazumi nagaruru namida
todomekanetsumo

Tōto nimo kimi ga nagekuto kikitsureba ne nomishi nakayu
aiomou ware wa

Yononaka no tsune naki koto wa shiruranwo kokoro tsukusuna
masurao nishite

516-7

Akitsushima Yamato no kuni wo amagumo ni iwafune ukabe
tomo ni he ni makai shiji nuki ikogitsutsu kunimi shi seshite
amorimashi harai tairage chiyo kasane iya tsugitsugini
shirashikuru Ama no Hitsugi to kamunagara waga Ōkimi no
amenoshita osametamaeba mononofu no yasotomonoo wo
nadetamai totonoetamai osukuni no yomo no hito womo
atesawazu megumitamaeba inishie yu nakarishi shirushi
tabi maneku mōshitamainu tamudakite koto naki miyo to
ametsuchi hitsuki to tomoni yorozuyo ni shirushitsuganzo
yasumishishi waga Ōkimi aki no hana shiga iroiro ni
meshitamai akirametamai sakamizuki sakayuru kyō no
ayani tōtosa

Aki no toki hana kusanaredo iro gotoni meshi akiramuru
kyō no tōtosa

518-9

Ashihiki no yatsuo no ue no tsuga no ki no iya tsugitsugini
matsu ga ne no tayuru koto naku aoniyoshi Nara no miyako ni

yorozuyo ni kuni shirasanto   yasumishishi waga Ōkimi no
kamunagara omohoshimeshite   toyo no akari mesu kyō no hi wa
mononofu no yasotomonoo no   shimayama ni akaru tachibana
uzu ni sashi himo tokisakete   chitose hogi hogitoyomoshi
eraerani tsukaematsuruwo   miruga tōtosa

Sumerogi no miyo yorozuyo ni   kaku shikoso meshi akirameme
tatsu toshinoha ni

520

Ametsuchi ni tarawashiterite   waga Ōkimi shikimasebakamo
tanushiki osato

521–2

Haru no nu ni kasumi tanabiki   uraganashi kono yūkage ni
uguisu nakumo

Waga yado no isasamuratake   fuku kaze no oto no kasokeki
kono yūbe kamo

523

Uraurani tereru harubi ni   hibari agari kokoroganashimo
hitori shi omoeba

524–6

Ōkimi no tō no mikado to   shiranuhi Tsukushi no kuni wa
ata mamoru osae no ki zoto   kikoshiosu yomo no kuni niwa
hito sawani michitewa aredo   tori ga naku Azumaonoko wa
idemukai kaerimi sezute   isamitaru takeki ikusa to
negitamai make no manimani   tarachine no haha ga me karete
wakakusa no tsuma womo makazu   aratama no tsukihi yomitsutsu
ashi ga chiru Naniwa no Mitsu ni   ōbune ni makai shiji nuki
asanagi ni kako totonoe   yūshio ni kaji hikiori
adomoite kogiyuku kimi wa   nami no ma wo iyukisagukumi
masakiku mo hayaku itarite   Ōkimi no mikoto no manima

masurao no kokoro wo mochite   arimeguri koto shi owaraba
tsutsumawazu kaerikimaseto   iwaibe wo tokobe ni suete
shirotae no sode orikaeshi   nubatama no kurokami shikite
nagaki ke wo machi kamo koin   hashiki tsumara wa

Masurao no yugi torioite   idete ikeba wakare wo oshimi
nagekiken tsuma

Tori ga naku Azumaotoko no   tsuma wakare kanashiku ariken
toshinoo nagami

527–9

Sumerogi no tōki miyo nimo   oshiteru Naniwa no kuni ni
amenoshita shirashimeshikito   ima no yo ni taezu iitsutsu
kakemakumo ayani kashikoshi   kamunagara waga Ōkimi no
uchinabiku haru no hajime wa   yachikusa ni hana sakinioi
yama mireba mi no tomoshiku   kawa mireba mi no sayakeku
mono gotoni sakayuru toki to   meshitamai akirametamai
shikimaseru Naniwa no miya wa   kikoshimesu yomo no kuni yori
tatematsuru mitsuki no fune wa   horie yori miobiki shitsutsu
asanagi ni kaji hikinobori   yūshio ni sao sashikudari
ajimura no sawagikioite   hama ni idete unabara mireba
shiranami no yae oruga ue ni   amaobune hararani ukite
ōmike ni tsukaematsuruto   ochikochi ni izari tsurikeri
sokidaku mo ogiro nakikamo   kokibaku mo yutakekikamo
koko mireba ube shi kamiyo yu   hajimekerashimo

Sakurabana ima sakari nari   Naniwa no umi oshiteru miya ni
kikoshimesu nabe

Unabara no yutakeki mitsutsu   ashi ga chiru Naniwa ni toshi wa
henubeku omohoyu

530–2

Ōkimi no mikoto kashikomi   tsuma wakare kanashikuwa aredo
masurao no kokoro furiokoshi   toriyosoi kadode wo sureba

389

tarachine no haha kakinade   wakakusa no tsuma toritsuki
tairakeku ware wa iwawan   masakikute haya kaerikoto
masode mochi namida wo nogoi   musebitsutsu kotodoi sureba
muratori no idetachigateni   todokōri kaerimi shitsutsu
iya tōni kuni wo kihanare   iya takani yama wo koesugi
ashi ga chiru Naniwa ni kiite   yūshio ni fune wo ukesue
asanagi ni he muke koganto   samorauto waga oru toki ni
harugasumi shimami ni tachite   tazu ga ne no kanashiku nakeba
harobaroni ie wo omoide   oisoya no soyo to narumade
nagekitsurukamo

Unabara ni kasumi tanabiki   tazu ga ne no kanashiki yoi wa
kunibe shi omohoyu

Ie omouto i wo nezu oreba   tazu ga naku ashibe mo miezu
haru no kasumi ni

533-7

Ōkimi no make no manimani   sakimori ni waga tachikureba
hahasoba no haha no mikoto wa   mimo no suso tsumiage kakinade
chichinomi no chichi no mikoto wa   takuzunu no shirahige no ue yu
namida tari nageki notabaku   kakojimono tada hitori shite
asatode no kanashiki waga ko   aratama no toshinoo nagaku
aimizuba koishiku arubeshi   kyō danimo kotodoi sento
oshimitsutsu kanashibiimase   wakakusa no tsuma mo kodomo mo
ochikochi ni sawani kakumii   harutori no koe no samayoi
shirotae no sode nakinurashi   tazusawari wakaregatenito
hikitodome shitaishimonowo   Ōkimi no mikoto kashikomi
tamahoko no michi ni idetachi   oka no saki itamuru gotoni
yorozutabi kaerimi shitsutsu   harobaroni wakare shi kureba
omou sora yasukumo arazu   kouru sora kurushikimonowo
utsusemi no yo no hito nareba   tamakiharu inochi mo shirazu
unabara no kashikoki michi wo   shimazutai ikogiwatarite
arimeguri waga kurumadeni   tairakeku oya wa imasane
tsutsumi naku tsuma wa mataseto   Suminoe no aga sumegami ni
nusa matsuri inorimōshite   Naniwazu ni fune wo ukesue

390

yasoka nuki kako totonoete   asabiraki wa wa kogidenuto
ie ni tsugekoso

Iebito no iwae nika aran   tairakeku funade wa shinuto
oya ni mōsane

Misora yuku kumo mo tsukai to   hito wa iedo iezuto yaran
tazuki shirazumo

Iezuto ni kai zo hirieru   hamanami wa iya shikushikuni
takaku yosuredo

Shimakage ni waga fune hatete   tsugeyaran tsukai wo namiya
koitsutsu yukan

538–40

Hisakata no Amanoto hiraki   Takachiho no take ni amorishi
Sumerogi no Kami no miyo yori   hajiyumi wo tanigirimotashi
makagoya wo tabasamisoete   Ōkume no masuratakeo wo
saki ni tate yugi toriōse   yama kawa wo iwane sakumite
fumitōri kunimagi shitsutsu   chihayaburu kami wo kotomuke
matsurowanu hito womo yawashi   hakikiyome tsukaematsurite
Akitsushima Yamato no kuni no   Kashihara no Unebi no miya ni
miyabashira futoshiritatete   amenoshita shirashimeshikeru
Sumerogi no Ama no Hitsugi to   tsugite kuru Kimi no miyo miyo
kakusawanu akaki kokoro wo   Sumera-be ni kiwametsukushite
tsukaekuru oya no tsukasa to   kotodatete sazuketamaeru
umi no ko no iya tsugitsugini   miru hito no kataritsugitete
kiku hito no kagami ni senwo   atarashiki kiyoki sono na zo
ohorokani kokoro omoite   munakoto mo oya no na tatsuna
Ōtomo no uji to na ni oeru   masurao no tomo

Shikishima no Yamato no kuni ni   akirakeki na ni ou tomonoo
kokoro tsutomeyo

Tsurugitachi iyoyo togubeshi   inishie yu sayakeku oite
kinishi sono na zo

391

Utsusemi wa kazu naki mi nari   yama kawa no sayakeki mitsutsu
michi wo tazunena

Wataru hi no kage ni kioite   tazunetena kiyoki sono michi
mata mo awan tame

543

Mitsubo nasu kareru mi zotowa   shireredomo nao shi negaitsu
chitose no inochi wo

544

Aounabara kaze nami nabiki   yukusa kusa tsutsumu koto naku
fune wa hayaken

545

Aratashiki toshi no hajime no   hatsuharu no kyō furu yuki no
iya shike yogoto

546-9

Wake ga tame waga te mo sumani   haru no nu ni nukeru tsubana zo
meshite koemase

Hiru wa saki yoru wa koinuru   nebu no hana kimi nomi mimeya
wake saeni miyo

Waga kimi ni wake wa kourashi   tabaritaru tsubana wo hamedo
iya yase ni yasu

Wagimoko ga katami no nebu wa   hana nomini sakite kedashiku
mi ni narajikamo

550-2

Amazakaru hina ni na kakasu   Koshi no naka kunuchi kotogoto
yama washimo shijini aredomo   kawa washimo sawani yukedomo

sumegami no ushihakiimasu   Niikawa no sono Tachiyama ni
tokonatsu ni yuki furishikite   obaseru Katakaigawa no
kiyoki se ni asa yoi gotoni   tatsu kiri no omoisugimeya
arigayoi iya toshinoha ni   yoso nomimo furisakemitsutsu
yorozuyo no kataraigusa to   imada minu hito nimo tsugen
oto nomimo na nomimo kikite   tomoshiburu gane

Tachiyama ni furiokeru yuki wo   tokonatsu ni miredomo akazu
kamukara narashi

Katakai no kawa no se kiyoku   yuku mizu no tayuru koto naku
arigayoi min

553–5

Asahi sashi sogai ni miyuru   kamunagara mina ni owaseru
shirakumo no chie wo oshiwake   amasosori takaki Tachiyama
fuyu natsu to waku koto mo naku   shirotae ni yuki wa furiokite
inishie yu arikinikereba   kogoshikamo iwa no kamusabi
tamakiharu ikuyo heniken   tachite ite miredomo ayashi
mine takami tani wo fukamito   ochitagitsu kiyoki kōchi ni
asa sarazu kiri tachiwatari   yū sareba kumoi tanabiki
kumoi nasu kokoro mo shinuni   tatsu kiri no omoisugusazu
yuku mizu no oto mo sayakeku   yorozuyo ni iitsugiyukan
kawa shi taezuba

Tachiyama ni furiokeru yuki no   tokonatsu ni kezute wataruwa
kamunagara tozo

Ochitagitsu Katakaigawa no   taenu goto ima miru hito mo
yamazu kayowan

556

Inishie yu hito no iikuru   oibito no otsu tou mizu zo
na ni ou taki no se

Waga na wamo china no iona ni   tachinutomo kimi ga na tataba
oshimikoso nake

558-9

Yasumishishi waga Ōkimi no   shikimaseru kuni no naka niwa
miyako shi omohoyu

Fujinami no hana wa sakari ni   narinikeri Nara no miyako wo
omohosuya kimi

560

Tsukuyo yoshi kawa no to kiyoshi   iza koko ni yukumo yukanumo
asobite yukan

561-3

Amagumo no mukabusu kuni no   mononofu to iwareshi hito wa
Sumerogi no Kami no mikado ni   to no he ni tachisamorai
uchi no he ni tsukaematsurite   tamakazura iya tōnagaku
oya no na mo tsugiyuku mono to   omochichi ni tsuma ni kodomo ni
kataraite tachinishi hi yori   tarachine no haha no mikoto wa
iwaibe wo mae ni sueokite   hitote niwa yū torimochite
hitote niwa nigitae matsuri   tairakeku masakiku maseto
ametsuchi no kami ni koinomi   ikanaran toshitsukihi nika
tsutsujibana nioeru kimi ga   kurotori no nazusaikonto
tachite ite machiken hito wa   Ōkimi no mikoto kashikomi
oshiteru Naniwa no kuni ni   aratama no toshi furumadeni
shirotae no koromode hosazu   asa yoi ni aritsuru kimi wa
ikasamani omoimaseka   utsusemi no oshiki kono yo wo
tsuyujimo no okite iniken   toki narazushite

Kinō koso kimi wa arishika   omowanuni hamamatsu no ue ni
kumo to tanabiku

Itsu shikato matsuran imo ni   tamazusa no koto dani tsugezu
inishi kimi kamo

Koto mo naku oikoshimonowo   oinami ni kakaru koi nimo
ware wa aerukamo

Koishinan nochi wa nani sen   ikeru hi no tame koso imo wo
mimaku horisure

Wagimoko wa tokoyo no kuni ni   sumikerashi mukashi mishiyori
ochimashinikeri

Ametsuchi no wakareshi toki yu   kamusabite takaku tōtoki
Suruga naru Fuji no takane wo   Amanohara furisakemireba
wataru hi no kage mo kakuroi   teru tsuki no hikari mo miezu
shirakumo mo iyukihabakari   tokijikuzo yuki wa furikeru
kataritsugi iitsugiyukan   Fuji no takane wa

Tago no ura yu uchiidete mireba   mashironi zo Fuji no takane ni
yuki wa furikeru

Sumerogi no Kami no Mikoto no   shikimasu kuni no kotogoto
yu washimo sawani aredomo   shimayama no yoroshiki kuni to
kogoshikamo Iyo no takane no   Isaniwa no oka ni tatashite
uta omoi koto omowashishi   miyu no ue no komura wo mireba
omi no ki mo oitsuginikeri   naku tori no koe mo kawarazu
tōki yo ni kamusabiyukan   idemashidokoro

Momoshiki no ōmiyabito no   Nigitazu ni funanori shiken
toshi no shiranaku

Mimoro no Kamunabiyama ni   ioe sashi shijini oitaru
tsuga no ki no iya tsugitsugini   tamakazura tayuru koto naku

aritsutsumo yamazu kayowan   Asuka no furuki miyako wa
yama takami kawa tōshiroshi   haru no hi wa yama shi migahoshi
aki no yo wa kawa shi sayakeshi   asagumo ni tazu wa midare
yūgiri ni kawazu wa sawagu   miru gotoni ne nomishi nakayu
inishie omoeba

Asukagawa kawayodo sarazu   tatsu kiri no omoisugubeki
koi ni aranakuni

573-4

Harubi wo Kasuga no yama no   takakura no Mikasa no yama ni
asa sarazu kumoi tanabiki ˈkaodori no manaku shiba naku
kumoi nasu kokoro isayoi   sono tori no katakoi nomini
hiru wamo hi no kotogoto   yoru wamo yono kotogoto
tachite ite omoi zo waga suru   awanu ko yueni

Takakura no Mikasa no yama ni   naku tori no yameba tsugaruru
koi mo surukamo

575-7

Inishie ni ariken hito no   shizuhata no obi tokikaete
fuseya tate tsumadoi shiken   Katsushika no Mama no Tekona no
okutsuki wo koko towa kikedo   maki no ha ya shigeritaruran
matsu ga ne ya tōku hisashiki   koto nomimo na nomimo ware wa
wasuraenakuni

Ware mo mitsu hito nimo tsugen   Katsushika no Mama no Tekona no
okutsukidokoro

Katsushika no Mama no irie ni   uchinabiku tamamo kariken
Tekona shi omohoyu

578-80

Yasumishishi wago Ōkimi no   tokomiya to tsukaematsureru
Saiganu yu sogai ni miyuru   okitsushima kiyoki nagisa ni
kaze fukeba shiranami sawagi   shio hireba tamamo karitsutsu

kamiyo yori shika zo tōtoki   Tamatsushimayama

Okitsushima ariso no tamamo   shiohi michite kakuroiyukaba
omohoenkamo

Waka no ura ni shio michikureba   kata wo nami ashibe wo sashite
tazu nakiwataru

581–3

Yasumishishi wago Ōkimi no   takashirasu Yoshinu no miya wa
tatanazuku aogakigomori   kawanami no kiyoki kōchi zo
harube wa hana sakioori   aki sareba kiri tachiwataru
sono yama no iya masumasuni   kono kawa no tayuru koto naku
momoshiki no ōmiyabito wa   tsuneni kayowan

Mi-Yoshinu no Kisayama no ma no   konure niwa kokoda mo sawagu
tori no koe kamo

Nubatama no yo no fukeyukeba   hisagi ouru kiyoki kawara ni
chidori shiba naku

584–5

Yasumishishi wago Ōkimi wa   Mi-Yoshinu no Akitsu no onu no
nu no he niwa tomi sueokite   miyama niwa ime tatewatashi
asagari ni shishi fumiokoshi   yūgari ni tori fumitate
uma namete mikari zo tatasu   haru no shigenu ni

Ashihiki no yama nimo nu nimo   mikaribito satsuya tabasami
midaritari miyu

586–7

Ametsuchi no tōkiga gotoku   hitsuki no nagakiga gotoku
oshiteru Naniwa no miya ni   wago Ōkimi kuni shirasurashi
miketsukuni hi no mitsuki to   Awaji no Nujima no ama no
wata no soko okitsu ikuri ni   awabitama sawani kazukide
fune namete tsukaematsurushi   tōtoshi mireba

397

Asanagi ni kaji no to kikoyu   miketsukuni Nujima no ama no
fune nishi arurashi

Yasumishishi waga Ōkimi no   kamunagara takashiraseru
Inaminu no Ōmi no hara no   aratae no Fujii no ura ni
shibi tsuruto amabune midari   shio yakuto hito zo sawanaru
ura wo yomi ube mo tsuri wa su   hama wo yomi ube mo shio yaku
arigayoi mimasumo shirushi   kiyoki shirahama

Okitsunami henami yasukemi   izari suto Fujie no ura ni
fune zo toyomeru

Inaminu no asaji oshinabe   sanuru yo no kenagaku areba
ie shi shinubayu

Akashigata shiohi no michi wo   asu yoriwa shita-emashiken
ie chikazukeba

Ajisahafu imo ga me karete   shikitae no makura mo makazu
kaniwa maki tsukureru fune ni   makaji nuki waga kogikureba
Awaji no Nujima mo sugi   Inamizuma Karani no shima no
shima no ma yu wagie wo mireba   aoyama no soko tomo miezu
shirakumo mo chie ni narikinu   kogitamuru ura no kotogoto
yukikakuru shima no sakizaki   kuma mo okazu omoi zo waga kuru
tabi no ke nagami

Tamamo karu Karani no shima ni   shimami suru u nishimo areya
ie mowazaran

Shimagakuri waga kogikureba   tomoshikamo Yamato e noboru
Ma-Kumanu no fune

Kaze fukeba nami ka tatanto   samorai ni Tsuta no hosoe ni
uragakuri ori

Masurao wa mikari ni tatashi   otomera wa akamo susobiku
kiyoki hamabi wo

Yasumishishi waga Ōkimi no   meshitamau Yoshinu no miya wa
yama takami kumo zo tanabiku   kawa hayami se no to zo kiyoki
kamusabite mireba tōtoku   yoroshinabe mireba sayakeshi
kono yama no tsukibanomikoso   kono kawa no taebanomikoso
momoshiki no ōmiyadokoro   yamu toki mo arame

Kamiyo yori Yoshinu no miya ni   arigayoi takashiraseruwa
yama kawa wo yomi

Haru no nu ni sumire tsumi nito   koshi ware zo nu wo natsukashimi
hitoyo nenikeru

Asu yoriwa haruna tsumanto   shimeshi nu ni kinō mo kyō mo
yuki wa furitsutsu

Ōbune wo kogi no susumi ni   iwa ni furi kaeraba kaere
imo ni yoritewa

Mitami ware ikeru shirushi ari   ametsuchi no sakayuru toki ni
aeraku omoeba

Iza kodomo hayaku Yamato e   Ōtomo no Mitsu no hamamatsu
machikoinuran

Okurara wa ima wa makaran   ko nakuran sono kano haha mo
wa wo matsuranzo

Ōkimi no tō no mikado to   shiranuhi Tsukushi no kuni ni
naku ko nasu shitaikimashite   iki danimo imada yasumezu
toshitsuki mo imada araneba   kokoro yumo omowanu aida ni
uchinabiki koyashinure   iwan sube sen sube shirani
iwaki womo toisake shirazu   ie naraba katachi wa aranwo
urameshiki imo no mikoto no   are wobamo ikani seyotoka
niodori no futari narabii   kataraishi kokoro somukite
ie sakariimasu

Ie ni yukite ikani ka aga sen   makurazuku tsumaya sabushiku
omohoyubeshimo

Hashikiyoshi kaku nomi karani   shitaikoshi imo ga kokoro no
sube mo sube nasa

Kuyashikamo kaku shiramaseba   aoniyoshi kunuchi kotogoto
misemashimonowo

Imo ga mishi ōchi no hana wa   chirinubeshi waga naku namida
imada hinakuni

Ōnuyama kiri tachiwataru   waga nageku okiso no kaze ni
kiri tachiwataru

Chichihaha wo mireba tōtoshi   meko mireba megushi utsukushi
yononaka wa kaku zo kotowari   mochidori no kakarawashimoyo
yukue shiraneba   ugegutsu wo nugitsurugotoku
fuminugite yuku chiu hito wa   iwaki yori narideshi hito ka
naga na norasane   ame e yukaba naga manimani
tsuchi naraba Ōkimi imasu   kono terasu hitsuki no shita wa

amagumo no mukabusu kiwami   taniguku no sawataru kiwami
kikoshiosu kuni no mahora zo   kanikakuni hoshiki manimani
shika niwa arajika

Hisakata no amaji wa tōshi   naonaoni ie ni kaerite
nari wo shimasani

613-4

Uri hameba kodomo omohoyu   kuri hameba mashite shinubayu
izuku yori kitarishi mono zo   manakai ni motona kakarite
yasui shi nasanu

Shirogane mo kugane mo tama mo   nani senni masareru takara
ko ni shikameyamo

615-6

Yononaka no sube naki mono wa   toshitsuki wa nagarurugotoshi
toritsuzuki oikuru mono wa   momokusa ni semeyorikitaru
otomera ga otomesabi suto   karatama wo tamoto ni makashi
yochikora to te tazusawarite   asobiken toki no sakari wo
todomikane sugushiyaritsure   minanowata kaguroki kami ni
itsu no ma ka shimo no furiken   kurenai no omote no ue ni
izuku yuka shiwa kakitarishi   masurao no otokosabi suto
tsurugitachi koshi ni torihaki   satsuyumi wo tanigirimochite
akagoma ni shizukura uchioki   hainorite asobiarukishi
yononaka ya tsuneni arikeru   otomera ga sanasu itado wo
oshihiraki itadoriyorite   matamade no tamade sashikae
saneshi yo no ikuda mo araneba   tazukazue koshi ni taganete
ka yukeba hito ni itowae   kaku yukeba hito ni nikumae
oyoshio wa kaku nomi narashi   tamakiharu inochi oshikedo
sen sube mo nashi

Tokiwa nasu kaku shimogamoto   omoedomo yo no koto nareba
todomikanetsumo

401

Kakemakuwa ayani kashikoshi   Tarashihime Kami no Mikoto
Karakuni wo muketairagete   mikokoro wo shizumetamauto
itorashite iwaitamaishi   matama nasu futatsu no ishi wo
yo no hito ni shimeshitamaite   yorozuyo ni iitsugu gane to
wata no soko okitsu-Fukae no   unakami no Kofu no hara ni
mitezukara okashitamaite   kamunagara kamusabiimasu
kushimitama ima no otsutsu ni   tōtokirokamo

Ametsuchi no tomoni hisashiku   iitsugeto kono kushimitama
shika shikerashimo

Amazakaru hina ni itsutose   sumaitsutsu miyako no teburi
wasuraenikeri

Uchihisasu miya e noboruto   tarachishi ya haha ga te hanare
tsune shiranu kuni no okuka wo   momoeyama koete sugiyuki
itsu shikamo miyako wo minto   omoitsutsu kataraioredo
onoga mi shi itawashikereba   tamahoko no michi no kumami ni
kusa taori shiba torishikite   tokejimono uchikoifushite
omoitsutsu nageki fuseraku   kuni ni araba chichi torimimashi
ie ni araba haha torimimashi   yononaka wa kaku nomi narashi
inujimono michi ni fushiteya   inochi suginan

Tarachishi no haha ga me mizute   obohoshiku izuchi mukiteka
aga wakaruran

Tsune shiranu michi no nagate wo   kurekure to ikani ka yukan
karite wa nashini

Ie ni arite haha ga torimiba   nagusamuru kokoro wa aramashi
shinaba shinutomo

Idete yukishi hi wo kazoetsutsu   kyōkyō to a wo matasuran

chichihahara wamo

Hitoyo niwa futatabi mienu   chichihaha wo okiteya nagaku
aga wakarenan

626-7

Kaze majiri ame furu yo no   ame majiri yuki furu yo wa
sube mo naku samukushi areba   katashio wo toritsuzushiroi
kasuyuzake uchisusuroite   shiwabukai hana hishibishini
shika to aranu hige kakinadete   are wo okite hito wa arajito
hokoroedo samukushi areba   asabusuma hikikagafuri
nunokataginu ari no kotogoto   kisoedomo samuki yo surawo
ware yorimo mazushiki hito no   chichihaha wa ue samukaran
mekodomo wa koite nakuran   kono toki wa ikani shitsutsuka
naga yo wa wataru   ametsuchi wa hiroshito iedo
aga tame wa sakuya narinuru   hitsuki wa akashito iedo
aga tame wa teri ya tamawanu   hito mina ka are nomiya shikaru
wakurabani hito towa aruwo   hitonami ni are mo nareruwo
wata mo naki nunokataginu no   miru no goto wawakesagareru
kakafu nomi kata ni uchikake   fuseio no mageio no uchi ni
hitatsuchi ni wara tokishikite   chichi haha wa makura no kata ni
mekodomo wa ato no kata ni   kakumiite urei samayoi
kamado niwa keburi fukitatezu   koshiki niwa kumo no su kakite
ii kashigu koto mo wasurete   nuedori no nodoyohioruni
itonokite mijikaki mono wo   hashi kiruto ieruga gotoku
shimoto toru satoosa ga koe wa   neyado made kitachi yobainu
kakubakari sube naki mono ka   yononaka no michi

Yononaka wo ushito yasashito   omoedomo tobitachikanetsu
tori nishi araneba

628-30

Kamiyo yori iitsutekuraku   soramitsu Yamato no kuni wa
Sumegami no   itsukushiki kuni   kotodama no sakihau kuni to
kataritsugi iitsugaikeri   ima no yo no hito mo kotogoto
me no mae ni mitari shiritari   hito sawani michitewa aredomo

takahikaru Hi no Mikado   kamunagara mede no sakari ni
amenoshita mōshitamaishi   ie no ko to erabitamaite
ōmikoto itadakimochite   Morokoshi no tōki sakai ni
tsukawasare makariimase   unabara no he ni mo oki nimo
kamuzumari ushihakiimasu   moromoro no ōmikamitachi
funanohe ni michibikimōshi   ametsuchi no ōmikamitachi
Yamato no Ōkunitama   hisakata no ama no misora yu
amagakeri miwatashitamai   koto owari kaeran hi wa
mata sarani ōmikamitachi   funanohe ni mite uchikakete
suminawa wo haetarugotoku   achikaoshi Chika no saki yori
Ōtomo no Mitsu no hamabi ni   tadahate ni mifune wa haten
tsutsumi naku sakiku imashite   haya kaerimase

Ōtomo no Mitsu no matsubara   kakihakite ware tachimatan
haya kaerimase

Naniwazu ni mifune hatenuto   kikoekoba himo tokisakete
tachihashiri sen

631-7

Tamakiharu uchi no kagiri wa   tairakeku yasukumo aranwo
koto mo naku mo mo naku aranwo   yononaka no ukeku tsurakeku
itonokite itaki kizu niwa   karashio wo sosogu chiu ga gotoku
masumasu mo omoki umani ni   uwani utsuto iu koto no goto
oinite aru waga mi no ue ni   yamai woto kuwaete areba
hiru wamo nagekaikurashi   yoru wamo ikizukiakashi
toshi nagaku yami shi watareba   tsuki kasane urei samayoi
kotogoto wa shinanato moedo   sabae nasu sawagu kodomo wo
utsutetewa shini wa shirazu   mitsutsu areba kokoro wa moenu
kanikakuni omoiwazurai   ne nomishi nakayu

Nagusamuru kokoro wa nashini   kumogakuri nakiyuku tori no
ne nomishi nakayu

Sube mo naku kurushiku areba   idehashiri inanato moedo
kora ni sayarinu

Tomibito no ie no kodomo no   kiru mi nami kutashi sutsuran
kinuwatara wamo

Aratae no nunoginu wodani   kisegateni kaku ya nagekan
sen sube wonami

Minawa nasu moroki inochi mo   takunawa no chihiro nimogato
negaikurashitsu

Shizutamaki kazu nimo aranu   mi niwa aredo chitose nimogato
omohoyurukamo

638–40

Yo no hito no tōtomi negau   nanakusa no takara mo ware wa
nani senni   waga naka no umareidetaru
shiratama no waga ko Furuhi wa   akaboshi no akuru ashita wa
shikitae no toko no he sarazu   tateredomo oredomo
tomoni tawabure   yūzutsu no yūbe ni nareba
iza neyoto te wo tazusawari   chichihaha mo ue wa na-sakari
sakikusa no naka niwo nento   utsukushiku shiga kataraeba
itsu shikamo hito to nariidete   ashikekumo yokekumo minto
ōbune no omoitanomuni   omowanuni yokoshimakaze no
nifubukani ooikinureba   sen sube no tadoki wo shirani
shirotae no tasuki wo kake   masokagami te ni torimochite
amatsukami aogi koinomi   kunitsukami fushite nukazuki
kakarazumo kakarimo   kami no manimani to
tachiazari ware koinomedo   shimashiku mo yokekuwa nashini
yayayayani katachi tsukuhori   asanasana iu koto yami
tamakiharu inochi taenure   tachiodori ashizuri sakebi
fushi aogi mune uchi nageki   te ni motaru aga ko tobashitsu
yononaka no michi

Wakakereba michiyuki shiraji   mai wa sen shitabe no tsukai
oite tōrase

Fuse okite ware wa koinomu   azamukazu tadani iyukite
amaji shirashime

405

Onoko yamo munashikarubeki   yorozuyo ni kataritsugubeki
na wa tatezushite

Hikoboshi wa Tanabatatsume to   ametsuchi no wakareshi toki yu
inaushiro kawa ni mukitachi   omou sora yasukaranakuni
nageku sora yasukaranakuni   aonami ni nozomi wa taenu
shirakumo ni namida wa tsukinu   kaku nomiya ikizukioran
kaku nomiya koitsutsu aran   saninuri no obune mogamo
tamamaki no makai mogamo   asanagi ni ikakiwatari
yūshio ni ikogiwatari   hisakata no Amanokawara ni
amatobuya hire katashiki   matamade no tamade sashikae
amata i mo neteshigamo   aki ni arazutomo

Kaze kumo wa futatsu no kishi ni   kayoedomo waga tōzuma no
koto zo kayowanu

Tabute nimo nagekoshitsubeki   Amanogawa hedaterebakamo
amata sube nami

Aki no nu ni sakitaru hana wo   oyobi ori kakikazoureba
nanakusa no hana

Hagi ga hana obana kuzubana   nadeshiko no hana
ominaeshi mata fujibakama   asagao no hana

Araora wo konka kojikato   ii morite kado ni idetachi
matedo kimasazu

Araora wa meko no nari woba   omowazuro toshi no yatose wo
matedo kimasazu

Shirakumo no Tatsuta no yama no   tsuyujimo ni irozuku toki ni
uchikoete tabi yuku kimi wa   ioeyama iyukisakumi
ata mamoru Tsukushi ni itari   yama no soki nu no soki miyoto
tomonobe wo agachi tsukawashi   yamabiko no kotaen kiwami
taniguku no sawataru kiwami   kunigata wo meshitamaite
fuyugomori haru sariyukaba   tobu tori no hayaku kimasane
Tatsutaji no okabe no michi ni   nitsutsuji no niowan toki no
sakurabana sakinan toki ni   yamatazu no mukae maiden
kimi ga kimasaba

Chiyorozu no ikusa naritomo   kotoage sezu torite kinubeki
onoko tozo omou

Namayomi no Kai no kuni   uchiyosuru Suruga no kuni to
kochigochi no kuni no minaka yu   idetateru Fuji no takane wa
amagumo mo iyukihabakari   tobu tori mo tobi mo noborazu
moyuru hi wo yuki mote kechi   furu yuki wo hi mote kechitsutsu
ii mo ezu nazuke mo shirazu   kusushikumo imasu kami kamo
Se no umi to nazukete arumo   sono yama no tsutsumeru umi zo
Fujigawa to hito no watarumo   sono yama no mizu no tagichi zo
hinomoto no Yamato no kuni no   shizume tomo imasu kami kamo
takara tomo nareru yama kamo   Suruga naru Fuji no takane wa
miredo akanukamo

Fuji no ne ni furiokeru yuki wa   minazuki no mochi ni kenureba
sono yo furikeri

Fuji no ne wo takami kashikomi   amagumo mo iyukihabakari
tanabikumonowo

Shinagadori Awa ni tsugitaru   azusayumi Sue no Tamana wa
munawake no hiroki wagimo   koshiboso no sugaruotome no
sono kao no kirakirashikini   hana no goto emite tatereba

tamahoko no michi yuku hito wa   onoga yuku michi wa yukazute
yobanakuni kado ni itarinu   sashinarabu tonari no kimi wa
arakajime onozuma karete   kowanakuni kagi sae matsuru
hito mina no kaku madoereba   uchishinai yoritezo imo wa
tawarete arikeru

Kanato nishi hito no kitateba   yonaka nimo mi wa tanashirazu
idetezo aikeru

656–7

Haru no hi no kasumeru toki ni   Suminoe no kishi ni ideite
tsuribune no toorau mireba   inishie no koto zo omohoyuru
Mizunoe no Urashima no ko ga   katsuo tsuri tai tsurihokori
nanuka made ie nimo kozute   unasaka wo sugite kogiyukuni
Watatsumi no kami no omina ni   tamasakani ikogimukai
aitoburai koto narishikaba   kakimusubi Tokoyo ni itari
Watatsumi no kami no miya no   uchi no he no taenaru tono ni
tazusawari futari iriite   oi mo sezu shini mo sezu shite
nagaki yo ni arikerumonowo   yononaka no orokabito no
wagimoko ni norite kataraku   shimashiku wa ie ni kaerite
chichihaha ni koto mo norai   asu no goto ware wa kinanto
iikereba imo ga ieraku   Tokoyo-be ni mata kaerikite
ima no goto awanto naraba   kono kushige hirakuna yume to
sokoraku ni katameshi koto wo   Suminoe ni kaerikitarite
ie miredo ie mo mikanete   sato miredo sato mo mikanete
ayashimito soko ni omowaku   ie yu idete mitose no hodo ni
kaki mo naku ie usemeyato   kono hako wo hirakite miteba
moto no goto ie wa aranto   tamakushige sukoshi hirakuni
shirakumo no hako yori idete   Tokoyo-be ni tanabikinureba
tachihashiri sakebi sode furi   koimarobi ashizuri shitsutsu
tachimachini kokoro keusenu   wakakarishi hada mo shiwaminu
kurokarishi kami mo shirakenu   yunayuna wa iki sae taete
nochi tsuini inochi shinikeru   Mizunoe no Urashima no ko ga
iedokoro miyu

Tokoyo-be ni sumubekimonowo   tsurugitachi shiga kokoro kara
ozo ya kono kimi

Shinateru Katashiwagawa no   saninuri no ōhashi no ue yu
kurenai no akamo susobiki   yamaai mochi sureru kinu kite
tada hitori iwatarasu ko wa   wakakusa no tsuma ka aruran
kashi no mi no hitori ka nuran   towamakuno hoshiki wagimo ga
ie no shiranaku

Ōhashi no tsume ni ie araba   uraganashiku hitori yuku ko ni
yado kasamashiwo

Shirakumo no Tatsuta no yama no   taki no ue no Ogura no mine ni
sakiooru sakura no hana wa   yama takami kaze shi yamaneba
harusame no tsugiteshi fureba   hotsue wa chirisuginikeri
shizue ni nokoreru hana wa   shimashiku wa chiri na-midariso
kusamakura tabi yuku kimi ga   kaerikurumade

Waga yuki wa nanuka wa sugiji   Tatsutahiko yume kono hana wo
kaze ni na-chirashi

Koromode Hitachi no kuni   futanarabu Tsukuba no yama wo
mimaku hori kimi kimaserito   atsukekuni ase kakinage
konone tori usobuki nobori   o no ue wo kimi ni misureba
o no kami mo yurushitamai   me no kami mo chihaitamaite
toki to naku kumo i ame furu   Tsukubane wo sayani terashite
ibukarishi kuni no mahora wo   tsubarakani shimeshitamaeba
ureshimito himo no wo tokite   ie no goto toketezo asobu
uchinabiku haru mimashiyuwa   natsukusa no shigekuwa aredo
kyō no tanushisa

Kyō no hi ni ikani ka shikan   Tsukubane ni mukashi no hito no
kiken sono hi mo

Uguisu no kaiko no naka ni   hototogisu hitori umarete

naga chichi ni nitewa nakazu   naga haha ni nitewa nakazu
unohana no sakitaru nube yu   tobikakeri kinakitoyomoshi
tachibana no hana wo ichirashi   hinemosu ni nakedo kikiyoshi
mai wa sen tōku na-yukiso   waga yado no hanatachibana ni
sumiwatare tori

Kakikirashi ame no furu yo wo   hototogisu nakite yukunari
aware sono tori

666–7

Kusamakura tabi no urei wo   nagusamoru koto mo aranto
Tsukubane ni noborite mireba   obana chiru Shizuku no tai ni
karigane mo samuku kinakinu   Niihari no Toba no ōmi mo
akikaze ni shiranami tachinu   Tsukubane no yokekuwo mireba
nagaki ke ni omoi tsumikoshi   urei wa yaminu

Tsukubane no susomi no tai ni   akita karu imogari yaran
momiji taorana

668–9

Washi no sumu Tsukuba no yama no   Mohakitsu no sono tsu no ue ni
adomoite otome otoko no   yukitsudoi kagau kagai ni
hitozuma ni ware mo majiran   waga tsuma ni hito mo kototoe
kono yama wo ushihaku kami no   mukashi yori isamenu waza zo
kyō nomiwa megushimo na-miso   koto mo togamuna

O no kami ni kumo tachinobori   shigure furi nuretōrutomo
ware kaerameya

670–1

Kotohiushi no Miyake no saki ni   sashimukau Kashima no saki ni
saninuri no obune wo make   tamamaki no okaji shiji nuki
yūshio no michi no todomi ni   mifunako wo adomoitatete
yobitatete mifune idenaba   hama mo seni okure namiite
koimarobi koi kamo oran   ashizurishi ne nomiya nakan
Unakami no sono tsu wo sashite   kimi ga kogiyukaba

Umitsuji no naginan toki mo   wataranan kaku tatsu nami ni
funade subeshiya

672–3

Tori ga naku Azuma no kuni ni   inishie ni arikeru koto to
ima madeni taezu iikuru   Katsushika no Mama no Tekona ga
asaginu ni aoeri tsuke   hitasao wo mo niwa orikite
kami danimo kaki wa kezurazu   kutsu wodani hakazu yukedomo
nishiki aya no naka ni tsutsumeru   iwaigo mo imo ni shikameya
mochizuki no miteru omowa ni   hana no goto emite tatereba
natsumushi no hi ni iruga goto   minatoiri ni fune kogugotoku
yukikagure hito no iu toki   ikubaku mo ikerajimonowo
nani sutoka mi wo tanashirite   nami no to no sawagu minato no
okutsuki ni imo ga koyaseru   tōki yo ni arikeru koto wo
kinō shimo mikenga gotomo   omohoyurukamo

Katsushika no Mama no i mireba   tachinarashi mizu kumashiken
Tekona shi omohoyu

674–6

Ashinoya no Unaiotome no   yatosego no kataoi no toki yu
obanari ni kami takumadeni   narabioru ie nimo miezu
utsuyū no komorite maseba   miteshigato ibusemu toki no
kakiho nasu hito no tou toki   Chinuotoko Unaiotoko no
fuseya taki susushikioi   aiyobai shikeru toki wa
yakidachi no tagami oshineri   shiramayumi yugi torioite
mizu ni iri hi nimo iranto   tachimukai kioishi toki ni
wagimoko ga haha ni kataraku   shizutamaki iyashiki waga yue
masurao no arasou mireba   ikeritomo aübeku areya
shishikushiro yomi ni matanto   komorinu no shitabaeokite
uchinageki imo ga inureba   Chinuotoko sono yo ime ni mi
toritsuzuki oiyukikereba   okuretaru Unaiotoko i
ame aogi sakebi orabi   tsuchi ni fushi kigami takebite
mokoroo ni maketewa arajito   kakihaki no odachi torihaki
tokorozura tomeyukikereba   yakaradomo iyukitsudoi
nagaki yo ni shirushi ni sento   tōki yo ni kataritsuganto

otomezuka naka ni tsukurioki   otokozuka konatakanata ni
tsukuriokeru yueyoshi kikite   shiranedomo niimo no goto mo
nenakitsurukamo

Ashinoya no Unaiotome no   okutsuki wo yukiku to mireba
ne nomishi nakayu

Tsuka no e no ko no e nabikeri   kikishi goto Chinuotoko nishi
yorinikerashimo

677

Haruyama no saki no oori ni   haruna tsumu imo ga shirahimo
mirakushi yoshimo

678–80

Amoritsuku Ame-no-Kaguyama   kasumi tatsu haru ni itareba
matsukaze ni ikenami tachite   sakurabana konokure shijini
okibe niwa kamo tsuma yobai   hetsube ni ajimura sawagi
momoshiki no ōmiyabito no   makaridete asobu fune niwa
kaji sao mo nakute sabushimo   kogu hito nashini

Hito kogazu arakumo shirushi   kazuki suru oshi to takabe to
fune no e ni sumu

Itsu no ma mo kamusabikeruka   Kaguyama no hokosugi ga moto ni
koke musumadeni

681

Narayama no konotegashiwa no   futaomo ni ka nimo kaku nimo
nejikebito no tomo

682–6

Tamahoko no michi ni idetachi   ashihiki no nu yuki yama yuki
niwatazumi kawa yukiwatari   isanatori umiji ni idete
fuku kaze mo ohoni wa fukazu   tatsu nami mo nodoni wa tatanu
kashikokiya kami no watari no   shikinami no yosuru hamabe ni

takayama wo hedate ni okite   iribuchi wo makura ni makite
ura mo naku koyaseru kimi wa   omochichi no manago nimo aran
wakakusa no tsuma mo aranto   ie toedo ieji mo iwazu
na wo toedo na danimo norazu   taga koto wo itooshimikamo
takanami no kashikoki umi wo   tada watariken

Omochichi mo tsuma mo kodomo mo   takadakani konto matsuran
hito no kanashisa

Iebito no matsuranmonowo   tsure mo naki ariso wo makite
fuseru kimi kamo

Iribuchi ni koyaseru kimi wo   kyōkyō to konto matsuran
tsuma shi kanashimo

Uranami no kiyosuru hama ni   tsure mo naku koyaseru kimi ga
ieji shirazumo

687–9

Yasumishishi waga Ōkimi no   takashikasu Yamato no kuni wa
Sumerogi no Kami no miyo yori   shikimaseru kuni nishi areba
aremasan miko no tsugitsugi   amenoshita shirashimasanto
yaoyorozu chitose wo kanete   sadameken Nara no miyako wa
kagiroi no haru nishi nareba   Kasugayama Mikasa no nube ni
sakurabana konokuregakuri   kaodori wa ma naku shiba naku
tsuyujimo no aki sarikureba   Ikomayama Tobuhi ga oka ni
hagi no e wo shigarami chirashi   saoshika wa tsuma yobitoyomu
yama mireba yama mo migahoshi   sato mireba sato mo sumiyoshi
mononofu no yasotomonoo no   uchihaete sato namishikeba
ametsuchi no yoriai no kagiri   yorozuyo ni sakaeyukanto
omoiirishi ōmiya surawo   tanomerishi Nara no miyako wo
aratayo no koto nishi areba   Ōkimi no hiki no manimani
harubana no utsuroi kawari   muratori no asadachiyukeba
sasutake no ōmiyabito no   fuminarashi kayoishi michi wa
uma mo yukazu hito mo yukaneba   arenikerukamo

Tachikawari furuki miyako to   narinureba michi no shibakusa

413

nagaku oinikeri

Natsukinishi Nara no miyako no   areyukeba idetatsu gotoni
nageki shi masaru

Akitsukami waga Ōkimi no   amenoshita Yashima no uchi ni
kuni washimo ōku aredomo   sato washimo sawani aredomo
yamanami no yoroshiki kuni to   kawanami no tachiau sato to
Yamashiro no Kaseyama no ma ni   miyabashira futoshikimatsuri
takashirasu Futagi no miya wa   kawa chikami se no to zo kiyoki
yama chikami tori ga ne toyomu   aki sareba yama mo todoroni
saoshika wa tsuma yobitoyome   haru sareba okabe mo shijini
iwao niwa hana sakioori   ana omoshiro Futagi no hara
ito tōto ōmiyadokoro   ube shikoso waga Ōkimi wa
kimi no mani kikashitamaite   sasutake no ōmiya koko to
sadamekerashimo

Mikanohara Futagi no nube wo   kiyomikoso ōmiyadokoro
sadamekerashimo

Yama takaku kawa no se kiyoshi   momoyo made kamishimiyukan
ōmiyadokoro

Waga Ōkimi Kami no Mikoto no   takashirasu Futagi no miya wa
momoki nasu yama wa kodakashi   ochitagitsu se no to mo kiyoshi
uguisu no kinaku harube wa   iwao niwa yamashita hikari
nishiki nasu hana sakioori   saoshika no tsuma yobu aki wa
amagirau shigure wo itami   sanitsurau momiji chiritsutsu
yachitose ni aretsugashitsutsu   amenoshita shirashimesanto
momoyo nimo kawarubekaranu   ōmiyadokoro

Izumigawa yuku se no mizu no   taebakoso ōmiyadokoro
utsuroiyukame

Futagiyama yamanami mireba   momoyo nimo kawarubekaranu

ōmiyadokoro

Otomera ga umio kaku tou   Kase no yama toki shi yukereba
miyako to narinu

Kase no yama kodachi wo shigemi   asa sarazu kinakitoyomosu
uguisu no koe

Komayama ni naku hototogisu   Izumigawa watari wo tōmi
koko ni kayowazu

699–701

Yasumishishi waga Ōkimi no   arigayou Naniwa no miya wa
isanatori umi katatsukite   tama hiriu hamabe wo chikami
asahafuru nami no to sawagi   yūnagi ni kaji no to kikoyu
akatoki no nezame ni kikeba   watatsumi no shiohi no muta
urasu niwa chidori tsuma yobi   ashibe niwa tazu ga ne toyomu
miru hito no katari ni sureba   kiku hito no mimaku horisuru
mikemukau Ajifu no miya wa   miredo akanukamo

Arigayou Naniwa no miya wa   umi chikami amaotomera ga
noreru fune miyu

Shio hireba ashibe ni sawagu   ashitazu no tsuma yobu koe wa
miya mo todoroni

702–4

Yachihoko no Kami no miyo yori   momofune no hatsuru tomari to
Yashimaguni momofunabito no   sadameteshi Minume no ura wa
asakaze ni uranami sawagi   yūnami ni tamamo wa kiyoru
shiramanago kiyoki hamabe wa   yukigaeri miredomo akazu
ube shikoso miru hito gotoni   kataritsugi shinubikerashiki
momoyo hete shinubaeyukan   kiyoki shirahama

Masokagami Minume no ura wa   momofune no sugite yukubeki
hama naranakuni

415

Hama kiyomi ura uruwashimi   kamiyo yori chifune no tomaru
Ōwada no hama

705

Okakitsu no asa wo hikihoshi   imo nane ga tsukuri kiseken
shirotae no himo womo tokazu   hitoe yuu obi wo mie yui
kurushikini tsukaematsurite   ima danimo kuni ni makarite
chichihaha mo tsuma womo minto   omoitsutsu yukiken kimi wa
tori ga naku Azuma no kuni no   kashikokiya   kami no misaka ni
nigitama no koromo samura ni   nubatama no kami wa midarete
kuni toedo kuni womo norazu   ie toedo ie womo iwazu
masurao no yuki no susumi ni   koko ni koyaseru

706–8

Inishie no masuraonoko no   aikioi tsumadoi shiken
Ashinoya no Unaiotome no   okutsuki wo waga tachimireba
nagaki yo no katari ni shitsutsu   nochi no hito no shinubi ni sento
tamahoko no michi no he chikaku   iwa kamae tsukureru tsuka wo
amagumo no sokie no kagiri   kono michi wo yuku hito gotoni
yukiyorite itachi nagekai   aru hito wa ne nimo nakitsutsu
kataritsugi shinubitsugi koshi   otomera ga okutsukidokoro
ware saeni mireba kanashimo   inishie omoeba

Inishie no Shinudaotoko no   tsumadoishi Unaiotome no
okutsuki zo kore

Kataritsugu karani mo kokoda   kohoshikiwo tadame ni miken
inishieotoko

709–11

Chichihaha ga nashi no manimani   hashimukau oto no mikoto wa
asatsuyu no keyasuki inochi   kami no muta arasoikanete
Ashihara no Mizuho no Kuni ni   ie namiya mata kaerikonu
tōtsukuni Yomi no sakai ni   hau tsuta no onoga mukimuki
amagumo no wakare shi yukeba   yamiyo nasu omoimadowai
iyu shishi no kokoro wo itami   ashigaki no omoimidarete

416

harutori no ne nomi nakitsutsu   ajisahafu yoru hiru iwazu
kagiroi no kokoro moetsutsu   nageku wakare wo

Wakaretemo mata mo aubeku   omohoeba kokoro midarete
waga koimeyamo

Ashihiki no arayamanaka ni   okuriokite kaerau mireba
kokorogurushimo

712

Inishie ni yana utsu hito no   nakariseba koko mo aramashi
tsumi no eda wamo

713

Kaku nomini arikerumonowo   hagi ga hana sakite ariyato
toishi kimi wamo

714

Watatsumi no oki ni mochiyukite   hanatsutomo uremuzo kore ga
yomigaerinan

715

Shiranuhi Tsukushi no wata wa   mi ni tsukete imada wa kinedo
atatakeku miyu

716

Yononaka wo nani ni tatoen   asabiraki kogiinishi fune no
ato nakigotoshi

717

Shiratama wa hito ni shiraezu   shirazutomo yoshi
shirazutomo ware shi shirereba   shirazutomo yoshi

Ie omouto kokoro susumuna   kazemamori yoku shite imase
arashi sono michi

Yūyami wa michi tazutazushi   tsuki machite imase waga seko
sono ma nimo min

Misora yuku tsuki no hikari ni   tada hitome aimishi hito no
ime nishi miyuru

Kamotori no asobu kono ike ni   konoha ochite ukitaru kokoro
waga mowanakuni

Niwa ni tatsu asa wo karihoshi   shikishinubu Azumaomina wo
wasuretamauna

Kimi nakuba na zo mi yosowan   kushige naru tsuge no ogushi mo
torantomo mowazu

Koko nishite ie yamo izuku   shirakumo no tanabiku yama wo
koete kinikeri

Waga inochi shi masakiku araba   mata mo min Shiga no Ōtsu ni
yosuru shiranami

Furu yuki no shirokami madeni   Ōkimi ni tsukaematsureba
tōtokumo aruka

Amenoshita sudeni ooite   furu yuki no hikari wo mireba
tōtokumo aruka

Aratashiki toshi no hajime ni   toyo no toshi shirusuto narashi
yuki no fureruwa

Ōmiya no uchi nimo to nimo   hikarumade furasu shirayuki
miredo akanukamo

730-1

Ametsuchi to aisakaento   ōmiya wo tsukaematsureba
tōtoku ureshiki

Ame niwamo iotsutsuna hau   yorozuyo ni kuni shirasanto
iotsutsuna hau

732-7

Mutsuki tachi haru no kitaraba   kaku shikoso ume wo oritsutsu
tanushiki oeme

Waga sono ni ume no hana chiru   hisakata no ame yori yuki no
nagarekurukamo

Ume no hana sakite chirinaba   sakurabana tsugite sakubeku
narinite arazuya

Waga sakari itaku kudachinu   kumo ni tobu kusuri hamutomo
mata ochimeyamo

Kumo ni tobu kusuri hamuyowa   miyako miba iyashiki aga mi
mata ochinubeshi

Ume no hana ime ni kataraku   miyabitaru hana to are mou
sake ni ukabekoso

738

Muko no ura no irie no sudori   hagukumoru kimi wo hanarete

419

koi ni shinubeshi

739

Ōbune ni imo noru mono ni   aramaseba hagukumi mochite
yukamashimonowo

740

Kimi ga yuku umibe no yado ni   kiri tataba aga tachinageku
iki to shirimase

741

Aki saraba aiminmonowo   nani shikamo kiri ni tatsubeku
nageki shimasan

742

Waga yueni omoi na-yaseso   akikaze no fukan sono tsuki
awan monoyue

743

Takubusuma Shiragi e imasu   kimi ga me wo kyō ka asu kato
iwaite matan

744

Shio matsuto arikeru fune wo   shirazushite kuyashiku imo wo
wakarekinikeri

745

Unabara wo yasoshimagakuri   kinuredomo Nara no miyako wa
wasurekanetsumo

746

Waga yueni imo nagekurashi   Kazahaya no ura no okibe ni
kiri tanabikeri

Yama no ha ni tsuki katabukeba   izari suru ama no tomoshibi
oki ni nazusau

Ware nomiya yobune wa koguto   omoereba okibe no kata ni
kaji no oto sunari

Asa sareba imo ga te ni maku   kagami nasu Mitsu no hamabi ni
ōbune ni makaji shiji nuki   Karakuni ni watariyukanto
tadamukau Minume wo sashite   shio machite miobikiyukeba
okibe niwa shiranami takami   urami yori kogite watareba
wagimoko ni Awaji no shima wa   yū sareba kumoigakurinu
sayo fukete yukue wo shirani   aga kokoro Akashi no ura ni
fune tomete ukine wo shitsutsu   watatsumi no okibe wo mireba
izari suru ama no otome wa   obune nori tsurarani ukeri
akatoki no shio michikureba   ashibe niwa tazu nakiwataru
asanagi ni funade wo sento   funabito mo kako mo koe yobi
niodori no nazusaiyukeba   Ieshima wa kumoi ni mienu
aga moeru kokoro naguyato   hayaku kite minto omoite
ōbune wo kogi waga yukeba   okitsunami takaku tachikinu
yoso nomini mitsutsu sugiyuki   Tama no ura ni fune wo todomete
hamabi yori uraiso wo mitsutsu   naku ko nasu ne nomishi nakayu
watatsumi no tamaki no tama wo   iezuto ni imo ni yaranto
hiriitori sode niwa irete   kaeshiyaru tsukai nakereba
moteredomo shirushi wo namito   mata okitsurukamo

Tama no ura no okitsushiratama   hirieredo mata zo okitsuru
miru hito wo nami

Aki saraba waga fune haten   wasuregai yosekite okere
okitsushiranami

Kore ya kono na ni ou Naruto no   uzushio ni tamamo karu tou
amaotomedomo

753

Ōkimi no mikoto kashikomi ōbune no yuki no manimani
yadori surukamo

754

Unabara no okibe ni tomoshi izaru hi wa akashite tomose
Yamatoshima min

755

Yū sareba akikaze samushi wagimoko ga tokiaraigoromo
yukite haya kin

756

Tabi ni aredo yoru wa hi tomoshi oru ware wo yami niya imo ga
koitsutsu aruran

757

Ama tobuya kari wo tsukai ni eteshigamo Nara no miyako ni
koto tsugeyaran

758–60

Sumerogi no tō no mikado to Karakuni ni wataru waga se wa
iebito no iwai mataneka tadami kamo ayamachi shiken
aki saraba kaerimasanto tarachine no haha ni mōshite
toki mo sugi tsuki mo henureba kyō ka kon asu kamo konto
iebito wa machikouranni tō no kuni imada mo tsukazu
Yamato womo tōku sakarite iwa ga ne no araki shimane ni
yadori suru kimi

Iwatanu ni yadori suru kimi iebito no izura to ware wo
towaba ikani iwan

Yononaka wa tsune kaku nomito wakarenuru kimi niya motona
aga koiyukan

Ametsuchi to tomoni mogamoto   omoitsutsu arikenmonowo
hashikeyashi ie wo hanarete   nami no ue yu nazusaikinite
aratama no tsukihi mo ki henu   karigane mo tsugite kinakeba
tarachine no haha mo tsumara mo   asatsuyu ni mo no suso hizuchi
yūgiri ni koromode nurete   sakiku shimo arurangotoku
idemitsutsu matsuranmonowo   yononaka no hito no nageki wa
aiomowanu kimi ni areyamo   akihagi no chiraeru nube no
hatsuobana kario ni fukite   kumobanare tōki kunibe no
tsuyujimo no samuki yamabe ni   yadori seruran

Hashikeyashi tsuma mo kodomo mo   takadakani matsuran kimi shi
shimagakurenuru

Momijiba no chirinan yama ni   yadorinuru kimi wo matsuran
hito shi kanashimo

Kashikokiya mikoto kagafuri   asu yuriya kae ga muta nen
imu nashinishite

Waga tsuma wa itaku koirashi   nomu mizu ni kago sae miete
yo ni wasurarezu

Tokidoki no hana wa sakedomo   nani surezo haha tou hana no
sakidekozuken

Chichihaha mo hana nimogamoya   kusamakura tabi wa yukutomo
sasagote yukan

Waga tsuma mo e ni kakitoran   itsuma moga tabi yuku are wa
mitsutsu shinuban

Ōkimi no mikoto kashikomi   iso ni furi unohara wataru
chichihaha wo okite

Naniwazu ni yosoiyosoite   kyō no hi ya idete makaran
miru haha nashini

Mizutori no tachi no isogi ni   chichihaha ni monowazu kenite
ima zo kuyashiki

Makebashira homete tsukureru   tono no goto imase hahatoji
omegawari sezu

Waro tabi wa tabi to omehodo   ii nishite ko mechi yasuran
waga mi kanashimo

Wasuranto nu yuki yama yuki   ware kuredo waga chichihaha wa
wasure senukamo

Chichihaha ga kashira kakinade   saku arete iishi kotoba zo
wasurekanetsuru

Ie nishite koitsutsu arazuwa   naga hakeru tachi ni naritemo
iwaiteshigamo

Michi no he no umara no ure ni   hao mame no karamaru kimi wo
hakareka yukan

Ashigaki no kumado ni tachite   wagimoko ga sode mo shiohoni
nakishizo mohayu

Ōkimi no mikoto kashikomi   idekureba wa nu toritsukite
iishi kona wamo

Sakimuri ni tatan sawagi ni   ie no imu ga narubeki koto wo
iwazu kinukamo

Arare furi Kashima no kami wo   inoritsutsu sumeramikusa ni
ware wa kinishiwo

Ashigara no misaka tamawari   kaerimizu are wa kueyuku
arashio mo tashi ya habakaru   Fuwa no seki kuete wa wa yuku
muma no tsume Tsukushi no saki ni   chimariite are wa iwawan
moromoro wa sakeku to maosu   kaerikumadeni

783–8

Kyō yoriwa kaerimi nakute   Ōkimi no shiko no mitate to
idetatsu ware wa

Ametsuchi no kami wo inorite   satsuya nuki Tsukushi no shima wo
sashite iku ware wa

Matsu no ke no namitaru mireba   iwabito no ware wo miokuruto
tatarishi mokoro

Amotoji mo tama nimogamoya   itadakite mizura no naka ni
aemakamakumo

Tsu no kuni no umi no nagisa ni   funa yosoi tashidemo toki ni
amo ga me mogamo

Yuko saki ni naminato erai   shiruhe niwa ko woto tsuma woto
okite tomo kinu

789

Chihayaburu kami no misaka ni   nusa matsuri iwau inochi wa
omochichi ga tame

790

Waga iwaro ni yukamo hito moga   kusamakura tabi wa kurushito
tsugeyaramakumo

791–2

Akagoma wo yamanu ni hakashi   torikanite Tama no Yokoyama
kashi yuka yaran

Kusamakura tabi no marune no himo taeba aga te to tsukero
kore no haru moshi

793-6

Asari suru ama no kodomo to hito wa iedo miruni shiraenu
umabito no ko to

Tamashima no kono kawakami ni ie wa aredo kimi wo yasashimi
arawasazu ariki

Matsuragawa kawa no se hikari ayu tsuruto tataseru imo ga
mo no suso nurenu

Haru sareba wagie no sato no kawato niwa ayuko sabashiru
kimi machigateni

797-8

Ōkimi no mikoto kashikomi nikibinishi ie wo okite
komoriku no Hatsuse no kawa ni fune ukete waga yuku kawa no
kawakuma no yasokuma ochizu yorozutabi kaerimi shitsutsu
tamahoko no michi yukikurashi aoniyoshi Nara no miyako no
Sahogawa ni iyukiitarite waga netaru koromo no ue yu
asazukuyo sayakani mireba tae no ho ni yoru no shimo furi
iwadoko to kawa no hi korite samuki yo wo ikou koto naku
kayoitsutsu tsukureru ie ni chiyo madeni kimasan kimi to
ware mo kayowan

Aoniyoshi Nara no ie niwa yorozuyo ni ware mo kayowan
wasuruto omouna

799

Kazahaya no Miho no urami no shiratsutsuji miredomo sabushi
naki hito omoeba

800

Yononaka wa munashiki mono to arantozo kono teru tsuki wa

426

michikake shikeru

Ametsuchi no kami mo tasukeyo   kusamakura tabi yuku kimi ga
ie ni itarumade

Tōtsuhito Matsurasayohime   tsumagoi ni hire furishi yori
oeru yama no na

Makuzu hau Kasuga no yama wa   uchinabiku haru sariyukuto
yamakai ni kasumi tanabiki   Takamado ni uguisu nakinu
mononofu no yasotomonoo wa   karigane no kitsugu konogoro
kaku tsugite tsuneni ariseba   tomo namete asobanmonowo
uma namete yukamashi sato wo   machigateni waga seshi haru wo
kakemakumo ayani kashikoshi   iwamakumo yuyushikaranto
arakajime kanete shiriseba   chidori naku sono Sahogawa ni
iwa ni ouru suga no ne torite   shinubugusa haraetemashiwo
yuku mizu ni misogitemashiwo   Ōkimi no mikoto kashikomi
momoshiki no ōmiyabito no   tamahoko no michi nimo idezu
kouru konogoro

Ume yanagi suguraku oshimi   Saho no uchi ni asobishi koto wo
miya mo todoroni

Isonokami Furu no mikoto wa   tawayame no madoi ni yorite
umajimono nawa toritsuke   shishijimono yumiya kakumite
Ōkimi no mikoto kashikomi   amazakaru hinabe ni makaru
furugoromo Matsuchi no yama yu   kaerikonukamo

Ōkimi no mikoto kashikomi   sashinarabu kuni ni idemasuya
waga se no kimi wo   kakemakumo yuyushi kashikoshi
Suminoe no arahitogami   funanohe ni ushihakitamai

tsukitamawan shima no sakizaki   yoritamawan iso no sakizaki
araki nami kaze ni awasezu   tsutsumi naku yamai arasezu
sumuyakeku kaeshitamawane   moto no kunibe ni

807-8

Chichigimi ni ware wa manago zo   hahatoji ni ware wa manago zo
mainoboru yasoujibito no   tamuke suru Kashiko no saka ni
nusa matsuri ware wazo makaru   tōki Tosaji wo

Ōsaki no kami no obama wa   sebakedomo momofunabito mo
sugu to iwanakuni

809

Yononaka wo tsune naki mono to   ima zo shiru Nara no miyako no
utsurou mireba

810-1

Akihagi wo tsumatou ka koso   hitorigo ni ko motarito ie
kakojimono waga hitorigo no   kusamakura tabi nishi yukeba
takatama wo shijini nukitari   iwaibe ni yū torishidete
iwaitsutsu waga omou ako   masakiku arikoso

Tabibito no yadori sen nu ni   shimo furaba waga ko hagukume
ame no tazumura

812-3

Soramitsu Yamato no kuni   aoniyoshi Nara no miyako yu
oshiteru Naniwa ni kudari   Suminoe no Mitsu ni funanori
tada watari hi no iru kuni ni   tsukawasaru waga se no kimi wo
kakemakumo yuyushi kashikoki   Suminoe no waga ōmikami
funanohe ni ushihakiimashi   funadomo ni mitatashimashite
sashiyoran iso no sakizaki   kogihaten tomaritomari ni
araki kaze nami ni awasezu   tairakeku ite kaerimase
moto no mikado ni

Okitsunami henami na-koshiso   kimi ga fune kogikaerikite
tsu ni hatsurumade

814

Asakayama kage sae miyuru   yama no i no asaki kokoro wo
waga mowanakuni

815

Katsumata no ike wa ware shiru   hachisu nashi shika iu kimi ga
hige nakigotoshi

816

Ōumi no okuka mo shirazu   yuku ware wo itsu kimasanto
toishi kora wamo

817–8

Hisakata no Amanokawara ni   kamitsuse ni tamahashi watashi
shimotsuse ni fune ukesue   ame furite kaze fukazutomo
kaze fukite ame furazutomo   mo nurasazu yamazu kimaseto
tamahashi watasu

Amanogawa kiri tachiwataru   kyōkyō to waga matsu kimi ga
funade surashimo

819

Kasuganu ni keburi tatsu miyu   otomera shi harunu no uhagi
tsumite nirashimo

*   *   *

820

Ōumi ni shima mo aranakuni   unabara no tayutau nami ni
tateru shirakumo

429

Yasumishishi wago Ōkimi   takaterasu Hi no Miko no
kikoshiosu miketsukuni   kamukaze no Ise no kuni wa
kuni mirebashimo   yama mireba takaku tōtoshi
kawa mireba sayakeku kiyoshi   minato nasu umi mo hiroshi
miwatasu shima wa nadakashi   koko woshimo maguwashimikamo
kakemakumo ayani kashikoki   Yamanobe no Ishi no hara ni
uchihisasu ōmiyatsukae   asahi nasu maguwashimo
yūhi nasu uraguwashimo   haruyama no shinai sakaete
akiyama no iro natsukashiki   momoshiki no ōmiyabito wa
ametsuchi hitsuki to tomoni   yorozuyo nimoga

Yamanobe no Ishi no mii wa   onozukara nareru nishiki wo
hareru yama kamo

Haru saraba kazashi ni sento   waga moishi sakura no hana wa
chiriinishikamo

Imo ga na ni kaketaru sakura   hana sakaba tsuneni ya koin
iya toshinoha ni

Komori nomi koureba kurushi   yama no ha yu idekuru tsuki no
arawasaba ikani

Koto shi araba Ohatsuseyama no   iwaki nimo komoraba tomoni
na-omoi waga se

Akigawari shirasutono minori   arabakoso waga shitagoromo
kaeshi tamawame

Shōji no futatsu no umi wo　itowashimi shiohi no yama wo
shinubitsurukamo

Hashidate no Kumaki no yara ni　Shiragiono otoshiire washi
kakete kakete na-nakashisone　ukiizuruyato min washi

Kashimane no Tsukue no shima no　shitadami wo ihiroi mochikite
ishi mochi tsutsuki yaburi　hayakawa ni araisusugi
karashio ni kokoto momi　takatsuki ni mori tsukue ni tatete
haha ni matsuritsuya mezuko no toji
chichi ni matsuritsuya mimezuko no toji

Itoko nase no kimi　oriorite mono ni iyukutowa
Karakuni no tora tou kami wo　ikedori ni yatsu tori mochiki
sono kawa wo tatami ni sashi　yaedatami Heguri no yama ni
uzuki to satsuki no hodo ni　kusurigari tsukauru toki ni
ashihiki no kono katayama ni　futatsu tatsu ichihi ga moto ni
azusayumi yatsu tabasami　himekabura yatsu tabasami
shishi matsuto waga oru toki ni　saoshika no kitachi nagekaku
tachimachini ware wa shinubeshi　Ōkimi ni ware wa tsukaen
waga tsunu wa mikasa no hayashi　waga mimi wa misumi no tsubo
waga mera wa masumi no kagami　waga tsume wa miyumi no yuhazu
waga kera wa mifude no hayashi　waga kawa wa mihako no kawa ni
waga shishi wa minamasu hayashi　waga kimo mo minamasu hayashi
waga migi wa mishio no hayashi　oitaru yatsuko waga mi hitotsu ni
nanae hana saku yae hana sakuto　mōshi hayasane mōshi hayasane

Oshiteruya Naniwa no oe ni　io tsukuri namarite oru
ashigani wo ōkimi mesuto　nani senni wa wo mesurameya

akirakeku waga shiru koto wo   utabito to wa wo mesurameya
fuefuki to wa wo mesurameya   kotohiki to wa wo mesurameya
kamokaku mo mikoto ukento   kyōkyō to Asuka ni itari
tatedomo Okina ni itari   tsukanedomo Tsukunu ni itari
himukashi no naka no mikado yu   mairikite mikoto ukureba
uma nikoso fumodashi kaku mono   ushi nikoso hananawa hakure
ashihiki no kono katayama no   momunire wo ioe hagitari
amateruya hi no ke ni hoshi   saizuruya karausu ni tsuki
niwa ni tatsu suriusu ni tsuki   oshiteruya Naniwa no oe no
hatsutari wo karaku tarikite   suebito no tsukureru kame wo
kyō yukite asu tori mochiki   waga mera ni shio nuritamai
mochihayasumo mochihayasumo

833–4

Ametsuchi no kami wa nakareya   uruwashiki waga tsuma sakaru
hikaru kami narihataotome   te tazusai tomoni aranto
omoishini kokoro tagainu   iwan sube sen sube sirani
yūdasuki kata ni torikake   shizunusa wo te ni torimochite
na-sakesoto ware wa inoredo   makite neshi imo ga tamoto wa
kumo ni tanabiku

Utsutsu nito omoiteshigamo   ime nomini tamoto makinuto
miruwa sube nashi

835–6

Tsukubane no niikuwamayo no   kinu wa aredo kimi ga mikeshi shi
ayani kihoshimo

Tsukubane ni yuki kamo furaru   ina wokamo kanashiki koro ga
ninu hosarukamo

837–8

Niodori no Katsushikawase wo   nie sutomo sono kanashikiwo
to ni tatemeyamo

A no oto sezu yukan koma moga Katsushika no Mama no tsugihashi yamazu kayowan

839

Tsukubane no otemokonomo ni   moribe sue haha i moredomo
tama zo ainikeru

840–1

Shinanuji wa ima no harimichi   karibane ni ashi fumashinan
kutsu hake waga se

Shinanu naru Chikuma no kawa no   sazareshi mo kimi shi fumiteba
tama to hirowan

842–4

Ikahoro no Yasaka no ide ni   tatsu nuji no arawaromademo
sane wo saneteba

Ikahone ni kami na-narisone   waga e niwa yue wa nakedomo
kora ni yoritezo

Ikahokaze fuku hi fukanu hi   arito iedo aga koi nomishi
toki nakarikeri

845

Shimotsukenu Aso no kawara yo   ishi fumazu sora yuto kinuyo
naga kokoro nore

846

Tsumuganu ni suzu ga oto kikoyu   Kamushida no tono no nakachi shi
togari surashimo

847

Suzu ga ne no hayuma umaya no   tsutsumii no mizu wo tamaena
imo ga tadate yo

433

Kono kawa ni asana arau ko nare mo ware mo yochi wozo moteru
ide ko tabarini

Omoshiroki nu woba na-yakiso furukusa ni niikusa majiri
oiba ouru gani

Ine tsukeba kagaru aga te wo koyoi moka tono no wakugo ga
torite nagekan

Tare zo kono ya no to osoburu niunami ni waga se wo yarite
iwau kono to wo

Ōkimi no mikoto kashikomi kanashiimo ga tamakura hanare
yodachi kinukamo

Misora yuku kumo nimogamona kyō yukite imo ni kotodoi
asu kaerikon

Takaki ne ni kumo no tsuku nosu ware saeni kimi ni tsukinana
takane to moite

Haru no nu ni kusa hamu koma no kuchi yamazu a wo shinuburan
ie no koro wamo

Aoyagi no hararo kawato ni　na wo matsuto semido wa kumazu
tachido narasumo

Okite ikaba imo wa maganashi　mochite yuku azusa no yumi no
yuzuka nimogamo

Okureite koiba kurushimo　asagari no kimi ga yumi nimo
naramashimonowo

Sakimori ni tachishi asake no　kanatode ni tabanare oshimi
nakishi kora wamo

Ashi no ha ni yūgiri tachite　kamo ga ne no samuki yūbe shi
na woba shinuban

Sakimori ni yukuwa taga se to　tou hito wo miruga tomoshisa
monomoi mo sezu

Sasa ga ha no sayagu shimoyo ni　nanae karu koromo ni maseru
kora ga hada wamo

Omou hito konto shiriseba　yaemugura ooeru niwa ni
tama shikamashiwo

Tama shikeru ie mo nani sen　yaemugura ooeru oya mo
imo to oriteba

Kado tatete to mo sashitaruwo   izuku yuka imo ga irikite
ime ni mietsuru

Kado tatete to wa sashitaredo   nusubito no horeru ana yori
irite mieken

Monomowazu michi yukinanmo   aoyama wo furisakemireba
tsutsujibana nioeotome   sakurabana sakaeotome
na wozomo wa ni yosu tou   wa wozomo na ni yosu tou
arayama mo hito shi yosureba   yosorutozo iu naga kokoro yume

Ikani shite koi yaman mono zo   ametsuchi no kami wo inoredo
wa wa omoi masu

Shikarekoso toshi no yatose wo   kiru kami no yochiko wo sugi
tachibana no hotsue wo sugite   kono kawa no shita nimo nagaku
naga kokoro mate

Ametsuchi no kami womo ware wa   inoriteki koi tou mono wa
katsute yamazukeri

Tsuginefu Yamashiroji wo   hitozuma no uma yori yukuni
onozuma shi kachi yori yukeba   miru gotoni ne nomishi nakayu
soko mouni kokoro shi itashi   tarachine no haha ga katami to
waga moteru masomikagami ni   akitsuhire oinamemochite
uma kae waga se

Izumigawa watarise fukami   waga seko ga tabiyukigoromo
hizuchinankamo

Masokagami moteredo ware wa   shirushi nashi kimi ga kachi yori
nazumiyuku mireba

Uma kawaba imo kachi naran   yoshieyashi ishi wa fumutomo
wa wa futari yukan

Ki no kuni no hama ni yoru tou   awabitama hiriwanto iite
Imo no yama Se no yama koete   yukishi kimi itsu kimasanto
tamahoko no michi ni idetachi   yūura wo waga toishikaba
yūura no ware ni noraku   wagimoko ya naga matsu kimi wa
okitsunami kiyoru shiratama   hetsunami no yosuru shiratama
motomutozo kimi ga kimasanu   hiriutozo kimi wa kimasanu
hisanaraba ima nanuka bakari   hayakaraba ima futsuka bakari
arantozo kimi wa kikoshishi   na-koiso wagimo

Tsue tsukimo tsukazumo ware wa   yukamedomo kimi ga kimasan
michi no shiranaku

Tadani yukazu ko yu Koseji kara   iwase fumi tomezo waga koshi
koite sube nami

Sayo fukete ima wa akenuto   to wo akete Ki e yukishi kimi wo
itsu toka matan

Kado ni ishi otome wa uchi ni   itarutomo itaku shi koiba
ima kaerikon

Hōshira ga hige no sorigui   uma tsunagi itaku na-hikiso
hōshi wa nakan

Dan-ochi ya shika mo na-iiso   satoosa ga etsuki hataraba
imashi mo nakan

Ōumi no nami wa kashikoshi   shikaredomo kami wo iwaite
funade seba ikani

Nami takashi ikani kajitori   mizutori no ukine ya subeki
nao ya kogubeki

Akatoki to yogarasu nakedo   kono oka no konure no ue wa
imada shizukeshi

Nishi no ichi ni tada hitori dete   menarabezu kainishi kinu no
akijikori kamo

Kotoshi yuku niisakimori ga   asagoromo kata no mayoi wa
tare ka torimin

Tamadare no osu no sukeki ni   irikayoikone
tarachine no haha ga towasaba   kaze to mōsan

Masurao no idetachi mukau   furusato no Kamunabiyama ni
akekureba tsumi no saeda ni   yū sareba komatsu ga ure ni
satobito no kikikourumadeni   yamabiko no aitoyomumadeni
hototogisu tsumagoi surashi   sayonaka ni naku

Tabi nishite tsumagoi surashi   hototogisu Kamunabiyama ni
sayo fukete naku

Watatsumi wa kusushiki mono ka   Awajishima naka ni tateokite
shiranami wo Iyo ni megurashi   imachizuki Akashi no to yuwa
yū sareba shio wo mitashime   akesareba shio wo hishimu
shiosai no nami wo kashikomi   Awajishima isogakuriite

itsu shikamo kono yo no akento   samorauni i no negateneba
taki no ue no Asanu no kigishi   akenutoshi tachitoyomurashi
iza kodomo aete kogiden   niwa mo shizukeshi

Shimazutai Minume no saki wo   kogitameba Yamato koishiku
tazu sawani naku

892

Minasoko no tama sae sayani   mitsubekumo teru tsukuyo kamo
yo no fukeyukeba

893

Yugi kakuru tomonoo hiroki   Ōtomo ni kuni sakaento
tsuki wa terurashi

894

Tōrubeku ame wa na-furiso   wagimoko ga katami no koromo
ware shita ni kitari

895

Inishie no koto wa shiranuwo   ware mitemo hisashiku narinu
Ame-no-Kaguyama

896

Imoragari waga kayoiji no   shinususuki ware shi kayowaba
nabike shinuhara

897

Koto toreba nageki sakidatsu   kedashiku mo koto no shitahi ni
tsuma ya komoreru

898

Ujigawa wo fune watasewoto   yobaedomo kikoezarurashi
kaji no to mo sezu

439

Ame wa furu kario wa tsukuru   itsu no ma ni Ago no shiohi ni
tama wa hiriwan

Ie sakari tabi nishi areba   akikaze no samuki yūbe ni
kari nakiwataru

Amaobune ho kamo hareruto   mirumadeni Tomo no urami ni
nami tateri miyu

Kasuga naru Mikasa no yama ni   tsuki no fune izu
miyabio no nomu sakazuki ni   kage ni mietsutsu

Wata no soko shizuku shiratama   kaze fukite umi wa arutomo
torazuwa yamaji

Fuyugomori haru no ōnu wo   yaku hito wa yakitaranekamo
waga kokoro yaku

Amagumo ni chikaku hikarite   naru kami no mireba kashikoshi
mineba kanashimo

Sakihai no ikanaru hito ka   kurokami no shiroku narumade
imo ga koe wo kiku

Harugasumi nagaruru nabeni   aoyagi no eda kuimochite
uguisu nakumo

Uchinabiku haru sarikureba   shinu no ure ni o ha uchifurite
uguisu nakumo

Ume ga e ni nakite utsurou   uguisu no hane shirotae ni
awayuki zo furu

Sakurabana toki wa suginedo   miru hito no koi no sakari to
ima shi chiruran

Itsu shikamo kono yo no aken   uguisu no kozutai chirasu
ume no hana min

Momoshiki no ōmiyabito wa   itoma areya ume wo kazashite
koko ni tsudoeru

Fuyu sugite haru shi kitareba   toshitsuki wa aratanaredomo
hito wa furiyuku

Mono mina wa aratashiki yoshi   tada hito wa furinurunomishi
yoroshikarubeshi

Harusame ni koromo wa itaku   tōrameya nanuka shi furaba
nanayo kojitoya

Konogoro no koi no shigekeku natsukusa no kariharaedomo
oishikugotoshi

Ware kosowa nikukumo arame waga niwa no hanatachibana wo
mi niwa kojitoya

Minazuki no tsuchi sae sakete teru hi nimo waga sode himeya
kimi ni awazushite

Akikaze no fukitadayowasu shirakumo wa Tanabatatsume no
amatsuhire kamo

Kono yūbe furikuru ame wa Hikoboshi no haya kogu fune no
kai no chiri kamo

Ashidama mo tadama mo yurani oru hata wo kimi ga mikeshi ni
nuiaenkamo

Ametsuchi no hajime no toki yu Amanogawa imukaiorite
hitotose ni futatabi awanu tsumagoi ni mono omou hito
Amanogawa Yasu no kawara no arigayou toshi no watari ni
sohofune no tomo nimo he nimo funayosoi makaji shiji nuki
hatasusuki motoha mo soyoni akikaze no fukikuru yoi ni
Amanogawa shiranami shinugi ochitagitsu hayase watarite
wakakusa no tsuma ga te makan to ōbune no omoitanomite
kogikuran sono tsuma no ko ga aratama no toshinoo nagaku

omoikoshi koi tsukusuran   fumitsuki no nanuka no yoi wa
ware mo kanashimo

Komanishiki himo toki kawashi   Amebito no tsumatou yoi zo
ware mo shinuban

Hikoboshi no kawase wo wataru   saobune no yukiyukite haten
kawazu shi omohoyu

925

Niwakusa ni murasame furite   kōrogi no naku koe kikeba
akizukinikeri

926

Haru wa moe natsu wa midori ni   kurenai no madarani miyuru
aki no yama kamo

927

Kimi ni koi shinaeurabure   waga oreba akikaze fukite
tsuki katabukinu

928

Aki no yo wo nagashito iedo   tsumorinishi koi wo tsukuseba
mijikakarikeri

929

Kōrogi no wa ga toko no be ni   nakitsutsu motona
okiitsutsu kimi ni kouruni   inegatenakuni

930

Hanahada mo yo fukete na-yuki   michi no he no yuzasa ga ue ni
shimo no furu yo wo

Ime no goto kimi wo aimite   amagirashi furikuru yuki no
kenubéku omohoyu

Tarachine no haha ni sawaraba   itazurani imashi mo ware mo
koto narubeshiya

Matsuranni itaraba imo ga   ureshimito eman sugata wo
yukite haya min

Waga seko ga sono na norajito   tamakiharu inochi wa sutetsu
wasuretamauna

Omowanuni itaraba imo ga   ureshimito eman mayobiki
omohoyurukamo

Aimitewa omo kakusaruru   monokarani tsugite mimakuno
hoshiki kimi kamo

Itsuwari mo nitsukitezo suru   itsu yorika minu hito kouni
hito no shini seshi

Omowasure danimo e suyato   tanigirite utedomo korizu
koi to iu yatsuko

Asanegami ware wa kezuraji   uruwashiki kimi ga tamakura
furiteshimonowo

Ametsuchi ni sukoshi itaranu   masurao to omoishi ware ya
ogokoro mo naki

Tachite ite tadoki mo shirazu   waga kokoro amatsusora nari
tsuchi wa fumedomo

Hito no mite kototogame senu   ime ni ware koyoi itaran
yado sasuna yume

Tokimori no uchinasu tsuzumi   yomimireba toki niwa narinu
awanakumo ayashi

Tomoshibi no kage ni kagayou   utsusemi no imo ga emai shi
omokage ni miyu

Oharida no Itada no hashi no   kuzurenaba keta yori yukan
na-koiso wagimo

Miyaki hiku Izumi no soma ni   tatsu tami no yasumu toki naku
koiwatarukamo

Naniwabito ashibi taku ya no   sushite aredo onoga tsuma koso
tokomezurashiki

Uma no to no todoto mo sureba   matsukage ni idetezo mitsuru
kedashi kimi kato

Tamachihau kami mo ware woba   utsutekoso shieya inochi no
oshikekumo nashi

Masode mochi toko uchiharai   kimi matsuto orishi aida ni
tsuki katabukinu

Wagimoko ni au yoshi wo nami   Suruga naru Fuji no takane no
moetsutsuka aran

Minatoiri no ashiwakeobune   sawari ōmi ima kon ware wo
yodomuto mouna

Hisakata no amatsu misora ni   teru tsuki no usenan hi koso
waga koi yamame

Ōumi no soko wo fukamete   musubiteshi imo ga kokoro wa
utagai mo nashi

955

Imo ga kado yukisugikanete   kusa musubu kaze fuki tokuna
mata kaeri min

956

Umasegoshi ni mugi hamu koma no   norayuredo naoshi kouraku
shinubikanetsumo

957

Kawakami ni arau wakana no   nagarekite imo ga atari no
se nikoso yorame

958

Mimoro wa hito no moru yama   motobe wa ashibi hana saki
suebe wa tsubaki hana saku   uraguwashiyama zo nakuko moru yama

959–60

Narukami no hikaoru sora no   nagatsuki no shigure no fureba
karigane mo imada kinakazu   Kamunabi no kiyoki mitaya no
kakitsuta no ike no tsutsumi no   momotarazu itsuki ga eda ni
mizue sasu aki no momijiba   makimotaru osuzu mo yurani
tawayame ni ware wa aredomo   hikiyojite eda mo tooni
uchitaori a wa mochite yuku   kimi ga kazashi ni

Hitori nomi mireba koishimi   Kamunabi no yama no momijiba
taorikeri kimi

961–3

Ashihara no Mizuho no Kuni ni   tamuke suto amorimashiken
ioyorozu chiyorozu kami no   kamiyo yori iitsugikitaru
Kamunabi no Mimoro no yama wa   haru sareba harugasumi tachi
aki yukeba kurenai niou   Kamunabi no Mimoro no kami no
obi ni seru Asuka no kawa no   mio hayami oitamegataki
iwamakura koke musumadeni   aratayo no sakiku kayowan

447

koto hakari ime ni misekoso   tsurugitachi iwaimatsureru
kami nishi maseba

Kamunabi no Mimoro no yama ni   iwau sugi omoisugimeya
koke musumadeni

Igushi tate miwa suematsuru   kamunushi no uzu no tamakage
mireba tomoshimo

964-5

Ono torite Niu no hiyama no   ki korikite ikada ni tsukuri
makaji nuki iso kogitamitsutsu   shimazutai miredomo akazu
Mi-Yoshinu no taki mo todoroni   otsuru shiranami

Mi-Yoshinu no taki mo todoroni   otsuru shiranami
tomarinishi imo ni misemaku   hoshiki shiranami

966

Ōmi no mi tomari yaso ari   yasoshima no shima no sakizaki
aritateru hanatachibana wo   hotsue ni mochi hikikake
nakatsue ni ikaruga kake   shizue ni hime wo kake
naga haha wo torakuwo shirani   naga chichi wo torakuwo shirani
isobaioruyo ikaruga to hime to

967-8

Ōkimi no mikoto kashikomi   miredo akanu Narayama koete
maki tsumu Izumi no kawa no   hayaki se wo sao sashiwatari
chihayaburu Uji no watari no   tagitsuse wo mitsutsu watarite
Ōmiji no Ōsakayama ni   tamuke shite waga koeyukeba
Sasanami no Shiga no Karasaki   sakiku araba mata kaeri min
michi no kuma yasokuma gotoni   nagekitsutsu waga sugiyukeba
iya tōni sato sakarikinu   iya takani yama mo koekinu
tsurugitachi saya yu nukidete   Ikagoyama ikani ka waga sen
yukue shirazute

Ametsuchi wo nageki koinomi   sakiku araba mata kaeri min

Shiga no Karasaki

969

Momokine Minu no kuni no　Takakita no Kukuri no miya ni
himukashi ni yukinan miya wo　arito kikite waga kayoiji no
Okisoyama Minu no yama　nabike to hito wa fumedomo
kaku yoreto hito wa tsukedomo　kokoro naki yama no
Okisoyama Minu no yama

970–1

Amahashi mo nagakumogamo　takayama mo takakumogamo
tsukuyomi no motaru ochimizu　itorikite kimi ni matsurite
ochi eshimu mono

Ame naruya tsukihi no gotoku　waga moeru kimi ga hi ni keni
oyuraku oshimo

972–3

Shikishima no Yamato no kuni ni　hito sawani michite aredomo
fujinami no omoimatsuwari　wakakusa no omoitsukinishi
kimi ga me ni koi ya akasan　nagaki kono yo wo

Shikishima no Yamato no kuni ni　hito futari aritoshi mowaba
nani ka nagekan

974–6

Akitsushima Yamato no kuni wa　kamukara to kotoage senu kuni
shikaredomo a wa kotoage su　ametsuchi no kami mo hanahada
waga omou kokoro shirazuya　yuku kage no tsuki mo heyukeba
tama kagiru hi mo kasanarite　omoekamo mune yasukaranu
kourekamo kokoro no itaki　sue tsuini kimi ni awazuba
waga inochi no ikeran kiwami　koitsutsumo ware wa wataran
masokagami tadame ni kimi wo　aimitebakoso waga koi yamame

Ōbune no omoitanomeru　kimi yueni tsukusu kokoro wa
oshikekumo nashi

449

Hisakata no miyako wo okite   kusamakura tabi yuku kimi wo
itsu toka matan

977-8

Inishiye yu iitsugikuraku   koi sureba yasukaranu mono to
tamanoo no tsugitewa iedo   otomera ga kokoro wo shirani
sowo shiran yoshi no nakereba   natsusobiku inochi katamake
karigomo no kokoro mo shinuni   hito shirezu motona zo kouru
ikinoo nishite

Shikushikuni omowazu hito wa   aramedomo shimashi mo ware wa
wasuraenukamo

979-80

Oharida no Ayuchi no mizu wo   ma nakuzo hito wa kumu tou
tokijikuzo hito wa nomu tou   kumu hito no ma nakiga goto
nomu hito no tokijikiga goto   wagimoko ni waga kourakuwa
yamu toki mo nashi

Omoiyaru sube no tazuki mo   ima wa nashi kimi ni awazute
toshi no henureba

981-2

Sashiyakan oya no shikiya ni   kakiuten yaregomo wo shikite
uchioran shiko no shikite wo   sashikaete nuran kimi yue
akanesasu hiru wa shimirani   nubatama no yoru wa sugarani
kono toko no hishito narumade   nagekitsurukamo

Waga kokoro yakumo ware nari   hashikiyashi kimi ni kourumo
waga kokoro kara

983-4

Uchihaete omoishi onu wa   tōkaranu sono satobito no
shime yūto kikiteshi hi yori   taterakuno tazuki mo shirazu
oramakuno okuka mo shirazu   nikibinishi waga ie surawo

450

kusamakura tabine no gotoku   omou sora yasukaranumonowo
nageku sora sugushienumonowo   amagumo no yuki no makumaku
ashigaki no omoimidarete   midareo no tsukasa wo namito
waga kouru chie no hitoe mo   hito shirezu motona ya koin
ikinoo nishite

Futatsu naki koi woshi sureba   tsune no obi wo mie musububeku
waga mi wa narinu

985

Waga seko wa matedo kimasazu   Amanohara furisakemireba
nubatama no yo mo fukenikeri   sayo fukete arashi no fukeba
tachitomari matsu waga sode ni   furu yuki wa kōriwatarinu
imasarani kimi kimasameya   sanakazura nochi mo awanto
nagusamuru kokoro wo mochite   misode mochi toko uchiharai
utsutsu niwa kimi niwa awazu   ime nidani auto miekoso
ame no tariyo ni

986–7

Uchihisatsu Miyake no hara yu   hitatsuchi ni ashi fuminuki
natsukusa wo koshi ni nazumi   ikanaruya hito no ko yue zo
kayowasu mo ago
ube na ube na haha wa shiraji   ube na ube na chichi wa shiraji
mina no wata kaguroki kami ni   mayū mochi asasa yuitari
Yamato no tsuge no ogushi wo   osaesasu uraguwashiko
sore zo waga tsuma

Chichihaha ni shirasenu ko yue   Miyakeji no natsunu no kusa wo
nazumikurukamo

988

Miwatashi ni imora wa tatashi   kono kata ni ware wa tachite
omou sora yasukaranakuni   nageku sora yasukaranakuni
saninuri no obune mogamo   tamamaki no okai mogamo
kogiwataritsutsumo   aikataramewo

451

Satobito no ware ni tsuguraku　naga kouru utsukushizuma wa
momijiba no chirimidaretaru　Kamunabi no kono yamabe kara
nubatama no kuroma ni norite　kawa no se wo nanase watarite
uraburete tsuma wa aikito　hito zo tsugetsuru

Kikazushite moda aramashiwo　nani shikamo kimi ga tadaka wo
hito no tsugetsuru

Shirakumo no tanabiku kuni no　aogumo no mukabusu kuni no
amagumo no shita naru hito wa　a nomikamo kimi ni kouran
a nomikamo kimi ni koureba　ametsuchi ni koto wo mitete
kourekamo mune no yameru　omoekamo kokoro no itaki
waga koi zo hi ni keni masaru　itsu washimo koinu toki towa
aranedomo kono nagatsuki wo　waga seko ga shinubi ni seyoto
chiyo nimo shinubiwatareto　yorozuyo ni kataritsugaeto
hajimeteshi kono nagatsuki no　sugimakuwo ita mo sube nami
aratama no tsuki no kawareba　sen sube no tadoki wo shirani
iwagane no kogoshiki michi no　iwadoko no nehaeru kado ni
ashita niwa ideite nageki　yūbe niwa irii koitsutsu
nubatama no kurokami shikite　hito no nuru umai wa nezuni
ōbune no yukurayukurani　omoitsutsu waga nuru yora wa
yomi mo aenukamo

Komoriku no Hatsuse no yama　aohata no Osaka no yama wa
hashiride no yoroshiki yama no　idetachi no kuwashiki yama zo
atarashiki yama no　aremaku oshimo

Takayama to umi kosowa　yama nagara kaku mo utsushiku
umi nagara shika tadanarame　hito wa hanamono zo
utsusemi yohito wa

Kono tsuki wa kimi kimasanto   ōbune no omoitanomite
itsu shikato waga machioreba   momijiba no sugite yukinuto
tamazusa no tsukai no ieba   hotaru nasu honokani kikite
ōtsuchi wo honoho to fumi   tachite ite yukue mo shirazu
asagiri no omoimadoite   tsuetarazu yasaka no nageki
nagekedomo shirushi wo namito   izuku nika kimi ga masanto
amagumo no yuki no manimani   iyu shishi no yuki mo shinanto
omoedomo michi shi shiraneba   hitori ite kimi ni kouruni
ne nomishi nakayu

Ashibe yuku kari no tsubasa wo   miru gotoni kimi ga obashishi
naguya shi omohoyu

Kokoro woshi Mukau no sato ni   okite araba Hakoya no yama wo
mimaku chikaken

Isanatori umi ya shinisuru   yama ya shinisuru
shinurekoso umi wa shio hite   yama wa karesure

Konogoro no waga koijikara   shirushitsume kū ni mōsaba
goi no kagafuri

Konogoro no waga koijikara   tabarazuba misatozukasa ni
idete utaen

Hitodama no saonaru kimi ga   tada hitori aerishi amayo wa
hisashiku omohoyu

APPENDICES

I. BIOGRAPHICAL NOTES

PRE-ŌMI AND ŌMI PERIODS (–667) (667–73)

Emperor Yūryaku (418–79)   The 21st Sovereign (456–79) ; celebrated for his valour and his predilection for poetry.   Besides the one long poem contained in the *Manyōshū*, a number of his verses are preserved in the *Kojiki* and the *Nihonshoki*.   The Emperor is also remembered as a patron of sericulture.

Emperor Jomei (593–641)   The 34th Sovereign (629–41). Immediately after his accession to the throne he despatched an embassy to China ; he devoted his attention also to internal administration, pacifying the eastern provinces and encouraging Buddhism.

Empress Kōgyoku (594–661)   The 35th Sovereign (641–45) ; Empress-consort of the Emperor Jomei and mother of the Emperors Tenji and Temmu.   Upon the death of her imperial husband, she ascended the throne as Empress-regnant.   After four years she abdicated in favour of the Emperor Kōtoku, upon whose death, however, she re-ascended the throne as Empress-regnant Saimei.   She died in 661 at her temporary palace in Kyūshū while on a military expedition in western Japan.

Empress Saimei   The 37th Sovereign (655–661).   See above under *Empress Kōgyoku*.

Emperor Tenji (626–71)   The 38th Sovereign (661–71) ; son of the Emperor Jomei.   The Emperor Tenji, while he was still Crown Prince under the successive reigns of the Emperor Kōtoku and the Empress Saimei, assisted in effecting a thorough centralization of power through the famous Reform of Taika.   His own rule, with the capital at Ōtsu in Ōmi Province, lasted for ten years, during which he perfected the various organs of government by introducing continental institutions and systems and laid down what became the prototypes of many of the laws, rituals, and governmental regulations of Japan.

Empress Iwa-no-himé (? –347)   Empress-consort of the 16th Sovereign, the Emperor Nintoku ; proclaimed Empress in 314, and died in 347.   Both the *Kojiki* and the *Nihonshoki* contain various legends woven about the poems exchanged between the Emperor and the Empress.

457

Empress Yamato-himé   Empress-consort of the Emperor Tenji, and granddaughter of the Emperor Jomei; she conducted the affairs of government for a time following the death of the Emperor in 671.

Prince Shōtoku (573–622)   Second son of the 31st Sovereign, the Emperor Yōmei; endowed with extraordinary intellectual power and perspicuity.   As Crown Prince under the Empress-regnant Suiko, his aunt, he administered the affairs of the state on her behalf.   He inaugurated the system of court caps and ranks, promulgated a constitution, and compiled a national history. Being an ardent follower of Buddhism, he erected temples in various provinces and extended relief to the poor.   For his cultural and religious works as well as for his benevolent rule he has long been an object of national adoration and worship.

Prince Arima (640–58)   Son of the 36th Sovereign, the Emperor Kōtoku.   In 658, after the death of his father, the young prince, then only 19 years old, was involved in a certain affair and condemned to death.

Prince Ikusa   No biographical data.   Lived in the reign of the Emperor Jomei.

Princess Nukada   Daughter of Prince Kagami and younger sister of Fujiwara Kamatari's wife.   As a favourite of the Emperor Temmu, Princess Nukada bore him Princess Toochi (?–678) and lived for a while at the Imperial Palace of Ōtsu, but passed her later life in Yamato.   The dates of her birth and death are unknown, but her life roughly coincides with the latter half of the 7th century.   She was the greatest of the women poets of her time.   The *Manyōshū* contains 3 long poems and 10 *tanka*, which bear witness to the abundant genius of the beautiful princess.

Princess Kagami (Ōmi Period)   Sister of Princess Nukada and wife of Fujiwara Kamatari.

Fujiwara Kamatari (614–69)   Lineal descendant of a hero prominent in the building of the empire, and founder of the great family of Fujiwara, which has prospered through all the ages down to the present.   Kamatari assisted the Emperor Tenji in carrying out the Reform of Taika.   He was appointed Prime Minister and granted the highest court rank of ' Taishokkan.'

Toneri Kiné   Presumably a court lady in the reign of the Emperor Tenji.

A Lady of the Court   Waited upon the Emperor Tenji.

ASUKA AND FUJIWARA PERIODS (673–86) (686–710)

Emperor Temmu (622–86)   The 40th Sovereign ; son of the Emperor Jomei, and younger brother of the Emperor Tenji.   He established the capital at Asuka in Yamato Province.   A brave and gifted ruler, he initiated the work of compiling a national history, which culminated in the completion of the *Kojiki* and the *Nihonshoki* in the Nara Period.

Lady Fujiwara (Asuka Period)   Daughter of Fujiwara Kamatari, who became a consort of the Emperor Temmu.   Prince Niitabé was her son.

Empress Jitō   (645–702)   The 41st Sovereign, and Empress-consort of the Emperor Temmu, to whom she bore Prince Kusakabé.   Upon the death of the Emperor Temmu in 686 she ascended the throne and abdicated ten years later in favour of her grandson, who became the Emperor Mommu.

Shihi, Old Lady (Fujiwara Period)   No biographical data.

Prince Ōtsu (663–86)   Son of the Emperor Temmu, and younger brother of Princess Ōku.   In 686, at the age of 24, the prince was condemned to death.   An accomplished scholar and poet, adept in writing both Japanese and Chinese verses, he was also skilled in martial arts.

Lady Ishikawa (Asuka–Fujiwara Period)   No biographical data.   All the ladies bearing the surname of Ishikawa remain unidentified.

Prince Yugé (? –699)   6th son of the Emperor Temmu.

Prince Shiki (Fujiwara Period)   In the Fujiwara Period there were two princes of the same name, one a son of the Emperor Tenji, and the other that of the Emperor Temmu ; there is no way of establishing the authorship of the six poems under that name contained in the *Manyōshū*.   According to history, Prince Shiki, son of the Emperor Tenji, was father of the 49th Sovereign, the Emperor Kōnin, and died in 716.

Princess Ōku (661–701)   Daughter of the Emperor Temmu. At the age of fourteen she became the Imperial Deputy to the Great Shrine of Isé, and served for thirteen years.   Her poems are an outpouring of her tender love for her brother, the ill-fated Prince Ōtsu.

Princess Tajima (? –708)   Daughter of the Emperor Temmu.

Prince Omi (Asuka Period)   Nothing is known of his lineage. In 676 he was sentenced to banishment.

459

Prince Yamakuma (? –723) Grandson of the Emperor Temmu, and son of Prince Osakabé.

Prince Niu (Fujiwara–Nara Period) No biographical data ; possibly identical with Princess Niu, who, it is recorded, was granted court rank in the reign of the Emperor Shōmu.

Princess Tamochi (Fujiwara Period) Possibly consort, or a relative, of Prince Kauchi who died in 689 in Kyūshū, where he was Governor-General of the Dazaifu.

Wife of Tagima Maro (Fujiwara Period) No biographical data.

Kakinomoto Hitomaro (Fujiwara Period) Nothing is known of his life, save what may be gathered from the *Manyōshū*— namely that he was an official of low rank and died in Iwami, where he had spent his last years. It is presumed that his death occurred late in the Fujiwara Period or early in the Nara Period, and that he was then less than fifty years old. The *Manyōshū* contains scores of long poems and several hundred *tanka* by him, of which the one lamenting the death of Prince Takechi is at once the longest and the most powerful in the whole collection. Skilled in all kinds of composition, narrative, descriptive or lyrical, and unsurpassed in the beauty and vigour of language and loftiness of spirit, Hitomaro was indisputably the greatest of the Manyō poets ; he has been known to posterity as *kasei*, or ' Saint of Poetry.'

Yosami, Wife of Hitomaro Probably a village girl of Tsunu in Iwami.

Ōtomo Tanushi (Fujiwara Period) Second son of Yasumaro, and younger brother of Tabito. It seems that he died young.

Ōtomo Miyuki (? –701) Elder brother of Yasumaro ; distinguished himself in the war of 672.

Furu Tamuké (Fujiwara Period) No biographical data.

Naga Okimaro (Fujiwara Period) A poet of wit and humour, of whose life little is known. His poems include those composed on the occasion of the progress of the Dowager Empress Jitō to the province of Mikawa.

Takechi Furuhito (Fujiwara Period) No biographical data. It is possible he was no other than Takechi Kurohito listed below.

Takechi Kurohito (Fujiwara Period) Served under the Empress Jitō and the Emperor Mommu. Besides accompanying his Sovereigns in their progresses, he journeyed far and wide over the country, and has left some excellent travel poems, by virtue of which he occupies an important place in the history of Japanese poetry.

Okisomé Azumabito (Fujiwara Period) No biographical data.

Osakabé Otomaro (Fujiwara Period) No biographical data. The *Manyōshū* contains only one poem by him, which was composed on the occasion of the journey of the Emperor Mommu to Naniwa.

Mikata Shami (Fujiwara–Early Nara Period) *Shami* being a title for a Buddhist monk of lower rank the name is sometimes believed to have been that of one Yamada Mikata during the period of his religious vocation. He studied in Korea and was later appointed, together with Yamanoé Okura and others, Tutor to the Crown Prince. Some Chinese poems by him are also extant.

Daughter of Sono Ikuha (Fujiwara–Early Nara Period) No biographical data.

Wife of Go Dan-ochi (Fujiwara Period) No biographical data.

Lady Fuki Attended upon Princess Toochi, daughter of the Emperor Temmu. No biographical data.

Workman of the Fujiwara Palace An unidentified workman employed in the construction of the new Imperial Palace at Fujiwara, to which the capital was transferred from Asuka in 694. It is, however, believed by some commentators that the actual author of the poem ascribed to the workman was one of the officials.

Palace-Guards of the Crown Prince Hinamishi The Crown Prince Hinamishi was no other than Prince Kusakabé, son of the Emperor Temmu. It is conjectured that Kakinomoto Hitomaro might have been one of the composers of the notable group of 23 elegiac *tanka* on the death of the prince.

NARA PERIOD (710–84)

Empress Gemmyō (661–721) The 43rd Sovereign. The 4th daughter of the Emperor Tenji, she became consort of Prince Kusakabé and bore him the Emperor Mommu, upon whose untimely death she succeeded to the throne. In 710 the Empress transferred the capital to Nara, which was to remain the Imperial City for the next seventy-five years. It was the Empress who ordered the compilation of the *Kojiki* and also caused the *Fudoki* (Topographical Records) to be presented to the court from various provinces.

461

Princess Minabé (Fujiwara–Early Nara Period)   Daughter of the Emperor Tenji, and elder sister of the Empress Gemmyō.

Empress Genshō (680–748)   The 44th Sovereign.   Granddaughter of the Emperor Temmu and daughter of Prince Kusakabé, and elder sister of the Emperor Mommu.   She ascended the throne in 715, and abdicated nine years later in favour of the Emperor Shōmu.

Emperor Shōmu (701–56)   The 45th Sovereign.   Son of the Emperor Mommu, he was enthroned in 724.   An ardent Buddhist, the Emperor constructed at Nara the Tōdai-ji Temple with its Great Buddha, and established monasteries in various provinces.   The Tempyō Era covering the twenty-five years of his reign marks the golden age of culture and enlightenment in the history of ancient Japan.

Empress Kōken (718–70)   The 46th Sovereign.   Daughter of the Emperor Shōmu and the Empress Kōmyō ; was enthroned in 749.   In 758 she abdicated in favour of the Emperor Junnin, but re-ascended the throne in 764 as the Empress Shōtoku and reigned till death.   Like her father she was an earnest believer in Buddhism.

Emperor Junnin (733–65)   The 47th Sovereign.   Grandson of the Emperor Temmu, and son of Prince Toneri ; was enthroned in 758.   After six years on the throne he abdicated and went to live on the Island of Awaji, where he died.

Empress Kōmyō (701–60)   Consort of the Emperor Shōmu, and mother of the Empress-regnant Kōken.   She was installed Crown Princess at the age of sixteen and became Empress in 729.   As a devoted follower of Buddhism she extended her benevolence to the poor, the sick and the old.   She was also a scholar of Chinese literature and a skilled calligrapher.

Prince Toneri (? –735)   The third son of the Emperor Temmu.   The prince early displayed extraordinary intelligence and wisdom ; compiled the *Nihonshoki* by imperial command ; became Acting Prime Minister in 729.

Prince Hozumi (? –715)   The fifth son of the Emperor Temmu ; was appointed Acting Prime Minister in 705, and remained in his post until his death.

Princess Ki   Daughter of the Emperor Temmu and younger sister of Prince Hozumi.

Prince Yuhara (Middle Nara Period)   Grandson of the Emperor Tenji and son of Prince Shiki.   He is a notable poet of the late Manyō style.

462

Prince Aki (Middle Nara Period) Great-grandson of the Emperor Tenji, gransdon of Prince Shiki, and son of Prince Kasuga.

Prince Ichihara (Middle–Late Nara Period) Son of Prince Aki, he inherited the poetic aptitude that had marked his family for generations. In 763 the Prince was made Chief Superintendent for the construction of the Tōdai-ji Temple. An autograph letter of his is preserved in the Shōsō-in Treasury.

Prince Nagaya (676–729) Grandson of the Emperor Temmu, and son of Prince Takechi. Appointed Minister of the Left in 724, but condemned to death through false accusation. Fond of Chinese poetry, he often invited makers of Chinese verse to his mansion. Chinese poems of his own composition are extant.

Prince Funado (? –757) Grandson of the Emperor Temmu, and son of Prince Niitabé. Another reading of the Chinese characters for the name is ' Michinoya.'

Prince Kadobé (? –745) Great-grandson of the Emperor Temmu, and son of Prince Kauchi. He was made Mayor of Nara, the capital, in 737. Two years later he assumed the status of a subject. At the time of his death in 745 he was Superintendent of the Imperial Property, though at one time he is known to have occupied the post of Governor of Izumo Province. It is said that there was another Prince Kadobé—a descendant in the fourth generation of the Emperor Jomei.

Prince Atsumi (Late Nara Period) Nothing is known of his lineage.

Prince Odai Descended to the status of a subject. There are two poems by him, which, it is said, he was fond of singing at banquets to the accompaniment of the *koto*.

Prince Takamiya (Middle Nara Period) Nothing is known of the Prince save that from one of his poems referring to the Brahmin Prelate we may infer roughly the period in which he lived.

Princess Takata (Late Nara Period) Great-granddaughter of Prince Naga who was a son of the Emperor Temmu.

Princess Hirokawa (Late Nara Period) Granddaughter of Prince Hozumi, who was a son of the Emperor Temmu.

Tajihi Kunihito (Middle Nara Period) In 783 he was an official concerned with tax affairs.

Tajihi Kasamaro (Early Nara Period) No biographical data. His poems were composed during his travels in Kii and Kyūshū.

Tajihi Yanushi (Middle Nara Period)   At one time he was an official in the Bureau of Imperial Property.

Tajihi — (Middle Nara Period)   No biographical data.

Tajihi Takanushi (Late Nara Period)   Little is known of his life.

Ishikawa Kimiko (Early Nara Period)   In 721 he was relieved of his office as Governor of Harima Province and called back to the court to serve as a chamberlain.

Taguchi Masuhito (Early Nara Period)   Governor of Kamitsuké Province in 708 ; was appointed a captain of the Imperial Guards in the following year.

Ono Oyu (? –738)   In the early years of the Tempyō Era he was in Kyūshū, serving under Ōtomo Tabito as a third rank official of the Dazaifu.   Later he became the Vice Governor-General.

Kasa Kanamura (Early Nara Period)   One of the members of the same family group to which the other notable Manyō poets such as Monk Manzei (or Kasamaro) belonged.   The *Manyōshū* contains nearly fifty poems by him composed between 715 and 733.   He was a contemporary of Yamabé Akahito, and accompanied his Sovereign on various journeys.   Many of his poems are panegyrics of the imperial rule.

Isonokami — (Early Nara Period)   Possibly to be identified as Isonokami Otomaro, listed elsewhere.

Lady Kasa (Late Nara Period)   Probably a member of the family of Kasa Kanamura, or of Kasamaro (Monk Manzei). Her 29 *tanka* addressed to Ōtomo Yakamochi are preserved in the *Manyōshū*.

Takahashi — (Middle Nara Period)   No biographical data. The poem mourning his wife was written in 744.

Kuramochi Chitosé (Early Nara Peiod)   No biographical data. His poems were composed between 723 and 725 on the occasions of the imperial progresses which he accompanied.

Kosé Sukunamaro (Middle Nara Period)   *Sashōben* (chief of a section in the government) in 737.

Fujiwara Hirotsugu (? –740)   The eldest son of Umakai ; appointed official of the third rank in the Dazaifu in 738.   In 740 he memorialized the Throne, criticizing the government, and raised an army of rebellion.   He was soon captured and put to death.

Abé Okina   No biographical data.   Even the period in which he lived is not known.

Ikeda — It is believed by some that this was Ikeda Mahira, who was the second in command of the expeditionary force sent to eastern Japan in 787. Defeated in battle, he was dismissed from office, but in consideration of his meritorious act of rescuing the troops from drowning during a battle he was allowed to retain his court rank.

Ōmiwa Okimori (Late Nara Period) No biographical data.

Nakatomi Yakamori (Middle Nara Period) For having clandestinely married, contrary to rule, Sanu Chigami, a court attendant of low rank, he was banished to the province of Echizen. He did not share in the Amnesty of 740, but was pardoned afterwards and made a government official. There are a number of *tanka* which were exchanged between Yakamori and Chigami.

Sanu Chigami (Middle Nara Period) Served in the Bureau of the Princess Imperial Deputy at the Great Shrine of Isé. All communication with men was under a ban at the Bureau. Her relations with Nakatomi Yakamori led to the latter's banishment. An intensity of feeling, characteristically feminine, pervades her poems.

Lady Abé (Early–Middle Nara Period) No biographical data.

Lady Heguri (Late Nara Period) No biographical data. Her poems are addressed to Ōtomo Yakamochi.

Ōtomo Tabito (665–731) The ancestry of the illustrious house of Ōtomo is traced back to a military leader in the mythological age, whose grandson was also a distinguished general under the Emperor Jimmu, the founder of the empire. Tabito himself was appointed, in 720, commander-in-chief of an expeditionary force which was despatched to subjugate a fierce tribe in Kyūshū. In 728 he became Governor-General of the Dazaifu and went to live in Kyūshū, where he lost his wife. In 730 he returned to Nara as Grand Councillor of State, and died in the following year. With a few exceptions all his poems included in the *Manyōshū* are the works of the years subsequent to his appointment to the Governor-Generalship of the Dazaifu. The 13 poems in praise of saké are noted for their distinctly Chinese flavour and touch of melancholy, while those on his bereavement and solitude in old age are considered masterpieces that give him an exalted place as a poet.

Manzei (Early–Middle Nara Period) While still a layman he was called Kasamaro. Appointed Governor of Mino Province in 706 ; received an increase in fee in recognition of his service in constructing the Kiso Highway in 714 ; and appointed

465

concurrently Governor of Owari Province in 715 ; he enjoyed a high reputation as a good administrator. In 719 he was made Inspector-General over the three provinces of Owari, Mikawa and Shinano, and promoted in the following year to an important post in the Central Government. In 721 he became a monk and assumed the name of Manzei. He became the Chief Commissioner for the construction of the Kwanzeon-ji Temple in Kyūshū in 723.

Ōtomo Sukunamaro (Early–Middle Nara Period) The 3rd son of Yasumaro, and younger brother of Tabito and Tanushi. Inspector-General of Aki and Suhō Provinces in 819 ; he was also *Udaiben*, a court official of high rank.

Lady Ōtomo of Sakanoé (Middle–Late Nara Period) Daughter of Yasumaro ; younger sister of Tabito, Tanushi and Sukunamaro and an aunt of Yakamochi. She married Ōtomo Sukunamaro and bore him 'Lady Ōtomo of Sakanoé's Elder Daughter,' and other children. She was an outstanding poetess of the Tempyō Era, who adorned the declining period of the Ōtomo family. Her poems reveal a keen intellect and tender maternal love.

Ōtomo Yakamochi (718–85) The eldest son of Tabito. At the age of twenty-three he was appointed a court official in charge of palace-guards, and at twenty-nine Governor of Etchū Province, whence he returned to Nara in 751 as Junior Councillor of State. In 754 he entered the Department of War as an official of the 3rd rank. He was soon promoted to the post of Vice-Minister of War and then to *Uchūben* (bureau-chief in the Central Government) ; but relegated to Inaba Province as Governor in 758. Thenceforward he led a chequered career, marked, however, by frequent promotions and demotions. Finally he was appointed Senior Councillor of State and Steward to the Crown Prince, and was concurrently made Commander-in-chief of the Eastern Expeditionary Force. He died in 785. Shortly afterwards, because of a crime committed by a distant relative of his, not only was he posthumously deprived of his office and rank, but the great and ancient family of Ōtomo was broken up. Thus, the stormy vicissitudes of fortune that had attended his life, followed him even beyond the grave. The large number of his poems in the *Manyōshū*, totalling about 500, were all composed before 759 when he was forty-two years old. It is supposed that his later works were all lost, though there might well have been many excellent verses emanating from a

466

mind matured with age and experience. Nevertheless, Yakamochi who followed in the footsteps of Hitomaro, Akahito, and
Okura, has left scores of good poems revealing his love of nature,
tenderness, and loyalty, and profound insight into human affairs.
His rare genius is manifested in the several *tanka* composed in 753
which represent the fine lyricism that characterized the poetry of
the closing years of the Nara Period.

Lady Ōtomo of Tamura Daughter of Sukunamaro. So
called because she lived in the village of Tamura.

Lady Ki (Middle–Late Nara Period) Ojika was her given
name. She became consort of Prince Aki, a great-grandson of
the Emperor Tenji.

Ōtomo Ikenushi (Late Nara Period) Genealogy unknown,
though he belonged to the same family as Yakamochi. While
the latter was Governor of Etchū Province, he served under him
as a third-rank official. Later, he held a similar post in the
province of Echizen. We find him back in Nara in 753 as an
official of the city.

Ōtomo Azumabito (Late Nara Period) Assistant Chief of
the Metropolitan Police Board in 775.

Lady Ōtomo of Sakanoé's Elder Daughter (Late Nara
Period) Daughter of Sukunamaro and Lady Sakanoé. She was
married to Yakamochi and lived awhile in Etchū Province,
where her husband was Governor.

Ōtomo Yotsuna (Middle Nara Period) A member of the
Ōtomo clan. While Tabito was Governor-General of the Dazaifu, Yotsuna held under him an office connected with the affairs
of the frontier-guards.

Ōtomo Minaka (Middle Nara Period) Vice-Ambassador to
Shiragi in 736 ; official of the third rank in the Dazaifu in 745.

Ōtomo Momoyo (Middle Nara Period) In the beginning of
the Tempyō Era he was under Tabito at the Dazaifu, as an official of the fourth rank. In 743 he became second in command
of the garrison in Kyūshū, and occupied various provincial posts
at later times.

Ōtomo Miyori (?-774) In 730 he was made Governor of
Bungo under Tabito, and later was appointed Vice-Minister of
Justice, and also Governor of other provinces.

Yamabé Akahito (Early–Middle Nara Period) Little is
known of the poet save that, accompanying the Emperor Shōmu,
he travelled over various provinces, and died probably in 736.
He is unsurpassed in *tanka*, his long poems being comparatively

brief. In contrast to Hitomaro, the poet of passion, Akahito wrote nature poems marked with limpidity and grace of style. His poem on Mount Fuji is one of the best known of his works. With Hitomaro, he has been known as a ' Saint of Poetry.'

Hanishi Mitōshi Otherwise known as Shibimaro. A court official connected with the palace night watch and imperial retinue.

Ama-no-Inukai Okamaro (Middle Nara Period) No biographical data. At the command of the Emperor Shōmu he composed the celebrated poem in praise of his Sovereign's rule.

Yamanoé Okura (Fujiwara–Middle Nara Period) In 701 he journeyed to China as a member of the embassy headed by Awata Mahito, and returned with newly acquired knowledge and learning. In 721 he was made Tutor to the Crown Prince, and later Governor of Chikuzen Province, under Tabito. It appears that he died in 733 at the age of seventy-four. His works include a few Chinese compositions in verse and prose. They are notable for their philosophic and ethical strains. The poems on his children and on the sufferings of the poor are especially famous. He is also believed to be the compiler of the *Ruiju-Karin* (Forest of Classified Verses) which is no longer extant, but which is often mentioned in the Original Notes of the *Manyōshū*.

Takahashi Mushimaro (Early Nara Period) It is known that during the years 717–23, he was in the service of the provincial government of Hitachi, under Governor Fujiwara Umakai. Most likely he contributed not a little towards the making of the *Hitachi Fudoki* (Topographical Record of Hitachi), which was completed at that time. Specializing in legendary subjects such as Urashima, he possessed a distinctive style of his own.

Owari — (Early Nara Period) No biographical data.

Kamo Taruhito (Fujiwara–Early Nara Period) No biographical data.

Sena Gyōmon (Early Nara Period) Of Korean descent, he held an official post as Professor of Chinese Classics and was the recipient of imperial gifts, which were granted for the encouragement of learning. He also wrote Chinese poems, some of which are extant.

Tsuki — (Fujiwara Period) No biographical data.

Tanabé Sakimaro (Middle Nara Period) In 748 he went to Etchū as a messenger from the Minister of the Left, Tachibana Moroé, to the Governor of the Province, Ōtomo Yakamochi. He was then a court official connected with the imperial saké-brewery.

468

Wakamiya Ayumaro (Middle Nara Period)　No biographical data.

Kon Myōgun (Middle Nara Period)　The name is sometimes written Yo Myōgun.　Kon Myōgun was a man of Korean descent, and a retainer of Ōtomo Tabito.

Tsukan (Middle Nara Period)　A priest.　No biographical data.

Monk of the Gango-ji Temple　The Gango-ji was one of the ' Seven Great Temples of Nara,' and also one of the first Buddhist temples ever built in Japan, having been completed in 588.　Originally it stood on Makami Plain of Asuka, but was moved to Nara in 718.　The name of the monk is not known.

Kojima, a Young Woman of Tsukushi (Early Nara Period)　Evidently she lived in the city of the Dazaifu when Tabito was stationed there as Governor-General.

Ōyakemé, a Young Woman of Buzen (Late Nara Period) No biographical data.

Ato Tobira, a Young Woman (Late Nara Period)　No biographical data.

Taniha Ōmé, a Young Woman (Late Nara Period)　No biographical data.

Young Woman of Hitachi (Early Nara Period)　No biographical data.

Young Woman of Harima (Early Nara Period)　No biographical data.

Hozumi Oyu (Early Nara Period)　Assistant Director of the Board of Ceremonies in 718.　For some offence he was banished to the Island of Sado in 734, but allowed to return to Nara in 740. In 744 he was Assistant Director of the Imperial Property Bureau, and had in his charge the Kuni Palace during the Sovereign's absence.

Tachibana Moroé (684–757)　Descendant of the 30th Sovereign, the Emperor Bitatsu, he assumed the status of a subject and was given the surname of Tachibana in 736.　Minister of the Left in 743 ; and Governor-General of the Dazaifu in 746.

Ki Kiyohito (? –753)　At imperial command he compiled a national history of Japan in 714.　Together with Yamada Mikata and Yamanoé Okura he was made Tutor to the Crown Prince in 721.　Assistant Director of the Board of Palace Rites and Peerages and concurrently Professor of Literature in 741.

Fujii Moroai (Middle Nara Period)　Governor of Sagami in 747.

Kosé Natemaro (?-753) In 737 he was made the director of the office in charge of making Buddhist images. Grand Councillor of State in 749.

Ishikawa Toshitari (688–762) Descended from Takeshiuchi Sukuné. A great-grandson of Soga Murashi, Prime Minister. In 735 he became Governor of Izumo, and was awarded honours for his meritorious services. Appointed Governor-General of the Dazaifu in 753. A mortuary tablet, describing his career, was excavated in 1820.

Lord Ki (Middle Nara Period) In 730 he was Vice Governor-General of the Dazaifu under Ōtomo Tabito. His given name is not known, though he is sometimes identified as Ki Obito.

Sakiko of the Chō Family (Middle Nara Period) In 730 he was a government physician attached to the Dazaifu.

Tanabé Akiniwa (Middle Nara Period) A member of the suite of the embassy despatched to Shiragi in 736.

Yuki Yakamaro (Middle Nara Period) A member of the suite of the embassy despatched to Shiragi in 736. Died of the plague on the way.

Mibu Utamaro (Middle Nara Period) A member—third in rank—of the embassy despatched to Shiragi in the summer of 736. After a difficult voyage he returned to Nara in the autumn of the following year. Governor of Tajima in 750 ; and Director of the Bureau of Foreign Affairs and Buddhist Temples.

Fujii Kooyu (Middle Nara Period) A member of the embassy despatched to Shiragi in 736.

Frontier-Guards and Family (Late Nara Period) :—

Mononobé Akimochi from *Tōtōmi* Mononobé was the name of a clan in which military service was a hereditary profession.

Wakayamatobé Mumaro from *Tōtōmi* Sent from the family of a clerk in the provincial government.

Hasetsukabé Mamaro from *Tōtōmi*
Hasetsukabé Kuromasa from *Tōtōmi*
Mononobé Komaro from *Tōtōmi*
Hasetsukabé Hitomaro from *Sagami*
Mariko Ōmaro from *Sagami*
Udobé Ushimaro from *Suruga*
Sakatabé Obitomaro from *Suruga*
Tamatsukuribé Hiromé from *Suruga*
Akino Osamaro from *Suruga*

Hasetsukabé Inamaro from *Suruga*

Father of Kusakabé Minaka from *Kazusa*

Hasetsukabé Tori from *Kazusa*

Osakabé Chikuni from *Kazusa*

Mononobé Tatsu from *Kazusa*

Wakatoneribé Hirotari from *Hitachi*

Ōtoneribé Chifumi from *Hitachi*

Shidoribé Karamaro from *Hitachi*

Imamatsuribé Yosofu from *Shimousa*   A minor officer at the head of ten men.

Ōtabé Aramimi from *Shimotsuké*   A minor officer at the head of ten men.

Mononobé Mashima from *Shimotsuké*   A minor officer at the head of ten men.

Tsumori Okurusu from *Shimotsuké*

Hasetsukabé Taruhito from *Shimotsuké*

Kisakibé Isoshima from *Shimousa*

Kamutobé Kooshio from *Shinano*

Ōtomobé Fushimaro from *Kamitsuké*

Ujibé Kuromé   Wife of a frontier-guard from *Musashi*.

Kurahashibé Otomé   Wife of Mononobé Mané from *Musashi*.

Isonokami Otomaro (? –750)   Son of Isonokami Maro, Minister of the Left.   In 738 he was promoted to a high post in the government, but in the following year he was banished to Tosa Province because of a love affair.   Later, he received a pardon, and was appointed Senior Councillor of State and concurrently chief of administrative affairs of the court.   He was also a writer of Chinese verse, and it is said that there existed a collection in two books of his Chinese poems composed during his banishment.

Wife of Isonokami Otomaro   Presumably Kumé Wakamé who, it appears, was a lady attendant at the court.

II. CHRONOLOGICAL TABLE

A.D.	Emperors	Year of Reign	
479	Yūryaku	23	Death of Emperor Yūryaku.
588	Sushun	1	Gango-ji Temple completed.
593	Suiko*	1	Prince Shōtoku named Regent. Shitennō-ji at Naniwa built.
604		12	Constitution established by Prince Shōtoku.
607		15	Embassy, including students and monks, despatched to Sui Court. Hōryū-ji Temple built by Prince Shōtoku.
608		16	Embassy from Sui Court arrives; embassy to Sui Court despatched.
614		22	Embassy to Sui Court despatched.
620		28	A National History compiled by Prince Shōtoku.
622		30	Death of Prince Shōtoku.
628		36	Death of Empress Suiko.
630	Jomei	2	Embassy to T'ang Court despatched.
632		4	Embassy from T'ang Court arrives; monks return.
639		11	Monks return.
640		12	Students return.
641		13	Death of Emperor Jomei.
		Year of Era	
645	Kōtoku	Taika 1	Abdication of Empress Kōgyoku. Soga Emishi and his son Iruka killed. Taika era: for the first time the era is named.

* Empress

A.D.	Emperors	Year of Era	
646		2	Reform of Taika. Court removed from Asuka to Naniwa in Settsu.
653		Byakuchi 4	Embassy to T'ang Court despatched.
654		5	Embassy to T'ang Court despatched. Death of Emperor Kōtoku.
655	Saimei*	1	Embassy to Shiragi despatched. Accession of Empress Saimei at the Palace of Asuka.
659		5	Embassy to T'ang Court despatched.
661		7	Imperial fleet despatched to save Kudara; the Empress visits Kyūshū.
664	Tenji	3	Death of Empress Saimei. Frontier-guards posted in Tsushima, Iki and Tsukushi.
665		4	Embassy to T'ang Court despatched. Many people from Kudara naturalized.
667		6	Court removed to the Palace of Ōtsu in Ōmi.
668		7	Embassy to Shiragi despatched.
669		8	Death of Fujiwara Kamatari. Embassy to T'ang Court despatched.
670		9	Embassy to Shiragi despatched.
671		10	Death of Emperor Tenji.
672	Kōbun	1	War of Jinshin. Death of Emperor Kōbun.
673	Temmu	1	Court removed to the Palace of Kiyomihara at Asuka.
675		3	Embassy to Shiragi despatched.
676		4	Embassy to Shiragi despatched.
681		9	A National History compiled by imperial order.

A.D.	Emperors	Year of Era	
			Embassy to Shiragi despatched.
684		12	Embassy to Shiragi despatched.
686		Shuchō 1	Death of Emperor Temmu.
			Rebellion and death of Prince Ōtsu.
687	Jitō*	1	Embassy to Shiragi despatched.
689		3	Death of Crown Prince Kusakabé.
693		7	Embassy to Shiragi despatched.
694		8	Court removed to the Palace of Fujiwara.
695		9	Embassy to Shiragi despatched.
696		10	Death of Prince Takechi.
697	Mommu	1	Abdication of Empress Jitō.
700		4	Embassy to Shiragi despatched.
701		Taihō 1	Embassy to T'ang Court despatched.
			Code of Taihō promulgated.
702		2	Death of ex-Empress Jitō.
703		3	Embassy to Shiragi despatched.
704		Keiun 1	Embassy to Shiragi despatched.
706		3	Embassy to Shiragi despatched.
707		4	Death of Emperor Mommu.
710	Gemmyō*	Wadō 3	Court removed to Nara.
712		5	*Kojiki* (Records of Ancient Matters) Completed.
			Embassy to Shiragi despatched.
713		6	*Fudoki* (Topographical Records) ordered to be compiled by provinces.
715		Reiki 1	Death of Prince Hozumi.
			Abdication of Empress Gemmyō.
716	Genshō*	2	Embassy to T'ang Court despatched.
			Death of Prince Shiki.
718		Yōrō 2	Embassy to Shiragi despatched.
			Gango-ji Temple removed to Nara.
			Code of Taihō revised by Fujiwara Fubito and others by imperial order.

A.D.	Emperors	Year of Era		
719			3	Embassy to Shiragi despatched.
720			4	*Nihonshoki* (Chronicles of Japan) completed.
721			5	Death of ex-Empress Gemmyō.
722			6	Embassy to Shiragi despatched.
723			7	Death of Prince Yamakuma.
				The monk Manzei despatched to Tsukushi to build the Kanzeon-ji Temple.
724	Shōmu	Jinki	1	Abdication of Empress Genshō.
				Embassy to Shiragi despatched.
727			4	Embassy from Po-hai arrives for the first time.
729		Tempyō	1	Fujiwara Kōmyō-shi proclaimed Empress.
				Prince Nagaya put to death by imperial order.
731			3	Death of Ōtomo Tabito.
732			4	Embassy to Shiragi despatched.
733			5	Embassy to T'ang Court despatched.
735			7	Death of Prince Toneri.
				'Brahmin Prelate' arrives.
736			8	Embassy to Shiragi despatched.
				Prince Kazuraki granted the surname of Tachibana.
739			11	Embassy from Po-hai arrives.
740			12	Court removed to the Palace of Kuni.
				Rebellion of Fujiwara Hirotsugu.
				Embassy to Shiragi despatched.
741			13	Kokubun-ji (provincial temples) ordered to be built in provinces.
744			16	Death of Prince Azumi.
745			17	Court removed to Nara.

A.D.	Emperors	Year of Era	
748		20	Construction begun of the Great Buddha at the Tōdai-ji Temple. Death of Prince Kadobé. Death of ex-Empress Genshō.
749	Kōken*	Tempyō-Kampō, Tempyō-Shōhō 1	Great Buddha completed at the Tōdai-ji Temple. Abdication of Emperor Shōmu. Gold offered from Michinoku for gilding the Tōdai-ji Buddha.
751		3	The *Kaifūsō* completed.
752		4	Embassy to T'ang Court despatched. Embassy from Po-hai arrives.
753		5	Embassy to Shiragi despatched.
754		6	Ganjin, a monk from T'ang Court, arrives.
756		8	Death of ex-Emperor Shōmu.
757		Tempyō-Hōji 1	Death of Prince Funado. Death of Tachibana Moroé.
758	Junnin	2	Embassy from Po-hai arrives. Abdication of Empress Kōken.
759		3	Embassy from Po-hai arrives.
760		4	Death of Empress Kōmyō. Death of 'Brahmin Prelate.'
762		6	Embassy from Po-hai arrives.
764		8	Rebellion of Emi Oshikatsu. Abdication of Emperor Junnin.
765	Shōtoku*	Tempyō-Jingo 1	Death of ex-Emperor Junnin.
770	Kōnin	Hōki 1	Death of Empress Shōtoku.
771		2	Embassy from Po-hai arrives.
773		4	Embassy from Po-hai arrives.

477

A.D.	Emperors	Year of Era	
776		7	Embassy from Po-hai arrives.
777		8	Embassy to T'ang Court despatched.
778		9	Embassy from Po-hai arrives.
779		10	Embassy from Po-hai arrives.
781		Ten-ō 1	Abdication of Emperor Kōnin.
784	Kammu	Enryaku 3	Court removed to Nagaoka in Yamashiro.
785		4	Death of Ōtomo Yakamochi.
794		13	Court removed to Heian-kyō (Kyōto) in Yamashiro.

III. FINDING LIST

Poems in the order as they are found in the original work and their numbers according to the *Kokka Taikan* (*K. T.*) are given in the left column, and their corresponding numbers in the present translation (*our number*) in the right column.

K.T.	Our number	K.T.	Our number	K.T.	Our number
		42	82	104	40
(Book I)		43	73	105	54
1	1	45	83	106	55
2	2	46	84	107	48
3	4	47	85	108	49
4	5	48	86	115	60
5	23	49	87	116	61
6	24	50	206	117	242
8	25	51	51	118	243
13	9	52	207	123	198
14	10	53	208	124	199
15	11	57	203	125	200
16	26	58	204	126	178
17	27	61	205	127	179
18	28	63	603	129	177
22	202	64	52	131	88
23	62	71	195	132	89
24	63	75	260	133	90
25	38	76	231	135	91
28	41	77	232	136	92
29	74	79	797	137	93
30	75	80	798	140	136
31	76			141	21
32	185	(Book II)		142	22
33	186	85	12	147	16
36	77	86	13	148	17
37	78	87	14	149	18
38	79	88	15	150	37
39	80	95	32	151	35
40	81	103	39	152	36

K.T.	Our number	K.T.	Our number	K.T.	Our number
153	19	211	110	270	187
155	30	212	111	271	188
159	42	217	112	273	189
160	43	218	113	274	190
161	44	219	114	275	191
163	56	220	115	278	279
164	57	221	116	287	724
165	58	222	117	288	725
166	59	223	135	296	280
167	94	224	137	297	281
168	95	225	138	303	130
169	96	230	308	304	131
170	97	231	309	305	192
171	209	232	310	306	254
176	210			310	262
177	211	(Book III)		315	354
181	212	235	118	316	355
184	213	236	45	317	567
185	214	237	46	318	568
186	215	238	182	319	651
188	216	239	119	320	652
189	217	240	120	321	653
194	98	242	50	322	569
195	99	250	121	323	570
196	100	251	122	324	571
197	101	252	123	325	572
198	102	253	124	327	714
199	103	254	125	328	282
200	104	255	126	329	558
201	105	256	127	330	559
204	193	257	678	331	356
205	194	258	679	336	715
207	106	259	680	337	604
208	107	264	128	338	357
209	108	265	183	339	358
210	109	266	129	340	359

K.T.	Our number	K.T.	Our number	K.T.	Our number
341	360	420	67	475	418
342	361	421	68	476	419
343	362	422	69	477	420
344	363	423	64	478	421
345	364	424	65	479	422
346	365	425	66	480	423
347	366	428	132	481	323
348	367	431	575	482	324
349	368	432	576	483	325
350	369	433	577		
351	716	434	799	(Book IV)	
364	283	438	370	485	6
365	284	440	371	486	7
368	306	442	800	487	8
369	307	443	561	488	29
371	263	444	562	489	31
372	573	445	563	496	133
373	574	446	372	497	134
375	246	448	373	500	201
377	247	449	374	505	349
379	386	450	375	506	350
380	387	451	376	509	273
381	718	452	377	510	274
382	271	453	378	514	351
383	272	455	713	521	722
387	712	460	388	527	390
388	890	461	389	532	385
389	891	462	409	534	255
390	245	464	410	535	256
396	313	465	411	541	267
412	257	466	412	543	285
415	20	467	413	544	286
416	47	468	414	545	287
417	70	469	415	546	288
418	71	470	416	547	289
419	72	474	417	548	290

K.T.	Our number	K.T.	Our number	K.T.	Our number
549	801	723	397	888	622
555	379	724	398	889	623
557	601	728	428	890	624
559	564	731	557	891	625
560	565	741	429	892	626
571	560			893	627
573	383	(Book V)		894	628
574	384	793	380	895	629
594	314	794	605	896	630
596	315	795	606	897	631
600	316	796	607	898	632
602	317	797	608	899	633
603	318	798	609	900	634
604	319	799	610	901	635
605	320	800	611	902	636
607	321	801	612	903	637
608	322	802	613	904	638
619	391	803	614	905	639
620	392	804	615	906	640
632	248	805	616		
650	566	813	617	(Book VI)	
651	393	814	618	907	291
652	394	815	732	908	292
661	395	822	733	909	293
670	252	829	734	913	326
671	253	847	735	914	327
688	396	848	736	917	578
694	269	852	737	918	579
695	270	853	793	919	580
709	719	854	794	920	294
710	720	855	795	921	295
711	721	859	796	922	296
715	424	871	802	923	581
718	425	880	619	924	582
719	426	886	620	925	583
722	427	887	621	926	584

K.T.	Our number	K.T.	Our number	K.T.	Our number
927	585	1005	597	1088	140
928	297	1006	598	1089	820
929	298	1009	236	1091	894
930	299	1016	333	1096	895
931	328	1018	717	1121	896
932	329	1019	805	1129	897
933	586	1020		1138	898
934	587	1021	806	1154	899
935	300	1022	807	1161	900
936	301	1023	808	1182	901
937	302	1034	556	1232	882
938	588	1042	259	1235	883
939	589	1045	809	1263	884
940	590	1047	687	1264	885
941	591	1048	688	1265	886
942	592	1049	689	1269	141
943	593	1050	690	1271	142
944	594	1051	691	1275	150
945	595	1052	692	1281	151
948	803	1053	693	1295	902
949	804	1054	694	1317	903
956	381	1055	695	1336	904
968	382	1056	696	1369	905
971	649	1057	697	1411	906
972	650	1058	698		
973	234	1062	699	(Book VIII)	
974	235	1063	700	1418	53
978	641	1064	701	1421	677
979	399	1065	702	1424	599
985	249	1066	703	1427	600
988	258	1067	704	1435	264
989	250			1442	275
994	430	(Book VII)		1444	268
995	400	1068	139	1453	303
996	602	1082	892	1454	304
1001	596	1086	893	1455	305

K.T.	Our number	K.T.	Our number	K.T.	Our number
1456	334	1739	655	1811	676
1457	335	1740	656		
1460	546	1741	657	(Book X)	
1461	547	1742	658	1812	146
1462	548	1743	659	1814	147
1463	549	1747	660	1821	907
1479	431	1748	661	1830	908
1494	432	1753	662	1840	909
1500	401	1754	663	1855	910
1507	433	1755	664	1873	911
1508	434	1756	665	1879	819
1509	435	1757	666	1883	912
1511	3	1758	667	1884	913
1520	642	1759	668	1885	914
1521	643	1760	669	1917	915
1522	644	1764	817	1937	888
1537	645	1765	818	1938	889
1538	646	1766	181	1984	916
1552	251	1777	723	1990	917
1572	436	1780	670	1995	918
1602	437	1781	671	2015	148
1622	408	1785	311	2041	919
1629	438	1786	312	2052	920
1630	439	1790	810	2065	921
1656	404	1791	811	2089	922
1657	405	1800	705	2090	923
1658	240	1801	706	2091	924
		1802	707	2160	925
(Book IX)		1803	708	2177	926
1665	33	1804	709	2240	149
1666	34	1805	710	2298	927
1682	143	1806	711	2303	928
1699	144	1807	672	2310	929
1701	145	1808	673	2336	930
1714	218	1809	674	2342	931
1738	654	1810	675		

K.T.	Our number	K.T.	Our number	K.T.	Our number
		2645	946	3241	968
(Book XI)		2651	947	3242	969
2352	152	2653	948	3245	970
2355	153	2661	949	3246	971
2357	154	2667	950	3248	972
2364	887	2695	951	3249	973
2368	155	2824	863	3250	974
2375	156	2825	864	3251	975
2376	157	2838	957	3252	976
2382	158			3253	175
2386	159	(Book XII)		3254	176
2401	160	2855	172	3255	977
2418	161	2875	940	3256	978
2419	162	2887	941	3260	979
2421	163	2912	942	3261	980
2425	164	2998	952	3268	229
2433	165	3004	953	3269	230
2442	166	3028	954	3270	981
2491	167	3056	955	3271	982
2495	168	3096	956	3272	983
2496	169	3117	865	3273	984
2497	170	3118	866	3280	985
2498	171			3295	986
2513	173	(Book XIII)		3296	987
2514	174	3222	958	3299	988
2517	932	3223	959	3303	989
2526	933	3224	960	3304	990
2531	934	3227	961	3305	867
2546	935	3228	962	3306	868
2554	936	3229	963	3307	869
2572	937	3232	964	3308	870
2574	938	3233	965	3314	871
2578	939	3234	821	3315	872
2641	943	3235	822	3316	873
2642	944	3239	966	3317	874
2644	945	3240	967	3318	875

K.T.	Our number	K.T.	Our number	K.T.	Our number
3319	876	3460	851	3690	760
3320	877	3480	852	3691	761
3321	878	3510	853	3692	762
3322	879	3514	854	3693	763
3324	219	3532	855	3724	339
3325	220	3546	856	3733	340
3327	221	3567	857	3748	341
3328	222	3568	858	3750	342
3329	991	3569	859	3753	343
3331	992	3570	860	3758	344
3332	993			3767	345
3339	682	(Book XV)		3772	346
3340	683	3578	738	3774	347
3341	684	3579	739	3776	348
3342	685	3580	740		
3343	686	3581	741	(Book XVI)	
3344	994	3586	742	3786	823
3345	995	3587	743	3787	824
		3594	744	3791	223
(Book XIV)		3613	745	3792	224
3350	835	3615	746	3793	225
3351	836	3623	747	3794	226
3386	837	3624	748	3795	227
3387	838	3625	276	3797	228
3393	839	3626	277	3803	825
3399	840	3627	749	3806	826
3400	841	3628	750	3807	814
3414	842	3629	751	3809	827
3421	843	3638	752	3811	330
3422	844	3644	753	3812	331
3425	845	3648	754	3813	332
3438	846	3666	755	3816	244
3439	847	3669	756	3820	265
3440	848	3676	757	3824	184
3452	849	3688	758	3835	815
3459	850	3689	759	3836	681

K.T.	Our number	K.T.	Our number	K.T.	Our number
3840	337	3969	447	4102	473
3841	338	3970	448	4103	474
3846	880	3971	449	4104	475
3847	881	3972	450	4105	476
3849	828	3978	451	4106	477
3851	996	3979	452	4107	478
3852	997	3980	453	4108	479
3853	440	3981	454	4109	480
3854	441	3982	455	4110	481
3856	266	3985	456·	4111	482
3858	998	3986	457	4112	483
3859	999	3987	458	4113	484
3861	647	4000	550	4114	485
3865	648	4001	551	4115	486
3878	829	4002	552	4122	487
3880	830	4003	553	4123	488
3885	831	4004	554	4124	489
3886	832	4005	555		
3889	1000	4006	459	(Book XIX)	
		4007	460	4139	490
(Book XVII)		4011	461	4140	491
3897	816	4012	462	4150	492
3922	726	4013	463	4153	493
3923	727	4014	464	4154	494
3925	728	4015	465	4155	495
3926	729	4029	466	4160	499
3940	352			4161	500
3942	353	(Book XVIII)		4162	501
3957	496	4081	406	4164	502
3958	497	4083	407	4165	503
3959	498	4086	467	4166	504
3962	442	4094	468	4167	505
3963	443	4095	469	4168	506
3964	444	4096	470	4169	507
3965	445	4097	471	4170	508
3966	446	4101	472	4199	509

K.T.	Our number	K.T.	Our number	K.T.	Our number
4206	510	4292	523	4374	784
4211	511			4375	785
4212	512	(Book XX)		4377	786
4214	513	4293	233	4383	787
4215	514	4321	764	4385	788
4216	515	4322	765	4398	530
4220	402	4323	766	4399	531
4221	403	4325	767	4400	532
4227	196	4327	768	4402	789
4228	197	4328	769	4406	790
4236	833	4330	770	4408	533
4237	834	4331	524	4409	534
4240	241	4332	525	4410	535
4245	812	4333	526	4411	536
4246	813	4337	771	4412	537
4247	336	4342	772	4417	791
4254	516	4343	773	4420	792
4255	517	4344	774	4425	861
4260	180	4346	775	4431	862
4262	278	4347	776	4465	538
4264	237	4352	777	4466	539
4265	238	4357	778	4467	540
4266	518	4358	779	4468	541
4267	519	4360	527	4469	542
4272	520	4361	528	4470	543
4273	730	4362	529	4486	239
4274	731	4364	780	4514	544
4284	261	4370	781	4516	545
4290	521	4372	782		
4291	522	4373	783		

INDEX

Names of poets are printed in bold type.   The references
are to pages.

A

abalone, 152, 153, 236
Abé, Lady, 115
Abé Okina, 112
Abo, God of, 6n
Ajifu (Field), 102; Palace of, 232
Ainus, 81n
Akahito, see **Yamabé**
Akashi, 49n
Akashi, Straits of, lxii, 49, 194
Aki, Prince, 88, 89
Aki, plain of, 30
Akino Osamaro, 252
Akitsu, 28, 192
Akitsu-kami, xliii
Alnus japonica, 67n
Ama-no-Inukai Okamaro, 197
Amaterasu Ōmikami, xxxix, 47n
Anacreontic verses, xlv
animals, lxiii
Anonymous, 23, 67, 87, 128, 259,
264, 271
*Anthologie de la Littérature Japonaise
des Origines au 20ᵉ Siècle,* lxxix
Anthologie Japonaise, lxxix
Arao, 213
Arima, Mount, 124
Arima, Prince, 8
Arima Hot Springs, lii
asagao, 213n
Asaka, 265
Asaka, Prince, 132
Ashigara, 233, 254

Ashiki, 185
Ashinoya, 224
Ashinoya, Maiden of, 234
Aso River, 280
Aston, G., lxxix
Asuka, xxxiv, lx, lxi, 36, 37
Asuka and Fujiwara Periods, lxxi
Asuka, Palace of, 20, 189
Asuka, Princess, 37
Ato Tobira, 238
Atsumi, Prince, 91
auchi, lxv
Awaji, 48n, 49n, 94, 102, 193,
245, 289
aya, xlviii
ayu, 132, 147, 259
ayui (leg-ties), xlix
Aya District, 9
Ayuchi, 63, 308
Azuma, 93, 234
Azuma Uta, 278
Azumi Mikuni, 257
azusa, 4n

B

bamboo, lxiv, 172
Bamboo-Cutter, Old, 74
bead-tree, 199
bed, sweep the, 301, 310
Beggar Songs, 275
Beowulf, xiii
Bigamy, 154
Biwa, Lake, lxi, 5n, 50n
Bonneau, G., lxxx

Bosom-soothing Stones, 202
Boys' Festival, liv
boxwood, 168, 239
Brahmin Prelate, xxxvi, 91n
bu, 202
Buddha, xliv, 200 ; Way of, 179
Buddha's Foot Stone Poem, xx
Buddhism, xiii, xxx, xxxviii, xliv
bush-clover, 67, 161, 212, 229n, 236, 249, and *passim*

C

Cædmon, xiii
camellia, lxiv, 302
Central Asia, xxxi
Chamberlain, B. H., lxxix
cherry-flowers, 142, 284, 293
Cherry-Flower Maid, lxviii
Chigami, Sanu, lvii, see Sanu
Chikuma River, lxi, 279
Chikuzen, 202, 213
China, xxix, xxx, xlvi, 96, 103, 112, 160, 197, 207, 264, 265 ; embassy to, lviii, 264
Chinu, 167, 224
Chinese literature, lxix
chisa-tree, 155
chōka, xx
Chuangtsu, xlvii
Chūrō, 60
Chu Tsu, xix
cicada, lxiii, 135
Classical Poetry of the Japanese, The, lxxix
clothing, xlviii
coiffeur, xlix
'Collection of Ancient Poems,' xvii, 287
Confucianism, xiii, xxix, xxxviii, xliv, xlvi
Confucius, xiv
cormorant-fishing, 29, 147

crab, 276
crane, 64, 103, 176, 189, 191 and *passim*
cricket, 87, 296
crinum, 51
cryptomeria, lxv, 54
cuckoo, 135, 136, 143, 146, 164, 165, 220, 288
Cynewulf, xiii

D

Daihangan, 247
Dazaifu, xxxvi, 50n, 118, 119, 185, 213
Dialogue poem, lvii, 58, 283
dew-drops, 137
Dichtergrüsse aus dem fernen Osten, lxxix
Dickins, F. V., lxxix
divination, xli
Divorce, Seven Causes permitting, 153 ; Three Cases prohibiting, 154
Divine Wind, 21, 271
domestic animals, lxiii
domesticated birds, lxiii
dragon, lxiii
Dragon God, 17
dream, xli

E

Early Palace Style, xxiv
Eastland, lviii, 93, 151, 173
Eastland Poems, xxv
Echizen, 49n
eel, 138
eighty, 244, 259, 304
eighty clans, 168, 261
elixir, lxviii, 242, 306
elm, lxv
Emishi, xxxii
Etchū, 115, 153

490

evil spirits, xli

F

Feast of the Blue Horse, liv
Feast of New-tasting, lv, see *Ni-inamé-sai*
five virtues, 199
Florenz, K., lxxix
folk-song, xiv, lxxiii
foot-divination, xli
foot-wear, xlix
fox, 62
frontier-guard, xiv, lviii, 173n, 176
Fuji, Mount, lx, 187, 215, 301
Fujié Bay, 49
Fujii, 69
Fujii Bay, 192
Fujii Moroai, 240
Fujiwara Fusamaé, 82n
Fujiwara Fusasaki, 65
Fujiwara Hirotsugu, 112
Fujiwara Kamatari, xxxiii, 10, 13
Fujiwara Kiyokawa, 83, 84
Fujiwara, Lady, 17
Fujiwara, Palace of, 20, 67, 69
Fujiwara Maro, 124
Fujiwara Period, xiii
Fujiwara Sukunamaro, 251
Fujiwara Umakai, 82n, 214
Fujiwara Yatsuka, 211
Fujiwara Yoritsuné, lxxv
Fukaé, 202
Fuki, Lady, 66
Funado, Prince, 90
fur, xlviii
Furu Tamuké, 61
Furuhi, 210
Fusé Hitonushi, 252
Fusé Lake, lxi, 166
Fushimi, 53

Futagami Mountain, 22, 144, 145, 148
Futagi Palace, 230, 231
Fuwa, 39, 254

G

Gamō, 277n
Gango-ji Temple, Monk of the, 237
Gemmyō, Empress, xxiv, 81
'Genryaku Comparative Texts,' lxxiv
Genshō, Empress, 81, 88n
Geschichte der japanischen National-literatur, lxxx
Go Dan-ochi, Wife of, 66
God's Wind, 40
Graeco-Roman civilization, xxxi
Great Buddha, xxxvii
Great Purification, lv
grebes, 198, 245
Greek Anthology, The, xv
guide-knot, 22

H

Haétsuki (River), lxi
hagi, 67n, 74, 129, 229, 264, see bush-clover
haiku, xxiii, lxxviii
hakama, xlviii
Hakoya, 313n
Han Empire, xxxi
Hanishi Mitōshi, 197
haniwa, lxx
Haniyasu, 3n, 41, 69, 226n
hanka (envoy), xx
harai, xl, see purification
Harima Province, 49n 21n,
Harima, a Young Woman of, 239
hart, 275
Harvest Festival, 84n, 241

Hasetsukabé Hitomaro, 251
Hasetsukabé Inamaro, 253
Hasetsukabé Kuromasa, 251
Hasetsukabé Mamaro, 250
Hasetsukabé Taruhito, 256
Hasetsukabé Tatsumaro, 185
Hasetsukabé Tori, 253
Hashibito Oyu, 4
Hata-otomé, 277
Hata Iwataké, 150
Hatsusé, lxi, 24, 30, 51, 312
Hatsusebé, Princess, 36
hawk(s), lxiii, 147, 161
Hayahito, 58
Hayato, xxxv
Heavenly River, lv, 34, 212, 295
Heguri, Lady, 115
Heian Period, xvi
hemp, xlviii, 223, 234, and *passim*
Hi, 57
Hijikata, Maiden of, 51
Hikitsu, 247
Hikuma Plain, 67
Himeshima, 260
Hinamishi, Prince, 31, 34
Hiraga Motoyoshi, lxxviii
hiré (scarf), xlix
Hirokawa, Princess, 92
Hirumé, Goddess, 34
hisagi-tree, 192
Hitachi, xxxv, 278
Hitachi, a Young Woman of, 239
hitodama, 314n
Hitomaro, see Kakinomoto
'Hitomaro Collection,' xvii, xxiv, 52
Holland, lxxviii
Homer, xxii
Horié Canal, lxi
horse stumbling, xli, 97
Hozumi, Prince, 22, 23, 85

Hozumi Oyu, 240, 305n
Hsuantsung, xxxiv

I

Ichihara, Prince, 89
Ichihi Ford, 62
ichihi-tree, 275
Ié-no-shima, 94
Ikago, Mount, 305
Ikaho, 279, 280
Ikeda—, 113
Iki, 248
Ikoma, lxi
Ikuji, 89, 133
Ikusa, Prince, 9
Imaki, Prince, 92
Imamatsuribé Yosofu, 255
Imizu (River), lxi, 146, 160
Imo-Sé Mountains, 98
Imperial House, xxviii, xxxii, xliii, lv
Imperial Rescript, 150, 154, 197
Inaba Province, xxvi
Inabizuma, 94
Inami, 6, 50, 193
Inamizuma, 194
India, xxxi
Inland Sea, lxii
introductory verse, xxi, lxx
Inukai Kiyohito, 256
Iohara, 96
Irago (Island), 23
iris, lxv
Iruka, xxxii
Isaniwa, hill of, 188
Isaya (River of Doubt), 5
Isé, 23, 30, 88, 271
Isé, Shrine of, 21, 40n, 66
Ishikawa Kimiko, 96, 239
Ishikawa, Lady, 19, 59
Ishikawa Taruhito, 121, 260
Ishikawa Toshitari, 241

Isonokami Otomaro, 104, 239, 262
Isonokami Shrine, 25n
Isonokami Yakatsugu, 90
Itō, Sachio, lxxviii
Iwamaro, 138
Iwami, xxxv, 31, 33, 51
Iwa-no-himé, Empress, 6
Iwaré, 23, 73 ; Iwaré Pond, 19
Iwashiro, 8
Iwata, Prince, 23, 24
Iwata Field, 248
Iyo, lii, 188
Izanagi, 50n
Izanami, 50n
Izumi (River), lxi, 68, 162, 305
Izumo, xxxv, 6n, 90

J

January 7th, liv
January 15th, liv
January 16th, liv
Japanese morality, lviii
Japanese Poetry, lxxix
jewelled broom, liv
Jimmu, Emperor, 27
Jingu, Empress, xxix, 203
Jinki (era), 98, 99, 213, 219n, 260
Jinshin, War of, 27n, 39n, 60
Jitō, Empress, xxiv, 17, 19, 20, 30, 39n, 67
Jomei, Emperor, xxv, 3, 4, 9
joshi (introductory verse), xxi
juniper, 119
Junnin, Emperor, 84

K

Kachinu, plain of, 63
Kadobé, Prince, 90
kagai, lx, 222
Kagami, Princess, 12
kagerō, 43, 228

Kagu, Mount (Kagu-yama), lx, 3, 5, 18, 41, 54, 69, 226, 290
Kahara Temple, 274
Kaifūsō, xlix
Kaiyuan (era), xiii
kake kotoba (pivot-word), xxi
kakibé, xxvii, xxviii
Kakinomoto Hitomaro, xx, xxiv, xxxvi, lxxi, 27
Kako River, 49n
Kamako, xxxii
Kami, hill of, 189
Kamiichi, 89
Kamioka, 18
Kamishima, 227
Kamitsuké(nu), 96, 279
Kamitsukenu Suruga, 257
Kamo Taruhito, 226
Kamochi Masazumi, lxxvi
Kamokimi, 67
Kamo-yama, 51
Kamunabi, Mount, lx, lxi, 77, 189, 303, and *passim*
Kamunabi River, 91
Kamutobé Kooshio, 256
kana, xviii
Kanamura, see **Kasa**
' Kanamura Collection,' xvii, 104
kao-bana, 138
kao-dori (*k.*-bird), 190, 229
Kara, 75, 96, 245, 248, 275
Karadomari, 247
Karani Island, 194
Karasaki (Cape), 14, 27, 33, 305
Kariji, Lake, 48
Karma, xlv
Karu, Prince, 30
Karu, pond of, 85
Kasa Kanamura, 97, 104
'Kasa Kanamura Collection,' xvii, 104
Kasa, Lady, 106

Kasé, 230, 231
Kashihara, 27, 179
Kashiko, 263
Kashima, Shrine of, xl, 254
Kashimané, 274
Kashiwadebé, 260
Kasuga (Hill), lxi
Kasuga Plain (or Field), lix, lxiv, 124, 190
Kasuga Shrine, 84
Katakai River, 183
Katori Nahiko, lxxviii
Katsumata, 266
'Katsura MS.', lxxiv, lxxvii
Kauchi, Prince, 26
Kawachi, 218
Kawashima, Prince, 36n
Kazahaya, 244
Kazuraki, Prince, 82, 266
Kazurako, lxviii
Kehi, 49n
Keichū, lxxv
Kei-no, 49n
Keiun, 20
Ki, 241
Ki (Province), 13, 98, 191, see Kii
Ki Kiyohito, 240
Ki, Lady, 181
Ki, Princess, 85
Kibi Province, 44
Kii, lii, lxii, 61n, and *passim*, see Ki (Province)
kin, 202
Kinohé, 37, 39n, 73
Kisa (River), 116
Kisakibé Isoshima, 256
Kiyomi, Cape, 96
Kiyomi Palace, 35
Kiyomihara, 60n
Klaproth, lxxviii
Kofu, 202

Kogi, lxiii, lxiv, see *Manyōshū Kogi*
Kōgyoku, Empress, xxxii, 4
Kohata, 7
Kōhon Manyōshū, lxxvii
Kojiki, xvi
Kojima, 121, 238
Kokashū, xvii
Kōken, Empress, 83, 174n
Kokinshū, xiii, lxxiv, lxxx
Kokin Wakashū, xiii
Kokka Taikan, xv
Koma, 75, 296
Kōmyō, Empress, 84
Konkōmyō-gyō, xliv
Kon Myōgun, 236
konote-gashiwa, 227n
Korea, xxv, xxviii, xxix, and *passim*
Kosé, 68, 286
Kosé Natemaro, 241
Kosé Sukunamaro, 111
Koshi, xxxv, 105, 128, 141, 157, and *passim*
koto, 91, 140, 274, 276, 290
kotoagé, 59n
kotodama, 59n
Kudara, King of, xxix
Kudara Plain, 41
Kukuri, 306
Kumaki Sea, 274
Kumanu, 51, 195
Kuni, li, 132, 230
Kuni-no-miyatsuko, 250
Kurahashibé Aramushi, 257
Kurahashibé Otomé, 257
Kuramochi —, Wife of, 110
Kuramochi Chitosé, 109
Kusakabé, Prince, 30n
Kusakabé Minaka, Father of, 253
kushiro, xlix
kuzu vine, xlviii, 213, 261

494

Kyōto, 7n, 12n
Kyūshū, xxxv, xxxvi, lviii, 50n,
    and *passim*

L

Lady of the Court, 14
Land-allotment Law, xxxii
Laotsu, xlvii
lark, 172
leg-ties, 55, see *ayui*
Lespedeza, xlviii, 67
Li Po, xiii
Liang, xxxi
lily, lxv, 158
Lopu, 258
Lorenzen, Alfred, lxxx
lotus, 266
love poems, lxxii

M

magical spells, xli
Makami Plain, 39
Makimuku, lx, 53
makura kotoba (pillow-word), xxi
Mallotus japonicus, 192
Mama of Katsushika, 190, 223, 279
Manchuria, xxxvi
mandarin-ducks, li, 57
Manners and customs, xlvii ff.
Manu, 106
Manyō Daishōki, lxxv
manyō-gana, xviii
Manyōshū, xiii, xv, lxvii, lxxiii,
    lxxvi, 61n, and *passim*; Com-
    pilation of, xv ff.; Language
    of, lxix ff.; Translation of,
    lxxviii ff.
Manyōshū Kogi, lxxvi, see *Kogi*
Manyōshū Kenkyū Nempō, lxxvii
Manyōshū Ryakugé, lxxvi
Manzei, 122, 237
March 3rd, liv

Mariko Ōmaro, 251
Masaoka, Shiki, lxxviii
*Masterpieces of Japanese Poetry
    Ancient and Modern*, lxxx
Matokata, xxii, 67
Matsuchi, 263
Matsuho, 49n
Matsura (River), lxi, 258
Matsura, Maidens of, lxviii
May 5th, liv
medicine hunt, liv, 275
Meiji era, lxxviii
melon, 200
Mercurialis leiocarpa, xlviii, 218n
metempsychosis, xlv
Michinoku, 107n, 150, 152
Mifuné, Mount, 20, 99, 109
Miho Bay, lxii, 96
Mika-no-hara, 99, 132n
Mikasa, lxi, 190, 291
Mikata Shami, 65
Mikawa, 23n, 67
Mimana (in Korea), 261n
Mimiga, 17
Miminashi, Mount, lx, 5, 69
Mimoro, 77
Mimoro, Mount, 302, 303
mina, 74n
Minabé, Princess, 81
Minamoto Sanetomo, lxxvii
Minamoto Shitagō, lxxiv
Minu, Prince, 73
Minu Province, 184
Minumé, 48, 119, 233, 245, 289
Mirror Mountain, 12, 26
miru, 33
Misaka, 256
Miscanthus sinensis, lxv, 137
Mishima Field, 148
misogi, xl, lv
Mitsu, lxii, 93, 197, 244, and
    passim

Miwa, lx, 11, 52n, 61
Miyaké, 222, 310
Miyamori, Asatarō, lxxx
Mizuki, 121
mo, xlviii, 30n
Mommu, Emperor, xxv, 20, 64
Mononobé Akimochi, 250
Mononobé Komaro, 251
Mononobé Mané, 257
Mononobé Mashima, 255
Mononobé Tatsu, 253
Moon God, 86, 87
Moroé, see **Tachibana**
Muko Bay, 243
mulberry, lxiv, 264, 278, and
  passim
Munakatabé Tsumaro, 213
Muro, spa of, lxii, 8n
Mushimaro, see **Takahashi**
'Mushimaro Collection,' xvii, 215

N

Nabari, 26
Naga, Prince, 48
Naga Okimaro, 61, 67
Nagahama, 149
Nagai, 244
Nagara, Palace of, 101
Nagato, 244
Nagaya, Prince, 89
Nago, 155
Naka, 46
Naka-no-ōé, Prince, xxxii
Nakatomi, clan of, xxxii
Nakatomi Yakamori, xxv, lvii,
  113
Naniwa, li, lx, lxi, 95, 175
Naniwa, Palace of, 20, 101, 232
nanoriso, 94n
Nara, xxxiv, li, 11, 97, 185, 228,
  259, 264, and *passim*
Nara Period, xiii, xvi, xxiii, xxxvi,

lxxi, and *passim*
Naruto, 246
Natsumi, 86
Nature, Outlook on, lix ff.
Nether World, 211, 224
New Year's Day, liii, 181, 240
'night-thrush,' 9, 207, see *nué*
Nigitazu, 10, 189
Nihonshoki, xvi, 28n, 66n
Niikawa, 182
Niinamé-sai, xl, 84n
Niitabé, Prince, 266
Ninnō-gyō, xliv
Nintoku, Emperor, xxiv, 6,
  174n
Nirvana, 274
Nirvana Sutra, 57n
nishiki, xlviii
Niu, Mount, 304
Niu, Prince, 24
norito, xl
nué, lxiii, 9n, see 'night-thrush'
Nujima, 48, 193, 194
Nukada, Princess, lxxiii, 10, 13
nusa, xxxix, 263

O

ōbarai, liv
Ochinu, plain of, 36, 37
Odai, Prince, 91
Ogami (River), lxi
Ogura Mountain, 3, 219
Ōhara, 17
Oharida, 308
Ohatsusé Mountains, 273
Ōjin, Emperor, 85n
Okada, Tetsuzō, lxxx
Okamoto-no-miya, 4n
Ōkaru, 42n, 53
Okazaki, Tōmitsu, lxxx
Okinaga Kunishima, 254
Okiso Mountains, 306

Okisomé Azumabito, 64
Ōku, Princess, lvi, lxxiii, 21
Ōkumé-nushi, 151
Okura, see Yamanoé
omens, 7n
Omi, Prince, 23
Ōmi, 5, 8, 11, 22, 193, and *passim*
Ōmiwa Okimori, 113
Ōnamuchi, 154
Ono Imoko, xxx
Ono Oyu, 97
Ōnu, 149, 199
Onu Tamori, 180
oracles, 111
orange-blossoms, 24, 136, 153, and *passim*
orange-tree, lxv, 66, 136, 284, 304, and *passim*
Ōsaka, lxi, 20n, 197n
Osakabé Chikuni, 253
Osakabé Otomaro, 64
Ōsaki, 263
Oshikabé, Prince, 36, 53
Ōshima, lxii
osuhi, xlviii
Ōtabé Aramimi, 255
Ōtomo, xvi, xxiv, xxxv, lxxii, 133, 151, 152, 179, 197, 290
Ōtomo Azumabito, 184
Ōtomo Ikenushi, 140, 182
Ōtomo Kojihi, 96
Ōtomo Kumagori, 204
Ōtomo Minaka, 185
Ōtomo Miyori, 187
Ōtomo Miyuki, 60
Ōtomo Momoyo, 187
Ōtomo of Sakanoé, Lady, lxxii, 123, 128, 129
Ōtomo of Sakanoé's Elder Daughter, 129, 134, 136, 137, 165n, 184
Ōtomo Sadehiko, 261

Ōtomo Sukunamaro, 59, 122
Ōtomo of Tamura, Lady, lvi, 129
Ōtomo Tabito, xxiv, xxxvi, xlvii, lxxii, 116, 122, 241, 242, 267
Ōtomo Tanushi, 59, 60
Ōtomo Yakamochi, xvi, xxiv, xxxvi, lxxii, 106, 115, 130, 181, 182, 241
Ōtomo Yotsuna, 184
Ōtomobé Fushimaro, 257
Ōtoneribé Chibumi, 254
Ōtsu, Prince, lvi, 19, 21, 22
Ōtsu, 45
Ou, 90
Owari —, 225
Owari Okuhi, 153
Oxherd, lv, 211, 295
Ōyakemé, 238

P

pardanthus, 122
peach-blossoms, lxiv, 160, and *passim*
pearls, 152, 153, 166, 246, 283, 292, and *passim*
Peng-lai, 112
Persia, xxxi
Pfizmaier, August, lxxix
Pierson, J. L., lxxx
pillow-words, lxix, see *makura kotoba*
pine-branches, binding of, 8
pine-tree, lxv, 89, 255, and *passim*
plants, lxiv ff.
plum-blossoms, lxiv, 128, 242, 293, and *passim*
poetry festival, liv
Po-hai, xxxvi, 180
Political and social background, xxvii ff.

Poverty, Dialogue on, 205
Primitive and Mediaeval Japanese Texts, lxxix
purification, 243, 248, see *misogi*

R

Rahula, 200
rain, lxvii, 159
rainbow, 279
Rat, Day of, liv
Realm of Nothingness, 313
Reform of Taika, xxvii, xxix
Reiki (era), 104
renga, xx, lxxv
Revon, M., lxxix
rhetorical devices, xix ff.
ri, 203
rice-offering, 278n, 281
Rigan, 123
River of Heaven, 54, 267, see Heavenly River
Rosny, L. de, lxxix
Ruiju-Karin, xvii
ryō, 202

S

Saburu girl, 155
Sado (Isle of), 240n, 305n
Sagaraka Hills, 108
Saheki, 151
Saiga, 191
Saho, lxi, 90, 124, 127, 131, 134, 162, 259, 262
Saikaidō, 82n, 214
Saimei, Empress, 5n, 10n
sakaki, xxxix, 123
Sakamoto Hitogami, 250
Sakatabé Obitomaro, 252
saké, xlvii, 82, 117, 304, and *passim*
Sakiko, 242
' Sakimaro Collection,' xvii, 228

saki-kusa, 210
Sakurada, 63
Sakura-ko, 272
Sami, 46n
Saminé, island of, 46
sandals, xlix
San-indō, 82n
Sanscrit, lxxv
Sanu, 61
Sanu Chigami, xxv, lxxiii, 113
Sanuki, 9, 46
Sasaki, Nobutsuna, lxxvii
Sasanami, 45, 62, 63, 305, and *passim*
Sasara Field of Heaven, 25
Sata, 70
Sayo of Matsura, 261
Scarf-Waving Hill, lxviii, 261
Sé (lake), 215
Sea God, 128, 217, 245
sedōka, xx
Sekigahara, 39
Sena Gyōmon, 227
Sengaku, lxxv
sericulture, liv
Settsu, lxi, 185
Seventh Night, lv, 211, 267, 295
shaku, 202
Shibutani, Cape, 145, 167
Shidoribé Karamaro, 254
Shiga, lxi, 5n, 14, 22, 45, 239, 305
Shigatsu, 45
shiguré, lxvii
Shihi, Lady, 19
Shika, 96, 213
Shiki, Prince, 20
Shi King, xiv
shii, 9
Shimaki, Akahiko, lxxviii
Shimanoshō, 36n
shimé, xli
Shimofusa Province, 278

498

Shimotsuké Province, 280
Shinano Province, lxi, 279
Shingū, 61n
Shinsen Manyōshū, lxxiv
Shinto, xxx, xxxviii, xliii, and *passim*
Shinto litanies, xxi
Shiotsu, Mount, 97
Shiragi, xxxvi, 123, 203, and *passim*; embassy to, 242
Shiragi hatchet, 274
shishō, 153
shizu, xlviii
Shoku-nihongi, 61n
Shōmu, Emperor, 82, 84, 98n
Shōsō-in, xxxvii
Shōtoku, Prince, xxx, xliv, xlvii, 8
Shuchō (era), 30
Siebold, lxxviii
silk, xlviii
silk-tree, 181
silkworm(s), lxiii, 57
singing-frogs, lxiii, 91, 101, 109, 189, and *passim*
' Six Dynasties,' xxx
sleeves, turn back one's, 9, 139, and *passim*
snow, 17, 65, 181, 182, 188, 278
Snow-viewing banquet, 240
Sogas, xxviii
Sōgi, lxxv
song-feast, liv
Sono Ikuha, 65
staggerbush, li, lxiv, 22, 302
Suga, hill of, 149
sugi, 25, see cryptomeria
Sui dynasty, xxix, xxx, xxxi
Suiko, Empress, xxiv
Sukunahikona, 154
Suminoé, 54, 74, 110; Gods of, xl, 177, 263, 265

Sumiyoshi, 177n
sun, 202
suriginu, xlviii
Suruga, 96
susuki, 30, 162, 249, 290, see *Miscanthus*
' Sutra of the Benign King,' xliv
' Sutra of the Golden Light,' xliv
Suzu, 149, 152
sweet flag, lxv, 153

T

Tabito, see **Ōtomo**
taboo, xli
Tachi, Mount, 182, 183, see Tateyama
tachibana, 156, 171
Tachibana, 82
Tachibana Akemi, lxxviii
Tachibana Chikagé, lxxvi
Tachibana Moroé, 171, 240, 266n
Tachibana Naramaro, 84n
Tagi, 184
Tagima Maro, Wife of, 26
Tago, bay of, 97
Taguchi Masuhito, 96
Taguchi Ōto, 255
tahé, 75
' tail flower,' 30n, 213, 221, see *susuki*
Taitsung, Emperor (of Wei), 117
Tajihi —, 95
Tajihi Agatamaro, 120
Tajihi Agatamori, 82n
Tajihi Hironari, 207
Tajihi Kasamaro, 93
Tajihi Kunihito, 93
Tajihi Takanushi, 96
Tajihi Yanushi, 95
Tajima, Princess, 22

499

Tajimamori, 156
Takachiho, Peak of, 178
Takahara, Well of, 8
Takahashi—, 108
Takahashi Mushimaro, xxxvi, lxxii, 214
Takaichi District, 36, 42, 67n, 85n
Takamado, lxi, 104, 137, 261
Takamiya, Prince, 91
Takashima, 63
Takata, Princess, 92
Takayasu Tanemori, 112n
Takazen, Mount, 33
Také (in Isé), 67
Takechi, Prince, 23, 39
Takechi Furuhito, lxxi, 62
Takechi Kurohito, 62, 67
Takemikazuchi-no-Kami, 254n
Taketori no Oji, 74
Tako, 166
taku, xlviii, 45, 75n, 176
Takuno, 33
Tama (river, hill), lxi, 257
Tamana, Maiden, 216
Tamatsukuribé Hiromé, 252
Tamatsu-shima, 191
Tambaichi, 25n
Tamochi, Princess, 26
Tanakami, 68
Tanabata Matsuri, lv, 211n
Tanabé Akiniwa, 246
'Tanabé Sakimaro Collection,' 228
T'ang customs, xlviii
T'ang dynasty, xiii, xxix, xxxi
Tango, liv, lv, lxv
Taniha Ōmé, 238
tanka, xx, and *passim*
Taoism, xiii, xlvii
Taoistic influence, xlv, lxviii
Tateyama, lx, see Tachi (Mount)

Tatsuta, Mount, lx, 8, 219
Tatsuta(hiko), lxi, 219
Tekona, 190, 223
Temmu, Emperor, xxxiv, 17, 18
Tempyō (era), xxiv, xxv, xliv, 82, 103, 130, 207
Tempyō-Hōji (era), 84, 180
Tempyō-Kampō (era), 150, 158
Tempyō-Shōhō (era), 90, 96, 160, 169, 171, 250
Tenji, Emperor, lxi, lxxi, 5, 7, 8, 10, 11, 14, 27n
Thirty-six Master Poets, lxxiv
Thoughts and beliefs, xxxviii ff.
Three Hills, xxxix, 5, 6n
Three Hundred Manyō Poems, lxxx
'Three Kingdoms,' xxx
three principles, 199
thunder, 58, 280, 292, 302
Thunder Hill, 47, 189n
Tienpao (era), xiii
tigers, 39, 275
Tōdaiji-temple, xxxvii
toga-tree, 100, see *tsuga*-tree
Tōkaidō, 82n
Toko Mountain, 5
Tokugawa Mitsukuni, lxxv
Tokugawa Munetaké, lxxviii
Tomi, 126
Tomo, lxii, 119
Toné (River), lxi
Toneri, 67
Toneri, Prince, 85
Toneri Kiné, 14
Toochi, Princess, 66
tortoise-shell, xli, 110
Tosa, 262, 263
Tōsandō, 82n
Tōtōmi Province, 67, 250
Toyo, 26
Toyo-no-akari, xl, 84n
Tōzato Onu, 74

Tsi, xxxi
Tsu, 44
tsuga-tree, 145, 171, 189
Tsukan, 236
Tsuki —, 227
Tsukuba, Mount, lx, 93, 220, 221, 222, 278, 279
Tsukushi, xxxvi, lxii, 50, 61, 93, 172, 197, 237, 250, 255, and *passim*
Tsumori Okurusu, 255
tsurubami, 156
Tsuruga, xxxvi
Tsushima, 213, 214
Tu Fu, xiii
tutelary god, liv

U

Uchi, plain of, 4
Udobé Ushimaro, 252
Uétsuki, 72
uguisu, lxiii, 140, 165, 220, and *passim*, see warbler
uji (clan), xxvii
Ujibé Kuromé, 257
uji-bito, xxvii
uji-no-kami, xxvii
Uji River, lxi, 50, 53, 291, 305
Ujima, Mount, 89
Umashiné, 236n
Unai, Maiden, lxviii, 167, 224, 234
Unebi, lx, 5, 27, 42, 69, 179
unemé, 20n, 44, 88n, 266
unohana, lxv, 143
urabé, xli
Urashima, lxviii, 216
Utatsu, 46n

V

Vega (star), lxvi
versification, xix ff.

violets, 92, 196

W

Wadō (era), 81, 259, 260
Waka, lxii, 191
Wakamiya Ayumaro, 236
Wakatoneribé Hirotari, 254
Wakayamatobé Mumaro, 250
Waley, Arthur, lxxix
warbler, 141, 293, see *uguisu*
wasuré-gai, 246
Watari Hill, 33
Wazami Field, 39
Wazuka, Mount, 132
Weaver Maid, xlix, lv, lxvi, 211
Wei, xxxi
Wên Hsuan, xix
'West Hongan-ji Temple Book,' lxxiv
wizard, 53, 81
'words, lift up,' 59, 307, see *kotoagé*
wistaria, 166
'word-soul,' 207, see *kotodama*
Wuhsia, 258

Y

Yachihoko-no-Kami, 233n
Yakami, 33
Yakamochi, see **Ōtomo**
Yakushi-ji temple, xx
Yama, 81
yama-ai, 218n
Yamabé Akahito, xxiv, lx, lxxii, 187
'Yamabito Tsuminoé,' lxviii
yamabuki, 91n
Yamada Kimimaro, 149
Yamakuma, Prince, 23
Yamamura, 81
Yamanoé Okura, xvii, xxxvi, xlvii, lxxii, 197, 214

501

Yamashina, 12
Yamashiro, lvii, 11n, 108, 230, 285, 291, and *passim*
Yamato, xix, lx, 3, 20, 21, 59, 169, 179, 207, 289, 307, and *passim*
Yamato-himé, Empress, lxxi, 7
Yamato Plain, 5n
Yasu Beach, 295; plain of, 120
Yasumiko, 13
Yezo, xxxv
Yodo River, 5on
Yokoyama, 66
Yomi, 224, 235, see Nether World
Yōrō (era), 88n, 99
Yōrō Waterfall, lxviii
Yosami (wife of Hitomaro), 51
Yoshida Oyu, 138

Yoshino River, 2on
Yoshinu, lii, lx, lxi, 17, 20, 28, 29, 69, 71, 86, 89, 99, and *passim*
Yoshinu, Palace of, 71, 116, 196, and *passim*
yū, xxxix, 40, 57, 310
Yū River, 29
Yuan Ku, 76n
yūdachi, lxvii
Yugé, Prince, 20, 53, 64
Yuhara, Prince, 86, 87
Yuki Yakamaro, 246, 248
Yūryaku, Emperor, xiv, xxiii, xxv, lxxi, 3
Yūtai Sinyung, xix
Yuzuki, 52
yūzutsu (Venus), lxvi